ECONOMIA AND ESCHATOLOGY

With best wishes & prayers!

Fr. Abraham Mulamoottil

3-9-2014

Fr. Stelyios has conducted a meticulous study of two theological themes central to the liturgical life of the Church—sacrificial economy and eschatology. He has applied them masterfully to the Rite of the Prothesis and, by extension, to the Divine Liturgy, of which the former is a mini-representation. I strongly recommend this most edifying book to all avid readers, clergy and laity alike.

+Metropolitan Methodios of Boston
Greek Orthodox Metropolis of Boston, MA

We are grateful to Fr. Stelyios Muksuris for providing us with a thoughtful study on an important but little known and rarely studied element of the Orthodox liturgical tradition, the Prothesis Rite, which involves the preparation of the eucharistic elements. Fr. Muksuris sheds considerable light on the theological presuppositions, the historical development, and the practical implications of the Prothesis Rite, thereby enriching our knowledge of the Divine Liturgy, the sacred rite by which the Orthodox Church celebrates the sacrament of the holy Eucharist. In the process, he exposes the reader to the writings of the great liturgical commentators of the Byzantine era, especially those of Saints Nicholas Cabasilas and Symeon of Thessaloniki that are vital to our understanding of the Orthodox liturgy.

Alkiviadis C. Calivas, Th.D.
Professor Emeritus of Liturgics
Holy Cross Greek Orthodox School of Theology, Brookline, MA

In an age when discussion about liturgical reform in the Orthodox Church raises much interest, all contributions to the study of liturgy are of great value. The meticulous research evident in this study promises to render it an important resource in this endeavor, delving into the liturgical theology of the Liturgy's Preparatory Rites.

Lewis J. Patsavos, Th.D.
Professor Emeritus of Canon Law
Holy Cross Greek Orthodox School of Theology, Brookline, MA

In *Economia and Eschatology*, Fr. Stelyios has provided for us a masterly theological synthesis on the Preparatory Rites of the Divine Liturgy. Building particularly on the work of St. Symeon of Thessalonika († 1429), the last liturgical commentator of the Byzantine Empire, Fr. Stelyios offers a panorama of the meaning of these rites and situates them within the wider sphere of Orthodox theology and liturgy.

Steven Hawkes-Teeples, S.E.O.D.
Assistant Professor of Liturgy
St. Louis University, St. Louis, MO

Fr. Stelyios Muksuris' book successfully covers an important lacuna in the field of Byzantine liturgical studies. Dense and systematic, yet clear and straightforward, this book provides a comprehensive and significant hermeneutical tool for understanding the theological significance of the Prothesis Rite.

Stefanos Alexopoulos, Ph.D.
Professor of Liturgy
Ecclesiastical Academy, Athens, Greece

The issue of the function and significance of the Byzantine mystagogical commentaries on the liturgy has been an apple of contention among contemporary Byzantine liturgiologists. In this context, Fr. Muksuris's examination of such commentaries referring specifically to the Prothesis Rite is a breath of fresh air. With his eloquent pen he has managed to harmonize seamlessly hitherto disparate views on the function of these mystagogical explanations. Indeed, his impeccable scholarship has shown how the two main poles of this tradition, the historical/typological Antiochene school and the allegorical/ anagogical Alexandrian school are synthesized in the hermeneutical tradition regarding the Prothesis Rite. Besides this, however, this work is, as of now, the best and only work available on the Prothesis service in English. Fr. Muksuris has thus eliminated a serious lacuna in English literature on the subject. This work is therefore an absolute necessity in the library of any serious student of the Byzantine rite.

Philip Zymaris, Th.D.
Assistant Professor of Liturgics
Holy Cross Greek Orthodox School of Theology, Brookline, MA

ECONOMIA AND ESCHATOLOGY

LITURGICAL MYSTAGOGY
IN THE BYZANTINE PROTHESIS RITE

Stelyios S. Muksuris, Ph.D.

HOLY CROSS ORTHODOX PRESS

Brookline, Massachusetts

Published by Holy Cross Orthodox Press
50 Goddard Avenue
Brookline, Massachusetts 02445

ISBN: 978-1-935317-41-8
ISBN: 1-935317-41-5

Icon of St. Nicholas Cabasilas and St. Symeon of Thessalonike before the Holy Prothesis, by Iconographer George Kordis, used with permission.

Library of Congress Cataloging-in-Publication Data

Muksuris, Stelyios S.
  Economia and eschatology : liturgical mystagogy in the Byzantine prothesis rite / Stelyios S. Muksuris, Ph.D.
     pages cm
  Includes bibliographical references.
  ISBN-13: 978-1-935317-41-8
  ISBN-10: 1-935317-41-5
  1. Orthodox Eastern Church--Liturgy. 2. Mystagogy. 3. Eschatology. I. Title.
  BX350.M858 2013
  264'.019--dc23
                                                        2013019513

CONTENTS

Preface   ix

Introduction   xv
   BYZANTINE LITURGICAL MYSTAGOGY

Chapter One   1
   A NEW TRANSLATION OF THE PROTHESIS RITE

Chapter Two   19
   THE LIFE AND LITURGICAL WORKS OF ST. NICHOLAS
   CABASILAS AND ST. SYMEON OF THESSALONIKE: A
   CRITICAL SURVEY

Chapter Three   33
   A HISTORICAL OVERVIEW OF THE PREPARATION OF THE
   EUCHARISTIC GIFTS

Chapter Four   53
   A THEOLOGY OF *ECONOMIA*: SACRIFICE IN EASTERN
   LITURGY

Chapter Five   79
   ESCHATOLOGY AND ITS RELATION TO EASTERN LITURGY

Chapter Six   107
   THE MYSTICAL PROTHESIS I: BLOODLESS IMMOLATION
   OF THE LAMB

Chapter Seven   133
   THE MYSTICAL PROTHESIS II: TWO KINGDOMS
   OF SAINTS UNITED

Chapter Eight   165
   THE MYSTICAL PROTHESIS III: THE FINAL PREPARATION
   IN THE VEILING AND PRAYER

Chapter Nine   195
  THE PROTHESIS RITE AS IMAGE OF THE ANAPHORA

Conclusion   215
  LITURGICAL MYSTAGOGY AS THE EXPERIENCE OF DIVINE
    REALITY

Appendix   227
  THE RELATION OF THE PROTHESIS RITE TO THE
    EUCHARISTIC LITURGY: AN ARCHITECTURAL AND
    ICONOGRAPHIC APPROACH

Bibliography   236

About the Author   253

PREFACE

At its deepest and thus most effective level, liturgical mystagogy cannot be anything but experiential. Too often in Eastern forms of worship, excessive attention is given to a mere explanation of the symbolic forms within a rite. Traditionally, this was the role of mystagogy in the early Church, namely, to offer a deeper spiritual exegesis of Scripture to neophytes already initiated through holy baptism. Needless to say, such an intellectual engagement would ideally motivate and thus transform the new Christian to the ways of Christ as he followed the precepts of the Gospel. In the Divine Liturgy, however, exegesis that offers answers in a representational sense (A stands for B, C actually means D, and the like) is inadequate, from both a theological and pastoral perspective.

The Eucharistic Liturgy does not simply expose us to the Mystery of God's love and salvation in Jesus Christ, nor is its primary aim to secure for us an intellectual understanding of divine concepts and higher theories, as enticing as these may be. By necessity, the Liturgy raises us to a sublime participation in the Christ event in a profoundly holistic manner that fulfills our every expectation and aspiration. In other words, the Liturgy "personalizes" the Christ event for us by suspending time and space as we know it and by bringing heaven to earth, thus allowing us to engage in the singular event of salvation on both a cosmic and personal level. This face-to-face encounter with the Lord, this experience of mystery, makes personal transformation possible because at its highest level conversion cannot be a mere intellectual exercise. Rather, conversion is an ongoing event, a continuous experience of fellowship with God. Succinctly put, it is life itself, and the Liturgy of the Church, by its intrinsically experiential character, facilitates this transformation of man in God. As Dermot Lane put it so well, "God comes to man in experience. We receive God in experience. We do not project, create or posit God in experience. Rather we find God, already there ahead of us, in human experience."[1]

The Byzantine liturgical mystagogue was never complacent with a rudimentary exegesis of ritual forms. Each wrote his commentary on the Divine Liturgy as if he were standing directly before the divine mystery itself and describing the very vision of this mystery. This is nowhere more obvious than in St. Symeon of Thessalonike's remarkable commentary on the completed prothesis rite in his monumental work, *On the Sacred Liturgy*. Here Symeon envisions upon the holy paten a microcosm of God's Kingdom that is permeated by the divine presence. Surrounding the Lamb of God are particles for the saints, the living, and the dead, all of whom constitute the redeemed community of faith as well as the transformed cosmos. This eschatological image of God's family, as it were, "God among men and God in the midst of gods, made divine from Him who is truly God by nature", is expressed throughout the Eucharistic Liturgy and, most especially, in the very gathering together of God's people before the divine throne to worship and share fellowship with the Lord and with one another, thus all the while securing their deification. For the saintly Archbishop of Thessalonike, it is this entrance into the transformative mystery of God, encompassing the economia of the divine sacrifice and the inauguration of the eschatological Kingdom, which is experienced in the Divine Liturgy in its fullness and expressed as a sort of miniaturization, or σμικρογραφία, in the Preparatory Rites that precede its celebration.

The composition of this book began over a decade ago as my doctoral dissertation, in a field that I have come to embrace most passionately—liturgical theology. Having grown up in the Church all my life, I have always sought an appreciation of the Church's ritual, but one that surpasses a mere intellectual cognizance of what is done and what ritual items and rubrics represent. The Liturgy needs to touch people's lives in a profound way that is at once experiential and transformative. And people committed to Christ Jesus must allow their lives to be touched by the Liturgy in a meaningful way that will awaken them to the reality of what it means to be a Christian of love, prayer, and service—a "little Christ" capable of changing the world for the better.

Too often we are passive recipients of God's graces, simple bystanders witnessing the Christ event in our liturgical worship and soaking up the manifold blessings that come our way in, sadly, a utilitarian sense that focuses only on our personal needs and desires. We choose to be complacent with simplistic explanations that satisfy our curiosities and pique our inter-est in the sensationalistic and impressively beautiful. As intended mirrors of the divine, however, we frequently fall short of our calling to reflect and actively channel these graces to a world in desperate need of them because we ourselves have not allowed God to transform us as we encounter Him in worship. Hence, Eastern liturgical worship, by its sublime expressivity, must inspire in us a commitment to participate in the mystagogy that flows through the Eucharistic Liturgy and to relate it to our own lives. In the end liturgy, in its optimal expression, *is* theology—a dialogue about God with God, with ourselves, and with one another.

ACKNOWLEDGEMENTS

Many individuals who share my intense love for Eastern Liturgy and liturgical theology have contributed immensely to the completion of this book. I shall begin with my academic mentors, to whom I wish many more healthy and productive years in the service of God. Fr. Alkiviadis C. Calivas, Professor Emeritus of Liturgics at Holy Cross Greek Ortho-dox School of Theology in Brookline, MA, provided for me my first systematic exposure to the study of liturgical worship as a student of the-ology. He instilled in me a profound love for the worship and rites of the Church in a unique manner that engaged both my mind and heart. His lectures at Seminary, always well organized and presented, were the ones I knew I could never miss. I thank him for his mentorship and friendship over the years.

The Rt. Rev. Archimandrite Robert F. Taft, Professor Emeritus of Lit-urgy at the Pontifical Oriental Institute in Rome, and the world's premier liturgiologist in Eastern Liturgy, has been "my professor outside the class-room." I never once had the distinct privilege to take a class with him (such are the misfortunes of life), but I have read his meticulously researched works throughout my tenure as a postgraduate student and so feel as though I have always known his work. In recent years, after being inducted into the international Society of Oriental Theology and attending confer-ences in which Fr. Taft offered the keynote lecture, I met him in person and have developed both a professional relationship and friendship with him (we are both New Englanders, after all) that I deem priceless. Among other things, I am also indebted to him for endorsing me before the faculty and administration of the Byzantine Catholic Seminary in Pittsburgh to teach Liturgical Theology, a ministry that I have now been honored to execute for the past five years.

Fr. Andrew Louth, Professor of Patristics and Byzantine Studies in the Department of Theology and Religion at Durham University, UK, served as my Ph.D. thesis advisor from 2000–2008. He also served as my M.Litt. advisor for another work in liturgical theology (1997–2000), which I have not yet published: *The Anaphorae of the Liturgy of the Apostles Sts. Addai and Mari and the Byzantine Liturgy of St Basil the Great: A Comparative Study.* I thank him for helping me to develop a critical theological mind, whose purpose is always to seek the truth responsibly and to embrace it whole-heartedly. His patience with my shortcomings and his unwavering encouragement, in good times and challenging moments, saw this work through. I am grateful for his academic mentorship and his friendship.

I would be remiss in not acknowledging the academic and spiritual guidance provided me by my former professor and very dear friend, Dr. Lewis J. Patsavos, Professor Emeritus of Canon Law (and fellow Cantabrigian). His positivity and sincerity have been a well of inspiration and strength to me, both personally and professionally.

I wish to extend my gratitude to several of my academic colleagues in the *Societas Orientalium Liturgiarum, Societas Liturgica*, the Orthodox Theological Society in America, and the American Academy of Religion, too numerous to mention here by name, for their friendship, support, and fellowship over the years. Three dear friends, however, academic brothers and fellow graduates of HC/HC, need special recognition for their constant encouragement of my work and academic growth: Fr. Stefanos Alexopoulos, Professor of Liturgy at the Ecclesiastical Academy in Athens, Greece; Fr. Philip Zymaris, Assistant Professor of Liturgics at Holy Cross Greek Orthodox School of Theology; and Dr. Anton Vrame, Director of the Greek Orthodox Archdiocese Department of Religious Education and Director of Holy Cross Orthodox Press, for seeing this book to print.

Special thanks also to my technical editor and production manager, Konstantine Pietronuto, and others associated with Holy Cross Orthodox Press for their meticulous and careful handling of my manuscript, for their helpful suggestions, and their excellent cooperation. What you are currently holding in your hands is a result of their expertise and dedication.

A special acknowledgment of gratitude to His Eminence Archbishop Demetrios of America, my former professor of Old Testament Studies at Holy Cross, for inspiring in me the love of learning, research, and academic excellence. I am most indebted also to His Eminence Metropolitan Methodios of Boston, my spiritual father and former President of Hellenic College and Holy Cross, under whose *omophorion* I matured into early adulthood as a seminarian and later priest. I thank him sincerely for always insisting on excellence and gracefulness in the execution of the divine services of the Church. For as I came to understand and appreciate from him, the celebrant's faith and love must be accompanied by a manner of celebration that is at once dignified and appropriate to God, which conveys a meaningfulness capable of transforming human lives. I likewise venerate filially the right hand of my former bishop, spiritual father, and friend, His Eminence Maximos, former Metropolitan of Pittsburgh, under whom I served as his Administrative Assistant for five years. I thank him for his humble spirit, his exemplary Christian paradigm, his brilliant mind, and for sustaining my family and me all these years with a love that I would be so fortunate to emulate only minimally in my own life. I shall never forget our endless conversions on virtually every topic under the sun, from family life to the Basilian anaphora (a personal favorite of mine which quickly became his also). And finally, special thanks to His Eminence Metropolitan Savas of Pittsburgh, for his encouragement not only to complete my doctoral dissertation with Durham but also to assure its eventual publication. To all these hierarchs who have impacted me in such positive ways, I pray that the Lord God grant them many years!

The long and arduous journey toward the publication of this book would never have been completed were it not for the prayers and support of one of the most charismatic hierarchs in recent times, who sadly is no longer with us. His Beatitude Archbishop Christodoulos of Athens and All Greece, now in God's Kingdom, endorsed my work as a liturgiologist most enthusiastically during my one-year research sabbatical in Greece and never allowed me to forget it. Our numerous conversations together in his office gave me a sense of direction in my priestly diakonia and pride in my academic endeavors. He was a leader of leaders, a true priest of God, a confidant, and a beautiful friend. A brilliant man with great wisdom and love for the Church, his people, and his clergy, His Beatitude left this transient world too early and his absence is felt all over, especially now during these troubling times in Greece. We know, however, that his prayers continue to flow melodically before God's Throne, interceding to assure our welfare and salvation. May his memory be eternal!

I extend my gratitude to my brother clergy and their families, who over the years sustained me through their prayers and their friendly concern and support. I would be remiss in not thanking by name Fr. Nicholas M. Kastanas, my father confessor, former professor, and dear friend, who was the first person I met as a new seminarian at HC/HC. Over the years, our friendship blossomed and culminated when Fr. Nick assumed the pastorship of my home parish in Arlington, MA, where he continues to serve to this day. Nowhere have I met such a positively minded and gracious servant of the Lord. I also wish to thank the faithful of the communities I was privileged to serve over the years, throughout the Archdiocese of America and Greece, for patiently bearing with me during my postgraduate studies and for accepting the reality of my "dual career" as both a priest and professor, serving both the Church and the Academy.

With sincere filial affection I venerate the hands of my two earliest heroes without whom I would not be here today—my beloved mother Katina and my late father Sotiris Muksuris. Through all the hardships we endured together as a family, from Constantinople to Boston and beyond, you never once gave up, but with undying trust in God and in each other you persevered and moved forward, teaching me that where God and faith are there is success and happiness. This book is my personal testimony to this greatest lesson in life, which I learned at your feet. I love you.

And to all my friends and relatives, especially my in-laws Stamatis and Anastasia Petromilonakis of Athens, Greece, who have stood by me throughout my life and believed in me, I express to you my heartfelt gratitude and love. Each of you is in some way responsible for the success of this book. Stay gold, each one of you.

I must conclude by saving the best for last, as it were. To my best friend, wife, and soul mate Georgia, I say "thank you" from the bottom of my heart for your undying support and your exemplary patience during this long journey. When my light was about to go out, you spoke up emphatically and kept the flame burning, believing in me when I could not or would not. Nothing I can ever do or say can adequately match the gift of your love toward me and our family. In like manner and for the same reasons, I embrace my beautiful daughter Katerina for bearing with me all these years and for making us so proud of you, both as an academic achiever and as a beautiful human being with the right values and virtues. I love you more than words can express.

Any shortcomings and imperfections in this book are solely my responsibility, for to God alone is to be attributed all perfection and thanksgiving and glory, world without end.

Pittsburgh, Pennsylvania
May 5, 2013
Feast of the Great and Holy Pascha

NOTE

1. Dermot A. Lane, *The Experience of God: An Invitation to Do Theology* (New York, 1981), p. 14.

INTRODUCTION

Within the penetrating liturgical treatises of St. Symeon of Thessalonike, one particular phrase captures quite succinctly the very essence of the mystagogy of the Byzantine Divine Liturgy. Addressing his clergy regarding the mystical significance of the preparatory rite known as the *prothesis*, the Archbishop of Thessalonike seems to extend his exegesis to define the entire eucharistic experience. He observes: "Through this sacred sacrifice, both holy angels and men together have been united to Christ, and in Him have they been sanctified and they unite us to Him."[1] The implication here of a more immediate and intimate reality—the union of heavenly and earthly beings to Christ and to one another, here and now—forms the very cornerstone of Byzantine liturgical mystagogy.

LITURGICAL MYSTAGOGY: A THEOLOGICAL BASIS

In the Eastern celebration of the Eucharist, both the material and spiritual worlds, eternity and history, intersect during the Church's mystical worship and embrace the realm of the other. Surpassing all rational thought, liturgical mystagogy intends to raise the spiritual consciousness of the worshipper, from a trivial vision of the ritual acts conducted in the church to a deeper comprehension of the meaning behind those acts. More importantly, however, mystagogy does not simply claim to be an exercise in symbol identification; it attempts to convey the invisible divine presence through the visible human act. The classic Augustinian definition of μυστήριον is most applicable here: A mystery is when "one thing is seen, another understood" (*aliud videtur, aliud intelligitur*).[2]

The Byzantine notion of mysticism involves "an immediate experience or intuitive knowledge of the divine that surpasses rational, logical perceptions and knowledge as well as 'normal' religious consciousness."[3] The role of mystagogy[4] centers upon *leading* and *guiding* the neophyte or Christian worshipper more deeply into this understanding and experience of the divine.

In order for mystagogy to succeed and before man can truly be initiated into the divine mystery, he must first establish contact with that particular source or setting in which God has chosen to reveal Himself. Following the Alexandrian Origen's line of thinking, the central mystery of Christ the Logos is at once veiled and unveiled in the "two articles of clothing" associated with His person; namely, His flesh (the Incarnation event) and the Holy Scriptures.[5] Regarding the Incarnation, A. Verheul writes: "Christ himself is thus the great, the pre-eminent sign: his material bodily nature both hides and reveals his invisible divine Person. For the first time in him the material-bodily condition has become the bearer of a divine reality, of a divine power, yea, of the divine Person himself."[6] As mysteries that derive from the central mystery of Christ, nature and the Scriptures, both associates of the material world, possess their own distinct μυσταγωγίαι, or methods of revealing the Logos. These mystagogies take a variety of forms but are typically found in the priceless philosophical treatises and scriptural exegetical works attributed to the brilliant and critical minds of both the Eastern and Western Church Fathers.

Likewise the Church, in its sacramental liturgies and most especially in the Eucharist, constitutes a further mystery, in that Christ the Logos is simultaneously hidden in and revealed by the liturgical sign within the rite. The liturgical sign essentially fulfills three purposes, the first of which involves this initial revelation of the invisible and divine via the medium of the visible and material. As soon as the mystery is made known to the worshipper, he then enters into union with it, thus completing the second phase. Verheul comments, "The person who stands behind the sign, who made it a sign, comes to meet the person who approaches it as a sign."[7] Finally, the concealing character of the liturgical sign hinders one from knowing fully the mystery and coming into direct contact with it. This partial union of the two sides of the sign—God and man—helps to awaken in man an irresistible yearning for a deeper intelligence and union.

> The sign undoubtedly makes us know, but, by the very incompleteness of the knowledge that it bestows, suggests and invites to a complete knowledge and union, which it makes us long for and which will one day make the sign superfluous. Thus viewed the sign is always a pledge

or foretaste of a coming full realization and has naturally only a provisional character.[8]

Hence, the third function of the liturgical sign serves to entice man to a fuller contact with God, precisely because of its incompleteness. One notices here the eschatological implications of this particular purpose. The liturgical sign within the Church on earth invariably leads man to a partial vision of the Kingdom, but at the consummation of the age, the sign will be excessive since the fullness of the Kingdom will have been attained.

Through the implement of liturgical mystagogy, this contiguity between heaven and earth and between God and man makes it possible for each realm, on either side of the Church, to interpenetrate the domain of the other. Verheul writes: "In the visible world the invisible world is present to us, and by means of the visible world we participate in the invisible world."[9] For example, in the Liturgy, the chief celebrant does not simply execute the responsibilities of a minister but is himself transformed into the very icon of Christ (*imago Christi*), who Himself preaches the truth of the Gospel, and who, through the priest, "offers and is offered." The Divine Liturgy then is not simply a *memorial* celebration in the historical sense, but the very *actualization* of this celebration, made alive and effectual for the Church that solemnly participates in the eucharistic mystery. Fr. Robert Taft summarizes this "full" meaning of *anamnesis* rather succinctly, correctly identifying the grace of God and the collective faith of the Church as the two necessary catalysts, the *sine qua non*, which validate and activate liturgical mystagogy.

> Thereby, the supper of the Lord has become the messianic banquet of the kingdom, and our earthly ritual a participation in this heavenly worship. This is possible by the power of the Holy Spirit. By this worship we confess our faith in the saving death and resurrection of the Lord. It is indeed a memorial of all Christ did for us, not in the sense of a ritual reenactment of a past event in its several historical phases, but as an anamnesis of the total mystery that is Christ in its present efficacy, the eternal intercession before the throne of God of Christ our high priest. Its force is rooted in our Trinitarian faith. Its efficacy is the work of the Holy Spirit, sent by the will of the Father, through the hands of the priest, to bring us Christ as He did in the incarnation.[10]

In a very true sense, one may even say that mystagogy "incarnates" the heavenly Kingdom into the earthly Church: Christ, as High Priest before the throne of God, likewise assumes the presidency of the liturgical synaxis and draws the attention of all people to His life, passion, death, and resurrection, as well as to the imminence of His second and glorious return. And by His dual presence (i.e. in both heaven and on earth),[11] Christ's saving power transforms man and raises him to a vision and union with God.

The theological basis for Byzantine liturgical mystagogy follows precisely the rationale behind the use of icons in the Eastern Christian tradition: the incarnation of the Son of God. Taft, acknowledging the parallel growth of mystagogy and the theological doctrine behind Eastern iconography, states: "I believe it is an equally important period in the growth of liturgical piety, where the same dynamics were at work, producing in mystagogy a realism parallel to that in religious art."[12] God chooses to become a part of the material world He created—a world of inherent goodness—in order to raise mankind to God. In St. John of Damascus' words: "I do not worship matter; I worship the Creator of matter who became matter for my sake, who willed to take His abode in matter; who worked out my salvation through matter."[13] The execution of iconography requires the physical pre-appearance or preexistence, as it were, of a person or object, perceptible to the physical senses, before its artistic depiction can be rendered through material means. The same applies to mystagogy, which necessitates the appearance of Christ in the flesh in order to transfer His real presence into the signs and symbols that permeate the Divine Liturgy. "For now that since his Resurrection Christ is invisible to us, the sign character of his divinized humanity has passed into the holy signs of the liturgy. What was made possible through the Incarnation has become actuality in the liturgy of the Church."[14] Christ's epiphany in the flesh sanctifies the physical world, consecrating the objects and gestures and rites of the Church to serve as the media through which God communicates with His people. In Verheul's words, "The same divine and redeeming power that operated in the visible humanity of Christ is now present and operative in the signs of the sacraments and sacramentals."[15]

LITURGICAL MYSTAGOGY IN THE BYZANTINE TRADITION

Liturgical scholars agree that not unlike the Scriptures, "the rites of the Church await an exegesis and a hermeneutic and a homiletic to expound, interpret, and apply their multiple levels of meaning in each age. Mystagogy is to liturgy what exegesis is to scripture."[16] Indeed, the important cosmopolitan centers of Alexandria and Antioch, aside from creating two distinct approaches to the person of Christ and the interpretation of Holy Scripture, also proposed two unique approaches to liturgical mystagogy: (1) a "literal" (historical/typological) method (the Antiochene school); and (2) a "spiritual" (mystical/allegorical) method (the Alexandrian school).[17]

In the first method, there exists a strong correlation between the liturgical rites and the saving acts of Christ's life. Early proponents of this view include such Fathers as Cyril of Jerusalem, John Chrysostom, and Theodore of Mopsuestia, the last two of whom were students of Diodore of Tarsus (d. AD 394).

On the other hand, the allegorical Alexandrian mystagogical school envisions the Liturgy as surpassing history and time—indeed, the physical world—in order to lead the worshipper to the spiritual and mystical realities of the invisible world. Early proponents of this position include Clement of Alexandria, his pupil, the great Origen, and Dionysios the Areopagite (whose fifth century *Ecclesiastical Hierarchy* systemized early Alexandrian mystagogy).

The preliminary work of these and other early Christian writers gradually paved the way for the eventual development of the ever-important Byzantine mystagogical commentaries that followed. The Byzantine mystagogues traditionally number five: Maximos the Confessor (d. 662) and Symeon of Thessalonike (d. 1429), both of whom followed the Alexandrian method of liturgical exegesis; and Germanos of Constantinople (d. 730), Nicholas of Andida (eleventh century), and Nicholas Cabasilas (d. 1391), all proponents of Antiochene liturgical interpretation.

It must be emphasized quite strongly that the overall intent of both mystagogical methods of interpretation is fundamentally identical: to elevate the worshipper to an encounter with the living God through their own distinctive interpretation of the Divine Liturgy. Furthermore, this common purpose suggests quite convincingly that each mystagogical system should not be viewed as mutually exclusive of the other, but rather as complementary, insofar as history and the *eschaton*, heaven and earth, converge into a single reality during the mystical and sublime celebration of the Divine Liturgy. Bornert cautions: "*Mais il ne faudrait ni exagérer la cohésion interne des deux tendances, ni forcer leur opposition réciproque.*"[18] Both schools differ in their emphasis toward interpreting the inherent mysticism of the Liturgy, but the common denominator between them is clearly their intent to surpass the material symbol or act, thereby allowing the worshipper to enter into the divine reality and to attain salvation and sanctification. In this sense, neither view can ever be perceived as mutually exclusive.

THE UNIQUENESS OF THE BYZANTINE PROTHESIS RITE

A distinctive feature in the modern celebration of the Byzantine Divine Liturgy, as in other Oriental liturgies, is the prothesis rite, "a sort of 'fore-mass',"[19] to use Taft's deliberate characterization, in which the eucharistic elements of bread and wine are prepared in an elaborate private ceremony prior to the beginning of the Eucharist. A look at history indicates that this rite developed gradually from a very simple preparation and transfer of the gifts prior to the beginning of the Eucharist proper (i.e. following the dismissal of the Catechumens and before the Great Entrance) into a complex series of symbolic actions, biblical recitations, commemorations, and prayers, conducted before the commencement of the Liturgy. The highly symbolical nature of this preliminary rite, with its reenactment of Christ's self-sacrifice through the preparation of the Lamb and chalice, as well as the hierarchical arrangement of particles around the Lamb to signify the eschatological reality of the Church, affirms a sublime mystagogy taken up in the writings of the later Byzantine writers.

This formalized prothesis rite either appears in or is commented upon by several late Byzantine manuscripts,[20] the most important of which, for the purposes of this study, are: (1) the *Diataxis*[21] of Patriarch Philotheos Kokkinos of Constantinople (fourteenth century); (2) the *Explanation of the Divine Liturgy*[22] by St. Nicholas Cabasilas; and (3) *On the Sacred Liturgy*[23] and *Interpretation of the Church and the Liturgy*,[24] by St. Symeon of Thessalonike. Whereas Philotheos' *Diataxis* offers exclusively a step-by-step description of the proper execution of the prothesis rite, one finds in the commentaries of Cabasilas and Symeon a combination of the ceremonial and the mystagogical significance behind the ritual acts and prayers.

A dominant theme that evidently saturates every section of this elaborate prothesis rite is the *economia* of salvation, fulfilled through Christ's ultimate sacrifice upon the Cross. From the very outset of the rite, the Church, through the celebrant priest, proclaims the *anamnesis* ("remembrance") of the Lord's *economia*, fulfilled through the series of subsequent ritual acts over the bread and chalice, each action corresponding to either a stage or aspect of Christ's passion and death. One viable approach to the term ἀνάμνησις, when used in this liturgical context, is to understand it not as a simple remembrance of a past event, but rather as a "'re-calling' or 're-presenting' before God of an event in the past, so that it becomes *here and now operative by its effects*."[25] One observes here a clear example within the Byzantine Liturgy of the inherent realism required by liturgical mystagogy.

The notion of sacrifice, however, does not refer solely to the events surrounding Christ's final days on earth, but properly includes His entire life as a sacrificial offering to God the Father. As Dix writes:

> His sacrifice was something which began with His Humanity and which has its eternal continuance in heaven. . . . Calvary has here

become only the final moment, the climax of the offering of a sacrifice whose opening is at Bethlehem, and whose *acceptance* is in the resurrection and ascension and in what follows beyond the veil in heaven.[26]

This inclusion of other significant "historical" events in the life of Christ, such as His birth, is consistent with the popular view (to be examined later in this study) that the prothesis likewise comprises a commemoration of the Incarnation. Cabasilas understands Christ's entry into the world not as an isolated event, but as one intimately connected to His passion; indeed, the initiation of a life of self-offering. He writes: ". . . it [the bread of the prothesis] has become an offering, since it represents our Lord during the first phase of his life on earth, when he became an oblation."[27] Symeon of Thessalonike is more direct than Cabasilas in associating the prothesis rite with the Nativity, although he too places the majority of the emphasis on Christ's sacrifice upon the Cross. He writes: "But the prothesis also represents both the cave and the manger" ("Ἀλλὰ καὶ ἡ πρόθεσις τύπον ἐπέχει τοῦ σπηλαίου τε καὶ τῆς φάτνης").[28] Nevertheless, the passion theme, centered on Christ's sacrifice, clearly dominates the rite. Cabasilas offers the following argument in support of the passion's centrality:

> What is this commemoration? How do we remember the Lord in our liturgy? Which of his actions, which stages of his life, are called to mind? In other words, what are we to recall concerning him and his life? That he raised the dead, that he gave sight to the blind, that he ruled the tempests, that he fed thousands with a few loaves, thus showing himself to be God Almighty? By no means. Rather, we must remember those events which seem to denote nothing but weakness: his Cross, his Passion, his Death—these are the happenings which he asks us to commemorate. And how can we know this? It is the interpretation of St. Paul [cf. 1 Corinthians 11.26], who understands so well all that concerns Christ.[29]

Another preeminent theme that permeates the prothesis rite and is very intimately affiliated with Christ's *economia* is the eschatological reality that the Lord's self-sacrifice has established for the Church and the world. Each individual salvific act within history (the Cross, the Empty Tomb, the Ascension, and Pentecost) essentially builds upon the previous event and anticipates the advent of the eternal *αἰών*, or "age," which originates from history but is simultaneously beyond measurable time. The *eschaton* ("the end"), known alternately as the "Day of the Lord," is, as Dix observes, the Church's

> answer to the agonising problem of history, with its apparent chaos of good and evil. This completion of history, . . . does not interrupt

history or destroy it; it fulfils it. All the divine values implicit and fragmentary in history are gathered up and revealed in the *eschaton*, which
is 'the End' to which history moves.[30]

In one sense, this *eschaton* is an imminent reality, waiting to be fulfilled
at an indeterminate point in the future. However, for the early Christians
of Jewish extraction, this reality had already been manifested in Christ's
life, death, and resurrection. Hence, the primitive Church believed quite
insistently that it was living in the final days, earnestly awaiting the Second
Coming of her risen Lord.

> When the Messiah had in solid historical fact—'under Pontius Pi-
> late'—offered Himself in sacrifice that the whole will of God might
> be done, the supreme crisis of history had occurred . . . in His Person
> the 'Age to come' has been inaugurated, in which the Kingship of God
> is unquestionable and unchallenged. In Him—in His human life and
> death—the rule of God in all human life had been proclaimed abso-
> lute and perfectly realised.[31]

The Byzantine Church embraces both of these eschatological angles
and expresses them liturgically in the prothesis rite. The sacrificial Lamb of
God is extracted from the offering bread (*prosphora*) and marked with the
signs of His passion, undergoing numerous incisions and piercings. The
Lamb is then transferred to the circular paten (*diskos*), soon to be encircled
by His Church, represented by the numerous bread particles incised from
other prosphorae in honor of the Theotokos, the orders of angels and saints,
and the living and dead. Christ's self-sacrifice, depicted through the physical markings on the Lamb, heralds the inauguration of His Kingdom: a reality in which time and eternity, earth and heaven, material and immaterial
beings intersect, visualized in the gifts of bread and wine ritually prepared
during the prothesis rite. Symeon of Thessalonike makes an extraordinary
reference to this eschatological vision when he writes:

> But let us understand how also through this divine symbol and
> through the work of the holy proskomide we see Jesus himself and his
> Church all as one, in the middle him the true light, [and the Church]
> having gained eternal life, illumined by him and sustained. For he,
> through the bread, is in the middle; his Mother, through the [trian-
> gular bread] particle, is to [his] right; the saints and angels [smaller
> triangular particles] are on [his] left; and below is the pious gathering
> of all who have believed in him [small particles]. And this is the great
> mystery: God among men and God in the midst of gods, made divine
> from him who is truly God by nature, who was incarnated for them.

> And this is the future kingdom and the polity of eternal life: God with
> us, seen and communed.[32]

One can conceive then how the two themes of economia and eschatology
are necessarily interdependent and expressed as such in the prothesis rite.
Christ's sacrifice ushers in the eschatological reality, as the Lamb itself is initially mutilated by the series of symbolic incisions before being surrounded
by "so great a cloud of witnesses" (Heb 12:1),[33] drawn to Him throughout
history and at the consummation of time.

OBJECTIVES OF THE BOOK

It is the intent of this study to identify and affirm the powerful economic
(sacrificial) and eschatological character of the Byzantine Divine Liturgy's
prothesis rite, through a comprehensive examination of the later Byzantine
mystagogical commentaries of St. Nicholas Cabasilas and St. Symeon of
Thessalonike. The richly typological symbolism that pervades the prothesis
serves as a clear indication of how a once exclusively practical rite assumed,
in time, a profound theological dimension.

One crucial aim of this study will be to prove, through the performance
of the rite, the necessary interdependence between Christ's sacrificial passion, achieved within historical time and the visible world, and the eschatological reality, to be experienced in its fullness at the consummation of
time. In one sense, the former gives viability to the latter, as the sequence of
rubrical actions in the prothesis exhibits quite clearly (the Lamb is prepared
before the other particles are added to the paten). However, the Church, as
the community of faith which forever celebrates her Lord's extreme sacrifice, constantly has her attention transfixed toward the *eschaton*, the final,
extra-historical "event" of the divine economy which definitively affirms the
lordship of Christ over all existence. It is this "event," at the threshold of
eternity, that accomplishes the final transformation and glorification of the
world to which the Church has aspired since her inception.

A final concern of this book will be to substantiate the patristic claim
that the prothesis rite, with its extensive and vivid imagery, is a reflection of
the entire eucharistic liturgy, both in form and theological significance. Cabasilas makes this bold affirmation by advancing the theme of Christ's sacrifice throughout the Church's entire eucharistic worship,[34] while Symeon
calls the proskomide προοίμια τῆς ἱερουργίας ("introduction of the sacred
work," i.e. the liturgy).[35] Ioannes Fountoules summarizes both approaches
well by writing: "The entire performance of the proskomide consists of a

mini-sketch (σμικρογραφία) of the Divine Liturgy and is embodied theologically and liturgically within its confines."³⁶

René Bornert has written: "In the celebration of the Divine Liturgy, as in the cult of sacred images, the Byzantine Church has expressed her soul."³⁷ One can surely extend this celebration to encompass the prothesis rite as well, and still envision the sublime theology which reveals the Church's very mind and ethos; indeed, her very *raison d'être*. It is the ardent intent of this book to attain this revelation through a comprehensive study of the mystagogical wealth of this prothesis rite.

NOTES

1. Symeon of Thessalonike, Περὶ τῆς Θείας Μυσταγωγίας (*On the Sacred Liturgy*) 94; PG 155.281B. The Greek text follows: "Τῇ θυσίᾳ ταύτῃ τῇ ἱερᾷ, πάντες ὁμοῦ ἄγγελοί τε καὶ ἄνθρωποι ἅγιοι ἡνώθησαν τῷ Χριστῷ, καὶ ἐν αὐτῷ ἡγιάσθησαν καὶ τούτῳ ἡμᾶς ἐνοῦσιν."All translations of Symeon throughout this book, unless otherwise specified, are mine.

2. Augustine of Hippo, *Homily* 272.16; PL 38.1247. The full text reads: "Ista fratres dicuntur sacramenta, quia in eis aliud videtur, aliud intelligitur." Ambrose of Milan offers an identical statement in defining allegory as used in the exegesis of Scripture: "Allegoria est cum aliud geritur et aliud figuratur" (Ambrose, *De Abraham* I.4.28; PL 14.432). See also A. Verheul, *Introduction to the Liturgy: Towards a Theology of Worship* (London, 1968), 104.

3. *The Oxford Dictionary of Byzantium*. vol. 2. Ed. Alexander P. Kazhdan (New York, 1991), 1431.

4. As the term implies, μυσταγωγία(μυστήριον, 'mystery'; ἀγωγή, 'initiation') refers specifically not to the mystery itself, but rather to the method or mechanism that facilitates this attainment of mystical knowledge or experience. It is commonly known in the Byzantine East that the μυσταγωγίαιwere those "commentaries . . . interpretationsof liturgical rites that apply to liturgy the multilevel patristic method of scriptural exegesis" (Ibid., vol. 1, 488).

5. For a more detailed examination of Origen's mystagogical views, see René Bornert, *Les commentaires byzantins de la Divine Liturgie du VIIe au XVe siècle* (Paris, 1965), 56–57.

6. Verheul, 109.

7. Ibid., 105.

8. Ibid.

9. Ibid., 107.

10. Robert F. Taft, "The Liturgy of the Great Church: An Initial Synthesis of Structure and Interpretation on the Eve of Iconoclasm", in *Dumbarton Oaks Papers* 34–35 (Washington, D.C., 1980-1981), vol. 58. Reprinted in Robert F. Taft, *Liturgy in Byzantium and Beyond* (Brookfield, 1995).

11. This simultaneous presence in both heaven and earth is expressed in the Divine Liturgy, during the prayer before the elevation of the Host: "ὁ ἄνω τῷ Πατρὶ συγκαθήμενος καὶ ὧδε ἡμῖν ἀοράτως συνών" ("You who are seated above with the Father and are invisibly here with us"; translation mine). See the critical text of the Liturgy of St. John Chrysostom in P.N. Trembelas, ed., Αἱ τρεῖς λειτουργίαι κατὰ τοὺς ἐν Ἀθήναις κώδικας (*The Three Liturgies According to the Athens Codices*). *Texte und Forschungen zur byzantinisch-neugriechischen Philologie* (Athens, 1935), 129.

12. Ibid., 59.

13. John of Damascus, *On the Divine Images* I.16; see also *On the Divine Images: Three Apologies Against Those Who Attack the Divine Images*. trans. David Anderson (Crestwood, 1980), 23.

14. Verheul, 109.

15. Ibid., 110.

16. Taft, *The Liturgy of the Great Church*, 59.

17. Taft correlates liturgical mystagogy with the Western allegorical tradition of scriptural exegesis, applying a specific terminology for each approach. He indicates that the literal method, utilizing the standard of typology, explains the Old Testament historical events as possessing their real meaning only in relation to Christ. On the other hand, the 'spiritual' method of interpreting Scripture is understood under three aspects: (1) the *allegorical*, or dogmatic aspect, in which the entire OT refers to the mystery of Christ and the Church in hidden symbols and words; (2) the *tropological*, or moral and spiritual aspect, which relates the allegorical sense of the mystery of Christ to everyday Christian living and behavior; and (3) the *anagogical*, or eschatological aspect, which refers to the contemplation of the consummation of the age and the final establishment of the Kingdom of God. See ibid., 59–60.

18. Bornert, 52. "But one would have neither to exaggerate the internal cohesion of the two tendencies, nor to force their reciprocal opposition." Translation mine.

19. Robert F. Taft, *The Great Entrance: A History of the Transfer of Gifts and Other Pre-anaphoral Rites of the Liturgy of St. John Chrysostom* (Rome, 1978), 257.

20. In most cases, the manuscripts include the prothesis rite either prefacing the Divine Liturgy or incorporated directly into the liturgical formulary. Taft indicates that certain extant *diataxeis* (see note 21 below) contained only the prothesis rite. See Taft, *The Great Entrance*, xxxv. Trembelas' list of liturgical codices number eighty-nine, dating between the eighth-ninth centuries (*Barberini Codex 336*) and up through the eighteenth, the majority of which are contained in the National Library of Athens (Ἐθνικὴ Βιβλιοθήκη Ἀθηνῶν) and the Byzantine Museum of Athens (Βυζαντινὸ Μουσεῖο Ἀθηνῶν). The prothesis rite received its final form in the fifteenth century, as evidenced by Symeon of Thessalonike. See Αἱ τρεῖς λειτουργίαι, vii–viii.

21. The *diataxis* appeared as a new liturgical source in the twelfth century, geared toward describing the ceremonial of the Divine Liturgy specifically through the combination of the liturgical text with rubrical directions. Up through the fifteenth century, Taft indicates that these sources multiplied chiefly within monastic communities, "probably because of the desire to impose the new developments in the ritual of the prothesis rite" (R. Taft, *The Great Entrance*, xxxv). He furthermore states

that in certain manuscripts, the new prothesis developments were incorporated directly into the liturgical text, while in others the text remained untouched, and the prothesis rite was simply attached to the beginning of the Liturgy as a "Diataxis of the Divine Liturgy" (ibid.). These interesting observations reveal not only the gaining prevalence of the prothesis in the Byzantine East, but also imply the inherent intricacy of the prothesis rite as a 'mini-mass' in itself.

Of the various liturgical *diataxeis* circulating during this period, the most influential was clearly that of Philotheos Kokkinos, written when he was still the abbot of the Great Lavra monastic community on Mt. Athos. Following his elevation to the patriarchal throne of Constantinople in 1353, his *Diataxis* gained widespread prominence, not only throughout the Greek world but also among the Slavic churches. Ibid., xxxvi–xxxvii.

22. PG 150.368–492.

23. PG 155.253–304.

24. PG 155.697–749.

25. Dix, 161.

26. Ibid., 242.

27. Nicholas Cabasilas, *A Commentary on the Divine Liturgy*. trans. J.M. Hussey and P.A. McNulty (London, 1960), 34; PG 150.380D.

28. Symeon of Thessalonike, *On the Sacred Liturgy* 85; PG 155.264C.

29. Hussey and McNulty, trans., 36; Cabasilas, *Commentary* 7; PG 150.384A.

30. Dix, 258.

31. Ibid., 259.

32. Symeon of Thessalonike, *On the Sacred Liturgy* 94; PG 155.285AB. I have added brackets solely for clarification.

33. Henceforth, all New Testament references will derive from the Revised Standard Version (RSV) of the Bible, whereas the Septuagint (LXX) will be used for Old Testament passages.

34. "These words [Luke 22:19] pronounced by the priest apply not only to the bread, prepared at the prothesis, but also to the whole liturgy; he begins with this commemoration and ends with it." See Hussey and McNulty, trans., 35; Cabasilas, *Commentary* 7; PG 150.381D.

35. Symeon of Thessalonike, *On the Sacred Liturgy* 83; PG 155.261B.

36. Ioannes M. Fountoules, Ἀπαντήσεις εἰς λειτουργικὰς ἀπορίας [*Answers to Liturgical Questions*] vol. 3 (Athens, 1994), 43. Translation mine.

37. Bornert, 7. Translation mine.

1

A NEW TRANSLATION OF
THE PROTHESIS RITE

THE MODERN TEXT OF THE PROTHESIS RITE WITH
ENGLISH TRANSLATION

The following text includes the Greek original and my own English translation of a contemporary prothesis rite, as it is celebrated according to
the Byzantine liturgical tradition of the Eastern Orthodox Church. It derives from the 2001 *Hieratikon,* or *Priest's Service Book,* published by Apostolike Diakonia, the official publishing house of the Church of Greece. All
the constitutive sections of the book have been radically revised and greatly
improved by the editor, Fr. Constantine Papayiannis, whose significant efforts have yielded a text free from inaccuracies and inconsistencies, while at
the same time remaining true to the ritual practices of the Late Byzantine era
which reflected, for the most part, the final phase of the prothesis' expansion
into its current form and was the period in which Sts. Nicholas Cabasilas and
Symeon of Thessalonike, contemporaries of Patriarch Philotheos Kokkinos
and his renowned *Diataxis* of the Divine Liturgy, lived and wrote their liturgical commentaries. We shall thus adhere strictly to this document.

A few editorial comments are necessary here. The brackets in the juxta-
posed translation below provide peripheral information meant to give clar-
ity to an expression or word with no direct English equivalent and thus best
left in the original language. The parentheses, on the other hand, include a
word or phrase implied in the Greek but necessary in the English rendition
so as to avoid any vagueness or mistranslation. It is important to note that
the Old Testament scriptural texts used in the prothesis rite are in almost
every case identical to those in the Septuagint. Consequently, I have included the LXX reference in brackets following the text. Finally, endnotes
give extended contextual data that cannot realistically be bracketed.

Ἡ Ἀκολουθία τῆς Προθέσεως
(Ἀποστολικὴ Διακονία, 2001)

The Service of the Prothesis[1]
(Apostolike Diakonia, 2001)

ΠΡΟΣΕΥΧΗ ΤΩΝ ΛΕΙΤΟΥΡΓΩΝ
(ΑΚΟΛΟΥΘΙΑ ΤΟΥ «ΚΑΙΡΟΥ»)

PRAYER OF THE CELEBRANTS[2]
(SERVICE OF "KAIROS")

Μετὰ τὴν ϛ′ ᾠδὴν τῶν κανόνων (ἢ συνηθέστερον ψαλλομένων τῶν καθισμάτων τοῦ Ὄρθρου) ὁ ἱερεὺς καὶ ὁ διάκονος ἐξέρχονται διὰ τῶν πλαγίων θυρῶν καὶ ποιήσαντες μετάνοιαν πρὸ τοῦ θρόνου ἔρχονται ἐνώπιον τῆς Ὡραίας Πύλης οὔσης κεκλεισμένης καὶ προσκυνοῦσι τρὶς λέγοντες καθ᾽ ἑαυτόν· Ὁ Θεός, ἱλάσθητί μοι τῷ ἁμαρτωλῷ καὶ ἐλέησόν με. Εἶτα λέγει ὁ διάκονος χαμηλοφώνως·

Εὐλόγησον, δέσποτα.

Ὁ ἱερεύς· Εὐλογητὸς ὁ Θεὸς ἡμῶν . . .

Ὁ διάκονος· Ἀμήν.

Ὁ ἱερεύς· Δόξα σοι, ὁ Θεός . . . Βασιλεῦ οὐράνιε . . .

Ὁ διάκονος τὸ Τρισάγιον κ.τ.λ.

Ὁ ἱερεύς· Ὅτι σοῦ ἐστιν ἡ Βασιλεία . . .

Ὁ διάκονος· Ἀμήν.

Καὶ λέγουσι τὰ τροπάρια ταῦτα.

Ὁ ἱερεύς·

Ἐλέησον ἡμᾶς, Κύριε, ἐλέησον ἡμᾶς· πάσης γὰρ ἀπολογίας ἀποροῦντες, ταύτην σοι τὴν ἱκεσίαν ὡς Δεσπότῃ οἱ ἁμαρτωλοὶ προσφέρομεν· ἐλέησον ἡμᾶς.

Ὁ διάκονος· Δόξα Πατρί.

Κύριε, ἐλέησον ἡμᾶς· ἐπὶ σοὶ γὰρ πεποίθαμεν· μὴ ὀργισθῇς ἡμῖν σφόδρα, μηδὲ μνησθῇς τῶν ἀνομιῶν ἡμῶν· ἀλλ᾽ ἐπίβλεψον καὶ νῦν ὡς εὔσπλαγχνος καὶ λύτρωσαι ἡμᾶς ἐκ τῶν ἐχθρῶν ἡμῶν· σὺ γὰρ εἶ Θεὸς ἡμῶν καὶ ἡμεῖς λαός σου· πάντες ἔργα χειρῶν σου καὶ τὸ ὄνομά σου ἐπικεκλήμεθα.

Ὁ ἱερεύς· Καὶ νῦν.

After the 6th ode of the canons (or more commonly during the chanting of the kathismata of the Orthros) the priest and the deacon exit the side doors and, making a prostration before the throne, they come in front of the Beautiful Gate, which is completely closed, and they make three venerations, each one saying to himself: O God, be gracious to me the sinner and have mercy on me. Then the deacon says in a low voice:

Bless, master.

The priest: Blessed is our God . . .

The deacon: Amen.

The priest: Glory to you, O God . . . O heavenly King . . .

The deacon [says] the Trisagion, etc.

The priest: For yours is the kingdom . . .

The deacon: Amen.

Then they say these hymns.

The priest:

Have mercy on us, O Lord, have mercy on us; for lacking every defense, we sinners offer to you as Master this plea: have mercy on us.

The deacon: Glory to the Father.

Lord, have mercy on us, for we have hoped in you; do not be exceedingly angry with us, nor remember our transgressions; but look upon us now as the compassionate one and rescue us from our enemies; for you are our God, and we are your people, (we are) all the works of your hands, and we have called upon your name.

The priest: Both now.

Τῆς εὐσπλαγχνίας τὴν πύλην ἄνοιξον ἡμῖν (καὶ ἀνοίγεται τὸ καταπέτασμα τῆς Ὡραίας Πύλης), εὐλογημένη Θεοτόκε· ἐλπίζοντες εἰς σὲ μὴ ἀστοχήσωμεν· ρυσθείημεν διὰ σοῦ τῶν περιστάσεων· σὺ γὰρ εἶ ἡ σωτηρία τοῦ γένους τῶν χριστιανῶν.

Ὁ διάκονος· Κύριε, ἐλέησον ιβʹ.

Καὶ προσκυνοῦσι τὰς ἁγίας εἰκόνας λέγοντες.

Εἰς τὴν εἰκόνα τοῦ Χριστοῦ·

Τὴν ἄχραντον εἰκόνα σου προσκυνοῦμεν, ἀγαθέ, αἰτούμενοι συγχώρησιν τῶν πταισμάτων ἡμῶν, Χριστὲ ὁ Θεός· βουλήσει γὰρ ηὐδόκησας ἀνελθεῖν ἐν τῷ σταυρῷ, ἵνα ρύσῃ οὓς ἔπλασας τῆς δουλείας τοῦ ἐχθροῦ. Ὅθεν εὐχαρίστως βοῶμέν σοι· χαρᾶς ἐπλήρωσας τὰ πάντα, ὁ Σωτὴρ ἡμῶν, παραγενόμενος εἰς τὸ σῶσαι τὸν κόσμον.

Εἰς τὴν εἰκόνα τῆς Θεοτόκου·

Εὐσπλαγχνίας ὑπάρχουσα πηγή, συμπαθείας ἀξίωσον ἡμᾶς, Θεοτόκε· βλέψον εἰς λαὸν τὸν ἁμαρτήσαντα· δεῖξον ὡς ἀεὶ τὴν δυναστείαν σου· εἰς σὲ γὰρ ἐλπίζοντες, τὸ Χαῖρε βοῶμέν σοι, ὥς ποτε ὁ Γαβριήλ, ὁ τῶν ἀσωμάτων ἀρχιστράτηγος.

Εἰς τὴν εἰκόνα τοῦ Προδρόμου·

Μνήμη δικαίου μετ᾽ ἐγκωμίων· σοὶ δὲ ἀρκέσει ἡ μαρτυρία τοῦ Κυρίου, Πρόδρομε· ἀνεδείχθης γὰρ ὄντως καὶ προφητῶν σεβασμιώτερος, ὅτι καὶ ἐν ρείθροις βαπτίσαι κατηξιώθης τὸν κηρυττόμενον· ὅθεν τῆς ἀληθείας ὑπεραθλήσας, χαίρων εὐηγγελίσω καὶ τοῖς ἐν ᾅδῃ Θεὸν φανερωθέντα ἐν σαρκί, τὸν αἴροντα τὴν ἁμαρτίαν τοῦ κόσμου καὶ παρέχοντα ἡμῖν τὸ μέγα ἔλεος.

Καὶ εἰς τὴν εἰκόνα τοῦ ἁγίου τοῦ ναοῦ τὸ ἀπολυτίκιον αὐτοῦ·

Open to us the gate of compassion (*and the veil of the Beautiful Gate is opened*), O blessed Theotokos; hoping in you, may we not fail; through you may we be delivered from tribulation; for you are the salvation of the generation of Christians.

The deacon: Lord, have mercy (*12 times*).

And they venerate the holy icons saying:

Toward the icon of Christ:

Your pure icon we venerate, O good one, asking for forgiveness of our faults, O Christ God; for by your will you deigned to ascend upon the cross, in order to deliver those whom you fashioned from the slavery of the enemy. Wherefore we cry out to you in thanksgiving: you filled all things with joy, O our Savior, coming to save the world.

Toward the icon of the Theotokos:

Being the well of mercy, make us worthy of your compassion, O Theotokos; look upon the people who have sinned; show your might as always, for hoping in you we cry to you, Rejoice, as Gabriel, the chief leader of the bodiless, had done once.

Toward the icon of the Forerunner:

The memory of the righteous (is marked) with praises, but for you the witness of the Lord is sufficient, O Forerunner; for truly you were shown forth more eminent than the prophets, for you were made completely worthy to baptize in the streams the one who is proclaimed; wherefore you have struggled greatly for the truth, rejoicing to evangelize even those in hades, (preaching) God appearing in the flesh, taking away the sin of the world, and granting to us great mercy.

And toward the icon of the saint of the church his dismissal hymn:

Καὶ ἔρχονται πάλιν πρὸ τῆς Ὡραίας Πύ-
λης· καὶ λέγει ὁ διάκονος· Τοῦ Κυρίου
δεηθῶμεν. Κύριε, ἐλέησον. Καὶ ὁ ἱερεὺς κλίνας τὴν κεφαλὴν λέγει τὴν εὐχὴν
ταύτην·

Κύριε, ἐξαπόστειλον τὴν χεῖρά σου ἐξ
ὕψους κατοικητηρίου σου καὶ ἐνίσχυσόν
με εἰς τὴν προκειμένην διακονίαν σου, ἵνα,
ἀκατακρίτως παραστὰς τῷ φοβερῷ βήμα-
τι, τὴν ἀναίμακτον ἱερουργίαν ἐπιτελέσω.
Ὅτι σοῦ ἐστιν ἡ δύναμις καὶ ἡ δόξα εἰς τοὺς
αἰῶνας τῶν αἰώνων.

Ὁ διάκονος· Ἀμήν.

Ὁ ἱερεύς· Δόξα σοι, Χριστὲ ὁ Θεός, ἡ ἐλπὶς
ἡμῶν, δόξα σοι.

Ὁ διάκονος· Δόξα, καὶ νῦν. Κύριε, ἐλέησον
γ΄. Δέσποτα ἅγιε, εὐλόγησον.

Καὶ ὁ ἱερεὺς τὴν μικρὰν ἀπόλυσιν·

Χριστὸς ὁ ἀληθινὸς Θεὸς ἡμῶν, ταῖς
πρεσβείαις τῆς παναχράντου καὶ παναμώμου ἁγίας αὐτοῦ Μητρός, τῶν ἁγίων ἐνδόξων καὶ πανευφήμων ἀποστόλων, τοῦ ἁγίου (τοῦ ναοῦ), τοῦ ἐν ἁγίοις πατρὸς ἡμῶν
Ἰωάννου ἀρχιεπισκόπου Κωνσταντινουπόλεως τοῦ Χρυσοστόμου, (ἢ τοῦ ἐν ἁγίοις πατρὸς ἡμῶν Βασιλείου ἀρχιεπισκόπου
Καισαρείας τοῦ μεγάλου καὶ οὐρανοφάντορος) καὶ πάντων τῶν ἁγίων ἐλεήσαι καὶ
σώσαι ἡμᾶς ὡς ἀγαθὸς καὶ φιλάνθρωπος.

Δι᾽ εὐχῶν τῶν ἁγίων πατέρων ἡμῶν,
Κύριε Ἰησοῦ Χριστὲ ὁ Θεός, ἐλέησον ἡμᾶς.

Ὁ διάκονος· Ἀμήν.

Καὶ αἰτησάμενοι διὰ κλήσεως τῆς κεφαλῆς
συγχώρησιν παρὰ τοῦ λαοῦ εἰσέρχονται διὰ
τῶν πλαγίων εἰς τὸ Ἱερὸν λέγοντες ἕκαστος·
Εἰσελεύσομαι εἰς τὸν οἶκόν σου, προσ-
κυνήσω πρὸς ναὸν ἅγιόν σου ἐν φόβῳ σου.

Καὶ προσκυνήσαντες τρὶς ἐνώπιον τῆς ἁγίας
Τραπέζης ἀσπάζονται ὁ μὲν ἱερεὺς τὸ ἱ. Εὐαγγέλιον καὶ τὴν ἁγίαν Τράπεζαν, ὁ δὲ διάκονος
μόνον τὴν ἁγίαν Τράπεζαν.

And they come again before the Beautiful Gate; and the deacon says: Let us pray to the Lord. Lord, have mercy. And the priest bowing his head says this prayer:[3]

Lord, send out your hand from the height of your abode and strengthen me for your present ministry, so that standing uncondemned before your fearful bema, I may conduct this bloodless holy work. For yours is the power and glory to the ages of ages.

The deacon: Amen.

The priest: Glory to you, O Christ God, our hope, glory to you.

The deacon: Glory, both now. Lord, have mercy (3 times). Holy master, bless.

And the priest (says) the small dismissal:

May Christ our true God, through the intercessions of his all-pure and all-blameless holy Mother, of the holy glorious and all-praiseworthy apostles, of saint (of the church), of our father among the saints John Chrysostom, Archbishop of Constantinople, (or of our father among the saints Basil the Great and revealer of heaven, Archbishop of Caesarea) and of all the saints, have mercy on us and save us as one who is good and loves man.

Through the prayers of our holy fathers, Lord Jesus Christ God, have mercy on us.

The deacon: Amen.

And asking for forgiveness from the people by the bowing of their head they enter into the Altar through the sides [doors], each one saying: I shall enter into your house, I shall worship toward your temple in your fear.

And making three venerations before the holy Table, the priest kisses the holy Gospel and the holy Table and the deacon only the holy Table.

ΕΝΔΥΣΙΣ ΚΑΙ ΝΙΨΙΣ ΧΕΙΡΩΝ

Εἶτα λαβόντες ἕκαστος τὸ στιχάριον προσκυνοῦσι τρὶς πρὸς ἀνατολὰς λέγοντες· Ὁ Θεός, ἱλάσθητί μοι τῷ ἁμαρτωλῷ καὶ ἐλέησόν με.

Καὶ ὁ μὲν διάκονος κρατῶν τὴν στολὴν αὐτοῦ προσέρχεται εἰς τὸν ἱερέα λέγων· Εὐλόγησον, δέσποτα, τὸ στιχάριον σὺν τῷ ὀραρίῳ. Ὁ ἱερεὺς εὐλογεῖ αὐτὰ λέγων· Εὐλογητὸς ὁ Θεὸς ἡμῶν... Καὶ ὁ διάκονος ἀσπασάμενος ἕκαστον ἄμφιον καὶ λέγων·

Ἀγαλλιάσεται ἡ ψυχή μου ἐπὶ τῷ Κυρίῳ· ἐνέδυσε γάρ με ἱμάτιον σωτηρίου καὶ χιτῶνα εὐφροσύνης περιέβαλέ με· ὡς νυμφίῳ περιέθηκέ μοι μίτραν καὶ ὡς νύμφην κατεκόσμησέ με κόσμῳ.

Εἰς τὸ ὀράριον·

Ὁ θέλων γενέσθαι μέγας ἐν ὑμῖν, ἔσται ὑμῶν διάκονος.

Εἰς τὸ δεξιὸν ἐπιμάνικον·

Ἡ δεξιά σου, Κύριε, δεδόξασται ἐν ἰσχύϊ· ἡ δεξιά σου χείρ, Κύριε, ἔθραυσεν ἐχθρούς· καὶ τῷ πλήθει τῆς δόξης σου συνέτριψας τοὺς ὑπεναντίους.

Εἰς τὸ ἀριστερόν·

Αἱ χεῖρές σου ἐποίησάν με καὶ ἔπλασάν με· συνέτισόν με καὶ μαθήσομαι τὰς ἐντολάς σου.

Καὶ ἀπελθὼν εἰς τὸν νιπτῆρα νίπτεται τὰς χεῖρας αὐτοῦ λέγων·

Νίψομαι ἐν ἀθῴοις τὰς χεῖράς μου καὶ κυκλώσω τὸ θυσιαστήριόν σου, Κύριε, τοῦ ἀκοῦσαί με φωνῆς αἰνέσεώς σου καὶ διηγήσασθαι πάντα τὰ θαυμάσιά σου. Κύριε, ἠγάπησα εὐπρέπειαν οἴκου σου καὶ τόπον σκηνώματος δόξης σου· μὴ συναπολέσῃς μετὰ ἀσεβῶν τὴν ψυχήν μου καὶ μετὰ ἀνδρῶν αἱμάτων τὴν ζωήν μου, ὧν

VESTING AND WASHING OF THE HANDS[4]

Then each receiving [taking] the sticharion, they make three venerations toward the east saying: O God, be gracious to me the sinner and have mercy on me.

The deacon, holding his vestments, comes to the priest saying: Bless, master, the sticharion with the orarion. *The priest blesses them saying:* Blessed is our God ... *And the deacon, kissing the hand of the priest, wears his vestments, kissing each vestment and saying:*

My soul shall rejoice in the Lord; for he has clothed me with the garment of salvation and has dressed me with the robe of joy; he has placed a crown on me as on a bridegroom, and adorned me with ornaments as a bride. [Is 61.10]

For the orarion:

He who wants to become great among you, let him be your servant. [Mt 20.26]

For the right epimanikon:

Your right hand, O Lord, has been glorified in strength; your right hand, O Lord, has destroyed enemies; and in the abundance of your glory you have shattered the adversaries to pieces. [Ex 15.6]

For the left (epimanikon):

Your hands have made me and fashioned me; teach me and I shall learn your commandments. [Ps 118.73]

And coming to the water basin, he washes his hands saying:

I shall wash my hands in innocence and encompass your altar, O Lord, to hear the voice of your praise and to declare all your wonders. O Lord, I have loved the beauty of your house and the dwelling place of your glory; destroy not my soul together with the ungodly nor my life with bloody men, in whose hands are iniquities; their right hand

ἐν χερσὶν ἀνομίαι, ἡ δεξιὰ αὐτῶν ἐπλήσθη δώρων. Ἐγὼ δὲ ἐν ἀκακίᾳ μου ἐπορεύθην· λύτρωσαί με, Κύριε, καὶ ἐλέησόν με· ὁ πούς μου ἔστη ἐν εὐθύτητι· ἐν ἐκκλησίαις εὐλογήσω σε, Κύριε.

Καὶ μετὰ τοῦτο ἔρχεται εἰς τὴν Πρόθεσιν καὶ εὐτρεπίζει τὰ ἱερὰ σκεύη. Ὁ δὲ ἱερεὺς ἐνδύεται ἐπίσης τὴν στολὴν αὐτοῦ εὐλογῶν καὶ ἀσπασάμενος ἕκαστον ἄμφιον καὶ λέγων·

Εἰς τὸ στιχάριον·

Ἀγαλλιάσεται ἡ ψυχή μου ...

Εἰς τὸ ἐπιτραχήλιον·

Εὐλογητὸς ὁ Θεός, ὁ ἐκχέων τὴν χάριν αὐτοῦ ἐπὶ τοὺς ἱερεῖς αὐτοῦ ὡς μύρον ἐπὶ κεφαλῆς τὸ καταβαῖνον ἐπὶ πώγωνα, τὸν πώγωνα τοῦ Ἀαρών, τὸ καταβαῖνον ἐπὶ τὴν ᾤαν τοῦ ἐνδύματος αὐτοῦ.

Εἰς τὴν ζώνην·

Εὐλογητὸς ὁ Θεός, ὁ περιζωννύων με δύναμιν καὶ ἔθετο ἄμωμον τὴν ὁδόν μου.

Εἰς τὸ δεξιὸν ἐπιμάνικον·

Ἡ δεξιά σου, Κύριε, δεδόξασται ...

Εἰς τὸ ἀριστερόν·

Αἱ χεῖρές σου ἐποίησάν με ...

Εἰς τὸ ἐπιγονάτιον (ἐὰν ἔχῃ ἐκκλησιαστικὸν ὀφφίκιον)·

Περίζωσαι τὴν ῥομφαίαν σου ἐπὶ τὸν μηρόν σου, δυνατέ, τῇ ὡραιότητί σου καὶ τῷ κάλλει σου καὶ ἔντεινε καὶ κατευοδοῦ καὶ βασίλευε ἕνεκεν ἀληθείας καὶ πρᾳότητος καὶ δικαιοσύνης, καὶ ὁδηγήσει σε θαυμαστῶς ἡ δεξιά σου.

Εἰς τὸ φελώνιον·

Οἱ ἱερεῖς σου, Κύριε, ἐνδύσονται δικαιοσύνην καὶ οἱ ὅσιοί σου ἀγαλλιάσονται.

Καὶ οὕτως ἀπελθὼν νίπτεται καὶ αὐτὸς τὰς χεῖρας λέγων·

is filled with bribes. But I have walked in innocence; rescue me, O Lord, and have mercy on me; my foot will stand on level ground; in the congregations I shall praise you, O Lord. [Ps 25.6–12]

And after this, he comes to the Prothesis and prepares the holy vessels. And the priest likewise wears his vestments, blessing and kissing each vestment and saying:

For the sticharion:

My soul shall rejoice ...

For the epitrachelion:

Blessed is God, who pours out his grace upon his priests as myrrh upon the head that descends upon the beard, the beard of Aaron, that descends to the edge of his garment. [Ps 132.2]

For the zone:

Blessed is God, who girds me with power and has made my way blameless. [Ps 17.33]

For the right epimanikon:

Your right hand, O Lord, has been glorified ...

For the left (epimanikon):

Your hands have made me ...

For the epigonation (if he has an ecclesiastical offikion):

Gird your sword upon your thigh, O mighty one, in your comeliness and your beauty and bend your bow and prosper and reign for the sake of truth and meekness and righteousness, and your right hand shall guide you wondrously. [Ps 44.4–5]

For the phelonion:

Your priests, O Lord, shall be dressed in righteousness and your holy ones shall rejoice. [Ps 131.9]

And likewise coming to the water basin, he too washes his hands saying:

Νίψομαι ἐν ἀθῴοις τὰς χεῖράς μου . . .

ΠΡΟΕΤΟΙΜΑΣΙΑ ΤΩΝ ΤΙΜΙΩΝ ΔΩΡΩΝ

Μετὰ ταῦτα ἐλθόντες εἰς τὴν Πρόθεσιν προσκυνοῦσι τρὶς λέγοντες· Ὁ Θεός, ἱλάσθητί μοι τῷ ἁμαρτωλῷ καὶ ἐλέησόν με.

Εἶτα λέγει ὁ διάκονος· Εὐλόγησον, δέσποτα.

Καὶ ὁ ἱερεύς· Εὐλογητὸς ὁ Θεὸς ἡμῶν πάντοτε . . .

Καὶ λαβὼν τὴν προσφορὰν ὑψοῖ αὐτὴν μετὰ τῆς λόγχης λέγων·

Ἐξηγόρασας ἡμᾶς ἐκ τῆς κατάρας τοῦ νόμου τῷ τιμίῳ σου αἵματι· τῷ σταυρῷ προσηλωθεὶς καὶ τῇ λόγχῃ κεντηθεὶς τὴν ἀθανασίαν ἐπήγασας ἀνθρώποις. Σωτὴρ ἡμῶν, δόξα σοι.

Εἶτα σφραγίζει ἐκ τρίτου τὴν προσφορὰν διὰ τῆς λόγχης λέγων εἰς ἑκάστην σφράγισιν·

Εἰς ἀνάμνησιν τοῦ Κυρίου καὶ Θεοῦ καὶ Σωτῆρος ἡμῶν Ἰησοῦ Χριστοῦ.

Ὁ διάκονος· Πάντοτε, νῦν καὶ ἀεὶ καὶ εἰς τοὺς αἰῶνας τῶν αἰώνων. Ἀμήν.

Ἀκολούθως ὁ ἱερεὺς ἐμπηγνύει τὴν λόγχην εἰς τὸ δεξιὸν μέρος τῆς σφραγῖδος, ἐν ᾧ ἐστι τὸ IC, καὶ ἀνατέμνων λέγει·

Ὡς πρόβατον ἐπὶ σφαγὴν ἤχθη.

Εἰς δὲ τὸ ἀριστερόν, ἐν ᾧ ἐστι τὸ XC·

Καὶ ὡς ἀμνὸς ἄμωμος, ἐναντίον τοῦ κείροντος αὐτὸν ἄφωνος, οὕτως οὐκ ἀνοίγει τὸ στόμα αὐτοῦ.

Εἰς τὸ ἄνω μέρος·

Ἐν τῇ ταπειώσει αὐτοῦ ἡ κρίσις αὐτοῦ ἤρθη.

Εἰς τὸ κάτω·

Τὴν δὲ γενεὰν αὐτοῦ τίς διηγήσεται; Ὁ διάκονος· Ἔπαρον, δέσποτα.

I shall wash my hands in innocence . . .

PREPARATION OF THE PRECIOUS GIFTS

After these, coming to the Prothesis they make three venerations saying: O God, be gracious to me the sinner and have mercy on me.

Then the deacon says: Bless, master.

And the priest: Blessed is our God always . . .

And taking the prosphora he lifts it with the lance saying:

You have purchased us from the curse of the law by your precious blood; nailed to the cross and pierced by the lance, you have made immortality gush forth for men. O our Savior, glory to you.[5]

Then he seals [crosses] the prosphora three times with the lance saying at each sealing:

In remembrance of our Lord and God and Savior Jesus Christ.

The deacon: Always, now and forever and to the ages of ages. Amen.

Consequently, the priest inserts the lance into the right side of the seal, where the IC [portion] is, and cutting he says:

As a sheep he was led to the slaughter. [Is 53.7]

And into the left, where the XC [portion] is:

And as a blameless[6] lamb before its shearer (is) silent, so he also opens not his mouth. [Is 53.7]

Into the top section:

In his humility his judgment was taken away. [Is 53.8]

Into the bottom section:

Who shall tell of his generation? [Is 53.8]

The deacon:[7] Lift up, master.

Καὶ ὁ ἱερεὺς ἐπαίρει διὰ τῆς λόγχης τὸν ἀμνὸν λέγων·

And the priest lifts up the Lamb with the lance saying:

Ὅτι αἴρεται ἀπὸ τῆς γῆς ἡ ζωὴ αὐτοῦ.

For his life is lifted up from the earth. [Is 53.8]

Καὶ θέτει αὐτὸν ὕπτιον ἐν τῷ δισκαρίῳ.

And he places it upside down on the paten.

Ὁ διάκονος· Θῦσον, δέσποτα.

The deacon: Sacrifice, master.

Ὁ ἱερεὺς θύει αὐτὸν χαράσσων σταυρὸν βαθέως διὰ τῆς λόγχης καὶ λέγων·

The priest slices it, making a deep incision crosswise with the lance and saying:

Θύεται ὁ ἀμνὸς τοῦ Θεοῦ, ὁ αἴρων τὴν ἁμαρτίαν τοῦ κόσμου, ὑπὲρ τῆς τοῦ κόσμου ζωῆς καὶ σωτηρίας.

The Lamb of God, who takes away the sin of the world, is sacrificed for the life and salvation of the world.

Καὶ στρέφει ἐπάνω τὸ ἕτερον μέρος, ἤτοι τὸ ἔχον τὴν σφραγῖδα.

And he turns the other part upward, that is, the one having the seal.

Ὁ διάκονος· Νύξον, δέσποτα.

The deacon: Pierce, master.

Καὶ ὁ ἱερεὺς νύττει τὸν ἄρτον διὰ τῆς λόγχης ὑπὸ τὸ ὄνομα IC λέγων·

And the priest pierces the bread with the lance beneath the name IC saying:

Εἰς τῶν στρατιωτῶν λόγχῃ αὐτοῦ τὴν πλευρὰν ἔνυξε· καὶ εὐθέως ἐξῆλθεν αἷμα καὶ ὕδωρ· καὶ ὁ ἑωρακὼς μεμαρτύρηκε καὶ ἀληθινή ἐστιν ἡ μαρτυρία αὐτοῦ.

One of the soldiers pierced his side with a spear, and at once there came out blood and water; and he who has seen it has borne witness and his witness is true. [Jn 19.34–35]

Ὁ διάκονος ἐγχέει εἰς τὸ ἅγιον ποτήριον νᾶμα καὶ ὕδωρ λέγων·

The deacon pours wine and water into the holy chalice saying:

Εὐλόγησον, δέσποτα, τὴν ἁγίαν ἕνωσιν.

Bless, master, the holy union.

Καὶ ὁ ἱερεὺς εὐλογεῖ αὐτὰ λέγων·

And the priest blesses them saying:

Εὐλογημένη ἡ ἕνωσις τῶν ἁγίων σου πάντοτε, νῦν καὶ ἀεὶ καὶ εἰς τοὺς αἰῶνας τῶν αἰώνων. Ἀμήν.

Blessed is the union of your holy things always, now and forever and to the ages of ages. Amen.

Εἶτα λαβὼν ἑτέραν προσφορὰν λέγει·

Then taking another prosphora he says:

Εἰς τιμὴν καὶ μνήμην τῆς ὑπερευλογημένης, ἐνδόξου δεσποίνης ἡμῶν, Θεοτόκου καὶ ἀειπαρθένου Μαρίας, ἧς ταῖς πρεσβείαις πρόσδεξαι, Κύριε, τὴν θυσίαν ταύτην εἰς τὸ ὑπερουράνιόν σου θυσιαστήριον.

In honor and memory of our most-blessed, glorious lady, the Theotokos and ever-virgin Mary, through whose intercessions accept, O Lord, this sacrifice upon your super-celestial altar.

Καὶ τέμνει ἐξ αὐτῆς τὴν μερίδα τῆς Θεοτόκου καὶ θέτει αὐτὴν εἰς τὰ δεξιὰ τοῦ Ἀμνοῦ λέγων·

And he cuts from this the particle of the Theotokos and places it to the right of the Lamb saying:

Παρέστη ἡ βασίλισσα ἐκ δεξιῶν σου ἐν ἱματισμῷ διαχρύσῳ, περιβεβλημένη, πεποικιλμένη.

Εἶτα λαβὼν τρίτην προσφορὰν (ἢ τὴν αὐτήν, ἐλλείψει ἄλλης) ἐξάγει ἐξ αὐτῆς ἐννέα μερίδας πρὸς τιμὴν τῶν ἁγίων καὶ θέτει αὐτὰς εἰς τὰ ἀριστερὰ τοῦ Ἀμνοῦ εἰς τρεῖς τάξεις ἀνὰ τρεῖς μερίδας ἐκ τῶν ἄνω πρὸς τὰ κάτω, ἤτοι τὴν δευτέραν κάτωθεν τῆς πρώτης, τὴν τρίτην κάτωθεν τῆς δευτέρας, τὴν τετάρτην πλησίον τῆς πρώτης, τὴν πέμπτην πλησίον τῆς δευτέρας κ.ο.κ., λέγων·

Εἰς τὴν α΄ μερίδα·

Εἰς τιμὴν καὶ μνήμην τῶν παμμεγίστων ταξιαρχῶν Μιχαὴλ καὶ Γαβριὴλ καὶ πασῶν τῶν ἐπουρανίων δυνάμεων ἀσωμάτων.

Εἰς τὴν β΄ μερίδα·

Τοῦ τιμίου καὶ ἐνδόξου προφήτου, προδρόμου καὶ βαπτιστοῦ Ἰωάννου, τῶν ἁγίων ἐνδόξων προφητῶν Μωσέως καὶ Ἀαρών, Ἠλιοὺ καὶ Ἐλισσαίου, Δαβὶδ καὶ Ἰεσσαί, τῶν ἁγίων τριῶν Παίδων καὶ Δανιὴλ τοῦ προφήτου καὶ πάντων τῶν ἁγίων προφητῶν.

Εἰς τὴν γ΄ μερίδα·

Τῶν ἁγίων ἐνδόξων καὶ πανευφήμων ἀποστόλων Πέτρου καὶ Παύλου, τῶν Δώδεκα καὶ τῶν Ἑβδομήκοντα καὶ πάντων τῶν ἁγίων ἀποστόλων.

Εἰς τὴν δ΄ μερίδα·

Τῶν ἐν ἁγίοις πατέρων ἡμῶν, μεγάλων ἱεραρχῶν καὶ οἰκουμενικῶν διδασκάλων Βασιλείου τοῦ Μεγάλου, Γρηγορίου τοῦ Θεολόγου καὶ Ἰωάννου τοῦ Χρυσοστόμου, Ἀθανασίου καὶ Κυρίλλου, Νικολάου τοῦ ἐν Μύροις καὶ πάντων τῶν ἁγίων ἱεραρχῶν.

Εἰς τὴν ε΄ μερίδα·

Τοῦ ἁγίου πρωτομάρτυρος καὶ ἀρχιδιακόνου Στεφάνου, τῶν ἁγίων μεγάλων

The queen stood at your right hand, clothed and adorned in a garment of pure gold.

Then taking a third prosphora (or the same one, if there is no other) he takes out from it nine particles in honor of the saints and he places them to the left of the Lamb in three columns of three particles each from the top to the bottom, that is, the second one beneath the first, the third beneath the second, the fourth next to the first, the fifth next to the second, etc., saying:

For the first particle:

In honor and memory of the exceedingly great commanders Michael and Gabriel and all the heavenly bodiless powers.

For the second particle:

Of the honorable and glorious prophet, forerunner and baptist John, the holy glorious prophets Moses and Aaron, Elijah and Elisha, David and Jesse, the holy Three Children and Daniel the prophet, and all the holy prophets.

For the third particle:

Of the holy, glorious and all-praiseworthy apostles Peter and Paul, the Twelve and the Seventy, and all the holy apostles.

For the fourth particle:

Of our holy fathers among the saints, great hierarchs and ecumenical teachers Basil the Great, Gregory the Theologian, and John Chrysostom, Athanasios and Cyril, Nicholas of Myra, and all the holy hierarchs.

For the fifth particle:

Of the holy first martyr and archdeacon Stephen, the holy great martyrs George the

μαρτύρων Γεώργίου τοῦ Τροπαιοφόρου, Δημητρίου τοῦ Μυροβλήτου, Θεοδώρου τοῦ Τήρωνος καὶ Θεοδώρου τοῦ Στρατηλάτου, τῶν ἱερομαρτύρων Χαραλάμπους καὶ Ἐλευθερίου καὶ πάντων καὶ πασῶν τῶν ἁγίων μαρτύρων.

Εἰς τὴν ς' μερίδα·

Τῶν ὁσίων καὶ θεοφόρων πατέρων ἡμῶν Ἀντωνίου, Εὐθυμίου, Σάββα, Ὀνουφρίου, Ἀθανασίου τοῦ ἐν τῷ Ἄθῳ καὶ πάντων καὶ πασῶν τῶν ὁσίων.

Εἰς τὴν ζ' μερίδα·

Τῶν ἁγίων καὶ θαυματουργῶν ἀναργύρων Κοσμᾶ καὶ Δαμιανοῦ, Κύρου καὶ Ἰωάννου, Παντελεήμονος καὶ Ἑρμολάου καὶ πάντων τῶν ἁγίων ἀναργύρων.

Εἰς τὴν η' μερίδα·

Τῶν ἁγίων καὶ δικαίων θεοπατόρων Ἰωακεὶμ καὶ Ἄννης, τοῦ ἁγίου (τῆς ἡμέρας), οὗ καὶ τὴν μνήμην ἐπιτελοῦμεν.

Εἰς τὴν θ' μερίδα·

Τοῦ ἐν ἁγίοις πατρὸς ἡμῶν Ἰωάννου ἀρχιεπισκόπου Κωνσταντινουπόλεως τοῦ Χρυσοστόμου (ἢ Βασιλείου ἀρχιεπισκόπου Καισαρείας τοῦ μεγάλου καὶ οὐρανοφάντορος), καὶ πάντων τῶν ἁγίων, ὧν ταῖς ἱκεσίαις ἐπίσκεψαι ἡμᾶς, ὁ Θεός.

Εἶτα ἐξάγει μερίδας ὑπὲρ τῶν ζώντων καὶ τίθησιν αὐτὰς ὑποκάτω τοῦ Ἀμνοῦ πρὸς τὰ δεξιὰ λέγων·

Μνήσθητι, Δέσποτα φιλάνθρωπε, πάσης ἐπισκοπῆς ὀρθοδόξων, τοῦ ἀρχιεπισκόπου ἡμῶν (δεῖνος), τοῦ τιμίου πρεσβυτερίου, τῆς ἐν Χριστῷ διακονίας καὶ παντὸς ἱερατικοῦ καὶ μοναχικοῦ τάγματος [ἐν τοῖς μοναστηρίοις· τοῦ πατρὸς ἡμῶν (δεῖνος) ἱερομονάχου] καὶ πάσης τῆς ἐν Χριστῷ ἡμῶν ἀδελφότητος.

Καὶ μνημονεύει τοῦ χειροτονήσαντος αὐτὸν ἀρχιερέως, ἐὰν εἶναι ἐν τῇ ζωῇ, καὶ ὧν ἔχει ζώντων κατ' ὄνομα καὶ ἐπιλέγει·

Triumphant, Demetrios the Myrrh-flowing, Theodore the Recruit and Theodore the Commander, the priest-martyrs Haralambos and Eleftherios, and all the holy [male and female] martyrs.

For the sixth particle:

Of our righteous and God-bearing fathers Anthony, Euthymios, Sabbas, Onouphrios, Athanasios of Athos, and all the [male and female ascetics] righteous.

For the seventh particle:

Of the holy and miraculous unmercenaries Kosmas and Damian, Kyros and John, Panteleimon and Hermolaos, and all the holy unmercenaries.

For the eighth particle:

Of the holy and righteous ancestors of God Joachim and Anna, of Saint *(of the day)*, whose memory we commemorate.

For the ninth particle:

Of our holy father among the saints John Chrysostom, Archbishop of Constantinople *(or* Basil the Great and revealer of heaven, Archbishop of Caesarea) and all the saints, through whose supplications visit us, O God.

Then he takes out particles for the living and places them below the Lamb toward the right saying:

Remember, O loving Master, every diocese of the Orthodox, our archbishop *(name)*, the honorable presbyterate, the diaconate in Christ and every priestly and monastic order [*in the monasteries:* our father *(name)* the priest-monk] and all our brother-hood in Christ.

And he commemorates the hierarch who ordained him, if he is alive, and by name all the living and he adds:

Καὶ πάντων τῶν ἀδελφῶν ἡμῶν, οὓς προσεκάλεσω εἰς τὴν σὴν διακονίαν διὰ τῆς σῆς εὐσπλαγνίας, φιλάνθρωπε Δέσποτα.

Ἀκολούθως ἐξάγει μερίδας ὑπὲρ τῶν κεκοιμημένων καὶ θέτει αὐτὰς ὑποκάτω τοῦ Ἀμνοῦ πρὸς τὰ ἀριστερὰ λέγων·

Ὑπὲρ μνήμης καὶ ἀφέσεως τῶν ἁμαρτιῶν τῶν μακαρίων καὶ ἀοιδίμων κτιτόρων τῆς ἁγίας Ἐκκλησίας (ἢ τῆς ἁγίας μονῆς) τάυτης.

Καὶ μνημονεύει τοῦ χειροτονήσαντος αὐτὸν ἀρχιερέως, ἐὰν ἔχῃ κοιμηθῆ, καὶ ὧν ἔχει κεκοιμημένων, καὶ ἐπιλέγει·

Καὶ πάντων τῶν ἐπ᾽ ἐλπίδι ἀναστάσεως ζωῆς αἰωνίου, τῶν τῇ σῇ κοινωνίᾳ κεκοιμημένων ὀρθοδόξων πατέρων καὶ ἀδελφῶν ἡμῶν, φιλάνθρωπε Κύριε.

Μνημονεύει δὲ καὶ ὁ διάκονος ὧν βούλεται ζώντων καὶ κεκοιμημένων.

Τελευταῖον δὲ αἴρει ὁ ἱερεὺς μερίδα ὑπὲρ ἑαυτοῦ καὶ θέτει αὐτὴν μετὰ τῶν μερίδων τῶν ζώντων λέγων·

Μνήσθητι, Κύριε, καὶ τῆς ἐμῆς ἀναξιότητος· καὶ συγχώρησόν μοι πᾶν πλημμέλημα ἑκούσιόν τε καὶ ἀκούσιον.

Εἶτα ὁ διάκονος λαβὼν τὸ θυμιατήριον καὶ βαλὼν θυμίαμα λέγει πρὸς τὸν ἱερέα·

Εὐλόγησον, δέσποτα, τὸ θυμίαμα.

Εἶτα ὁ ἱερεὺς εὐλογῶν λέγει τὴν εὐχὴν τοῦ θυμιάματος·

Θυμίαμά σοι προσφέρομεν, Χριστὲ ὁ Θεὸς ἡμῶν, εἰς ὀσμὴν εὐωδίας πνευματικῆς· ὃ προσδεξάμενος εἰς τὸ ὑπερουράνιόν σου θυσιαστήριον, ἀντικατάπεμψον ἡμῖν τὴν χάριν τοῦ παναγίου σου Πνεύματος.

Ὁ διάκονος θυμιῶν τὸν ἀστερίσκον λέγει·

Στερέωσον, δέσποτα.

And all our brothers, whom you have called to your service through your compassion, O loving Master.

Consequently, he takes out particles for those who have fallen asleep and places them beneath the Lamb toward the left saying:

For the memory and forgiveness of the sins of the blessed and ever-memorable builders of this holy Church (*or* holy monastery).

And he commemorates the hierarch who ordained him, if he has fallen asleep, and all those who have fallen asleep, and he adds:

And all who in hope of the resurrection of eternal life have fallen asleep in communion with you, our Orthodox fathers and brothers, O loving Lord.

And the deacon commemorates the living and dead which he wants.

And finally the priest lifts up a particle for himself and places it with the particles of the living saying:

Remember also, O Lord, my unworthiness and forgive me every transgression both voluntary and involuntary.

Then the deacon takes the censer and placing incense (in it) says to the priest:

Bless, master, the incense.

And the priest blessing says the prayer of the incense:

We offer incense to you, O Christ our God, as a scent of spiritual fragrance; receiving it upon your super-celestial altar, send down to us in return the grace of your all-holy Spirit.

The deacon censing the asteriskos says:

Make firm, master.

Καὶ ὁ ἱερεὺς θέτει τὸν ἀστερίσκον ἐπὶ τοῦ δίσκου λέγων·

Τῷ λόγῳ Κυρίου οἱ οὐρανοὶ ἐστερεώθησαν καὶ τῷ πνεύματι τοῦ στόματος αὐτοῦ πάσα ἡ δύναμις αὐτῶν.

Ὁ διάκονος θυμιῶν τὸ πρῶτον κάλυμμα λέγει·

Εὐπρέπισον, δέσποτα. Ὁ δὲ ἱερεὺς καλύπτει δι' αὐτοῦ τὸν ἅγιον δίσκον λέγων·

Ὁ Κύριος ἐβασίλευσεν, εὐπρέπειαν ἐνεδύσατο· ἐνεδύσατο Κύριος δύναμιν καὶ περιεζώσατο.

Ὁ διάκονος θυμιῶν τὸ δεύτερον κάλυμμα λέγει· Κάλυψον, δέσποτα. Ὁ δὲ ἱερεὺς καλύπτει δι' αὐτοῦ τὸ ἅγιον ποτήριον λέγων·

Ἐκάλυψεν οὐρανοὺς ἡ ἀρετή σου, Χριστέ, καὶ τῆς αἰνέσεώς σου πλήρης ἡ γῆ. Ὁ διάκονος θυμιῶν τὸν ἀέρα λέγει· Σκέπασον, δέσποτα. Ὁ δὲ ἱερεὺς καλύπτει ἀμφότερα τὰ ἅγια λέγων·

Σκέπασον ἡμᾶς ἐν τῇ σκέπῃ τῶν πτερύγων σου· ἀποδίωξον ἀφ' ἡμῶν πάντα ἐχθρὸν καὶ πολέμιον· εἰρήνευσον ἡμῶν τὴν ζωήν· Κύριε, ἐλέησον ἡμᾶς καὶ τὸν κόσμον σου καὶ σῶσον τὰς ψυχὰς ἡμῶν ὡς ἀγαθὸς καὶ φιλάνθρωπος.

Ὁ διάκονος· Εὐλόγησον, δέσποτα.

Καὶ ὁ ἱερεὺς λαβὼν τὸ θυμιατήριον θυμιᾷ τὴν Πρόθεσιν λέγων ἐκ γ'·

Εὐλογητὸς ὁ Θεὸς ἡμῶν, ὁ οὕτως εὐδοκήσας· δόξα σοι.

Ὁ δὲ διάκονος ἐπιλέγει ἑκάστοτε·

Πάντοτε, νῦν καὶ ἀεὶ καὶ εἰς τοὺς αἰῶνας τῶν αἰώνων. Ἀμήν.

Εἶτα λέγει ὁ διάκονος·

Ἐπὶ τῇ προθέσει τῶν τιμίων δώρων τοῦ Κυρίου δεηθῶμεν. Κύριε, ἐλέησον.

Καὶ ὁ ἱερεὺς τὴν εὐχήν.

And the priest places the asteriskos upon the paten saying:

By the word of the Lord the heavens were made firm and by the breath of his mouth all their power. [Ps 32.6]

The deacon censing the first veil says:

Beautify, master. And the priest covers with it the holy paten saying:

The Lord has reigned, he has clothed himself with beauty; the Lord has clothed and girded himself with power. [Ps 92.1]

The deacon censing the second veil says: Cover, master. And the priest covers with it the holy chalice saying:

Your virtue, O Christ, covered the heavens, and the earth (is) full of your praise.

The deacon censing the aer says: Shelter, master. And the priest covers both holy vessels saying:

Shelter us under the shelter of your wings; drive away from us every enemy and adversary; pacify our lives; Lord, have mercy on us and your world and save our souls as (one who is good) and loves man.

The deacon: Bless, master.

And the priest, taking the censer, censes the Prothesis three times saying:

Blessed is our God, who has so deigned; glory to you.

And the deacon adds each time:

Always, now and forever and to the ages of ages. Amen.[8]

Then the deacon says:

Upon the offering of the precious gifts let us pray to the Lord. Lord, have mercy.

And the priest the prayer.

ΕΥΧΗ ΤΗΣ ΠΡΟΘΕΣΕΩΣ

Ὁ Θεός, ὁ Θεὸς ἡμῶν, ὁ τὸν οὐράνιον ἄρτον, τὴν τροφὴν τοῦ παντὸς κόσμου, τὸν Κύριον ἡμῶν καὶ Θεὸν Ἰησοῦν Χριστὸν ἐξαποστείλας σωτῆρα καὶ λυτρωτὴν καὶ εὐεργέτην, εὐλογοῦντα καὶ ἁγιάζοντα ἡμᾶς· αὐτὸς εὐλόγησον τὴν πρόθεσιν ταύτην καὶ πρόσδεξαι αὐτὴν εἰς τὸ ὑπερουράνιόν σου θυσιαστήριον. Μνημόνευσον ὡς ἀγαθὸς καὶ φιλάνθρωπος τῶν προσενεγκάντων καὶ δι᾽ οὓς προσήγαγον, καὶ ἡμᾶς ἀκατακρίτους διαφύλαξον ἐν τῇ ἱερουργίᾳ τῶν θείων σου μυστηρίων.

Ὅτι ἡγίασται καὶ δεδόξασται τὸ πάντιμον καὶ μεγαλοπρεπὲς ὄνομά σου, τοῦ Πατρὸς καὶ τοῦ Υἱοῦ καὶ τοῦ ἁγίου Πνεύματος, νῦν καὶ ἀεὶ καὶ εἰς τοὺς αἰῶνας τῶν αἰώνων. Ἀμήν.

Καὶ μετὰ τοῦτο ποιεῖ μικρὰν ἀπόλυσιν λέγων·

Δόξα σοι, Χριστὲ ὁ Θεός, ἡ ἐλπὶς ἡμῶν, δόξα σοι.

Ὁ διάκονος· Δόξα, καὶ νῦν. Κύριε, ἐλέησον γ΄. Δέσποτα ἅγιε, Εὐλόγησον.

Ὁ ἱερεὺς τὴν μικρὰν ἀπόλυσιν·

Χριστὸς ὁ ἀληθινὸς Θεὸς ἡμῶν, ταῖς πρεσβείαις τῆς παναχράντου καὶ παναμώμου ἁγίας αὐτοῦ Μητρός, τοῦ ἐν ἁγίοις πατρὸς ἡμῶν Ἰωάννου ἀρχιεπισκόπου Κωνσταντινουπόλεως τοῦ Χρυσοστόμου, (ἢ Βασιλείου ἀρχιεπισκόπου Καισαρείας τοῦ μεγάλου καὶ οὐρανοφάντορος) καὶ πάντων τῶν ἁγίων, ἐλεήσαι καὶ σώσαι ἡμᾶς, ὡς ἀγαθὸς καὶ φιλάνθρωπος.

Δι᾽ εὐχῶν τῶν ἁγίων πατέρων ἡμῶν, Κύριε Ἰησοῦ Χριστὲ ὁ Θεός, ἐλέησον ἡμᾶς. Ὁ διάκονος· Ἀμήν.

Καὶ προσκυνήσαντες ἐκ τρίτου ἀσπάζονται τὰ τίμια δῶρα, ὁ μὲν ἱερεὺς τὸ ἅγιον δισκάριον, τὸ ἅγιον ποτήριον, καὶ τὸν ἐπὶ τοῦ ἀέρος σταυρόν, ὁ δὲ διάκονος τὸ κάτω μέρος τοῦ ἀέρος.

PRAYER OF THE PROTHESIS

O God, our God, who sent forth as food for the entire world, the heavenly bread, our Lord and God Jesus Christ as savior and deliverer and benefactor, blessing and sanctifying us; do you the same bless this prothesis, and accept it upon your super-celestial altar. As a good and loving one, remember those who have brought forth offerings and those for whom they were brought forth, and protect us without condemnation in the holy work of your divine mysteries.

For sanctified and glorified is your all-honorable and magnificent name, of the Father and the Son and the Holy Spirit, now and forever and to the ages of ages. Amen.

And after this he does the small dismissal saying:

Glory to you, O Christ God, our hope, glory to you.

The deacon: Glory, both now. Lord, have mercy (3 times). Holy master, bless.

And the priest (says) the small dismissal:

May Christ our true God, through the intercessions of his all-pure and all-blameless holy Mother, of our father among the saints John Chrysostom, Archbishop of Constantinople, (or Basil the Great and revealer of heaven, Archbishop of Caesarea) and of all the saints, have mercy on us and save us as one who is good and loves man.

Through the prayers of our holy fathers, Lord Jesus Christ God, have mercy on us. *The deacon:* Amen.

And making three venerations they kiss the precious gifts, the priest (kissing) the holy paten, the holy chalice and the cross on the aer, the deacon (kissing) the bottom section of the aer.

ΠΡΟΕΙΣΑΓΩΓΙΚΑ ΤΗΣ ΘΕΙΑΣ ΛΕΙΤΟΥΡΓΙΑΣ

Μετὰ τὴν ἀπόλυσιν τῆς Προθέσεως ὁ διάκονος (ἢ ὁ ἱερεὺς) θυμιᾷ τὴν Πρόθεσιν, τὴν
ἁγίαν Τράπεζαν καὶ ἀπὸ τῆς Ὡραίας Πύλης
τὰς εἰκόνας καὶ τὸν λαὸν καὶ αὖθις τὴν ἁγίαν
Τράπεζαν λέγων καθ' ἑαυτὸν τὰ τροπάρια·

Ἐν τάφῳ σωματικῶς, ἐν ᾅδῃ δὲ μετὰ
ψυχῆς ὡς Θεός, ἐν παραδείσῳ δὲ μετὰ
λῃστοῦ, καὶ ἐν θρόνῳ ὑπῆρχες, Χριστέ, μετὰ Πατρὸς καὶ Πνεύματος, πάντα
πληρῶν ὁ ἀπερίγραπτος.

Δόξα Πατρί.

Ὡς ζωηφόρος, ὡς παραδείσου ὡραι-
ότερος ὄντως καὶ παστάδος πάσης βασι-
λικῆς ἀναδέδεικται λαμπρότερος, Χριστέ,
ὁ τάφος σου, ἡ πηγὴ τῆς ἡμῶν ἀναστάσεως.

Καὶ νῦν.

Τὸ τοῦ Ὑψίστου ἡγιασμένον θεῖον
σκήνωμα, Χαῖρε· διὰ σοῦ γὰρ δέδοται ἡ
χαρά, Θεοτόκε, τοῖς κραυγάζουσιν· Εὐλογημένη σὺ ἐν γυναιξί, πανάμωμε Δέσποινα.

Μετὰ τοῦτο ἔρχονται ἐνώπιον τῆς ἁγίας
Τραπέζης, καὶ λέγει ὁ διάκονος·

Καιρὸς τοῦ ποιῆσαι τῷ Κυρίῳ· δέσποτα ἅγιε, εὐλόγησον.

Καὶ ὁ ἱερεὺς σφραγίζων τὴν κεφαλὴν αὐτοῦ
λέγει·

Εὐλογητὸς ὁ Θεὸς ἡμῶν πάντοτε, νῦν
καὶ ἀεὶ καὶ εἰς τοὺς αἰῶνας τῶν αἰώνων.

Ὁ διάκονος· Ἀμήν. Εὔξαι ὑπὲρ ἐμοῦ, δέσποτα ἅγιε.

Ὁ ἱερεύς·

Κατευθύναι Κύριος τὰ διαβήματά σου
εἰς πᾶν ἔργον ἀγαθόν.

Ὁ διάκονος· Μνήσθητί μου, δέσποτα ἅγιε.

Ὁ ἱερεύς·

INTRODUCTION TO THE DIVINE LITURGY

*After the dismissal of the Prothesis, the deacon
(or the priest) censes the Prothesis, the holy Table
and from the Beautiful Gate the icons and the
people and again the holy Table saying to himself
the hymns:*

Bodily you were in the grave, with
(your) soul You were in Hades as God, you
were in paradise with the thief, and you were
upon the throne, O Christ, with the Father
and the Spirit, filling all things, O indescribable one.

Glory to the Father.

Your tomb, O Christ, the source of our
own resurrection, has been shown forth as
lifebearing, as truly more beautiful than paradise and brighter than any royal bridal chamber.

Both now.

Rejoice, O sanctified dwelling of the
Most High; for through you, O Theotokos,
joy is given to those who cry out: Blessed are
you among women, O all-blameless Lady.

*After this they come before the holy Table, and
the deacon says:*

It is time [kairos] for the Lord to act.
Holy master, bless.

And the priest sealing [crossing] his head says:

Blessed is our God always, now and forever and to the ages of ages.

The deacon: Amen. Pray for me, holy
master.

The priest:

May the Lord direct your steps to every
good work.

The deacon: Remember me, holy master.

The priest:

Μνησθείη σου Κύριος ὁ Θεὸς ἐν τῇ βασιλείᾳ αὐτοῦ πάντοτε, νῦν καὶ ἀεὶ καὶ εἰς τοὺς αἰῶνας τῶν αἰώνων.

Εἶτα ὁ ἱερεὺς ὑψῶν τὰς χεῖρας λέγει·

Βασιλεῦ οὐράνιε, Παράκλητε, τὸ Πνεῦμα τῆς ἀληθείας, ὁ πανταχοῦ παρὼν καὶ τὰ πάντα πληρῶν, ὁ θησαυρὸς τῶν ἀγαθῶν καὶ ζωῆς χορηγός, ἐλθὲ καὶ σκήνωσον ἐν ἡμῖν καὶ καθάρισον ἡμᾶς ἀπὸ πάσης κηλῖδος καὶ σῶσον, ἀγαθέ, τὰς ψυχὰς ἡμῶν.

Καὶ προσκυνοῦσιν ἀμφότεροι ἐκ γ΄ λέγοντες·

Δόξα ἐν ὑψίστοις Θεῷ καὶ ἐπὶ γῆς εἰρήνη, ἐν ἀνθρώποις εὐδοκία (*τρίς*).

Κύριε, τὰ χείλη μου ἀνοίξεις καὶ τὸ στόμα μου ἀναγγελεῖ τὴν αἴνεσίν σου (*δίς*).

Καὶ ἀσπάζονται ὁ μὲν ἱερεὺς τὸ ἱερὸν Εὐαγγέλιον καὶ τὴν ἁγίαν Τράπεζαν, ὁ δὲ Διάκονος τὴν ἁγίαν Τράπεζαν καὶ τὴν χεῖρα τοῦ ἱερέως· καὶ οὕτως ἄρχονται τῆς Θ. Λειτουργίας.

Ἐὰν δὲ λειτουργῇ ὁ ἱερεὺς ἄνευ διακόνου, λέγει μόνον· Εὐλογητὸς ὁ Θεός ... Βασιλεῦ οὐράνιε ... Δόξα ἐν ὑψίστοις ... Κύριε, τὰ χείλη μου ... Προσκυνήσας δὲ καὶ ἀσπασάμενος τὸ ἱ. Εὐαγγέλιον καὶ τὴν ἁγίαν Τράπεζαν ἄρχεται τῆς Θ. Λειτουργίας.

May the Lord God remember you in his kingdom always, now and forever and to the ages of ages.

Then the priest lifting up his hands says:

O heavenly King, Advocate, Spirit of truth, present everywhere and filling all things, the treasury of good things and giver of life, come and dwell in us and cleanse us from every stain and save, O good one, our souls.

And together they make three venerations saying:

Glory to God in the highest and on earth peace, good will among men (*thrice*).

Lord, you will open my lips and my mouth will proclaim your praise (*twice*).

And the priest kisses the holy Gospel and the holy Table, the deacon kisses the holy Table and the hand of the priest; and thus they begin the Divine Liturgy.

But if the priest liturgizes without a deacon, he says only: Blessed is our God ... O heavenly King ... Glory to God in the highest ... Lord, you will open my lips ... And venerating and kissing the holy Gospel and the holy Table, he begins the Divine Liturgy.

NOTES

1. Constantinos Papayiannis, ed. Ἱερατικόν [*Priest's Service Book*], (Athens, 2001), 95–108.

The order is designed for a presbyter serving with a deacon and does not necessarily refer to any particular concelebration with a hierarch, only specifying that both celebrant priest and deacon make a reverence toward "the (episcopal) throne" on the solea (typically adjacent to the right choir), as a visible sign of the celebrants' submission to the authority of the bishop, who is the *typos* of God the Father in the local church and presides in His place (cf. Ignatios of Antioch, *Trallians* 3.1, *Sources chrétiennes* 10.96; *Magnesians* 6.1, *Sources chrétiennes* 10.82-84). The modern text reflects the liturgical celebrations in the *katholikon*, or main church, of a monastery, where it was not uncommon for the abbot to preside over the liturgical celebration from his stall near the choir, while the Divine Liturgy was conducted from the altar by the vested priest and deacon. The later Byzantine practice was copied by parish churches, in which a diocesan hierarch at times opted to preside from his stall (episcopal "throne") rather than serve as chief celebrant from the altar.

2. Patriarch Philotheos Kokkinos, in his fourteenth-century *Diataxis*, strongly advocates the necessity of proper preparation well before the commencement of the eucharistic liturgy, as early, in fact, as the preceding evening. Abstinence from evil thoughts and physical pleasures, reconciliation with enemies, and vigilant prayerfulness all indicate the solemnity with which the celebrant clergy must approach the Divine Liturgy. From a mystagogical perspective, it would appear that for Philotheos, the clergy are preparing for a "theophany," a vivid encounter with the living God, which would require a purification of body and soul in every manner possible. The words of the Lord have much relevance here: "So if you are offering your gift at the altar, and there remember that your brother has something against you, leave your gift there before the altar and go; first be reconciled to your brother, and then come and offer your gift" (Matt 5:23–24).

Symeon of Thessalonike likewise recapitulates the importance of the celebrant's preparedness and worthiness during the Eucharist, at the conclusion of his *Interpretation of the Divine Temple and Liturgy*, when he writes: "And so it is necessary that the priest watch himself in such very great works of God, and probe himself, . . . For if he has need of securing [the salvation] of others, how much more [must he do so] for himself; and if the one who eats and drinks unworthily, that is communes only, eats and drinks judgment upon himself, how much more does he who liturgizes unworthily. For this reason, . . . let our humility and love increase (for these are the works of the One who is sacrificed [in the liturgy] for us . . ." (Περὶ τοῦ Θείου Ναοῦ 103; PG 155.749B). Yet another indication of Symeon's concern for proper order in the liturgical rite and the spiritual welfare of his clergy is made clear when he writes: "And the priest in the altar, having first venerated the bishop, thus displaying his obedience and having been found worthy of blessing, conducts the proskomide. Because it is necessary that the blessing precede the divine works and that he [the priest] ask for forgiveness ("δεῖ γὰρ εὐχὴν προηγεῖσθαι τῶν θείων ἔργων, καὶ αἰτεῖσθαι συγχώρησιν"). See Symeon of Thessalonike, *On the Sacred Liturgy* 83 (PG 155.261A).

3. This prayer for worthiness, which concludes the preparatory rite of *kairos*, is, at least in modern usage, normally said by the chief celebrant for himself and, *by implication*, includes the other lower-ranking clergy.

4. A final preparation of the clergy on the day of the liturgical celebration takes the form of a combined ritual of prayer and vesting, immediately prior to the beginning of the prothesis. The first portion of the rite, called *kairos*, or "liturgical time," escorts the celebrant clergy from historical time (*chronos*) into the "endless time of God," realized during the celebration of the Holy Liturgy. By entering the "kairos of God," the priest sheds all worldly cares and ways in order to fully apply himself to the service of God's sublime altar. The rite consists of a section of opening prayers, the veneration of the icons on the iconostasis, a final prayer for worthiness, and the dismissal, followed immediately by the visible display of reconciliation between the clergy and laity.

Following their entrance into the altar, the priest and deacon both proceed to put on the vestments of their respective office, reciting psalm verses over each article as it is placed on their body. As special clothing worn only during divine services, the liturgical vestments of the clergy differ significantly from everyday clothing and serve as physical proof that the clergy have temporarily left behind the fallen and imperfect world of history and have passed into the "*kairos* of God," an apocalyptic image reminiscent of Revelation 4:4.

5. The *apolytikion*, or dismissal hymn, is sung during the Matins of Holy Friday.

6. In contrast to the prothesis text, the LXX citation from Isaiah 53:7 does not attach the epithet ἄμωμος ("blameless") to the word ἀμνός ("lamb"). This peculiarity is the only case in which the liturgical text of the prothesis rite and its corresponding scriptural citation differ.

7. Within the Byzantine Church, the deacon's primary role in the prothesis rite and the Divine Liturgy gradually evolved into a teletarchical one, in which he is chiefly responsible for maintaining the proper order and flow of the liturgical services. Evidence of this role is clearly found in his prefacing of a priestly prayer or action with a short petition or injunction, either to the higher clergy or people, prompting them to either pray or act. Ioannes Fountoules does not hesitate, on numerous occasions, to classify the deacon as τελετάρχης, or the one who directs the natural flow and conduct of the rite, thus maintaining the proper solemnity and decorum of the Liturgy. See Ioannes M. Fountoules, Ἀπαντήσεις εἰς λειτουργικὰς ἀπορίας [*Answers to Liturgical Questions*], vol. 3 (Athens, 1994), 60–61.

8. In accordance with proper Eastern liturgical practice, most blessings are shared by both priest and deacon, with the latter on occasion concluding ("now and forever") the proclamation of the former ("Blessed is God").

2

The Life and Liturgical Works of St. Nicholas Cabasilas and St. Symeon of Thessalonike: A Critical Survey

St. Nicholas Cabasilas

References to the life of St. Nicholas Cabasilas and critical expositions of his major writings are relatively few and limited to just the second half of the twentieth century.[1] Some of the details surrounding his life, such as the years of his birth and death and whether or not he was ordained, remain dubious. However, the noted sources unanimously acknowledge the fact that for the first phase of his life, Cabasilas devoted himself to addressing and, in his capacity as imperial statesman under Byzantine Emperor John VI Kantakouzenos, eradicating social injustice. As for the second part of his life, the active politician-turned-contemplative monk committed himself to theological writing that reflected not only the ecclesiastical and theological controversies of his day, but also the liturgical practices of the Medieval Byzantine Church.

Nicholas Cabasilas' birth year is conventionally placed around 1300 in the northern Greek port of Thessalonike, but other sources suggest the early 1320s, thus making him a contemporary of his good friend and fellow statesman Demetrios Kydones (1324–1397),[2] who attempted to reunite East and West but in the end converted himself to Roman Catholicism.[3] For the East, the fourteenth century was a trying time of great political unrest and upheaval. A civil war raged in Byzantium between the two prominent families of the Emperor John VI and his ward John V Palaiologos.[4] Cabasilas, friend and adviser to the former, is mentioned by John VI in his historical writings,[5] having been sent to the court of the emperor's second son Manuel in Beroia in 1346, when he was forced to abdicate the throne at the hand of John Palaiologos. In 1347, John returned to the throne and began the process of prepping his son Matthew to succeed him, a move that inevitably created new clouds of controversy between the two families. In 1355, John V seized full political power, and John VI retired permanently to a monastery, taking the name Joasaph and accompanied by his friend Cabasilas, whom he admired for his great wisdom in political and religious matters and for his commitment to the unmarried life.[6] From this point forward, Cabasilas embarked on the contemplative life, which rendered for the Church his two greatest literary works.

It is not entirely clear if Cabasilas ever did enter the priesthood,[7] although it is undisputed that he certainly did not succeed his maternal uncle Nilos Cabasilas as Archbishop of Thessalonike (1361–63), at least according to the lineage of successors following St. Gregory Palamas (1347–1359), the champion of hesychast mysticism. One factor possibly contributing to this ambiguity regarding his clerical status was his having adopted his prominent uncle's family name "Cabasilas" rather than his father's, which was "Chamaetos."[8] In any case, history indicates that Cabasilas entered the Manganon monastery near Constantinople,[9] where he was at the very least tonsured a monk together with John VI Kantakouzenos. The date of his death is also indistinct, though the year 1391 is often used, several years following the surrender of his native Thessalonike to the Ottoman Turks in 1387.[10]

CABASILAS AND PALAMITE HESYCHASM

Nicholas Cabasilas' Christocentric sacramentalism stands at the very core of the spiritual message of Palamite hesychast mysticism, which did not concern itself with the specific theological technicalities of the first eight centuries but with the experience of God via prayer on the highest level. The hesychast controversy, which ravaged the Eastern Church during the Late Byzantine era, essentially asked how theosis (deification) could be attained without breaking the distinction between the Creator and the creature. How was it possible for the mystics to attain a vision of God without gazing upon the divine essence?[11]

Cabasilas, a mystic himself, supported Palamas' hesychast theology, as is evident in his refutation of the latter's adversary Nikephoros Gregoras (c. 1295–c. 1360).[12] Although no direct references are made to the Palamite "energies – essence" distinction in any of his major writings, this does not rule out his commitment to the hesychast cause, nor does it imply that "there is nothing in *The Life of Christ* which is not entirely compatible with

Palamism."[13] Bobrinskoy and Lot-Borodine maintain the position that the important elements of hesychast theology are well preserved in Cabasilas, who understands union with God as the domain of all Christians and not just mystics, a union that is attainable through participation in the sacramental life of the Church and most especially in the Eucharist.

The mystical vision obtained in the Divine Liturgy is essentially man's exposure to the life in Christ, which, according to B. Bobrinskoy, translates into "the existential centre of attraction common to hesychasm and to the spirituality of Cabasilas."[14] Participation in this divine life, and especially through the medium of the Eucharist, renders for Cabasilas a seemingly very "literal" and "realistic" union with Christ, the most perfect and highest form of union allowable to and attainable by man. Cabasilas affirms this point when he writes: "It is clear, then, that Christ infuses Himself into us and mingles Himself with us. He changes and transforms us into Himself, as a small drop of water is changed by being poured into an immense sea of ointment."[15] Hence, the liturgical mystagogy of Nicholas Cabasilas possesses the same inner goal as Palamite mystical contemplation: participation in the divine life and attainment of a vision of God, but through the mystical experience of the eucharistic celebration.

THE MYSTAGOGICAL WORKS OF CABASILAS

Cabasilas offered to the Church two important mystagogical writings: *The Explanation of the Divine Liturgy*[16] and *The Life in Christ*.[17] Throughout his works, one notices Cabasilas' great familiarity with Scripture, especially the Book of Psalms. Even when he borrows directly from this book in his interpretations, the psalm is transposed in a Christological or eucharistic sense. In addition, the commentator refers several times to the *Ecclesiastical Hierarchy* of Pseudo-Dionysios, whose mystagogical theology was still very much appreciated and adhered to in fourteenth century Byzantium, especially the teaching on the correlation between the ecclesiastical hierarchy and the celestial hierarchy. Finally, Cabasilas' affinity to Gregory Palamas and hesychast theology explains both mystics' agreement that the sacraments recapitulate the entire economy of salvation, which leads them both to attach the same value to biblical and liturgical symbolism.[18]

CABASILAS' EUCHARISTIC THEOLOGY

As an advocate of the Antiochene method of historical interpretation, Cabasilas acknowledges that the liturgical ceremonies correspond to the events in the earthly life of Christ. Whereas the rite of consecration relives the Lord's death, resurrection, and ascension, the acts performed before the epiklesis correspond to his public life preceding His death.[19] Cabasilas also explains, not unlike his predecessors of the Antiochene tradition, that Christ's sacrifice finds numerous prefigurations in the Old Testament, among which are the sacrifice of Isaac by his father Abraham (Gen 22:1–19), the paschal lamb during the feast of Passover (Exod 12:1–13), and the Jewish temple sacrifices.

The notion of sacrifice is developed well in Cabasilas' works.[20] The "bloodless sacrifice" of the Eucharist, celebrated over and over again, is in fact the reliving of Christ's unique sacrifice upon the Cross. The very transmutation of the elements, through the Church's offering of the eucharistic prayer—and, more specifically for Cabasilas, the prayer of consecration— renders present the immolated Body and Blood of Christ upon the altar. This presence of Christ then in the elements allows the eucharistic sacrifice to "announce" His death and resurrection, transforming them into an effectual, present reality for the Church.[21]

Cabasilas identifies three stages of the eucharistic offering, highlighted by Gregory Dix in his *Shape of the Liturgy*:[22] (1) the people offer simple bread and wine to the clergy as their offering; (2) the celebrant prepares these gifts in the office of the prothesis and offers them to God at His altar; and (3) God consecrates these gifts and returns them back to the Church as the Body and Blood of Christ. The ascending movement reaches its full climax at the epiklesis. At this point, the consecrated gifts have shifted hands, and it is now God who condescends to offer Himself to the faithful as Holy Communion. Furthermore, the passage of the gifts through various stages of offering, attested to by their covering and unveiling during the prothesis rite and in the Divine Liturgy, verifies the reverence bestowed upon them by the Church.

Cabasilas dedicates a good portion of his treatises in addressing the controversial issue of the "point of consecration," the exact moment when the gifts are transformed into the Body and Blood of Christ. His defense of the epiklesis as that "moment" is primarily a response to the Latin Church's assertion that the moment lies within the Words of Institution.[23]

For Cabasilas, the consecration is effected by the descent of the Holy Spirit, who operates through the words and acts of the priest. In essence, all three Persons of the Holy Trinity actualize the consecration.[24] From the view of the Eastern Church, the Words of Institution do not contain an actual formula or petition that requests this transmutation of the bread and wine. To be sure, Christ's words are critical in that they provide the context within which the eucharistic sacrifice is offered. More importantly though, they authorize the Church to offer the Eucharist, thus rendering it valid: "Do this in remembrance of Me." Hence, the Institution Narrative within the Byzantine anaphora may be considered contextual and not effectual. Cabasilas further argues that the Words of Institution are not sufficient by themselves because they simply issue a command, which remains unfulfilled until action is taken by the Holy Spirit to consecrate the bread and wine. He writes:

> God said: "Be fruitful and multiply." What then? After these words do we need nothing more to achieve this, and is nothing else necessary for the increase of the human race? Is not marriage and conjugal union essential, and all the other cares which go with marriage, and without which it would be impossible for mankind to exist and develop? We consider marriage, therefore, necessary for the procreation of children. . . . And in the same way, here in the liturgy we believe that the Lord's words do indeed accomplish the mystery, but through the medium of the priest, his invocation, and his prayer.[25]

In his understanding of sacramental symbolism, Cabasilas acknowledges that the mystery of the economy is conveyed to the Church not only through the actual sacrifice of Christ, but also through the liturgical celebration that renders its salvific power effectual for the Church. This sacramental reality, however, also goes hand in hand with the practical and didactic nature of the rites, which Cabasilas does not neglect to point out. Hence, the Great Entrance makes possible the practical transfer of the prepared gifts from the table of oblation to the altar, but not at the expense of excluding the typological significance of the rite, which is to relive Christ's entry into Jerusalem and progression toward Golgotha. Likewise, there are rites in the Divine Liturgy that are purely symbolical, such as the office of the prothesis and the zeon. In any case, Cabasilas notes that participation in the Divine Liturgy involves being present at the rite, reaping the spiritual benefits found in the prayers and hymns and Scripture readings, as well as discovering the hidden meaning (the deeper mystagogy) behind the words and the liturgical gestures.

ST. SYMEON OF THESSALONIKE

Biographical information on the life of Symeon of Thessalonike[26] is likewise as scant as that for Nicholas Cabasilas, and the former certainly did not enjoy the renown in the Latin West as did the latter, whose polemical writings in both major aforementioned works reflected the Medieval Eastern mindset vis-à-vis Catholic Anselmian and liturgical theology. Nevertheless, Symeon's liturgical treatises represent the final great exposition of liturgical matters prior to the fall of the Byzantine Empire. His extensive and often detailed commentaries on the liturgical practices of fourteenth to fifteenth-century Byzantium provide invaluable information and insight for contemporary liturgical worship in the Eastern Church, which resembles very closely the external forms practiced during Symeon's lifetime.

Symeon was born in Constantinople sometime during the middle of the fourteenth century, although the exact year of his birth is uncertain. He probably received his name when he was tonsured a monk and in all likelihood was named after Symeon Metaphrastes (c. tenth century), whose *akolouthia* (service) he is credited with composing. As a monk he lived in a small cell, possibly in the Monastery of Xanthopouloi, and he became well known throughout ecclesiastical and political circles for his familiarity with the rites of the Great Church of Constantinople. Spending time in the patriarchal court as a consultant for liturgical matters, he was eventually consecrated archbishop of Thessalonike in 1416 or 1417. History records that Symeon fell ill during his episcopal tenure, a result of the administrative stresses and high demands of his office, but he recovered and began producing during this time the literary works that distinguished him as arguably the East's most detail-oriented commentator on liturgical services.

An unwavering conservative on both political and religious affairs, Symeon possessed an uncompromising loyalty to the Byzantine imperial court, at a time when Thessalonike was under siege by both the Venetians and the Ottoman Turks. It is believed that his staunch opposition to foreign forces invading his jurisdictional territory made him dislikable among many of his own people, who would gladly have surrendered sooner rather than later in order to avoid complete annihilation at the hands of their more powerful enemies. In 1423, Thessalonike eventually surrendered to the Venetians and in September of 1429 Symeon died, six months before his city fell to the Ottoman Empire.

THE LITURGICAL COMMENTARIES OF SYMEON AND SYMEON'S CONSERVATISM

As archbishop, Symeon possessed a wide range of political and religious interests, spanning such areas as history, liturgy, ethics, dogmatics, and pastoral theology. Interestingly, Symeon's liturgical works interrupt the long line of literal interpreters of the Divine Liturgy, resuming the Alexandrian allegorical tradition of Dionysios the Areopagite and Maximos the Confes-

sor.[27] As Bornert writes: "This return of Symeon of Thessalonike to Dionysius the Pseudo-Areopagite and to Maximos the Confessor proves that the
Byzantine mystagogical tradition did not evolve in a linear progression. It
presents itself rather as an oscillation between two poles, Alexandrian symbolism and Antiochene realism."[28]

Symeon's most important study of the Byzantine Liturgy may be divided into two distinct sections: *A Refutation of All Heresies* and *A Treatise
on the Sacraments*,[29] both of which seem to imitate Pseudo-Dionysius' *Ecclesiastical Hierarchy* and Cabasilas' *Life in Christ*. Both works are designed
in the form of a dialogue, taking place between a bishop and his clergy. The
Treatise on the Sacraments identifies the seven mysteries of the Church with
the seven gifts of the Holy Spirit. Symeon also adds to his list those services
that are not included in the original enumeration, i.e., the consecration of
a church, monastic profession, the divine office, and funerals for Christians. As Simmons states, Symeon's aptitude for marking out detail renders
him "a pioneer in extending this type of commentary in a systematic way
to virtually the whole range of persons, functions and things associated
with the sacraments and prayers of the Church."[30] Within this latter work,
the chapter entitled *On the Sacred Liturgy*,[31] as well as another independent
work, his *Interpretation of the Divine Temple and Liturgy*,[32] together provide the two best witnesses to Symeon's mystagogy. Unfortunately, these
two superlative liturgical commentaries—as well as most of Symeon's minor works—have not yet been translated into English, although they have
appeared in Latin, Modern Greek, Romanian, and Russian translations.

By all indications both from his content and writing style, Symeon
may be labeled a liturgical traditionalist, maintaining a conservative stance
toward matters of liturgical order. Hagia Sophia Cathedral in Thessalonike
was one of the only locations in the East where the ancient asmatic cathedral rite, albeit with minor modifications, was faithfully chanted until the
fall of the great see to the Ottoman Empire in c. 1430.[33] Symeon aggres-
sively resisted any attempts to adopt the popular monastic-based Jerusalem
Typikon, which was accepted virtually everywhere else in the Byzantine
East. This included the Great Church of Constantinople, where the hybrid
Studite office (a merging of the Palestinian monastic office and the cathedral rite) and the authentic cathedral order of services coexisted side by side
until the recapture of the capital city from the Latins following the Fourth
Crusade in 1204, after which the cathedral rite was never fully restored.[34]

Despite Symeon's conservatism in matters of liturgical worship, he oc-
casionally did sanction the exercise of leniency when dictated by pastoral
needs. Thus, for example, although the asmatic cathedral rite is "senior and

superior to the monastic rite" for Symeon, "he prescribed that certain sections of the daily offices should be shortened and troparia and kanons be added (on the model of the monastic practice) in order to satisfy his flock."[35]

LITURGICAL MYSTAGOGY IN SYMEON

The Archbishop of Thessalonike's understanding of liturgical mystagogy is very similar to that of Dionysius and Maximos. The symbol, as a spiritual reality, is engaged in the sensible and hidden by it. Through its use in the Liturgy, the symbol makes present the reality that it represents and is, in one sense, the most direct means of contact between the divine and human worlds. Symeon also acknowledges three stages of spiritual growth, achieved through the sacraments: purification (κάθαρσις), illumination (φώτισις), and deification (θέωσις), with the last level being fulfilled through participation in the Eucharist.[36]

Symeon of Thessalonike acknowledges a double element in each sacrament (i.e. the sensible rite which conveys spiritual grace), both of which manifest the two perfect natures of Christ.[37] The Eucharist is, furthermore, the prolongation of Christ's incarnation throughout history, as well as the constant memorial of His sacrifice upon the Cross. The liturgical symbol renders Christ present in the Liturgy and follows the fulfillment of the divine economy until the eschaton.[38]

For Symeon, the liturgical ceremonies of the Church also possess a twofold purpose. Even though they gradually introduce intelligible realities to the worshipper, they first unravel before his eyes the important stages of salvation history. This second feature, explains Symeon, seems to dominate the eucharistic celebration, but its purpose is achieved when it leads one to a higher contemplation of God and the angelic world.[39] Thus, the Lord's earthly Passion and His ultimate victory over sin and death, as commemorated in the Divine Liturgy, are not ends in themselves, events that will indelibly remain within the confines of human history. Rather, they usher in the new aeon, granting to the faithful a vision of the Kingdom of God and the celestial realities that are a part of it.[40]

Several important examples characteristic of Symeon's mystagogy may be found in the service of kairos and subsequently the vesting of the celebrants. First, the order of kairos progresses in a hierarchical manner, meaning from the bishop to the lower clergy. Even the bishop "takes kairos" from Christ, who is the central mystery of the Church and who authorizes the celebration of the Divine Liturgy. Second, the clerical vestments are representative of the glorious apparel that adorn the heavenly host and, as symbols, are themselves sacred in that they convey a hidden reality. For this reason does Symeon apparently attach a scriptural verse to each one, indicating the sanctity that they convey. Finally, the chief celebrant of the Eucharist is clearly the bishop, and Symeon's manner of directing the entire flow of the preparatory offices toward his person affirms this truth.

A second example occurs during the readings that follow the first entrance, and the second entrance with the gifts, during which the bishop stands in front of the altar and faces the people. The procession with the Gospel Book and the Scripture readings are conducted by the lower clergy, as is the Great Entrance. This "non-participatory status" of the bishop during these two instances is interesting, in that he seems to be relegating the presidency of the Liturgy to Christ Himself.[41]

The manner of distributing and partaking of Holy Communion is also significant, in that it follows the hierarchical model common amongst the Alexandrian commentators. The bishop is the first to commune himself (i.e. from the hand of Christ whom he mystically represents), after which he communes the lower clergy, who venerate his right hand and epigonation vestment. The laity, in turn, are communed by the deacon or priest.[42] Finally, the bishop concludes the Divine Liturgy by blessing the people and distributing the antidoron, or blessed bread, thus signifying that Christ is not only the "offerer and the offered" within the Divine Liturgy, but also the culmination of every Christian's journey into the mystagogy of the Faith.

NOTES

1. The most dependable bibliography includes the following sources: Ihor Ševčenko, "Nicholas Cabasilas' 'Anti-Zealot' Discourse: A Reinterpretation," in *Dumbarton Oaks Papers*, vol. 11 (1957), 79–171; Myrrha Lot-Borodine, *Un maître de la spiritualité byzantine au XIVe siècle: Nicolas Cabasilas* (Paris, 1958); the "Foreword" by R.M. French (viii–xi) and the translators' "Introduction" (pp. 1–22) in Nicholas Cabasilas, *A Commentary on the Divine Liturgy*, trans. J.M. Hussey and P.A. McNulty (London, 1960); René Bornert, *Les commentaires byzantins de la Divine Liturgie du VIIe au XVe siècle* (Paris, 1965); Panagiotes Nellas, Προλεγόμενα εἰς τὴν μελέτην Νικολάου τοῦ Καβάσιλα [*Introduction to the Study of Nicholas Cabasilas*], (Athens, 1968); Boris Bobrinskoy, "Nicholas Cabasilas: Theology and Spirituality", in *Sobornost*, vol. 5, no. 7 (1968), 483–505; Athanasios A. Angelopoulos, Νικόλαος Καβάσιλας Χαμαετός: Ἡ ζωή του καὶ τὸ ἔργον του [*Nicholas Cabasilas Chamaetos: His Life and His Work*], (Thessalonike, 1969); J.M. Hussey, "Symeon the New Theologian and Nicolas Cabasilas: Similarities and Contrasts in Orthodox Spirituality", in *Eastern Churches Review*, vol. 4 (1972), 131–40; the "Translator's Foreword" (pp. 9–15) and the "Introduction" by Boris Bobrinskoy (pp. 17–42, reprinted from *Sobornost*; cf. above)

in Nicholas Cabasilas, *The Life in Christ*, trans. Carmino J. deCatanzaro (Crestwood, 1974); and Constantine N. Tsirpanlis, *The Liturgical and Mystical Theology of Nicolas Cabasilas* (New York, 1979).

2. Ševčenko, 85–86.

3. C.J. deCatanzaro, "Translator's Foreword", in N. Cabasilas, *The Life in Christ*, 11.

4. The details surrounding this conflict may be obtained from George Ostrogorsky, *History of the Byzantine State* (New Brunswick, N.J., 1969), 499–533.

5. John Kantakouzenos, *Book of Histories* 4.16; PG 154.125AB.

6. R.M. French, "Introduction", in N. Cabasilas, *A Commentary on the Divine Liturgy*, ix.

7. Interestingly, when the patriarchal throne was vacated following the deposition of Kallistos, who refused to crown John VI's son Matthew in 1354, Cabasilas was chosen as one of the three candidates for patriarch, the other two being the metropolitans of Heraklea and Philadelphia. John, however, chose Philotheos of Heraklea as patriarch, thus assuring for Cabasilas a future devoid of administrative responsibilities, in which he could fully dedicate himself to his theological works. See ibid.

8. C.J. deCatanzaro, "Translator's Foreword", in N. Cabasilas, *The Life in Christ*, 9–10.

9. Ibid., 10.

10. Ibid.

11. Ibid., 11.

12. See *On the Nonsense of Gregoras* [*In Gregorae deliramenta*]; PG 150.355–362, a fragment of which exists in J.P. Migne but is now attributed to Cabasilas' uncle, Nilos Cabasilas.

13. C.J. deCatanzaro, "Translator's Foreword", in N. Cabasilas, *The Life in Christ*, 12.

14. Boris Bobrinskoy, "Introduction", in N. Cabasilas, *The Life in Christ*, 23.

15. Cabasilas, *The Life in Christ* IV.6 in PG 150.593; for the translation see also *The Life in Christ*, 123.

16. PG 150.367–492. Cabasilas' *Explanation of the Divine Liturgy* is a treatise of sacramental mysticism, in the strict sense. It serves as an invaluable complementary text to the fourth chapter of *The Life in Christ*, which deals with the Eucharist. The latter work includes sections on: (1) the general principles of the life in Christ; (2) baptism; (3) chrismation; (4) the Eucharist; (5) the consecration of the altar (church); and (6) two chapters on the synergy between divine grace and the human will. In this treatise, Cabasilas affirms that a life in Christ requires unity and membership in Him, and the means by which this unity is achieved is through the holy sacraments of the Church.

In his *Explanation*, St. Nicholas makes a distinction between "ἱστορία and θεωρία, understanding the first to mean an image of the earthly life of Christ. Θεωρία, on the other hand, attempts to discover the redemptive presence of Christ through the liturgical rites, whose purpose is to sanctify the human soul by converting the historical sacrifice of Christ into an effectual, grace-filled reality in the present.

Cabasilas is also credited with authoring two other important mystagogical works, which have remained unedited: *Explanation of the Sacred Vestments* ["εἰς τὴν ἱερὰν στολήν" and *Commentary on the Divine Liturgy*, the second of which seems to be a brief synopsis of the more famous *Explanation of the Divine Liturgy*. See Bornert, 216–18.

17. PG 150.493–726.

18. Bornert, 221–26.

19. In this regard, Cabasilas' interpretation of the liturgical acts and their connection to Christ's life is almost identical to that of Nicholas of Andida, which convincingly demonstrates the former's careful study of the *Protheoria* and his acceptance of his predecessor's historical mystagogy.

20. Hussey and McNulty, trans., 80–82. See also Bornert, 229–33.

21. Through the collective offering of the eucharistic prayer and consecration, Christ is made fully present for the *entire* Church and not simply for certain communicants based on their individual faith. For the Eastern Church, the concept of "subjective presence" is quite foreign to its liturgical theology.

22. Dix notes that the terminology used for the various modes of liturgical oblation is virtually standardized in the pre-Nicene Church. Thus, for example, the communicants "bring" (προσενεγκεῖν) the gifts to the deacon; the deacon "offers up" (ἀναφέρειν) the gifts upon the altar; and the bishop and his concelebrating presbyters "offer" (προσφέρειν) the gifts to God. Interestingly, all three infinitives are derivative forms of the verb φέρω ("I carry"; "I bear"). See Gregory Dix, *The Shape of the Liturgy* (London, 1945), 111.

23. According to Gregory Dix, the pre-Nicene Church never truly concerned itself with an actual "moment of consecration," since in its mind, it was the *entire* eucharistic celebration that fulfilled the Church's thanksgiving and made the transformation complete. Dix, however, seems to believe that traces of this idea of a "moment" first appear in the middle of the fourth century with Eastern writers such as Cyril of Jerusalem, Sarapion, and Athanasios of Alexandria and later in the West with Ambrose of Milan (p. 240). Dix makes an interesting point when he writes that unlike earlier anaphorae, none of the rites following the fourth century seemed to associate the idea of consecration with the offering of thanksgiving. He concludes: "The memory of the Jewish origin and meaning of the *eucharistia* had completely faded from the mind of the hellenised churches of the fourth century, which everywhere sought for the formula of consecration in the 'second half' of their various prayers" (p. 241), that is, following the *Post-Sanctus*.

This preoccupation with a "moment of consecration" may well have been the result of a shift in understanding the Eucharist. Whereas the early Church saw the eucharistic liturgy as its collective offering of thanksgiving to God through the worshippers' praise and reception of Holy Communion, the post-Nicene Church primarily possessed a vision of the Eucharist as a "living sacrifice," meant not only to be consumed but "feared" and venerated. St. Cyril of Jerusalem, in his catechetical explanations of the anaphora in use during the fourth century in the Holy Land, the Liturgy of St. James, calls the Eucharist "this same fearful and unbloody sacrifice" (ἡ φρικοδέστατος καὶ ἀναίμακτος θυσία). The insistence then on an actual presence of Christ within the gifts not only makes the "moment" concept more viable, but it also lends support to a future Byzantine mystagogy that would envision the entire life of Christ hidden and revealed in the celebration of the Divine Liturgy. See Dix, 192, 199–200.

24. *"La consécration des dons est une opération commune aux trois personnes; mais elle leur appartient à des degrés divers: elle part du Père; elle est réalisée par le Fils; et elle est achevée dans l'Esprit-Saint"* (Bornert, p. 234). The phraseology above is reminiscent of the Greek patristic tradition. Cf. St. Gregory of Nyssa, *Ad Ablabium quod non sunt tres dii* [*That There Are Not Three Gods*]; PG 45.125C.

25. Hussey and McNulty, trans., 72.

26. See the important critical work by the late Ioannes Fountoules, Τὸ λειτουργικὸν ἔργον τοῦ Συμεὼν τῆς Θεσσαλονίκης: συμβολὴ εἰς τὴν ἱστορίαν καὶ θεωρίαν τῆς θείας λατρείας [*The Liturgical Work of Symeon of Thessalonike: Symbolism in the History and Theory of Divine Worship*], (Thessalonike, 1968). For a summary of Symeon of Thessalonike's life and the forces that influenced his writing style and at times sharply opinionated content on liturgical matters, see: D. Balfour, "Symeon of Thessalonike as a Historical Personality", in *The Greek Orthodox Theological Review*, vol. 28 (1983), 55–72; idem. Ἁγίου Συμεὼν Θεσσαλονίκης, Ἔργα Θεολογικά [*Saint Symeon of Thessalonike: Theological Works*]. *Analecta Vlatadon*, vol. 34 (Thessalonike, 1981), 29–76; and idem. *Politico-Historical Works of Symeon Archbishop of Thessalonica. Wiener Byzantinistische Studien*, vol. 13 (Vienna, 1979); see also the helpful introduction in the only complete English translation to date of any of Symeon's works: Saint Symeon of Thessalonike, *Treatise on Prayer*, trans. Harry L.N. Simmons (Brookline, 1984); finally, Steven Hawkes-Teeples, *The Praise of God in the Twilight of the Empire: The Divine Liturgy in the Commentaries of St. Symeon of Thessalonika, [d.] 1429* (Rome, 1998).

27. Although both Cabasilas and Symeon were contemporaries of each other, and even though the latter was quite familiar with Nicholas' mystagogical interpretation of the Divine Liturgy, he possessed a different orientation altogether. Whereas Cabasilas was greatly influenced by St. John Chrysostom and his Antiochene realism, Symeon followed the Alexandrian symbolism of Pseudo-Dionysius and Maximos.

28. Bornert, 249. Translation mine. See also Nicholas P. Constas, "Symeon of Thessalonike and the Theology of the Icon Screen", in *Thresholds of the Sacred: Architectural, Art Historical, Liturgical, and Theological Perspectives on Religious Screens, East and West*, ed. Sharon E.J. Gerstel (Washington, DC, 2006), 165–66.

29. The work is actually subdivided into over twelve semi-independent treatises that discuss faith and ritual practices in the Byzantine Church. The first section deals with orthodoxy and heresy and later opens up to an interpretation of the sacraments and the symbolism of the church building and how sacred space is understood in Byzantine theology. See Constas, 166.

30. Simmons, trans., 4.

31. PG 155.253A–304C.

32. PG 155.697A–749C.

33. Alexander Lingas, "Festal Cathedral Vespers in Late Byzantium", in *Orientalia Christiana Periodica*, vol. 63 (1997), 421–55.

34. John Thomas and Angela Constantinides Hero, eds., *Byzantine Monastic Foundation Documents: A Complete Translation of the Surviving Founders' Typika and Testaments. Dumbarton Oaks Studies*, vol. 35 (Washington, DC, 2000), 86–87.

35. Simmons, trans., 5.

36. Symeon is here following Pseudo-Dionysios' *Ecclesiastical Hierarchy*.

37. Bornert, 258.

38. St. Symeon's interpretation of the Liturgy does not focus on the progression of Christ's earthly life, but chiefly on the events leading to the consummation of time. For example, the Small Entrance represents Christ's redemptive Incarnation. The bishop's ascent to the throne before the readings symbolizes the Ascension. The readings from Scripture provide an image of the proclamation of the Gospel to the ends of the earth. The dismissal of the Catechumens before the Great Entrance depicts the separation of the elect from the condemned. The Great Entrance denotes Christ's Second Coming, while the Creed and the kiss of peace signify the ultimate union of humans with the angels in the world to come. Therefore, one may say that the divine mysteries have first been prefigured in the Old Testament. Secondly, they have been manifested in Christ. Thirdly, they are rendered present in the Church during every liturgical celebration. Finally, they will be fulfilled at the end of the *aeon* in the heavenly Jerusalem. See Bornert, 260.

39. "Christ is still at the center of this contemplation; but it is less the Jesus of history than the Logos, the summit of intelligible beings" (Bornert, 251; translation mine). In a sense, history surrenders itself to the *eschaton*, which reveals the fullness of the divine truth once hidden during the earthly sojourn of the Son of God. This vision of salvation, with the insistence that it commences in history, seems to differentiate the mystagogical interpretation of Symeon from that of Pseudo-Dionysius.

40. Along the lines of the *Ecclesiastical Hierarchy*, the contemplation of the divine is structured hierarchically and proceeds from a higher, inner plane to a lower, outer one. The first order of angels closest to God, the seraphim and cherubim, participate directly in the divine light, which they convey to the next lower level of angels. Likewise, in the hierarchical structure of the Church, the bishops observe directly the divine mysteries of the Eucharist, which they in turn deliver to the lower clergy to contemplate, who finally convey them to the lay people. Cf. *Interpretation of the Divine Temple and Liturgy* 82; PG 155.732A.

41. The removal of the episcopal pallium, or *omophorion*, before the readings and, in modern practice, the vesting with the smaller *omophorion* at the Great Entrance, symbolizes this deference to the authority of Christ the Teacher and Christ the Suffering Servant. Another interpretation may well be that Christ Himself is initiating the Church into the mystery of His Gospel and Passion (marked by the two entrances), after which the chief minister of the Church, the bishop, is free to vest and act in the place of Christ.

42. In modern practice, the bishop communes both the priests and the deacons and may even proceed to commune the laity with his co-celebrants, depending upon necessity or preference. In some cases, the bishop may designate for the senior presbyter to commune the deacons, thus maintaining a more orderly hierarchical structure, in which God's grace is distributed to each order from the one immediately above it.

3

A HISTORICAL OVERVIEW OF THE PREPARATION OF THE EUCHARISTIC GIFTS

Throughout the centuries, the preparation of the eucharistic gifts in the Eastern Church has undergone extensive development, both in outward form and internal significance. All available historical evidence unanimously indicates a gradual evolution from a practical, non-ceremonial transfer of bread and wine to the altar table during the Great Entrance, to a highly symbolic and self-sustained rite prior to the commencement of the eucharistic liturgy. Thomas Pott, building upon the work of his mentor Robert Taft, observes that "it developed from a non-rite into a true office (ἀκολουθία) with a beginning and a dismissal, following the example of every other office."[1]

The evolution of this practical act of preparation into the prothesis ceremonial occurred as the result of numerous developments in theological thought, each of which shaped the Church's consciousness of how it understood the prothesis, and simultaneously affected the rubrical modifications made to the rite. While this evolution initially appeared relatively slow, especially during the centuries following Maximos the Confessor's *Mystagogia* (AD 628–630), the rate of change accelerated almost disproportionately at the beginning of the second millennium.[2] In sharp contrast to its earlier history, the profuse additions to the prothesis eventually required limitations to be enforced on such items as the commemoration of names, attested to by Patriarch Philotheos Kokkinos.[3]

The chronological influx of theological concepts not only led to the expansion of the prothesis rite in mystagogical terms, but also reinforced the idea of the prothesis as image of the historical and meta-historical economy: that is, the dominical sacrifice upon the Cross and the restoration of all creation at the *eschaton*. The sacrificial and eschatological tone of this pre-Liturgy preparation ritual becomes quite evident after one traces the prothesis' development throughout history.

Georges Descoeudres[4] has already accomplished the tedious task of outlining the complete history of the prothesis rite in all its practical and chronological facets and so, the present chapter will rely heavily on his research. A supplement to Descoeudres is the parallel work of Pott,[5] which attempts to identify those "aspects of history which can aid one to comprehend more easily the evolution of the rite."[6] Although the mystagogical connection between sacrifice and eschatology—a fundamental assertion of this book—lies outside of the scope of interest of either scholar, their work nevertheless acknowledges, to a degree, that both ideas are undeniably prevalent in the overall symbolism of the prothesis rite.

Three stages of development are discernible in the prothesis rite, each of which corresponds to one of three "horizons of symbolical understanding."[7] In other terms, each stage is marked by the introduction of either a specific liturgical instrument or prayer or special rubric, which not only builds upon a pre-existing theological premise but also shapes the Church's mystagogical thought by drawing on different emphases. Before embarking on a careful examination of these three phases, it is worth looking briefly at how the liturgical offering was conducted prior to its eventual formalization.

PREPARATION OF THE GIFTS IN THE ANCIENT CHURCH

The manner of preparing the eucharistic gifts in the primitive Church involved nothing more than their simple transfer to the altar table. There is no specialized manner of preparation, no "ritualization" of the gifts, and no elaborate transfer.[8] Gregory Dix's dramatic description of this act indicates a purely practical act with absolutely no symbolical value whatsoever attached to the bread or wine. Commenting on a pontifical Eucharist (the Christians of the first century could not fathom a Liturgy without the presence of the bishop anyway),[9] he writes that after the opening greeting by the bishop and the spreading of the linen cloth over the altar table by the deacon,

> The bishop is still seated on his throne behind the altar, across which he faces the people. His presbyters are seated in a semi-circle around him. All present have brought with them, each for himself or herself, a little loaf of bread and probably a little wine in a flask. . . . These oblations of the people, and any other offerings in kind which might be made, the deacons now bring up to the front of the altar, and arrange upon it from the people's side of it. The bishop rises and moves

forward a few paces from the throne to stand behind the altar, where he faces the people with a deacon on either hand and his presbyters grouped around and behind him. He adds his own oblation of bread and wine to those of the people before him on the altar and so (presumably) do the presbyters.[10]

Several significant points need be made. First, the preparation and transfer of the eucharistic gifts are very clearly related; in fact, they appear to be one and the same act! Second, this act of preparation is performed in the presence of the worshipping faithful and not in some remote area concealed from them. Third, both clergy and lay people make their offering openly together, thus reducing any doubt of an elitism or clericalism in the liturgical anaphora. Finally, the participation of the deacons in managing this manual act of the preparatory reception and transfer of the eucharistic gifts demonstrates that it was void of any inner mystagogical significance.

By the fifth century, the primitive manner of transferring the gifts to the altar table has become ritualized, as evidenced by the *Mystagogical Catecheses* of Theodore of Mopsuestia (d. AD 428), a series of homilies delivered by him in Syriac while he was presumably still a presbyter in Antioch prior to 392 or following his elevation to the episcopal see of Mopsuestia (392–428). The transfer now possesses both a practical and symbolical purpose. Taft quotes the famous passage at length (*Homily* 15.24ff.), but only excerpts representative of this shift in thought are provided below.

> It is the deacons who bring out this oblation . . . which they arrange and place on the awe-inspiring altar, . . . By means of the symbols we must see Christ who is now being led out and going forth to his passion, and who, in another moment, is laid out for us on the altar . . . And when the offering that is about to be presented is brought out in the sacred vessels, the patens and chalices, you must think that Christ our Lord is coming out, led to his passion . . . by the invisible hosts of ministers . . . who were also present when the passion of salvation was being accomplished. . . . And when they bring it out, they place it on the holy altar to represent fully the passion. Thus we may think of him placed on the altar as if henceforth in a sort of sepulchre, and as having already undergone the passion.
>
> They [the deacons who have spread the linen cloths upon the altar-sepulchre] show by this ritual the greatness of the body lying there . . . a body that will soon rise to an immortal nature.
>
> These things take place in complete silence because, although the liturgy has not yet begun, still it is fitting to watch the bringing out and deposing of such a great and wonderful object in recollection and fear and a silent and quiet prayer, without saying anything.

After he [the deacon] has finished his appointed service and ad-
monished all with his voice and exhorted them to recite the prayers
that are suitable to ecclesiastical gatherings, and while all are silent,
the priest begins the rite of the prothesis, and before all else he offers
prayer to God, . . .[11]

This early form of a "Great Entrance" in Theodore's day includes a
number of ritualistic innovations that are worth mentioning: (1) the sac-
rifice-burial symbolism; (2) the sacramental realism in which the gifts "are
already" the lifeless body of the immolated Christ (a crucial foundational
point for the mystagogical development of the prothesis rite, especially in
the writings of Cabasilas and Symeon of Thessalonike); (3) only the deacons participate in this new procession; (4) the transfer is performed in
utter silence; and (5) a prayer in preparation for beginning the anaphora—
an unprecedented new element—is introduced. Taft remarks that the term
"prothesis" used in Theodore's famed homily should not be understood in
the modern Byzantine sense, i.e. of a second preparatory rite following the
transfer, but refers rather to the prayer offered by the priest in order to worthily celebrate the anaphora, the prayer of *accessus ad altare*.[12]

The place from which this transfer of the eucharistic gifts begins is likewise noteworthy. The building that came to be known as the *skeuophylakion*
seems to be mentioned for the first time in the account of the fire that
destroyed the Great Church of Hagia Sophia in 404 (the predecessor to
the Emperor Justinian's sixth-century architectural masterpiece), in which
Chrysostom, a contemporary of Theodore, served as archbishop of Constantinople.[13] While the church building itself was devastated, the σκευωρία,
or οἰκίσκος, a separate, rotunda-like "small building" northeast of the main
church and unattached to it, was left unscathed.

The *skeuophylakion* replaced the more ancient *diakonikon*, an antecham-
ber located near the entrance of the church where the faithful would deposit
their offerings to the deacons. The deacons, in turn, were chiefly responsible for making sure the gifts donated were from the baptized faithful in
good standing and from no one else. They typically watched over the gifts,
selecting as much bread as needed, mixing the water with wine, and then
bringing the prepared gifts at the appointed time.[14] The *skeuophylakion* was
eventually replaced by the table of oblation, which was located within a side
chapel or *pastophorion*, at the northeast corner of the altar. Appearing in the
mid-sixth century, this prothesis chamber resulted because of "changes in
the offerings of the faithful and in the transfer of gifts. And these changes
are supposed to signal the 'introduction' of the Great Entrance into the
liturgy of the Great Church."[15]

What were these changes exactly and why had they taken place? To answer such questions is to provide some valuable insight into the evolution of the prothesis rite into an independent, specialized ceremony. From antiquity, prior to the formal synthesis of the Liturgy of the Word and the Eucharist in the fourth century,[16] the gifts were prepared and transported to the altar table following the opening peace of the presiding bishop, i.e. at the very beginning of the eucharistic celebration. When the liturgies were fused into one rite, all non-baptized catechumens who attended the didactic synaxis portion of the Christian gathering were dismissed before the formal commencement of the Eucharist. The gifts of the faithful were then brought forward and the anaphora began.

Taft writes, "With the abolition of the catechumenate, the distinction between the liturgies of the catechumens and that of the faithful lost all meaning, and there was no longer any need to hold off the preparation of the gifts until after the Liturgy of the Word."[17] He goes on to claim that this event triggered the placement of the preparation before the Liturgy of the Word in the Byzantine tradition, at least by the eighth or ninth century. Marco Mandalà similarly believes that the prothesis rite was shifted to before the Liturgy of the Word because it is, in essence, a liturgical ceremony that naturally must precede the Eucharist, for which it is a preparation. And since the elimination of the catechumenate led to the vague distinction between synaxis and Eucharist, the prothesis was moved to the beginning of the whole liturgical unit.[18]

This reassignment of the prothesis to before the actual beginning of the Divine Liturgy and in a secluded nook within the altar (the table of oblation) now gave the clergy more time and privacy to complete their preparation of the gifts, two key conditions conducive to the transformation of this once very simple, mechanical act into a complex, symbol-enriched ritual. As can be ascertained from the historical evidence, the process of preparation evolved from a public act visible to the entire Church into a private sacerdotal ceremony concealed from the eyes of the lay faithful. The contact with the altar that the laity initially enjoyed now became limited to a degree, although they still brought their gifts to church and passively observed the transfer of the "ritualized gifts" during the Great Entrance.

It is important to point out that the historical and architectural changes the Eastern Church experienced in its liturgical life—i.e. the abolition of the catechumenate and the replaccment of the external *diakonika* and *skeuophylakia* with the prothesis table inside the altar—were not the sole innovations that transformed the prothesis into a full-fledged liturgical rite replete with mystagogical content. There were several theological factors, substantial developments in theological thought, which also exerted a high level of influence on the rite's evolution. It is now time to turn to these developments in detail, by examining the three phases outlined by Descoeudres.

RITUALIZATION PHASE I—INTRODUCTION OF THE PROTHESIS PRAYER

The first stage, corresponding to the "first ritualization" of the rite, involves the introduction of the prayer of the prothesis (seventh century). The prayer regards Christ as the "heavenly bread" (τὸν οὐράνιον ἄρτον) and links Christ as such with the bread of the oblation, thus giving the latter a venerable status—i.e. an inherent realism—throughout the entire Divine Liturgy, even prior to the consecration! This realism then facilitates the addition of other elements, all of which further contribute to expand the mystagogy of the rite.

Theodore of Mopsuestia's revolutionary characterization of the Great Entrance as the procession of Christ to His place of death led the Church to interpret the Divine Liturgy as "an accomplishment of a resurrection whose passion and sacrifice have taken place even before the liturgy has begun."[19] This radical view was met with both acceptance and criticism. On the one hand, St. Maximos the Confessor (628–630), in his *Mystagogia*, lends support to this position by calling the entrance with the gifts "an entrance of sacred and venerable mysteries,"[20] implying a realism in which they already represent the crucified Lord. On the other hand, approximately a century before Maximos and a century after Theodore, Patriarch Eutychios of Constantinople (552–565, 577–582), in his *Sermon on Pascha and the Holy Eucharist*, sharply criticizes the reverence paid to the unconsecrated gifts at the Great Entrance. He writes:

> They act stupidly, who have taught the people to sing a certain psalmic chant (ὕμνον τινὰ ψαλμικόν) when the ministers are about to bring up to the altar the bread of oblation and the recently (ἀρτίως) mixed chalice. In this hymn, which they consider suitable to the action being performed, the people say that they bear in the king of glory (βασιλέα τῆς δόξης) and refer in this way to the things being brought up, even though they have not yet been consecrated by the high-priestly invocation. . . .[21]

The adverb ἀρτίως ("recently"), aside from its intended use above to support Eutychios' rejection of any mystagogical significance at the Great Entrance, indicates that only the bread was "ritually" prepared at the prothesis and that the chalice was prepared just prior to the Great Entrance. In essence, the preparation of the chalice involved the mixing of wine with hot water at the Great Entrance, so that the wine would remain warm after the anaphora and during Holy Communion. Otherwise, any mixing at the prothesis would render a "colder" chalice by the end of the Liturgy and would thus require a second mixing. Pott admits that although the number of times and the moment when the wine and water were mixed varied from place to place, the established practice in the Great Church of Constantinople called for the initial mixing of wine and regular water at the prothesis and the further addition of hot water after the consecration and before Communion, i.e. at the rite of the *zeon*.[22] Taft writes: "This may be why the traditional Constantinopolitan prothesis prayer is a prayer *over the bread only*."[23] Further evidence to support this position is found in the canonical writings of Patriarch Nikephoros of Constantinople (806–815), who says, "it is not necessary to make a seal [i.e. bless with the sign of the Cross] over the holy chalice at the prayer in the skeuophylakion."[24] In any case, it is quite clear that the unconsecrated gifts had already acquired a mystical realism and were shown a reverence that would be fulfilled at the consecration later during the anaphora.

The first major stage in the ritualization of the prothesis rite was the introduction of the prayer of the prothesis, which seems to have appeared some time between Maximos' *Mystagogy* (first quarter of the seventh century) and the *Barberini Codex 336* (mid-eighth century).[25] In this prayer, originally recited after the bread had been placed upon the paten (in modern practice, after the bread and wine have been thoroughly prepared, following the commemorations and just prior to the dismissal), God, who has sent Christ into the world as the "heavenly bread" (John 6:51), is asked to bless and accept upon His heavenly altar the offering prepared below in His earthly temple. The prayer then beseeches the Lord to remember those who have made this offering and those for whom it was made. It concludes with a request to preserve without condemnation the clergy who are about to celebrate the Liturgy.

What is most interesting about this prayer is the description of Christ as the "heavenly bread" (ὁ οὐράνιος ἄρτος). Building upon the general consensus that the unconsecrated material gifts of bread and wine have acquired a distinct representative value of the suffering Christ led to His death at the Great Entrance, the mystagogical link between the bread of oblation and the Lord is made by pronouncing Him as the "heavenly bread." Consequently, the inherent realism implied by the prayer led to the addition of other mystagogical elements, related in some way to the Lamb of God who, both rubrically on the paten and theologically, occupies the central place in the Church.

RITUALIZATION PHASE II—INTRODUCTION OF THE LANCE

The second stage encompasses the introduction of the liturgical lance into the prothesis, a novelty that involved marking the oblation bread with the emblems of Christ's suffering, simultaneously incorporating the chalice into the overall mystagogy of the rite. The lance's use is attested to for the first time by Patriarch Germanos of Constantinople (715–730). Its introduction into the Byzantine Divine Liturgy is most likely related to the transfer from Jerusalem to Constantinople of the actual spear that pierced the side of Christ, in the year 614.[26] The historical significance of this ancient relic, combined with the piety shown toward it as having touched the very Body of the Lord, gradually led to the development of a sharp iron knife (σίδηρον), a smaller-scale replica of the famous lance, to be used in an array of liturgical movements symbolizing the sacrifice of the "heavenly bread."

The use of the lance to excise the Lamb from the prosphora loaf was accompanied by the Messianic verse from Isaiah 53:7, completing the liturgical act both visually and verbally: "he was led as a sheep to the slaughter, and as a lamb before the shearer is dumb, so he opens not his mouth." And since the spear was used by the centurion at the foot of the Cross to pierce the side of Christ, from which flowed blood and water, the last of the incisions on the Lamb integrates the addition of wine and water into the chalice, with the accompanying verse from John 19:34: "One of the soldiers pierced his side with a spear and at once came out blood and water." Hence, the preparation of the chalice is now fully synthesized with that of the bread, and both acts now fall within the confines of the prothesis rite.

Interestingly enough, these new innovations, namely, the prayer of the prothesis, the use of the lance, and the accompanying verses, are absent from subsequent euchologies for several centuries up until the fourteenth.[27] This fluidity could be the result of a possible resistance by some to a ritualization of the preparation of the gifts, but it was more likely because the rite was traditionally overseen by the deacons, and was thus considered an already established rite whose main elements were already familiar to the celebrant clergy.[28] Furthermore, another viable argument is that different *diataxeis* often fulfilled different purposes. For example, a *diataxis* of an episcopal Liturgy would surely not mention any aspect of the prothesis rite (since the bishop does not fully participate in the Liturgy until the Small Entrance), whereas a *diataxis* for a presbyterial Liturgy might.

What appears to be most significant in this stage of development is Germanos' insistence on

> the offering as an antitype not only of the person of Christ, but also of the event culminating in the history of salvation. If in the first stage, according to the interpretation of the prayer of the prothesis, the bread had to symbolically represent Christ, now the preparation of the bread and wine is a prophetic anticipation of this event that mystically and in fact will be accomplished in the anaphora.[29]

Again, both of these stages are fundamentally rooted in Theodore of Mopsuestia's insistence that it is the already sacrificed Christ, carried in procession, that is represented by the eucharistic gifts at the Great Entrance.

RITUALIZATION PHASE III—FURTHER PREPARATIONS, INCENSE, AND PARTICLES

This third stage of the prothesis' development—clearly the most eventful of the three—sees the addition of elements best labeled as secondary, which have no practical value in the preparation of the gifts for the Eucharist. The first two phases, predominantly linked with the procession to the altar, have initiated "a certain theological logic/manner of thinking" (*une certaine logique théologique*),[30] upon which the rapid modifications of the third stage are based. During this final period, the prothesis matures into an independent, self-sustaining rite.

In this final phase, following the end of iconoclasm, the additions to the rite multiply at an accelerated rate and are chronologically very close to each other. Among the significant developments are: the more specialized preparation of the Lamb and the chalice, the offering of incense, the multiplication of loaves and particles commemorating the saints as well as the living and dead, and the organization of the particles into categories corresponding to the celestial hierarchy.

By the third quarter of the twelfth century, the preparation of the paten and the chalice and the offering of incense are all well-established elements in the prothesis. Descoeudres remarks that in Leo Toscan's Latin translation of the Divine Liturgy of St. John Chrysostom (1173–1178), the preparation of the bread and chalice has the exact same form they have today, but the rite still lacks the commemorations of the saints and the living and dead.[31]

The prothesis is understood as the prophetic anticipation of Christ's economy, celebrated in full during the Eucharist proper.

Concerning the preparation of the bread, Toscan indicates a new innovation—namely, that four incisions are now made around the Lamb, each cut accompanied by one of the four verses from Isaiah. The verse from John 19:34 is no longer used with the symbolic piercing of the right side of the Lamb, but to interpret the mixture of wine with water.[32] As for the chalice, and in contrast to Germanos' witness, Toscan attests that wine and water are poured into the chalice when the appropriate word from John 19:34 is mentioned ("blood"; "water") and not when the side of the Lamb is pierced with the lance. This minor technicality in the rubrics was later abandoned, thus leading to the reattachment of the Johannine verse to the piercing with the lance, and assigning a new element, the benediction prayer over the chalice—"Εὐλογημένη ἡ ἕνωσις τῶν Ἁγίων σου . . ." ("Blessed is the union of Your holy things")—to the mixing of the wine and water.[33] With the recitation of the biblical verse and the prayer, one clearly sees that the contents of the chalice, like the bread, have acquired a similar mystagogical realism, more vivid perhaps than the one Germanos attempted to convey in his own interpretation of the prothesis rite over four hundred years before.

The incensing of the gifts at the prothesis seems to have begun during the ninth century,[34] and is mentioned by Anastasius the Librarian in his Latin translation of Patriarch Germanos' *Ecclesiastical History* (869–870). Initially, the rite of incense accompanied the prothesis prayer, probably in order to emphasize the sacrificial dimension of the offering.[35] Leo Toscan mentions, for the first time, that incense was also used for the ritualistic covering of the eucharistic gifts, which preceded the prayer.

In addition, a prayer over the incense was recited before the gifts were censed, a familiar practice in other parts of the Liturgy usually done by the senior celebrant. However, since the prothesis was by tradition the domain of the deacons, initially the covering of the gifts, along with the prayer of the incense and the censing itself, remained in their custody, but not for long. By the fourteenth century, the officiation of the prothesis rite passed over to the higher clergy, a *"tendance à la hiératisation"* within the Eastern Church that apparently began within monastic circles and affected not only the prothesis but other rites as well.[36]

The multiplication of the particles on the paten is the most significant innovation of this stage, and the one that finalizes the characterization of the prothesis as an autonomous rite. At the beginning of the twelfth century, written evidence[37] indicates the use of four prosphora loaves in the celebration of the prothesis. The first prosphora is offered in honor of Christ, from which is extracted the Lamb. From the remainder are excised particles in memory of the Mother of God, the celestial hierarchy of angels, St. John the Baptist, the apostles, prophets, bishops, and all the saints. One immediately notices here the deliberate hierarchical progression of the names, a list often dictated by personal preference, especially within monasteries. In fact, this subjectivity usually proved to be quite problematic, as it usually rendered an unconstrained and excessively long catalog of saints' names, a concern Philotheos Kokkinos attempted to regulate during his patriarchate.[38]

Pott points out that each commemoration of a name was in fact an intercessory petition, asking God, through the saint, to accept the sacrifice (i.e. prosphora) of the individual who brought his offering for the Liturgy.[39] If more than four loaves were available, the priest offered a prayer for the forgiveness of the sins of the living and dead. Whichever the case, the "drama" upon the paten, as it were, begins to take on a fresh new dimension. The prothesis has now become a sort of "private chapel," or "a mini-altar," upon which rests the immolated Lamb of God. Before Him, intercessory prayer to the saints, who are already "close" to God both spiritually and rubrically (i.e. their particles appear next to the Lamb on the paten), is offered for the expiation of man's sins.

The concept of making the eucharistic offering on behalf of another human being has already been encountered in the prayer of the prothesis, so the offering of prosphora with the commemoration of names cannot be considered a totally foreign idea. In fact, the fifth century *Testament of Our Lord* (1.19)[40] witnesses to the mentioning of the names of both those who offer gifts (bread, wine, *et al.*) and those for whom they are offered.

Within the ranks of the monastic communities, the offering of prosphora on behalf of others became a very popular practice. A veritable argument explaining the reason for this innovation lies in the fact that several powerful emperors and prominent members of Byzantine nobility were responsible for founding or restoring monasteries throughout the Empire. In return, they often requested that prosphora be offered in their name during the Divine Liturgy. This request was also honored for both the living and deceased monks of the monastery.[41]

Initially, the petitions for the living and dead were not combined with the list of saints from whom the Church sought intercession. However, as Pott explains, "But rather quickly, without doubt stimulated by the large popularity which the cult of saints enjoyed within monastic circles, one associated certain saints in the commemorations as intercessors."[42]

The commemoration of names in the prothesis is strikingly similar to the reading of the diptychs at various points during the Liturgy proper. In fact, Taft seems to think that both commemorations and diptychs mutually influenced each other.[43] The order of the dead preceding the living in the commemorations seems to have been borrowed from the sequence familiar in the diptychs. A little while later, the diptychs again seem to have provided the model for the prothesis to follow, namely, "the regrouping of saints in a single category of commemorations, destined to precede the category of the faithful."[44] The commemoration of the names at the prothesis, however, unlike the diptychs, was accompanied by the liturgical gesture of placing particles from each respective prosphora around the Lamb on the paten. This important rubric not only emphasized the inherent realism of the rite, but also led Symeon of Thessalonike to make his disclosure of the completed prothesis as a mystical image of the universe encircling its Creator.

Patriarch Nicholas III's prescription that the loaves be offered at the prothesis as intercession before the saints, took a radical turn on Mt. Athos in the twelfth century. The accession of the Athonite monk John to the patriarchal throne of Constantinople witnesses to the likelihood that the innovation was already in place on the Holy Mountain and was then brought to the Great Church by the hesychast patriarch. Essentially, the difference was that now, the saints mentioned in the prothesis were no longer perceived as playing an intercessory role for the expiation of the sins of the faithful. On the contrary, their names were now commemorated and the prosphora offered in their "honor and memory."[45] Even the preparation of the chalice, originally completed after the deposition of the particles, is now placed more sensibly before the commemorations, to make up a single unit with the preparation of the Lamb. By redirecting then the focus away from the paten, as it were, the particles representing the saints take on a different meaning: they no longer appear before the immolated Lamb as intercessors but as constitutive members of a celestial hierarchy in whose "honor and memory" the Eucharist is offered to God. This "reassignment" of the role of the saints is indicative of a shift from a more historical symbolism within the rite, focusing on the dynamic of intercession before the sacrifice of Christ, to an eschatological symbolism in which salvation history has culminated in the hierarchical arrangement of the heavenly and earthly realms around the throne of the Lamb of God. Such a promotion of a celestial hierarchy, emphasized later in Symeon of Thessalonike's mystagogical writings, appears in various ecclesiastical media, not only in the Liturgy itself but also in post-Iconoclastic liturgical art.[46] Pott writes: "The deceased or living faithful that one would wish to commemorate completes 'the economical system' or 'the history of salvation' represented on the paten, without there being anymore any explicit connection with the immolated lamb of God and the forgiveness of sins."[47] He adds:

> . . . the symbolic function of the particles for the saints and for the faithful underwent a real transformation: the idea of the celestial hierarchy had in effect eclipsed the more ancient system according to which the commemoration of the faithful was in direct connection with the gifts that had been offered in the light of the anaphora.[48]

In this final phase of the rite's symbolism, the prothesis is no longer envisioned as solely the prophetic anticipation of the anaphora to follow. Quite the contrary, it now encompasses the entire *economia* of salvation, from Christ's humble birth in Bethlehem to His Second Coming at the *eschaton*, where He sits in judgment before all heavenly and earthly beings gathered before Him.[49]

Following Nicholas of Andida's interpretation of the Liturgy in his *Protheoria* (eleventh century) as the representation of the entire life of Christ, the prothesis likewise does the same. The dramatization includes not simply Christ's passion, death, and resurrection, but also touches upon other significant historical events such as the virginal birth and Christ's hidden public life in Nazareth. This is affirmed, for example, by the practical eleventh-century introduction of the *asteriskos*, a sort of four-pronged metallic support placed on the paten and over which one of the smaller veils is draped to prevent the veil from touching the bread particles on the *diskos*. Its resemblance somewhat to a "star," according to Pott, initiated a symbolism in which it was identified as the star that appeared to the Magi at the birth of Christ.[50] However, this vague characterization conflicts with the more likely symbolization of the *asteriskos* as the firmament of heaven, especially when Psalm 32:6 accompanied its placement over the *diskos*. This second interpretation, presumably the more original of the two, coincides with the cosmic and eschatological imagery that highlights Symeon's commentaries and will be taken up afterward in this book.

This later tendency toward an "over-historicization" of the prothesis rite is likewise marked in some modern service books that include a dismissal for the prothesis, in which references to Christ's "birth in the cave" and "repose in a manger for our salvation" have been inserted. However, the newer and more critical *Hieratika*[51] have restored the original dismissal, allowing the historical element to remain in its simplified form, and in accordance solely with the witness of the Byzantine mystagogues.

In sum then, the historical development of the prothesis rite occurred simultaneously with parallel developments in theological thought, following a process that essentially allowed one particular change to lead quite naturally into the other. Pott elucidates quite well this natural flow by writing:

> We have observed how the rite of the prothesis developed on the horizon of a changing and increasingly important symbolic understanding. But it would be more correct to say that the development of the ritual and its interpretation went together: the interpretation, since Theodore of Mopsuestia, of the Great Entrance with the funeral procession of Christ already sacrificed, made the prepared gifts identify with the body of Christ, the lamb of God; the idea of the sacrifice of the lamb which is Christ called for the usage of the lance; the identification of the prothesis with Golgotha evoked the history of salvation represented on the paten and in the chalice; the idea of the history of salvation, embracing the entire universe, transformed the paten into a sort of Ark of Noah always collecting many commemorations which, in turn, evoked the image of the saved universe and the communion of saints; at the same time the idea of the history of salvation evoked the mysteries of the earthly life of Christ, conceived and born symbolically in the preparation of the bread and covered by the star of Bethlehem, which also must protect the hierarchical order represented by the particles of bread on the paten.[52]

It must be emphasized that throughout this complex development of the prothesis rite, especially in this final phase, no particular element or emphasis truly "eclipsed" the other, to the point of rendering it defunct in theory, as Pott correctly hypothesizes.[53] Despite Nicholas of Andida's new historical interpretation of the Liturgy and prothesis, Germanos' more ancient understanding of it as an immolation of the Lamb did not surrender its significance within the conscience of the Byzantine Church. Both views were equally acceptable and retained their importance. In fact, the differences are best understood as an issue of perspective and seen as complementary rather than contradictory. Indeed, both interpretations were well preserved in the witness of the liturgical manuscripts following the twelfth century, which included rubrics reflective of either position, without any intent of ignoring or undermining the other. Pott affirms this by writing: "*Les horizons de compréhension symbolique différents de la prothèse ne se sont donc pas succédés mais ils se sont superposés et ont continué à exister simultanément comme une interprétation à plusieurs niveaux d'un unique acte rituel.*"[54]

Hence, both sacrificial theology and eschatology came to coexist in a symbiotic, non-threatening, and mutually dependent union in the prothesis rite, projecting the crucified Lamb of history to be simultaneously the glorified Lamb of the *eschaton*, and drawing all of history to its final fulfillment in the eternal *aeon*.

ADDENDUM: PROTHESIS AND PROSKOMIDE— ETYMOLOGICAL DISTINCTIONS

The modern synonymous usage of both the terms prothesis and proskomide in Eastern liturgical language warrants a brief etymological and historical examination of both terms, highlighting their original nuances in definition that eventually led to their interchangeability.

The term πρόθεσις appears for the first time in the Septuagint translation of Scripture, referring to the shewbread (ἄρτος τῆς προθέσεως) of the Old Testament,[55] understood as the people's weekly offering set before the Lord. In Byzantine liturgical usage, the term possesses one of three connotations: (1) it often designates the specific ritualistic preparation of the gifts of bread and wine preceding the commencement of the Divine Liturgy; (2) it indicates the place in the altar where the gifts are prepared; and (3) the term sometimes refers to the actual gifts that have been prepared and await their transfer to the altar table. Whichever definition is espoused, the word's base meaning of "offering" (πρo + τίθημι, "I place toward/before"),[56] be it the act or the place or the actual offering itself, is not compromised.

Interestingly, the term, when referring to the dead, also has the connotation of "the public display of a dead man."[57] Although Theodore of Mopsuestia makes no mention of a preparatory ritual over the bread, his description nevertheless of the Great Entrance as symbolizing the procession of Christ to Golgotha possibly lends support to this secondary etymological claim. Pott remarks:

> The symbolical significance of the Great Entrance as the funeral procession of Christ is found to be attested to for the first time by Theodore of Mopsuestia (+426) and will result, at least in the Byzantine rite, in the interpretation of the liturgy as the accomplishment of a resurrection in which the passion and sacrifice have taken place even before the liturgy has begun.[58]

The term *prothesis* must not be confused with the Church's collective act of offering the gifts to God during the anaphoral section of the Liturgy. To be sure, the people do not offer bread and wine directly to God but present them first to the clergy in order to be "ritualized." In other words, the Church receives these gifts in their base form, which are then ritually prepared and set aside for their ultimate intended purpose. One may say that they are offered (by the people) in order to be brought (by the clergy) to God, who returns them back to His Church in the form of Holy Communion.

A synonymous term that likewise projects the aforementioned three definitions is προσκομιδή or προσκομιδία. Etymologically speaking and in sharp contrast to the idea of 'offering', *proskomide* derives from προσ + κομίζω ("I transport something, I distance it from somewhere to protect it, in order to safeguard it").[59] In antiquity, *proskomide* also refers to the dead and specifically means, "I transport the dead for burial."[60] In this case, the general sense is one of deliberate movement, from one place to another, in order to fulfill a specific purpose.

Taft proves that the term *proskomide* is synonymous with the idea of "offertory" and "anaphora" (or "eucharistic prayer"), as it appears in several manuscripts from as early as the fourth century and up until the seventh.[61] In the ancient manuscript tradition, the title "Prayer of the Proskomide," typically located after the Great Entrance—at the time, that is, when the gifts were initially made ready for their transport to the altar—is shown to apply to the entire eucharistic formulary that follows, i.e. the anaphora. After the twelfth century, *proskomide* was used to signify the rite of the prothesis, conferring upon it also the idea of offertory. This redefinition led to the erroneous idea that the "Prayer of the Proskomide" served as an actual offertory prayer, when in fact it was no more than a prayer of *accessus ad altare*,[62] in which the celebrant asked God to account him worthy of approaching the holy altar and performing the anaphora. The prayer's connection then to the anaphora was not seen as an actual offertory, but as a prelude to it, verbalizing the spiritual preparedness required of the celebrant prior to reciting the eucharistic prayer.

The synonymous use of both terms to designate the same rite certainly allows one to comprehend it as both a "pre-offering," as well as an act by which the prepared gifts are to be (or have already been) transported to the altar. On a mystagogical level, the symbolism of the rite as the display of the immolated Son of God at the table of oblation (Golgotha) and His subsequent transfer to the altar (tomb) from which His resurrection will occur, is also quite significant. However, this study, when referring to the complex preparatory rite of the eucharistic gifts, will utilize the term *prothesis*, for the simple reason that historically, *prothesis* was never used to specify the offertory itself, whereas *proskomide* was. Furthermore, the former does not hint at any transfer of gifts but rather specifies the independent rite of preparation that prefaces the Divine Liturgy. Any occasional usage then of the term *proskomide*, in place of *prothesis*, is solely for variety.

NOTES

1. Thomas Pott, *La réforme liturgique byzantine: étude du phénomène d'évolution nonspontanée de la liturgie byzantine* (Rome, 2000), 170. Translation mine. See also Robert F. Taft, *The Great Entrance: A History of the Transfer of Gifts and Other Pre-anaphoral Rites of the Liturgy of St. John Chrysostom* (Rome, 1978), 3ff.

2. Pott, 171.

3. Ibid., 188.

4. Georges Descoeudres, "Werden und Entwicklung des Prothesis-Ritus" (Chapter 6), in *Die Pastophorien im syro-byzantinischen Osten. Eine Untersuchung zu architektur- und liturgiegeschichtlichen Problemen* (Wiesbaden, 1983), 85–126.

5. Pott, 169–96.

6. Ibid. 171. Translation mine.

7. Descoeudres, 116–18.

8. Taft, *The Great Entrance*, 12. Justin Martyr (*Apologia* 1, 65) and Hippolytus of Rome (*Apostolic Tradition* 21) both express the simplicity of this preparation in the second century also.

9. Dix, *The Shape of the Liturgy* (London, 1945), 105, 134, and 285, specifically in his reference to the *fermentum*, or consecrated Host from the pontifical Liturgy, a piece of which was transported to the other area liturgies by the deacons in order to signify the unity between the bishop and his churches and to emphasize the centrality of the bishop's role as the Church's chief liturgist. See also John F. Baldovin, "The *Fermentum* at Rome in the Fifth Century: A Reconsideration", in *Worship*, vol. 79, no. 1 (2005), 38–53.

10. Dix, 104.

11. Theodore of Mopsuestia, *Catechetical Homily* 15.24ff; see also R. Tonneau and R. Devreesse, eds., *Les homélies catéchétiques de Théodore de Mopsueste* (Vatican City, 1949), 503ff; and Taft, *The Great Entrance*, 35–36. Taft also recognizes the following non-Byzantine sources as interpreting the procession of the gifts in a similar fashion (pp. 38–42): (1) the *Liturgical Homilies of Narsai* (d. 502), Homily 17; (2) the *Apostolic Constitutions* (late fourth century), Book 8, 12.3–4; (3) Pseudo-Dionysios (late fifth century), *Ecclesiastical Hierarchy* 3; PG 3.425, 427; and (4) the *Bibliotheca Rahmani Codex Syr. 303*, an eighth-ninth century Syriac account which describes a pre-seventh century Liturgy.

12. Taft, *The Great Entrance*, 38.

13. PG 47.35–36; 114.1188.

14. Taft, *The Great Entrance*, 32–33.

15. Ibid., 178–79.

16. Dix, 36–37. It is important to note that the primitive Church generally treated the Eucharist and the Synaxis (what later came to be known as the "Liturgy of the Catechumens") as separate Christian gatherings with distinct purposes. In St. Justin Martyr's *First Apology* (AD 155), as well as in St. Hippolytus of Rome's *Apostolic Tradition* (AD 215), two of the earliest non-biblical eucharistic witnesses, the Eucharist is shown to be preceded by the Synaxis on only one account. In all likelihood during the first century, the Synaxis, as the chief catechetical and kerygmatic tool of the bishop, took place during the week while the Eucharist was clearly celebrated on Sunday, the day of the Resurrection. However, it was not completely uncommon for the Synaxis to introduce the Eucharist after the second century, and by the fourth century, both services were fused into one rite and universally accepted as inseparable entities of the Liturgy, albeit with certain exceptions until the sixth century.

17. Taft, *The Great Entrance*, 15.

18. Marco Mandalà, *La protesi della liturgia nel rito Bizantino-Greco* (Grottaferrata, 1935), 60ff.

19. Pott, 172. Translation mine.

20. PG 91.693CD.

21. PG 86.2400A–2401B. English translation in Taft, *The Great Entrance*, 84–85.

22. Pott, 173, 179.

23. Taft, *The Great Entrance*, 274.

24. PG 100.856; Translation mine.

25. Taft, *The Great Entrance*, 274.

26. *Chronicon Paschale for the Year 614*, PG 92.988.

27. Pott, 175.

28. Ibid., 175–76.

29. Ibid., 176. Translation mine.

30. Ibid., 177.

31. Descoeudres, 87.

32. Ibid., 88.

33. Ibid., 88–89.

34. Pott, 179; Descoeudres, 96–97.

35. Descoeudres, 98–99.

36. Pott, 180; Descoeudres, 90, 113–14.

37. The sources bearing this information include a letter written by a priest from Crete to his metropolitan bishop Elias (residing at the time in Constantinople) and the metropolitan's written response, around 1120. In the letter, the priest wishes to believe that he is performing the rite of the prothesis correctly, following the established model by the deceased Patriarch Nicholas III Grammatikos (d. 1111). Cognizant, however, that the late patriarch's liturgical canons did not coincide with the more ancient *Ecclesiastical History* of Germanos and its derivatives, the Cretan priest attempts to reconcile his current practice with what he believed to be the more "correct" tradition. The metropolitan responds that Nicholas' rubrics take precedence, for the simple reason that the Great Church was following them also and because this was the established practice among the Byzantine churches of the East. See Pott, 181,

and René Bornert, *Les commentaires byzantins de la Divine Liturgie du VIIe au XVe siècle* (Paris, 1965), 146–48.

38. Pott, 188.

39. Ibid., 182.

40. *Testamentum Domini nostri Jesu Christi*. ed. J.E. Rahmani (Mainz, 1899), 24–25.

41. Pott, 183; Descoeudres, 106–07.

42. Pott, 183. Translation mine. He also mentions that Mary and the saint of the day were the first two figures who received a permanent place in the catalog of saints within the prothesis rite.

43. R. Taft, *The Diptychs: A History of the Liturgy of St. John Chrysostom*, vol. IV (Rome, 1991), 158–59.

44. Pott, 184. Translation mine.

45. Ibid., 185.

46. R. Taft, *The Byzantine Rite: A Short History* (Collegeville, 1992), 84–87, 89.

47. Pott, 185–86. Translation mine.

48. Ibid., 187. Translation mine.

49. Ibid., 186.

50. Ibid., 186, note 112.

51. Ἱερατικόν (*Priest's Service Book*). ed. Constantinos Papayiannis (Athens, 2001), 106; and Ἱερατικόν Α΄, περιέχον ἅπασαν τὴν τοῦ ἱερέως διάταξιν εἰς τὸν Ἑσπερινόν, τὸν Ὄρθρον, καὶ εἰς τὴν Θ. Λειτουργίαν τοῦ ἐν ἁγίοις πατρὸς ἡμῶν Ἰωάννου τοῦ Χρυσοστόμου, ὡς καὶ εἰς ἑτέρας ἱερᾶς ἀκολουθίας καὶ τελετάς [*Priest'sService Book (Volume 1), Containing the Entire Order of Service for the Priest, for Vespers, Matins and the Divine Liturgy of Our Father among the Saints JohnChrysostom, as Well as for Other Holy Services and Rites*], (Daphne, Holy Mountain, 1992), 90–91.

52. Pott, 189. Translation mine.

53. Ibid., 186ff.

54. Ibid., 187.

55. See Exod 40:23; 1 Kgs 21:6; 1 Chr 9:32, 23:29; and 2 Chr 4:19, 13:11. These ἄρτοι τῆς προθέσεως were a set of twelve loaves that were placed "before the Lord," on a table next to the altar of incense in the Temple, and were consumed by the priests alone later on in the week. See also *The Oxford English Dictionary*, vol. 9 (Oxford, 1933), 688.

56. Ioannes Stamatakos, ed. Λεξικὸν Ἀρχαίας Ἑλληνικῆς Γλώσσης [*Lexicon of the Ancient Greek Language*], (Athens, 1972), 832.

57. Ibid.

58. Pott, 172. Translation mine. Pott mistakenly calls Theodore of Mopsuestia's description of the entrance with the gifts a "funeral procession." Theodore is clear that the still *living* Christ is being led to the place of martyrdom—Golgotha—and that eventually, His lifeless body is laid out upon the altar, i.e., is entombed.

59. *Lexicon of the Ancient Greek Language*, 540, 847.

60. Ibid., 540.

61. Taft, *The Great Entrance*, 360–64. The same views are held by J. Mateos, *La célébration de la parole dans la liturgie byzantine* (Rome, 1971), 179; and A. Jacob, *Histoire du formulaire grec de la liturgie de Saint Jean Chrysostome* (unpublished doctoral dissertation), (Louvain, 1968), 282, 472–75. See also Descoeudres, xvi.

62. Pott, 170; Taft, *The Great Entrance*, 350–73; Mateos, 174–79; Descoeudres, 115.

4

A THEOLOGY OF *ECONOMIA*:
SACRIFICE IN EASTERN LITURGY

ETYMOLOGICAL CONSIDERATIONS OF *ECONOMIA*

A careful study of the origin of the term economia will reveal that it is generally linked with the concept of management or order. In a literal sense, economia derives from οἶκος ("house") and νόμος ("law"), signifying the order of law or lawful "management of a household or family, husbandry, thrift."[1] The verb form, οἰκονομέω, means (I) "manage as a house-steward, order, regulate."[2] Other "managerial" definitions include: "Ministration; management, charge, office";[3] "direction, governance of persons";[4] "abstract for concrete, ministry, ref. appointment of deacons to assist bishops . . . good management, thrift . . . operation, business, occupation . . . function . . . of administrative action, arrangement, procedure, system—of ecclesiastical discipline . . . ordinance, provision . . . administration, of alms . . . of ecclesiastical administration in general; . . . tenure of office of οἰκονόμος . . . disposition, organization, constitution."[5]

While this popular connotation seems to have been more limited in its scope, focusing primarily on the day-to-day operation of the family unit or immediate local community, the early Church broadened the meaning to encompass a yet greater family—humanity as a whole. In this wholly new Christian sense of the word, economia now equates the management of God's household, i.e. the Church and by extension, the human race, with the idea of the divine plan to save mankind, restore it, and unite it with God (cf. Eph 1:10; 3:2ff).

In regard to divine economy, the nuances are several: "dispensation, ordering; in general, of the natural order or natural laws . . . of divine dispensation in creation and providential ordering of world . . . of God's special dispensations or interpositions, especially of grace and mercy—in revelations, prophecies, and types . . . of divine grace or operation in sacraments—baptism, Eucharist . . . of the OT dispensation as a whole ... of Incarnation; as dispensation of divine purpose—ref. fact of Incarnation, virtually synonymous with ἐνανθρώπησις . . .";[6] "partic. ref. 'accommodation' or voluntary and contingent self-limitation of Son . . . Christol.; ref. Person of Word incarnate—ref. Christ's incarnate life and work, in general—ref. acts of Christ—ref. partic. of Passion and of Christ's redeeming activity in death and Resurrection—of other actions or events in Christ's life."[7]

SACRIFICE AS THE CORE ELEMENT IN THE DIVINE ECONOMIA

Liturgical scholars and theologians alike, when discussing the role of Jesus Christ in the history of salvation, very often associate the term "sacrifice" with "economia." The Golgotha event, undoubtedly central to the Christian soteriological position, is regarded as the ultimate expression of God's divine plan as "a secret and hidden wisdom of God (Θεοῦ σοφίαν ἐν μυστηρίῳ τὴν ἀποκεκρυμμένην), which God decreed before the ages for our glorification" (1 Cor 2:7). Although Saint Paul suggests in this particular passage that true and pious foreknowledge of this mystery would have dissuaded Jesus' persecutors from crucifying Him (1 Cor 2:8), he nevertheless identifies the sacrifice of Christ on the Cross as the necessary culmination and peak of God's efforts to reconcile mankind to Him.

Elsewhere in the New Testament, the shedding of Christ's blood is due cause for redemption and the forgiveness of sins (Eph 1:7), through which He has "made known to us in all wisdom and insight the mystery of his will, according to his purpose which he set forth in Christ as a plan for the fulness of time (κατὰ τὴν εὐδοκίαν αὐτοῦ ἣν προέθετο ἐν αὐτῷ εἰς οἰκονομίαν τον πληρώματος τῶν καιρῶν), to unite all things in him, things in heaven and things on earth" (Eph 1:9–10). The passage implies that the sacrificial act was the *sine qua non*, which completes and ultimately gives significance to God's dispensation to unite heavenly and earthly beings provisionally in the Liturgy before the final consummation of the age. Hence, Christ's death may be considered one component of God's overall economia, but its absolute and incontestable centrality gives worth to every other event of the divine dispensation, which either anticipates or derives its value from it.

TREATMENT OF SACRIFICE IN THE PATRISTIC WRITINGS

The early Christians uniquely envisioned the eucharistic sacrifice as a meal celebrating the renewal of God's covenant with His people. In the Last Supper accounts deriving from Matthew and Mark, John H. McKenna associates the Eucharist with the Sinai Covenant because of the references to the "blood of the covenant": "The 'liturgy' of Christ's life and death is presented as a covenant sacrifice which raises the Mosaic event to a higher plane and gives it new meaning."[8] By contrast, however, McKenna considers the Lukan-Pauline accounts of the Eucharist as reflective of the "bloodless covenant" revealed by God in Jeremiah 31:31-33, observing that Christians stretched the meaning of words like "sacrifice" "to include obedience to the gospel, works of charity, prayer and thanksgiving, all of which gave honor to God."[9] Hence, throughout the writings of the Church Fathers, the sacrificial notion of the Eucharist may be understood in one of two ways: either as the immolation of the victim, reenacted and relived within the Liturgy, or as the free, selfless response of the worshipper, who is prompted to act by the sacrifice of Christ.

Throughout the history of the Church, these two positions are reflected with relatively equal prominence within the early patristic tradition. The very early second-century *Didache*, or *Teaching of the Twelve Apostles*, exhorts the Christians to offer "pure sacrifice" in the Eucharist, making a direct reference to Malachi 1:11: "For from the risings of the sun to its goings down My name hath been glorified among the nations; and in every place incense is offered to My name, and a pure sacrifice—since My name is great among the nations, saith the Lord Almighty." By virtue of its connection to the aforementioned prophetic passage, the *Didache* text refers more so to the material "offerings" required for the Eucharist.[10] This realization is important and signifies that the author, and by extension the Early Church, were comfortable with the idea of the Eucharist as sacrifice.

The first statements on this sacrificial theme were penned by the Apostolic Fathers, each of whom, it would appear, were unwilling to completely abandon the notion of sacrifice as an institutionalized, ritualistic act which relives the immolation of the crucified Christ, although they were not exclusively bound to it.[11] Clement of Rome (AD 96), regards that real sacrifice is according to the will of God, and he arrives at this conclusion by suggesting a theology of divine acceptance,[12] opposing a philosophical criticism of sacrifice,[13] and stressing the obedience of Abraham and Isaac to God's initial will.[14] Furthermore, he adds a spiritual dimension to sacrifice by inserting "spiritualizing" texts from the Psalms in his chapters. Finally, he institutionalizes Christian sacrifice within the liturgical life of the Church, an attempt "to counteract what he perceived to be anti-institutional abuses or tenden-cies in the church."[15]

Ignatios of Antioch (d. AD 98–117) sees both the individual and the eucharistic community as temples and the altar upon which the Eucharist is offered as an image of the Church, with the one altar as a symbol of unity.[16] In his *Epistle to the Romans*, Ignatios accepts martyrdom as the expression of true sacrifice.[17]

The mid-second-century *Shepherd of Hermas* discusses sacrifice within the context of fasting,[18] and Polycarp of Smyrna (d. AD 156) endorses the aforementioned views,[19] adding a unique one of his own, namely, he identi-fies the individual with the altar of God, upon whom the sacrifice of love and mercy may be offered.[20]

The Apologists raise the Church's understanding of sacrifice to a newer and, expectedly, more sophisticated level in their attempt to treat the theme within a more theological context. For example, in Justin Martyr's two *Apologies*, written between AD 150–155, and in his *Dialogue with Trypho*, Justin develops his anti-sacrifice polemic, claiming the inappropriateness of offering material sacrifices to the spiritual God[21] and assessing this form of worship as demonic[22] but tolerated by God in the Old Testament.[23] None-theless, he adopts the theological connotations implied in Jewish temple sacrifices—namely, the divine acceptance of the sacrifice and atonement as the goal of ritualistic sacrifice—in order to construct his theology of Christ's sacrificial death as the Passover Lamb and offering for sin (Gen 49:11; Isa 53:7).[24] Finally, Justin defends the early Christians' act of offering the eucharistic sacrifice, highlighting that God is displeased by the wasted animal sacrifices made by pagans but is placated by the bloodless ritual celebration of the Eucharist which ultimately benefits man.[25] In fact, he observes how "superior" the Christian sacrifice is vis-à-vis the pagan of-fering in the eyes of God,[26] and he pinpoints the definition of sacrifice to the ritual act celebrated by Christians but *expressed in the context of prayer and thanksgiving*.[27] This fusion of a "sacrifice within the sacrifice" is most important for Eastern liturgy because it delineates the divine and human roles played in eucharistic worship. Both God and man offer themselves to one another as a sign of mutual affection and commitment to the greater cause of salvation.

Irenaeus of Lyons (end of the second century), in his *Against Heresies* and *The Proof of the Apostolic Preaching*, remarks that it is not God who needs sacrifices but we ourselves, offering them, as we do, continually for our benefit.[28] Deviating from Justin, Irenaeus also views Old Testament sac-rifices within a more positive light, considering them "as a providential preparation for Christian sacrifice."[29] Irenaeus' espousal of Old Testament sacrifices and his attempt to unite both Testaments makes sense in view of his polemic against the Gnostic heresiarchs of his time, whereas his contemporary Justin's disavowal of Old Testament blood offerings may be explained by his theological stance against the Jews.

Another significant point here is that for Irenaeus, the human body is not only the temple of God, but of Christ as well.[30] Here, in order to counter the opposing "spiritualistic" Gnostic view, he attempts to delineate a more specific material realism by emphasizing a realistic understanding of Christ's presence in the Eucharist. Most importantly, in regard to the sacrifice of Christ, the Bishop of Lyons affirms that this selfless act upon the Cross fulfills *in toto* the event of the Incarnation. In other words, Christ became flesh in order to offer Himself to the Father for the redemption of the human race. Among other things, Irenaeus writes:

> Because we are all connected with the first formation of Adam and were bound to death through disobedience, it was just and necessary that the bonds of death be loosed by him who was made man for us. Because death had established its dominion over the body, it was just and necessary that man who was once defeated by the body, should henceforth be free of its oppression. Thus, the Word became flesh in order that sin, destroyed by means of the same flesh through which it had gained its mastery and dominion, should no longer live in us. Thus did our Lord take up the same first formation [as Adam] in his incarnation, in order that he might offer it up in his struggle on behalf of his forefathers, and thus overcome through Adam what had stricken us through Adam.[31]

This intimate connection between Christ's birth and death, the latter being the natural consequence of the former, offers a plethora of invaluable insights in regard to Eastern liturgy and, most especially, to the prothesis rite. The later Byzantine introduction of the birth theme into the rite of preparation, coupled with the emblems of Christ's passion made by the various piercings of the Lamb, liturgically indicate the mutual and necessary dependency of each theme. In a liturgical sense, even before Christ is born in the flesh (at the prothesis) and appears to the world (at the Small Entrance), He has been marked with the symbols of His suffering, thus bestowing full significance on every event in His life leading up to Golgotha.

Irenaeus also takes up the Pauline theme of temple by describing the human body as the temple of Christ,[32] joining to it the concepts of universal priesthood and continuous sacrifice.[33] Unlike Justin's anti-Jewish and cultic polemic, Irenaeus establishes, at least in part, the basis of the Christian priesthood upon the Levitical. Hence, the eucharistic liturgy of the New Testament, in all its mystagogical significance, flows out of the Old Covenant, sharing the same "genus," as Daly says, but not the same "species":

> . . . the difference between Jewish and Christian sacrifice is one of "species," not "genus." For there are sacrifices now among the Christians just as there used to be among the Jews. But while the general class (genus) of sacrifice remains, their species has been changed, inasmuch as they are now offered "not by slaves but by free men."[34]

Finally, Irenaeus addresses the third Pauline concept of sacrifice, suggesting from the available evidence that "the eucharistic sacrifice is, as it was for Justin, the spiritualized one of prayers of praise and thanksgiving (*Against Heresies IV*, 29.1–32)."[35] Also, the influence of the Incarnation-sacrifice link in the East may be countered by Irenaean language (unfortunately available only in Latin) that quite possibly led to the concept and terminology of propitiation in the West.[36] Irenaeus speaks of man as the "agent" who seeks to appease God, the "recipient" of the propitiatory act. "However," observes Daly, "since Irenaeus is in general quite cognizant and respectful of the divine transcendence, it does not seem fair to assume on this evidence alone that he thinks favorably of propitiation in the sense of a creature presuming or hoping to exercise some control over God."[37]

With Hippolytus of Rome (third century AD), one also notes, as in Irenaeus, a similarly strong connection between events at Bethlehem and Golgotha.[38] Christ's birth leads Him to die and rise again, thus offering to God the Father both Himself and mankind. In this offering, Daly explains, we share by adoption what Christ possesses by nature; that is, deification.[39] In other words, Christ assumes the human condition and utilizes this medium of humanity in order to transform the fallen world and to assist the human person in assuming the divine.

Furthermore, the terms "offering" or "oblation" (προσφορά) begin to mean either the rite itself or the material gifts offered at the Liturgy. "For the idea of Christian sacrifice (i.e. sacrifices which Christians offer) had begun to shift away from the practical living of the Christian life toward the church's public liturgical celebration of the Eucharist."[40] Unfortunately, however, despite this unique modification in thinking about the eucharistic sacrifice in the writings of Hippolytus, no relation is ever established linking the ritual of sacrifice with the theology of Christ's sacrifice upon the Cross.

The last half of the second century produced a series of seven individual accounts of Christian martyrdom called the *Acts of the Martyrs*. Daly correctly claims that the concept of Christian martyrdom, rooted in Christ's own sacrificial death on the Cross, evolved naturally.[41] In fact, it is very difficult, if not senseless, not to make the same connection, namely, that Christ's blood sacrifice serves as the model upon which the bloodless eucharistic sacrifice is based. In the prothesis rite, the gradual lengthening of the commemoration of saints, in whose name the Eucharist will subsequently be offered, indicates not only the reverence the Church showed to its champions, but also its acknowledgement that the sacrifice of Christ to God the Father gave the impetus for the sacrifices made by these sainted individuals in the Name of Christ.

Several of the Alexandrian Fathers have commented on eucharistic sacrifice. Philo Judaeus (more commonly known as Philo of Alexandria, 20 BC–AD 50) represented a Jewish-Hellenistic viewpoint whose intent was to reconstruct Greek philosophical ideas and values within the framework of monotheistic Judaism and make the former compatible with the latter. This synthesis was anything but fully successful, as can be witnessed by Philo's views on sacrifice, in which his religious inclination dominates.[42] Following the allegorical method characteristic of the Alexandrians, Philo approaches his understanding of sacrifice by focusing on the soul's ascending progress toward God. Seven points from his stance on sacrifice stand out distinctly: (1) the Passover is a symbol of the soul's progress from things material to things spiritual; (2) true sacrifice is an offering of the whole self—body and soul; (3) the spiritual meaning of the ritual sacrifice—and not the external act itself—is what benefits the individual; (4) the purpose of the sacrifice is to first honor God and second to benefit the worshipper; (5) the person of the high priest is elevated and almost equated with the divine Logos; (6) ethical purity seems to be the absolute prerequisite that confers universal priesthood upon a worshipper; and (7) the temple, sanctuary, and altar are all used allegorically to refer to the soul, since "only the soul is created in God's image and likeness, and [that] therefore only the spiritual part of man can come close enough to the divine to become God's temple (*On the Creation* 69)."[43] Hence for Philo, sacrifice has become less of a "history-of-religions" material immolation and more of a spiritual prayer form, with the eucharistic thanksgiving prayer becoming the highest—and most valid—form of sacrifice.

The *Epistle of Barnabas* (c. AD 130), commonly accepted as a primary anti-Jewish polemic among the early Christians, provides some basic insights into the early Christian theology of sacrifice. The entire Old Testament, for example, only has meaning when its sole purpose is seen as revealing the advent of Christ. In this light, the ritual acts of sacrifice in Judaism are, according to *Barnabas*, completely meaningless, as the author endorses the prophetic criticism found in classical ritual texts such as Isaiah 1:11–13, Jeremiah 7:22–23, Psalm 51:19, and Zechariah 8:17. The epistle prefers rather the more spiritualistic theme of the Christian as the temple of God.

Clement of Alexandria (AD 140/150–211/215) is considered the first great proponent of the Alexandrian school of theological thought, and he has often been described as a "Christian Philo" because of his passionate dedication to the writings of his predecessor Philo Judaeus. However, he is well distinguished from Philo and the Gnostics of his time because of his complete acceptance of the doctrine of the Incarnation as well as his ardent belief in the Church as the depository of true and saving *gnosis*. His views on sacrifice may be summarized as twofold: (1) an emphasis on the spiritual aspect versus the ritualistic connotation; and (2) the Old Testament figures associated with sacrifice point to and derive their full meaning from Christ's sacrifice upon the Cross. Clement, in sharp contrast to other anti-Jewish polemical works, accepts the union and mutual support of both Old and New Testaments. For him, *gnosis* does not imply secretive knowledge but refers to the true, spiritual meaning of Scripture. Hence, a sacrifice acceptable to God is not limited to the specific, designated rites of the Jewish cult but rather derives from the proper living of the Christian life. Continuing on this theme, Clement writes: "We ought to offer God not costly sacrifices but such as he loves, and in that mixture of incense which is mentioned in the law. It consists of many tongues and voices in prayer [cf. Exod 30:34–36], . . ." (*Stromata* 7.6).[44]

Clement allegorizes the sacrifice of Christ through the use of various Old Testament references, all the while emphasizing that each image is a "type" of the Lord's future Passion (e.g. Christ is a "whole burnt offering"; Christ is the "Passover," the "Suffering Servant" and the "Lamb of God").[45] He is also typified in the person of the young Patriarch Isaac, Abraham's son, although Isaac's last-minute pardon absolved him from being immolated.[46]

Furthermore, as with Irenaeus and Hippolytus, Clement uses the Incarnation to fully place Christ's sacrifice in its proper perspective. The Incarnation mystery, as a central and necessary event within the configuration of the divine economia, possesses the notion that the incarnate God remains in complete control of His earthly life, from birth until death.

This voluntary characteristic of Christ's *economia*, from Bethlehem to Golgotha, is extended by Clement to include the widespread practice of Christians sacrificing their lives, either by holy living or through voluntary death, for the sake of the Gospel. He explains that the true Christian, possessing full "spiritual gnosis," is he who worships God "not in a specified place, or selected temple [cf. Mal 1:11], or at certain festivals and on appointed days, but during his whole life in every place."[47] Clement emphasizes the universal priesthood in the person of the "true Gnostic," who is "the sacred high priest of God."[48] As high priest, and in imitation of Christ the great High Priest, he not only fits the role of "offerer" of the sacrifice, but becomes also the "offering" itself.[49] In this sense, the Christian martyr exercises some sense of control over his destiny, although Clement completely shuns the rash enthusiasm toward any kind of martyrdom that is not rooted in godly love and faith. Unlike Irenaeus and Hippolytus, Clement does not seem to specifically make the connection between the sacrifice of the martyr—nor, for that matter, the whole life of the "true Gnostic" as sacrificial worship—and the Eucharist, although he does see the former two "sacrifices" as imitations of Christ's life and passion. Daly explains: "His concept of sacrifice is thus thoroughly spiritualized, but by no means radically dematerialized."[50]

The great Origen (AD 182–251) represents the culmination of the spiritualizing development in regard to the notion of sacrifice and has been labeled as the "great theologian of sacrifice."[51] The majority of Origen's extant works come from the Latin translations of Rufinus and Jerome (fifth century), which lack the reliability found in the Greek texts. Of the nearly 550 passages in Origen that address the theme of sacrifice (there are 340 Latin texts), 210 references appear in well-known Greek texts (*Commentary on Matthew*, *Exhortation to Martyrdom*, *Against Celsus*, and especially *Commentary on John*, and the fragmentary *Commentary on the Psalms*).[52] Fortunately, these Greek texts are adequate to indicate Origen's idea of sacrifice. Like his predecessor Clement of Alexandria, Origen looked favorably upon Old Testament sacrifices, which he strategically uses as a basis for his allegorical interpretation. For Origen, Christ remains the true Paschal Lamb of the new Israel, led to be slaughtered of His own volition in order to reconcile mankind to God by His own blood.[53] In this sense, Christ is both the High Priest who offers the sacrifice as well as the very sacrifice itself.

Origen, however, advances this fairly basic assertion a step further, in that he attempts to explain how the Church in its individual members shares together the sacrifice of Christ. It is here that Origen reveals his mode of spiritualizing thinking, namely, by introducing the significance of martyrdom as the Christian's most excellent form of sharing in the sacrifice of Christ.[54]

An interesting link may be drawn between the sacrifice of Christ and the martyrs with the Eucharist. St. John the Theologian envisions the holy martyrs standing next to the heavenly altar of sacrifice, centered around the slain Lamb (Rev 5:6ff. and 6:9–11),[55] an image very reminiscent of the eucharistic table. In this representation, the slaughtered Lamb of God, who removes the sin of the world, becomes the *sine qua non* of the Church's sacrificial theology, the point of reference from which any and every human sacrifice, be it in martyrdom or the proper living of the Christian life, derives its meaning.

What is strikingly appealing in this image gleaned from the Johannine text is that this "heavenly altar of sacrifice" ushers in the eschatological perspective, thus linking quite effectively the notion of the earthly and material Passover with the heavenly and spiritual Passover. Hence, the earthly ritual celebration, as a pattern and shadow of the heavenly sacrifice, looks to its consummation beyond history.[56] Although the sacrificed Lamb has been immolated once and for all within history, the full effects (i.e., consequences) will not be experienced until the dawning of the new *aeon*. However, in the repetitive celebration of the Eucharist, corresponding to the span of time between the historical Crucifixion and the eschatological Second Coming, the Church mystically relives the historical event each time. At the same time though, the faithful receive only a portion of the spiritual benefits in the Liturgy *as a provision* of those blessings that they will receive in full at the *eschaton*. Consequently the ἐφάπαξ nature of the Lamb's sacrifice produces profits to be enjoyed both in the earthly life and in the life to come.

Origen's spiritualizing approach then progresses away from ritualistic holocausts and Christian martyrdom to incorporate the very life of the Christian as another means of understanding sacrifice. People sacrifice not only when they surrender their bodies for the cause of Christ, but when they deliver up their wealth or personal resources out of deep love for others.[57] Surely, Origen surmises, it is not the amount of the offering that matters but rather that it is given in proportion to all that one is and has (cf. the widow's offering in Luke 21:1–4), and that it is given with one's whole strength.[58] This inner disposition is crucial to Origen's sacrificial approach, as he compares the conventional concept of sacrifice with Philo's—and later, the Clementine—allegorical notion of the sacrifice offered upon the altar of the heart. In summary, it appears that Origen's conception of sacrifice is devoid of any liturgical or ritualistic connection. On the contrary, it can only otherwise be seen as "a rite of the heart,"[59] a genuine self-offering made upon the altar within the temple of the body.

To recap the discussion, from this lengthy overview of the early patristic witnesses commenting on the popular Christian notion of sacrifice, one can plainly discern the presence, as well as legitimacy, of both the ritualistic and spiritualistic interpretations: the former being more or less Christ's offering of Himself to His Church through the Eucharist, and the latter being the individual Christian's response to Christ by living the truth of the Gospel. In fact, the affinity that some Fathers felt toward one particular interpretation does not indicate their complete rejection of the other but rather signifies where their emphasis lay. The incarnate Logos remained, and remains still, the model for the eucharistic sacrifice and the sacrifice of living the Christian life.

CONTROVERSIAL VIEWS OF SACRIFICE IN THE EASTERN CHURCH

The very same controversy that rampaged expansively in the West regarding the meaning of the eucharistic sacrifice—specifically the real presence of Christ in the Eucharist and the role of the celebrant in the Liturgy—was generally absent in the East. However, the Eastern churches were certainly not immune to doctrinal controversies regarding the Eucharist. Two particular arguments stand out among the Orthodox: (1) the question of whether the Eucharist is the image of Christ or His very reality—an issue disagreed upon and fought over during the course of the Iconoclast controversy in the Byzantine Empire during the eighth and ninth centuries; and (2) the twelfth-century debate over how Christ can receive the eucharistic sacrifice when He Himself is simultaneously this very sacrifice and the offerer of the sacrifice, stemming from the concluding line of the priestly prayer at the Cherubic Hymn: "Σὺ γὰρ εἶ ὁ προσφέρων καὶ προσφερόμενος καὶ προσδεχόμενος καὶ διαδιδόμενος . . ." ("For You are He who offers and is offered, who receives and is distributed"). A brief overview of the two controversies follows.

Controversy #1: The Eucharist—Reality or Image of Christ?

The Iconoclast controversy spanned a period of 120 years, and may be divided into two distinct periods: (1) the first period beginning with the Byzantine Emperor Leo III the Isaurian's blatant attack on the use of the holy icons in churches (c. AD 726) and ending in 787 with the Empress Irene calling the Seventh Ecumenical Council of Nicea, which formulated the theological justification for their ecclesiastical use; and (2) the second period, beginning with the resumption of persecution by Leo V the Armenian in 815 and ending with the final restitution of the icons by the Empress Theodora in 843, an event celebrated yearly by the Orthodox Church on the first Sunday in Great Lent.[60]

The Iconoclast repudiation of icons demonstrated a form of dualism, which understood matter and the entire material world as intrinsically evil. "They wanted a religion freed from all contact with what is material; for they thought that what is spiritual must be non-material."[61] The orthodox position claimed that such a rejection of holy images was simultaneously a deliberate rejection of the fundamental Christian doctrine of the Incarnation, in which Christ assumed our material humanity which is also worthy of transfiguration and salvation. In the words of St. John of Damascus, "The Word made flesh has deified the flesh."[62] As Timothy Ware insightfully observes, "If flesh became a vehicle of the Spirit, then so—though in a different way—can wood and paint."[63] As the Synodikon statement of the Seventh Ecumenical Council dictates, "The honor paid to the icon is conveyed to its prototype."[64] Hence, while true worship (λατρεία) is offered only to Christ as God, His material image is worthy of veneration (προσκύνησις), since the icon is *unequal to the divine essence* but accessible to humanity because of the "enfleshment" of God's Word.

How then does the Eucharist as a sacrifice factor into the Iconoclast debate? The Iconoclasts claimed that the Eucharist is the only proper *image of Christ's reality*, the only true *iconic representation* of the Son of God. What impelled this position? John Meyendorff takes a historical approach by commenting first that eucharistic communion after the fourth century became less frequent among the laity, since the lines separating the Church and secular society became less and less visible.[65] In other words, the Church saw a need to protect the Eucharist from the "crowd" of citizens in society that no longer represented the small closely-knit union of believers called the "people of God." Rationalizing this shift, some liturgical commentators began to look upon the Eucharist as "a system of *symbols* to be 'contemplated'; sacramental participation was thus gradually replaced with intellectual *vision.*'"[66]

The writings of pseudo-Dionysios seem to have been most influential in formulating this symbolic imagery around the Eucharist, although in a very superficial way. For Dionysios, the act of participating in the Liturgy and specifically in eucharistic communion symbolizes the union of one's mind with the divine God. Maximos the Confessor's reliance on Dionysian liturgical mystagogy leads the former into utilizing the terms "symbol" and "image" specifically for the very elements of the Eucharist. As a result of this patristic witness, the Iconoclasts interpreted the mystagogical writings of the aforementioned Fathers to suit their own position, namely, that the Eucharist is the only authentic and theologically correct icon of Christ.

The Orthodox contingent immediately rallied to prove that the Eucharist was not a symbol of Christ's reality but the very reality of Christ Himself. The major proponents were Patriarch Nikephoros of Constantinople and Theodore the Studite, who claimed that the Eucharist is not "type" but the very "truth,"[67] "the mystery which recapitulates the whole of the [divine] dispensation"[68] and "the flesh of God,"[69] of Christ "who came to save the very reality of human flesh by becoming and remaining 'flesh,' even after His glorification."[70] Hence, the Eucharist is not a symbolic sacrifice but a true sacrifice, since the consecrated eucharistic elements are not representative of the Lord's broken and glorified Body from a time already past, but mystically and truly become, by God's grace, the very same glorified flesh and blood here and now.

The Iconoclast idea of the inappropriateness of regarding the Eucharist as the real presence of Christ rather than as His image seems to derive from their response to the peculiar Origenistic notion that man communes with the *essence* of God when he partakes of Holy Communion. Objecting to this claim, the Iconoclasts argued that since such participation is impossible for mortals, it only makes sense for the Eucharist to be looked upon as the image, and not the reality, of Christ. The Orthodox position, while agreeing that participation in the essence of God for man is impossible, affirms that the Eucharist remains the highest and most sublime contact allowable to man by God. As such, writes Meyendorff, "The Eucharist is Christ's transfigured, life-giving, but still human, body, en-hypostasized in the Logos and penetrated with divine 'energies.'"[71] In these *energies* then, man experiences not an image of Christ but the fullness of the risen Lord, His very reality, which stops shy of His very essence as God. Meyendorff comments further:

> As a result of the iconoclastic controversy, Byzantine 'Eucharistic realism,' clearly departing from Dionysian terminology, was redirected along Christological and soteriological lines; in the Eucharist, man participates in the glorified humanity of Christ, which is not the 'essence of God' but a humanity still consubstantial to man and available to him as food and drink.[72]

Byzantine theology's rejection of the eucharistic sacrifice as symbol or image and its designation as Christ's real presence in the Liturgy establishes that the Eucharist is the celebration of the mystery of God's salvific economia, into which the faithful are led through their participation (i.e. by receiving Holy Communion). Icons are appropriately called symbols in that they visually engage the individual into a deeper understanding of the prototype depicted on it and his or her works. In the Eucharist, the communicant comes into the most sublime contact with the prototype of Christ, led not simply to remember Him but to relive Christ's life and to experience firsthand His manifold blessings through union with Him.

Controversy #2: Christ—Offerer or Receiver of the Eucharist . . . or Both?

A second controversy in regard to the Eucharist occurred in the Eastern Church during the middle of the twelfth century, with the claim made by a deacon named Soterichos Panteugenes that Christ cannot offer Himself in the eucharistic gifts and simultaneously receive them.[73] In making this bold claim, Soterichos conjured for himself a minority opinion that found virtually no patristic support whatsoever.

The patristic witness in support of the popularly accepted form of the prayer's conclusion is quite overwhelming, given the fact that the Fathers mentioned all lived and wrote well before the prayer was composed. The author of *On the Mystical Supper,* Theophilos of Alexandria (Cyril's uncle and predecessor), writes: ". . . He remains priest, and sacrifice, He who is Himself One who offers and is offered, and who receives (καὶ δεχόμενος), and who is distributed, not dividing into two persons (δύο πρόσωπα) the divine and inseparable . . . union of the all-honorable Trinity."[74]

Cyril of Jerusalem indicates how Christ retains His divine nature while simultaneously subjecting Himself to the state of humanity, observing the lawful customs of the Jews on the fortieth day following His birth. This legitimizes the claim then that as both God and man, He can simultaneously offer and receive sacrifices: ". . . let every [tongue] glorify the Child who is God, forty days old, and existing before the ages; a small child and the Ancient of Days; a nursing child and the Creator of the ages. I see an infant and I recognize God. . . ."[75] He continues: "I see an infant coming from Bethlehem toward Jerusalem, who is never separated from the heavenly Jerusalem. I see an infant brought to the temple as an earthly sacrifice in accordance with the law, but He accepts (δεχόμενον) the devout sacrifices of everyone in the heavens."[76] He adds: "He is the gift, as well as the temple; He is the High Priest, as well as the sacrificial altar, the altar of expiation. He it is who offers [προσφέρων], and He it is who is the sacrificed offered [προσφερόμενος] for the world."[77] And Cyril concludes: "He is the one who sacrifices [ὁ θύτης] and the one who is sacrificed [ὁ θυόμενος]; He who is offered up [ὁ ἀναφερόμενος] and He who accepts the sacrifice [καὶ αὐτὸς ὁ τὴν θυσίαν δεχόμενος]."[78]

In the West, Augustine of Hippo likewise comments on the double role of Christ as recipient and sacrifice:

And hence that true Mediator, in so far as, by assuming the form of servant, He became the Mediator between God and men, the man Christ Jesus, though in the form of God He received sacrifice together with the Father, with whom He is one God, yet in the form of a servant He chose rather to be than to receive a sacrifice, that not even by this instance any one might have occasion to suppose that sacrifice should be rendered to any creature.[79]

In another instance, commenting upon the biblical passage of Psalm 65:3 that makes reference to God forgiving the transgressions of His people, Augustine writes that propitiation of sins can only be achieved through some sacrifice, which for the Christian is the sacrifice of Christ, to whom the Bishop of Hippo prays, "Thou art the priest, Thou the victim; Thou the offerer, Thou the offering. . . ."[80]

The candidate for the patriarchal throne of Antioch, Soterichos the Deacon, together with his staunch supporters, the scholars Michael of Thessalonike, Nikephoros Basilakis, and Eustathios of Dyrrachios, as well as, in part, John the Italian and Eustratios of Nicea,[81] essentially rejected the theological legitimacy of the conclusion of the priestly prayer during the Cherubic Hymn, "For You are He who offers and is offered, who receives and is distributed."

The original sources that outline the positions of the debate and its final resolution are the following: (1) given facts surrounding the history of the Councils of 1156 and 1157, the synods convened in Constantinople that put an end to the controversy; (2) the Dialogue[82] of Soterichos with a certain Philon, composed by the former in between the convocation of both councils, in which he defends his position; (3) the patristic witnesses defending the orthodox doctrine; (4) the general decision of the councils[83]; and (5) the four anathemas that condemn Soterichos and outline the errors of his heretical teachings.

The orthodox position, backed by the overwhelming majority opinion of the Church Fathers, affirms that Christ does indeed offer Himself in the eucharistic sacrifice in His capacity as a human, but simultaneously He is capable of receiving the Eucharist in His capacity as God. Tchéremoukhine observes, "It is clear that the Lord Christ offered Himself according to His humanity and that He Himself accepted this sacrifice inasmuch as He is God, together with His Father and the Spirit."[84] Hence, the Synods of 1156 and 1157 indicate that the all-important distinction between Christ's two natures, the divine and human, renders this characterization of Christ as offerer and recipient accurate.

Soterichos' error in refusing to accept the Son as a recipient of the eucharistic sacrifice has rightly been called a Christological heresy. He mistakenly believed that the two different natures of Christ that offer and receive the sacrifice correspond to two different hypostases, or persons. Hence, if one hypostasis—and thus nature—offers a sacrifice (i.e. the Son), then only another hypostasis (nature) could receive it, which would necessarily be the Father.

This confusion of the natures of Christ with His hypostasis brought to the forefront of the debate Bishop Nicholas of Methone,[85] who championed the orthodox cause. Essentially, Nicholas refutes Soterichos' theology by stating that the two natures of Christ co-exist in the same hypostasis of the Son of God. The human nature of Christ, which by necessity belongs to the limited and material realm of humanity below, is capable of making a material offering to God. The divine nature of Christ, inseparable from the Godhead, remains in a position to accept the eucharistic offering. And since all three hypostases of the Holy Trinity share the same essence as God, all three receive the offerings made from below. "Said in another way, there exists no action of one of the Hypostases that is isolated or independent from the other two Persons."[86] Otherwise, to say that the Son cannot receive but only offer is to insinuate that He does not share the same essence as God and is a mere human, thus following the theological lines drawn by the early Church heretics Arius, Nestorius, and Eutyches.[87] Metropolitan Constantine of Kiev perhaps best expresses the most direct and comprehensive orthodox opinion formulated in 1156 at the synod that condemned Soterichos and his error. He writes:

> The living Sacrifice, more so the first one accomplished by Christ the Savior than those that were accomplished afterwards and up until now, were and are always offered not only to the Father without beginning from the Son, but also to the Word Himself who was incarnate; likewise, the Holy Spirit is not exempt from this honor owed to God. As for the sacrament, it has been and is offered everywhere to the one Godhead in three Persons (ὑποστάσεις). . . .[88]

Nicholas of Methone continues his refutation of Soterichos' position by rejecting the two "sanctifications" proposed by the latter, the first sanctification occurring at the Nativity and given by Christ and the second accomplished by the Father and occurring at the Crucifixion. Since the nature of the Father and the Son are one, there can only be one action (ἐνέργειαν) of grace, "as a natural, collective sequence,"[89] with the Crucifixion flowing consequentially from the Incarnation and both together comprising the one and only "sanctification."

Robert Taft indicates that the *Barberini Codex Gr. 336*, the oldest extant euchologion of the Eastern Church, includes the terms "ἁγιάζων" ("He who sanctifies") and "ἁγιαζόμενος" ("He who is sanctified") in the priestly prayer of the Cherubic Hymn,[90] rather than the more commonly accepted "προσδεχόμενος" and "διαδιδόμενος." Commenting on this particular version, Nicholas of Methone states that Christ's power to sanctify is associated with His divinity while His sanctification as an offering is achieved in His capacity as a human being. In fact, Christ's sanctification renders possible the same sanctification of man by Christ, because the only accessible bridge for man toward God is through the deified humanity of the resurrected Lord.

In summary then, Soterichos' Christological views, revealed in his unique understanding of the role of Christ as offerer and acceptor of the eucharistic sacrifice, was challenged and defeated by the Councils of 1156 and 1157. Although this particular debate was more limited in scope and spanned a briefer period of time than the Iconoclast controversy, nonetheless it challenged the Eastern perspective of sacrifice by placing into the forefront the question of Christ's role in the Eucharist. The overwhelming patristic evidence has shown quite clearly that as perfect man and high priest, Christ offers Himself and the eucharistic sacrifice to the entire Trinity—of which He is one and the same—and as God receives and consecrates and distributes the hallowed offering of Himself. Through the deified humanity then of the Logos, man also has access to God through his own personal participation in the divine Eucharist.

EASTERN PERSPECTIVES ON EUCHARISTIC SACRIFICE

Based upon the available patristic sources, it would appear that the Eastern view of sacrifice may best be delineated on the basis of four distinct perspectives, each of which contributes notably to the Church's mystagogical understanding of the prothesis rite and the sacrificial notions that pervade it. These four perspectives may be classified as: (1) the spiritual perspective, with an emphasis on the faith sacrifice of the individual worshipper, obtained at baptism, as the catalyst that makes the one-time sacrifice of Christ truly meaningful and effectual for the person and the Church; (2) the trinitarian view, popularized in the West by Robert Daly, which sees sacrifice as God's initiative—and not man's—to empty Himself (κένωσις), and incorporates most especially the sanctifying role of the Holy Spirit in the liturgical sacrifice; (3) the liturgical view of sacrifice, in which the idea of a "moment of consecration"—regarded in the West as occurring precisely during the Words of Institution and later countered in the East by highlighting the moment at the pneumatological epiklesis—is replaced by a more sensible "movement of consecration," in which the entire Eucharist is regarded as a series of ongoing and mutual sacrifices made between God and man that gradually consecrate the life of the latter; and (4) the very ancient and orthodox eschatological view, which links the eucharistic sacrifice of Christ, made upon the Cross and offered upon the altar table, with the notion of an eschatological banquet, celebrated in part now but fully at the completion of history.

In general, Eastern Christianity never succumbed to the need to explain the interrelationship between liturgical symbolism and realism. Hence, issues such as the eucharistic real presence of Christ and the exact manner of consecration were not, and could not be, explained in terms appealing to human rationale, inasmuch as Christ and the salvation He offered—as well as the means by which salvation is offered, i.e. the holy sacraments—remained central and real mysteries in the Church.

In the patristic mindset, as is quite evident from the writings of Cyril of Jerusalem, John Chrysostom, and Theodore of Mopsuestia, it is the faith of the Christian, obtained via the grace of holy baptism, which reveals the existent reality beyond what the physical senses perceive and allows the Christian to reap the spiritual benefits initiated by Christ's one-time sacrifice. More specifically, what Chrysostom means exactly by "believers" is not simply those who believe but those whose eyes of faith have been opened following their baptism into Christ: "Believers, therefore, are endowed with two kinds of eyes: bodily eyes and the eyes of faith. In fact, the thing that distinguishes Christians is precisely the fact that they also have the eyes of faith, which enable them to see those things that their bodily eyes are unable to see."[91] Likewise, even Theodore's classic mystagogical description of the Great Entrance derives its vividness and power from the inherent faith expected of each Christian. A portion of it clearly discloses Theodore's sacramental realism:

> And when they have brought (the particle of bread), they place it on the holy altar for the completion of the passion. We believe therefore that he (Christ) is now laid in a kind of tomb when he is placed on the altar and that he has already undergone the passion. . . . And when we see the oblation on the altar – as though some one after death had been laid in a kind of tomb – recollection then fills all present because what has taken place is awesome for all.[92]

The initiates in the Faith then, through their sacrifice of faith and commitment to the ways of the Kingdom, are able not only to envision the salvation God offers through the holy sacraments, unlike non-Christians, but they also have immediate access to the eschatological benefits made visible and attainable to them in symbol, albeit in part now. In faith, Christians not only witness Christ processing toward His passion, but they also become recipients of God's redeeming and saving power.

This view of sacrifice then, as active faith obtained through the grace of baptism, directly affects the Eastern Christian understanding of the prothesis rite in the sense that what is perceived during the rite does not qualify as one's personal imagination but rather as a mystical reality revealed to the celebrant priest who in faith prepares the gifts for their transfer and use in the Eucharist. In fact, St. Symeon of Thessalonike's exegetical work on the Divine Liturgy is typically replete with exhortations to the priests of his diocese to look beyond the external rubric and to behold the internal meaning and reality behind each mechanical act. "But let us understand," he asserts, "how also through this divine symbol and through the work of the holy proskomide we see Jesus himself and his Church all as one."[93]

Symeon, as a prominent and well-respected religious leader among bishops and priests, as well as their co-celebrant before God's holy altar, knew all too well that approaching the prothesis table prior to each Liturgy could very easily be reduced to a mechanical teleturgical exercise, an empty execution of rubrics void of symbolic meaning and vividness. This understanding of the prothesis could only be the result of looking upon the rite with the faculties of one's physical eyes, which are capable of perceiving only external appearances and material reality. Consequently, it is not surprising that the Archbishop of Thessalonike's mystical commentary on the prothesis rite and Divine Liturgy is intended to alleviate such a mundane understanding and hopefully induce the proper faith needed of the celebrant in order to experience more spiritual worship.

A second view of sacrifice in the Eastern tradition places the act of self-surrender not solely upon the shoulders of the Son of God, but rather sees sacrifice as belonging to all three members of the Holy Trinity and reciprocated by man who follows the example set first by God. To a certain degree, the trinitarian perspective resembles the previous view, inasmuch as both ultimately require a faith response by the celebrant or worshipper. As St. Paul affirms to the Romans, a Christian's sacrifice to God need not be the surrendering of his earthly life: "I appeal to you therefore, brethren, . . . to present your bodies as a living sacrifice, holy and acceptable to God, which is your spiritual [reasonable] worship [λογικὴν λατρείαν]" (Rom 12:1). This trinitarian perspective clearly accomplishes two things: (1) it dismisses the conventional history of religions view on sacrifice, which requires the destruction of a "scapegoat"—victim in order to appease an "angry" God; and (2) it transfers the initiative of true sacrifice from man to God, altering its meaning from destruction and appeasement to one of unconditional divine love. Indeed, this concept of sacrifice possesses a precedent in Holy Scripture and is, in fact, modeled after Christ's counsel to His disciples, "Greater love has no man than this, that a man lay down his life for his friends" (John 15:13).

In the eucharistic tradition of the East, a strong emphasis is placed upon the role of *all three Persons of the Holy Trinity* in the offering and, subsequently, consecration of the holy gifts. The consecratory Words of Institution in the Latin rite almost seem to draw the Church's attention only upon Christ as chief protagonist in the Eucharist. In the Eastern Liturgy, the insistence on the consecratory role of the Holy Spirit, who is invoked both to bring Christ to the Church and over the assembled Church in order to bring it to Christ,"[94] as well as the designation of Christ's Words of Institution as contextual rather than consecratory,[95] offsets this exclusive focus upon the Son and redistributes it equally among the Trinity.

Hence, the Father, in the divine economy, offers His Son to the world and the Son, in turn, offers Himself to the Father by accepting human death. Finally, the Holy Spirit makes possible the event of the Resurrection and thus offers Christ's salvation to the world through the Church established at Pentecost. Liturgically speaking, the Father bestows upon the Church the sacrificial Lamb in the form of bread and wine. Within the anaphoral prayers, specifically in the Words of Institution, the Lamb offers His flesh and blood to the Father. At the epiklesis, the Holy Spirit consecrates the offering and bestows it back to the Church as Holy Communion. In the wake of this divine initiative, the faithful surrender themselves in faith as they commune the Body and Blood of Christ, thus completing the "sacrificial circle" within the Eucharist.

For Eastern Christians, the Eucharist does not consist solely of a particular moment of consecration, in which the sacrifice of Christ has been accomplished, even though in the East, the designation of this moment to the descent of the Holy Spirit has assisted to counter the consecratory Words of Institution in the West. On the contrary, the Divine Liturgy *as a whole* has quite often been characterized as a "movement of consecration,"[96] made up of a series of ongoing and mutual sacrifices shared between God and man, with the intent of consecrating the life of the latter. The combination then of God's grace released freely upon the eucharistic community and authorized by His words to "do this in remembrance of me" (Luke 22:19), the prayers and hymns and rubrics, the spiritual disposition of the worshipper, and the general atmosphere of mysticism so central to Orthodox worship, are all sacrifices that contribute to the transformation and sanctification of the individual worshipper and the Church.

In this liturgical view of sacrifice, God offers Himself selflessly to the Church out of love, and the faithful in turn reciprocate the sacrifice by offering themselves and their "reasonable worship" to Him out of faith. This particular viewpoint fuses together the first two notions of sacrifice, as outlined already in the spiritual and trinitarian perspectives.

The Divine Liturgy is replete with several references to sacrifice that do not specifically refer to Christ's Passion. For example, in the Byzantine Liturgy of St. John Chrysostom, a portion of the priestly prayer concluding the post-Great Entrance litany reads: "Enable us to bring before You gifts and *spiritual sacrifices* ['θυσίας πνευματικὰς'] for our sins and for the transgressions of the people. Make us worthy to find grace in Your presence so that *our sacrifice* may be pleasing to You ['τοῦ γενέσθαι σοι εὐπρόσδεκτον τὴν θυσίαν ἡμῶν']. . . ."[97] The expression "spiritual sacrifices" follows the term "gifts" and is deliberately placed after the conjunction τε ("both and") to distinguish between the eucharistic sacrifice of the holy gifts and the spiritual sacrifice of the individual Christian.

In yet another example, during the beginning of the anaphora, the celebrant's injunction to "stand well" in order to "present the holy offering in peace" is met with the laic response: "Mercy and peace" ('Ἔλεος εἰρήνη).[98] God's offering of heavenly mercy and internal peace are reciprocated by the worshipper through his own appreciation toward God for His manifold gifts, an admiration articulated in doxological praise. The Divine Liturgy then, in keeping with this liturgical perspective on sacrifice, consists of several "moments of sacrifice," which together make effectual the sanctification and transformation of the Church and its faithful.

The final view of sacrifice that best reflects the Eastern position links the eucharistic sacrifice of Christ with an eschatological banquet, celebrated in partiality now, within the confines of history, but in its glorious fullness at the end of time. Generally speaking, the eschatological implications in the Eucharist, within the early patristic tradition, were quite apparent. Christ's sacrifice at Golgotha and the eschaton, into which the Church and the world were ushered following the Resurrection and Pentecost, were always considered part and parcel of God's overall economia of salvation. Theodore of Mopsuestia characteristically writes that "the fruit of the sacramental celebration consists in the blessings or gifts of the eschaton."[99] Just as the suffering of Christ and His triumph over death legitimized His earthly ministry and escorted in the final aion with the conception of the

Church, so too does the daily or weekly eucharistic banquet, feasted upon by the faithful during this eschaton, look forward to the eternal banquet of the Kingdom and release for the faithful the eschatological gifts of immortality, incorruptibility, and impassibility[100] here and now. Hence, this inchoative manner of receiving salvation now and provisionally for the future signifies that the eschatological gifts are simultaneously the content as well as the fruits of the sacrament, since the function of any sacrament (i.e. what it intends to achieve) derives from its nature (i.e. the reality of the event commemorated).[101]

Theodore likewise identifies the notion of sacrifice solely with the death of Christ, but reserves the Resurrection and all related post-Resurrection events with the theme of eschatological life. Significant here is the Last Supper shared by Christ with His disciples in the Upper Room, during which time He states: "I shall not drink again of this fruit of the vine until that day when I drink it new with you in my Father's kingdom" (Matt 26:29; cf. Mark 14:25 and Luke 22:18). This final earthly banquet of the incarnate Word brings to a close the epoch of fallen history but simultaneously institutes the eschatological banquet, which becomes for the Church the post-Resurrection eucharistic celebration. Christ models His death, His sacrifice for the world, upon the Eucharist, and henceforth commands His followers to partake of this "transitional" meal, that they too may share in the eschatological life and all its spiritual benefits. The eucharistic sacrifice then not only looks back to the historical immolation of the incarnate Word, commemorated at the Last Supper, but it also transcends history and looks forward to the eschatological banquet of the Kingdom since it is, in a provisional sort of way, the very same eschatological banquet in which the gifts of the Spirit are activated within the Church and richly distributed among the faithful. It is to this all-important theme of eschatology that this book now turns.

NOTES

1. *A Greek-English Lexicon*. Compiled by Henry G. Liddell and Robert Scott (Oxford, 1968), 1204.

2. Ibid. See also *A Patristic Greek Lexicon*. ed. G.W.H. Lampe (Oxford, 1961), 940–43.

3. Ibid., 940.

4. Ibid., 941.

5. Ibid.

6. Ibid.

7. Ibid., 942.

8. John H. McKenna, "Eucharist and Sacrifice: An Overview", in *Worship*, vol. 76, no. 5 (2002), 388.

9. Ibid., 389.

10. See the relevant chapter in Michael W. Holmes, ed. and trans., *The Apostolic Fathers: Greek Texts and English Translations* (Grand Rapids, 2007).

11. Robert J. Daly, *The Origins of the Christian Doctrine of Sacrifice* (Philadelphia, 1978), 85–87.

12. Clement of Rome, *Epistle to the Corinthians* 7.3–4.

13. Ibid., 52.1–4.

14. Ibid., 10.7; 31.3.

15. Daly, 85.

16. Ignatios of Antioch, *Epistle to the Ephesians* 5.2.

17. Idem. *Epistle to the Romans* 2.2; 4.1–2.

18. *Shepherd of Hermas* 5.3.

19. Polycarp of Smyrna, *Epistle to the Philippians* 1.2; 8.1; 9.2.

20. Ibid., 4.3.

21. Justin Martyr, *1 Apology* 10.1; 13.1; 10.1; 13.1; *Trypho* 10.3.

22. Idem., *1 Apology* 12.5; 9.1.

23. Idem., *Trypho* 19.3; 22.1; 92.4–5.

24. Daly, *Origins*, 88.

25. Justin Martyr, *1 Apology* 13.1.

26. Idem., *Trypho* 29.1.

27. *Trypho* 117.1–3. Athenagoras of Athens (c. AD 177), similarly to Justin Martyr, pleads his case against blood sacrifices but later goes on to endorse the merits of "bloodless sacrifice and reasonable worship" (ἀναίμακτον θυσίαν ... λογικήν ... λατρείαν); *Plea for the Christians*, 13.

28. Irenaeus of Lyons, *Against Heresies* 31.5.

29. Daly, *Origins*, 92.

30. Irenaeus of Lyons, *Against Heresies* V, 6.2.

31. Idem., *Proof of the Apostolic Preaching* 31; for the translation, see also Daly, *Origins*, 93–94, and footnote 7 on the bottom of p. 94.

32. Irenaeus of Lyons, *Against Heresies* V, 6.2.

33. Ibid., IV, 17.

34. Daly, *Origins*, 92.

35. Ibid., 96.

36. Ibid., 97.

37. Ibid.

38. Hippolytus of Rome, *Against Noetus*, 4.

39. Daly, *Origins*, 100.

40. Ibid., 133.

41. Ibid., 102.

42. Ibid., 105.

43. Ibid., 105. See also 106–09.

44. Clement of Alexandria, *Stromata* 7.6; see also Daly, *Origins*, 114.

45. Clement of Alexandria, *Stromata* 5, *Paedagogus* 2.8, *et al.*

46. Idem., *Stromata* 2.5; *Paedagogus* 1.5.

47. Idem., *Stromata* 7.7, *et passim.*

48. Ibid., 4.25.

49. Idem. *Protrepticus* 4.

50. Daly, *Origins*, 118.

51. Pierre Nautin, *Origène: sa vie et son oeuvre* (Paris, 1977), is an excellent guide to the person and theological writings of the Alexandrian Father.

52. Daly, *Origins*, 123.

53. Ibid., 124.

54. Origen, *Commentary on John* VI.59; XIII.13.

55. Ibid., VI.54.

56. Ibid., X.14.11–15.12; 18.13.

57. Idem., *Homilies on Leviticus* 2.4; *Homilies on Joshua* 2.1; *Commentary on the Psalms* 49.5.

58. Idem., *Commentary on Romans* IX (re: Rom 12:1); *Homilies on Leviticus* 5.12; *Commentary on the Psalms* 115; *Homilies on Numbers* 24.2; *Commentary on John* XIX.7–8.

59. Idem., *Homilies on Jeremiah* 18.10; *Commentary on John* VI.58; *Homilies on Leviticus* 1.5; 4.8; 5.3–4; *Homilies on Numbers* 24.2; *Against Celsus* VIII.17.

60. Timothy Ware, *The Orthodox Church* (New York, 1963), 39. See also the excellent article by Bradley Nassif, "Kissers and Smashers", in *Christian History*, Issue 54, vol. 16, no. 2 (1997) 20–23.

61. Ibid., 41.

62. St. John of Damascus, *On Icons* 1.21; PG 94.1253B.

63. Ware, 42.

64. Nassif, 23.

65. John Meyendorff, *Byzantine Theology: Historical Trends and Doctrinal Themes* (New York, 1979), 202.

66. Ibid.

67. Ibid., 203.

68. Ibid. See also Theodore the Studite, *Antirrheticus* I; PG 99.340A–C.

69. Meyendorff, 203. See also Nikephoros of Constantinople, *Antirrheticus* II; PG 100.336B–337A.

70. Meyendorff, 203.

71. Ibid.

72. Ibid.

73. Several studies meticulously address this debate within the twelfth century: Robert J. Taft, *The Great Entrance: A History of the Transfer of Gifts and Other Pre-anaphoral Rites of the Liturgy of St. John Chrysostom* (Rome, 1978), 119–48; René Bornert, *Les commentaires byzantins de la Divine Liturgie du VIIe au XVe siècle* (Paris, 1965), 215–44; A. Demetrakopoulos, ed. *Bibliotheca Ecclesiastica* (Leipzig, 1866), which presents the original Greek text of Nicholas the Bishop of Methone's argumentation versus Soterichos (Τοῦ αὐτοῦ Νικολάου ἐπισκόπου Μεθώνης ἀντίρρησις πρὸς

τὰ γραφέντα παρὰ Σωτηρίχου τοῦ προβληθέντος Πατριάρχου Ἀντιοχείας, περὶ τοῦ ʽΣὺ εἶ ὁ προσφέρων καὶ προσφερόμενος καὶ προσδεχόμενος'; *Of the same Nicholas bishop of Methone, objection to the writings by Soterichos the Patriarch-elect of Antioch, regarding the [conclusion of the prayer of the Cherubic Hymn] 'You are He who offers and is offered and who receives'*), although the text is difficult to follow on account of its run-on style and lack of proper paragraph indentations and topical designations; Paul Tchéremoukhine, "Le Concile de 1157 à Constantinople et Nicholas, Évêque de Methone", in *Messager de l'Exarchat du Patriarche Russe en Europe Occidentale* 67 (1969), 137–73; and Konstantinos M. Fouskas, Ὁ Νικόλαος Μεθώνης καὶ ἡ Διδασκαλία Αὐτοῦ περὶ Θείας Εὐχαριστίας [*Nicholas of Methone and His Teaching Regarding the DivineEucharist*], (Athens: n.p., 1992); and J. Gouillard, "Le Synodikon de l'Orthodoxie", in *Travaux et Mémoires* 2 (1967), 73–75.

74. Theophilos of Alexandria, *On the Mystical Supper*; PG 77.1029B.

75. Cyril of Jerusalem, *On the Presentation of Christ*; PG 33.1192B.

76. Ibid.

77. Ibid.

78. Ibid., PG 33.1193A.

79. Augustine of Hippo, *City of God*, X.20.

80. Idem., *Exposition on the Psalms*, LXV.6.

81. Fouskas, 99.

82. Niketas Choniates, *Treasures of the Orthodox Faith* 24; PG 140.143A–148C.

83. Ibid. PG 140.148C–153D (26 January, 1156) and PG 140.177B–202A (12–13 May, 1157).

84. Tchéremoukhine, 147. Translation mine.

85. For a comprehensive study of the theological argumentation, seeped in the writings of the Church Fathers and used by Nicholas of Methone to defeat the heretical viewpoints of Panteugenes, see: K.M. Fouskas, Ὁ Νικόλαος Μεθώνης καὶ ἡ Διδασκαλία Αὐτοῦ περὶ Θείας Εὐχαριστίας [*Nicholas of Methone and His Teaching Regarding the DivineEucharist*], (Athens, 1992), especially pp. 91–145.

86. Tchéremoukhine, 161. Translation mine.

87. Fouskas, 101–02, 110.

88. Tchéremoukhine, 141–42.

89. Fouskas, 111. Translation mine.

90. Taft, 136–37.

91. Enrico Mazza, *Mystagogy: A Theology of Liturgy in the Patristic Age*, trans. Matthew J. O'Connell (New York, 1989), 142.

92. Theodore of Mopsuestia, *Catechetical Homily* 15.26, 29, as quoted in E. Mazza, *Mystagogy*, vol. 61.

93. Symeon of Thessalonike, *On the Sacred Liturgy* 94; PG 155.285A.

94. Edward J. Kilmartin, "The Catholic Tradition of Eucharistic Theology: Towards the Third Millennium", in *Theological Studies*, vol. 55 (1994), 435.

95. Stylianos Muksuris, *The Anaphorae of the Liturgy of Sts. Addai and Mari and the Byzantine Liturgy of St. Basil the Great: A Comparative Study* (unpublished M.Litt. thesis), (Durham, 1999), 138–39.

96. Ibid., 259–61. See also Thomas Elavanal, *The Memorial Celebration: A Theological Study of the Anaphora of the Apostles Mar Addai and Mari* (Kerala, 1988), 216; and C.C. Richardson, "The So-Called Epiclesis in Hippolitus," in *Harvard Theological Review*, vol. 40 (1947), 108.

97. Emphasis mine. See *The Divine Liturgy of Saint John Chrysostom*, trans. Faculty of Hellenic College and Holy Cross Greek Orthodox School of Theology (Brookline, 1985), 17.

98. Ibid., 19. The Holy Cross faculty translation reads: "Mercy and peace", which most closely corresponds to the late eighth-century *Barberini Codex 336* manuscript: Ἔλεος εἰρήνη. See F.E. Brightman, ed. *Liturgies Eastern and Western* (Oxford, 1896), 321. The addition of θυσίαν αἰνέσεως ("a sacrifice of praise") in the Holy Cross text, however, is absent from *Barberini* but is included by Brightman in his modern rendition of the Byzantine Liturgy (p. 383).

99. Mazza, *Mystagogy*, 93.

100. Ibid., 94. See also Theodore of Mopsuestia, *Catechetical Homily* 14.2.

101. Mazza, *Mystagogy*, 97–98.

5

ESCHATOLOGY AND ITS RELATION TO EASTERN LITURGY

The purpose of this chapter is, in part, to trace the historical development of the eschatological concept in the theology of the Church, but
more so to identify and examine the strong eschatological undertones in
Eastern liturgical worship. Since the Church's theology is most visibly and
convincingly expressed in its liturgical life (in the East, theology and life
are inseparable and intricately intertwined), a study of eschatology cannot
properly be conducted without taking into consideration what ramifications this important article of faith has on Christians engaged in liturgical
prayer, both for their present lives and their future salvation.

The conventional and universally-accepted definition for the term "eschatology" is, quite literally, "the study of the last things, as they refer to
time" (from the Greek ἔσχατος, "what is last in time"). Within the Christian
tradition, eschatology finds its orientation in the future and specifically, in
the relative imminence of the Second Coming of the Son of God at the end
of human history. However, although eschatology anticipates the end of the
material world as known to mankind, it draws the attention of each believer
throughout the ages to adapt his current life in accordance with such future
expectations. J. Moltmann comments: "From first to last, and not merely
in the epilogue, Christianity is eschatology, is hope, forward looking and
forward moving, and therefore also revolutionizing and transforming the
present."[1] Hence, Christian life lived in the present pulsates with a continuous vision of God's Kingdom and a constant movement toward the
eschaton of God's final and permanent reign. Within liturgical worship, the
finality of the *eschaton*, along with its corresponding themes and benefits,
are experienced in part. In one sense, liturgical eschatology reveals to the

worshipper the future of the One who has come in the past at the Incarnation and continues to come in the present through the epicletic prayer at every eucharistic synaxis. In the writing of Karl Rahner, it is the *eisegesis*, or flowing movement, of the future reality into the present one.[2]

In his insightful study *Eucharist and Eschatology*, Geoffrey Wainwright attempts to demonstrate the eschatological dimension attached to the Christian Eucharist and to clarify how an awareness of that dimension assists one in understanding and practicing the sacrament. He makes the point that the Eucharist, within the confines of its weekly and even daily celebration, confirms a particular eschatological schema, so long as this schema takes note of certain points.[3] These general points are: (1) Christian eschatology proposes a polarity of the "already" and "not yet." In other words, the Eucharist, as an eschatological meal, is celebrated and partaken of with certain limitations. It is celebrated periodically (i.e. not continuously but on set days of the week), whereas the great banquet feast in the Kingdom will be eternal. In the Eucharist, only one portion of mankind honors God, but in the *eschaton* the honor paid to God will be universal. In this life, man falls into sins and repeats them; in the *eschaton*, man is set free from the power of sin (cf. Rom 6:6–8), and his joy is fulfilled; (2) Christian eschatology concerns the individual living in community. In the Eucharist, people come together to share the banquet meal here and now, but the Lord confronts each individual with either salvation or judgment, depending upon one's relationship within the greater community of faith; (3) Christian eschatology implies both a divine gift and its appropriation by humans, the gift being God's presence, or Kingdom (e.g. ". . . the kingdom of God has come upon you"; Matt 12:28); (4) Christian eschatology embraces both material and spiritual realms. The Eucharist of hallowed bread and wine confirms that the material creation is sacred, and it serves as the vehicle of communion that God intends between Himself as Spirit (John 4:24) and man as physical creature; (5) Christian eschatology is meant to be universal in scope, insofar as its overall purpose is the union and salvation of *all* humanity and *all* creation subject to the authority of God. In connection with the Eucharist though, Wainwright, for the sake of an "ecumenical liturgical ecclesiology," offers some daring and controversial proposals toward intercommunion among Christians, advocating leniency in sacramental matters;[4] (6) Christian eschatology allows progress and growth toward the Kingdom, since this vision of the future and the impending judgment prompt the faithful to conform their lives daily to the ways of God. The Eucharist is a constant endo-historical reminder of the dire significance of preparing oneself for the ecto-historical reality; and

(7) Christian eschatology includes a moment of judgment and renewal. Wainwright indicates that in the Eucharist, the Lord comes to judge and recreate, to present a "moment of judgement and renewal which is the projection of the cataclysm that will inaugurate the universal and incontestable reign of God."[5]

Prominence among these points must be granted to the Pauline concept of the "already and not yet," which appears throughout St. Paul's epistles but typically in conjunction with the grace of baptism, most especially in Colossians and Ephesians.[6] In Romans 6:1–11, Paul teaches that baptism in Christ, a sacramental act conducted in the present time, allows the Christian to share in Christ's own death upon the Cross, a historical event in the past. Unity in death, however, also presupposes unity in the resurrection, whose fullness for the baptized and faithful Christian will be experienced in the end time. Similarly, in Colossians 3:2–4: "Set your minds on things that are above, not on things that are on earth. For you have died, and your life is hid with Christ in God. When Christ who is our life appears, then you also will appear with him in glory." Once again, death is achieved "here and now," in baptism, but eternal life will be experienced in its totality at the Second Coming, even though unity with the risen Christ is actualized with the periodic celebration of the Eucharist.

Several images reflect this polarity between the Pauline "already and not yet" tension, by associating the present eucharistic celebration in the Church, within history, with the future banquet feast in the Kingdom, at the end of history. First, the Eucharist serves as a "taste" of the Kingdom to come. Taste implies the potential to experience fullness at a later time. "To taste is to relish, and to say that the eucharist provides a taste of the kingdom therefore allows us to express both the provisionality and yet the genuineness of the kingdom as it flavours the present."[7] Second, the Eucharist is a sign of the Kingdom for the present life insofar as it announces and initiates, but also furthers, its advent at the consummation of human history. Third, the Eucharist prefigures in its celebration the life of the Kingdom to come, even though it is rooted in the real events of human history. In other words, the eucharistic celebration serves as the very anamnesis of Christ's death and makes this commemoration of a past event readily accessible in the present. However, Christ's one-time sacrifice upon the Cross also activates the eternal benefits that follow the Resurrection, which will be experienced in their fullest form after the Second Coming. Finally, the Eucharist is a mystery of the Kingdom, an expression popularized by the Eastern Church Fathers in the third and fourth centuries. In the liturgical celebration, one simultaneously encounters both the hidden and visible natures of the Kingdom; that is, the fullness of God's presence concealed from human vision and understanding in the present life, and the observable portion of this Kingdom manifested through the liturgical rites of the Church. Wainwright remarks: "When the Mystery of God has been completed (Rev 10:7), sacraments will cease and the eucharist will give way to the vision of God in His incontestable kingdom."[8]

The Eastern churches essentially retained this tension between the present and future realities by incorporating the Pauline theology of the "here and not yet" into the Liturgy. The Eucharist then is the future final and incontrovertible salvation of man, to be attained outside of human history, previewed now, within the confines of human history.

HISTORICAL DEVELOPMENT OF THE ESCHATOLOGICAL CONCEPT IN THE CHURCH

Two important but related theories regarding the primitive eucharistic celebration and its intimate association to the *eschaton* dominated the first century Church. The Eucharist was viewed as the eschatological joy-meal of the church in Jerusalem. This vision of a celebratory feast involving substantial eating and drinking was an image well known to the Jews of Jesus' time. Jesus Himself makes reference to this euphoric banquet during the Passover celebration with His disciples, in which He extends the feasting into the next life: "I tell you, I will not drink of this fruit of the vine from now on until that day when I drink it anew with you in my Father's kingdom" (Matt 26:29).

In the second theory, the Eucharist was understood not solely as a memorial of the death of Christ but also as the very proclamation of His second glorious coming into the world. In his famous eucharistic chapter, Paul writes: "For whenever you eat this bread and drink this cup, you proclaim the Lord's death until he comes" (1 Cor 11:26). The imminence of the final establishment of God's Kingdom was very obvious to the early Christian community. The weekly eucharistic celebration helped to assure the Christians that the earthly banquet feast, although periodic, never properly ended and, in a sense, would eventually finds its continuation in the new age of God's final and supreme reign. Through the usage of the liturgical tool of anamnesis, a basic feature in all eucharistic liturgies, the Church acknowledges the twofold fact that Christ's final appearance in glory is still awaited at the sudden conclusion of history, and yet He still visits His people whenever they celebrate the Lord's Supper in His remembrance (cf. Matt 18:20). One sees then the intimate connection between the presence of Christ through anamnesis (εἰς τὴν ἐμὴν ἀνάμνησιν) and His final coming (ἄχρις οὗ ἂν ἔλθῃ). Christ's death is not proclaimed as an event of the past, but always within the context of the *Parousia*, that is, with the foreknowledge of the imminent Second Coming.

The development of the eschatological concept among the Israelites of the Old Testament naturally predated the formulation of Christian eschatology, which based itself on the same similar themes of future hope and expectation. For the Israelites, the existing covenant established between Yahweh and the people essentially defined the eschatological outcome. Unfaithfulness to the covenant relationship, which involved a violation of the horizontal and vertical relationships of the people with one another and God, respectively, would render forth the often-quoted "Day of the Lord," mentioned frequently in the prophetic writings (Isa 2:11,12; Hos 2:16; Joel 1:15; Amos 5:18; *et alia*). This fearful Day of the Lord for the Israelites was best understood as a particular moment or time *within history* in which divine retribution, directed toward the violators of the covenant relationship, would be experienced in its fullness. For the grave sins of complacency and apathy, the Lord would bring severe judgment and punishment upon the perpetrators. On a more positive note, the Day of the Lord also implied, for the small remnant that remained faithful to Him, hope and the restitution of prosperity.

In summary then, the development of the Old Testament eschatological concept as future expectation and hope, rooted in judgment for the wicked and salvation for the just, possessed such themes as "the Day of Yahweh and the remnant, the new exodus and conquest, the lordship of God [over all nations and not just Israel], the new heaven and new earth, and finally even the resurrection."[9]

For the Israelites, the community or family meal becomes the very affirmation of the covenant between themselves and their God (rooted in the Passover experience), as well as their reminder to honor and preserve this relationship. The notion of remembrance occupied a central place in the religious meal, because its role was essentially to remind the Israelites of God's past mercies and wonders in the lives of their ancestors as grounds for their own present obedience. By extension, the religious meal also sought to direct one's thoughts toward future blessings, stemming from a reverential regard of past figures and events in history, which in turn would assist in shaping one's present moral and religious behavior. In this regard, the meal takes on an apparent eschatological significance, insofar as future hopes and expectations are celebrated in the present, within the context of the memorial meal.

Similarly, the Eucharist, as a memorial meal, is also celebrated in a time of *hope*, preceding the Second Coming of Christ, whose first coming was seen as the expression of God's *promise*. The Church has always prayed daily for the Second Coming, as a final fulfillment of the Lord's first advent in the flesh. Geoffrey Wainwright writes: "At every eucharist the church is in fact praying that the parousia may take place at that very moment, and if the Father 'merely' sends His Son in the sacramental mode we have at least a taste of that future which God reserves for Himself to give one day."[10]

The Old Testament scriptures are replete with examples of memorial meals, which look forward to future blessings in the context of past and present ones. For example: (1) the first Passover meal in Egypt (Exod 12:1–28); (2) the meal at the making of the covenant on Mt. Sinai (Exod 24:9–11); (3) the sacred meals observed in the places of sacrifice (Deut 12:5–7, 17–18; 14:23, 26; 15:20; 27:7); (4) references to manna (Exod 16:4, 15; Ps 78:24f; Neh 9:15; Wis 16:20; 2 Ezek 1:19); (5) the meals mentioned in the wisdom literature (Prov 9:1–6; Ps 23:5; Song 5:1); and (6) the themes of feeding and feasting in the context of the future salvation (Isa 25:6–9).

From the inter-Testamental period, one encounters: (1) references to the abundance of food (2 Esd 8:52–54; 2 Bar 29:5); (2) references to new manna, especially in the Syriac Apocalypse of Baruch, in which a cryptic reference is made to the Messiah: "… the treasury of manna shall again descend from on high, and they will eat of it in those years, because these are they who have come to the consummation of time" (2 Bar 29:8); (3) future Messianic feasting in the Ethiopian Book of Enoch 62:13–16: "With that Son of Man shall they eat and lie down and rise up for ever and ever", a reference to the euphoric banquet in the Kingdom; and (4) two particular references found in the Qumran scrolls.[11]

Clearly, the model memorial meal for the Old Testament Jews was the Passover, in which God expects His people to recall their freedom from bondage and, upon the realization of this marvelous wonder, to anticipate their inheritance of the Promised Land. "This day shall be for you a memorial day, and you shall keep it as a feast to the Lord; throughout your generations you shall observe it as an ordinance for ever . . . And when you come to the land which the Lord will give you, as he has promised, you shall keep this service" (Exod 12:14, 25).

In the New Testament, the memorial meal maintains its eschatological significance, with any reference to "future blessings" revolving around the person of the resurrected Christ and occurring following the dawning of the new *aion*. Examples of feasting throughout the Gospels are likewise overwhelmingly abundant: (1) Matthew 8:11; Luke 13:29, in which future feasting is anticipated within the Kingdom of God; (2) Luke 6:21a; Matthew 5:6, in which the spiritual hunger of the present will be satisfied in the eschatological future; (3) the reference to "joy" (χαρά) in the Parable of the Talents (Matt 25:14–30) is understood as entering into the joyful banquet hall of the Kingdom; (4) the parabolic exhortation to vigilance in Luke 12:35–38, in which the Master invites his faithful servants to the table of the Kingdom where he serves them; (5) the various meals Jesus ate during His lifetime, with sinners and publicans (Matt 9:10–13, 11:19; Mark 2:15–17; Luke 5:29–32, 7:34, 15:1–2, 19:1–10), with His disciples (Mark 2:23–28) the plucking of corn from the cornfields on the Sabbath, as a sign of the dawning of the eschatological Sabbath; Matt 26:17–30, Mark 14:12–26, Luke 22:7–38, John 13: the institution of the Eucharist; Luke 24:30–35, John 21:9–13: the post-Resurrection meals of Christ with His disciples); (6) the feeding of the multitudes as a sign of the gathering of God's people in the *eschaton* (Matt 14:13–21, 15:32–39; Mark 6:30–44, 8:1–10; Luke 9:11–17; John 6:3–15); and (7) the image of feeding expressed in Jesus' conversation with the Syro-Phoenician woman, in which the "children's bread" refers to the faithful remnant of Israel and the "crumbs" to the blessings to be harvested by the Gentiles (Matt 15:21–28; Mark 7:24–30).

Christ's own involvement in meals during his lifetime essentially projects Him as the center and source of the act, from whom forgiveness of sins and eternal life flow. Consequently, since the fullness of such spiritual benefits can only be secured at the conclusion of one's earthly life, one may assume that such blessings belong to the eschatological, or meta-historical, reality of the age to come rather than to the historical present.

The reference to "daily bread" in the Lord's Prayer raises several interesting points in terms of linking the eucharistic bread to any form of future eschatological feasting. Following the fourth century, many churches during their celebration of the Eucharist customarily accepted the Lord's Prayer as the classic preparatory prayer preceding the reception of Holy Communion, for obvious reasons. Cyril of Jerusalem (c. AD 348) seems to be the first author to refer to the Lord's Prayer following the eucharistic prayer but before the fraction of the consecrated bread. The Clementine Liturgy (Book 8 of the *Apostolic Constitutions*) omits it, as does Chrysostom in his writings in Antioch a generation later. In the West, Ambrose of Milan (c. 395) makes reference to it in his *De sacramentis* vi.24, as does Augustine of Hippo. However, Rome does not apparently endorse this Eastern innovation until about the time of Gregory of Rome (595).[12]

"Our daily bread" is a commonly-accepted rendering of the original Greek text, τὸν ἄρτον ἡμῶν τὸν ἐπιούσιον, which presented problems of an etymological nature for Origen, who had not concerned himself with the Latin translation of "daily." He did not believe the term ἐπιούσιος was found in Greek literature or utilized colloquially but was somehow the product of the evangelists Matthew and Luke, in whose gospels the term appears (Matt 6:11; Luke 11:3). Origen defines it as "suited to our (rational) nature" and capable of imparting immortality to the one who partakes of it, since the bread is the very Logos of God.[13] For him, the "logical nature" of man essentially meant that man was capable of being fed spiritually by the Logos of God. Along similar lines, Origen, in good company with the likes of Jerome, Cyril of Alexandria, who identifies the Eucharist as "suited to the nature of the soul",[14] and the Syriac *Peshitta*, understands ἐπιούσιος as signifying that which is necessary for both bodily and spiritual existence (ἐπὶ + οὐσία).[15]

Another interpretation—and clearly the most ancient of those presented here—sees ἐπιούσιος as referring to the bread needed for the current day (ἐπὶ τὴν οὖσαν ἡμέραν) in order to support one's bodily existence. Chrysostom's rendering of Matthew 6:11 reads: "τουτέστι τὸν ἄρτον τὸν ἐπιούσιον, τὸν ἐφήμερον [*daily*]."[16] In this regard, the significance of the bread is reduced to a material substance that essentially supports physical life and is devoid of any spiritual qualities. However, such a rendering disqualifies the eschatological importance of the "daily bread" to which Christ makes reference in Matthew and Luke.

Jerome interpreted this bread as that which surpasses any other substance (*super-substantialis*) and whose qualities range from unique to excellent (περιούσιος).[17] Such bread surpasses human essence because it derives from the divine substance of the Logos, an ontological claim about the eucharistic bread that certainly incited many a future controversy in the West, especially with regard to consecration.

Within the Armenian tradition, a familiar interpretation is "everlasting bread," which quite possibly may come from an earlier Syrian understanding of the eucharistic bread as "constant" or "continual,"[18] carrying over beyond earthly life into the fullness of the Kingdom at the *eschaton*.

The final interpretation—and the one which Wainwright seemingly embraces most enthusiastically, though Origen rejected it—is the understanding of ἐπιούσιος as "the coming day" or "the next day" (from the infinitive ἐπιέναι, "to follow," "to succeed"), to which is attached a very viable reference to the eschatological reality of the future age. The term appears in several places throughout the Book of Acts (7:26, 16:11, 20:15, 21:18, 23:11), but in these pericopes it is mainly used in the context of the next calendar day or the immediate day just beginning. According to Wainwright, the fourth petition of the Lord's Prayer is understood as: "Give us *already now* the bread of the *future age*."[19] The eucharistic bread is the material and spiritual bread partaken of now in periodic fashion in the Church, but which will fill the faithful with eternal satisfaction in the Kingdom to come. Wainwright understands the eucharistic bread in its eschatological significance, namely, that it becomes in itself the harbinger of the several beneficences yet to come, delineated in the Lord's Prayer. He writes:

> To understand the fourth petition as a prayer for God to give already now the bread of the future age allows a consistent interpretation of the Lord's prayer . . . the disciples are taught to pray for the things that make up the kingdom (namely: the hallowing of God's name, the role of His will on earth, the forgiveness of sins), and for deliverance from the tribulation that precedes the kingdom's coming – and in this context the fourth petition can only mean 'Give us today the bread we are destined to have in the kingdom' and therefore be a prayer for the inbreaking of the kingdom.[20]

Following this concise review of the development of the eschatological concept from the Old Testament to the early Christian Church, it is now time to focus on several individual theological themes that are pertinent to understanding liturgical eschatology and its implementation in Eastern worship: (1) the eschatological significance of meal imagery in Eastern liturgy; (2) the Second Coming as the Church's ultimate hope and expectation in worship; (3) the partial fulfillment ("here and now") and imminence ("yet to come") of spiritual blessings and judgment experienced in the Church's worship; and (4) the popular Eastern concept of καιρός as God's time of salvation, which is infused into the χρόνος of the Church's liturgical celebration.

THEOLOGICAL THEMES IN LITURGICAL ESCHATOLOGY

The Eucharist is, for all intents and purposes, a celebratory meal-event that occurs within the confines of historical time. The Church understands the eucharistic liturgy never as an end to itself, but accepts it as a periodic and provisional act which looks forward to the final fulfillment of man's salvation in the risen Christ. Due to sin and, subsequently, man's whimsical nature in his faith commitment, the glorification of God in this life can hardly be a truly perpetual experience. Wainwright observes, "The eucharist is no more than provisional and anticipatory because God's glory is not yet *visibly* perceived, received and reflected by men and nature."[21] Nevertheless, the periodic, Sunday-to-Sunday celebration of the Eucharist on earth sets a pattern which Christians are expected to reproduce in order to live up to the perpetual eucharistic celebration of the eternal Kingdom. Similarly, God's divine glory can never be fully envisioned in this life through the faculty of physical sight; however, it can be perceived through faith, which reveals in part that which will appear in its fullness at the *eschaton*.

The vertical dimension of liturgical eschatology, illustrated richly in the Eastern Church's liturgical worship, hymnology, and church architecture, reminds man that he can enter eternity at any given moment during his earthly existence because of his vulnerability and constant susceptibility to physical death. At any moment then, each individual can be confronted with God's judgment. However, there is also an all-important horizontal dimension to eschatology that intersects the vertical plane, and which looks to regulating behavior as a means of preparation for salvation.

MEAL IMAGERY IN EASTERN WORSHIP

As previously indicated in this chapter, several references to eschatological meals and their importance abound in both the Old and New Testaments. The significance of the Eucharist as the Church's central eschatological meal is established primarily in St. Luke's Gospel (22:14–18) and St. Paul's First Letter to the Corinthians (11:26). Wainwright observes: "Having the form of a meal, the eucharist belongs to that universally known realm of spoken and acted imagery which describes and embodies the relation between God and men in terms of eating and drinking."[22] The Eucharist then identifies not only the connectedness between the present and future, but also the relational nature between God and man, revealing a relationship that is at once paternal and filial, respectively, and one that demands the provision of the former and the receptivity of the latter for survival.

Several Church Fathers identify the wine of the Kingdom as being drunk already in the wine of the Eucharist and so envision the Eucharist as the preparatory meal of the eschatological banquet.[23] Others, on the contrary, do not accept this traditional line of interpreting the eucharistic meal as provisionary for the eschatological future and interconnected with the meal of the Kingdom. For example, Irenaeus places the fulfillment of the drinking of new wine in the Kingdom (Luke 22:14–18) only in the *eschaton*,[24] although elsewhere he seems open to accepting the Eucharist as anticipatory of the final fulfillment.[25] Also, Augustine distinguishes between the "old wine" at Christ's institution of the Eucharist and the "new wine," which represents man's renewed and glorified body in the Kingdom.[26]

Five important conclusions then may be drawn regarding the centrality of the relational aspect of the Eucharist in the worship of the Church: (1) the eucharistic meal expresses both the difference and continuity between the present and future realities (the former experienced as a partial but real taste of the fullness of the latter); (2) the eucharistic meal displays the structure of the reality in which God binds Himself to man and man to God (i.e. God, by nature of His ultimate goodness, feeds man through the Eucharist and man's participation in the Eucharist secures for him forgiveness of sins and eternal life); (3) the eucharistic meal confirms not only the positive value of man but the inherent value of the material creation because it fulfills its "spiritual destiny," so to speak, of mediating communion between God and man; (4) the Eucharist becomes a sign of righteousness, showing men sitting at table with God in a right relationship (the vertical dimension); and (5) the eucharistic meal expresses the communal nature of God's Kingdom (the horizontal dimension),[27] prepared for the enjoyment of the righteous since the beginning of the world (cf. Matt 25:34).

Regarding the association of the Eucharist with meal imagery, Nicholas Cabasilas makes two interesting references to the Liturgy as the table that effects union with the living Christ. His first comment stems from his *Explanation of the Divine Liturgy*, in which he states that feeding on Christ is the ultimate source of joy for both the Christian who has departed this life in faith as well as for the Christian who remains alive on earth.

> Now the source of all delight and bliss to those who dwell in that place – whether you call it paradise, or Abraham's bosom, or the place free from sorrow and pain, which is full of light, and green and cool, or even if you call it the kingdom itself – is none other than this cup and this bread. For these are the Mediator, . . . and who now appears to us thus [in the consecrated elements of Holy Communion] . . . . Those who have not been joined to him in the union which his table can create, cannot enjoy any rest in that place, or receive there any good thing, great or small.[28]

From the passage above, it is clear that Cabasilas acknowledges Christ as food indeed to be consumed by the faithful in the context of the eucharistic celebration. In fact, the prayer over the proskomide (about which Cabasilas omits any substantial commentary regarding meal imagery) shows forth Christ as being the "heavenly bread sent down as food for the whole world" (τὸν οὐράνιον ἄρτον τὴν τροφὴν τοῦ παντὸς κόσμου).

A second incidence appears in *The Life in Christ*, in which Cabasilas expresses a distinction and continuity between both earthly and heavenly feasts. For the living, the Eucharist becomes their lifeline to the risen Lord because it allows them to experience in part now what they will experience in full in the future. For those who have discontinued their existence in the flesh, their reception of Holy Communion during their lifetimes infuses them with true life in God, which began at a certain point in their bodily existence and is simply perpetuated into eternity. The passage from Cabasilas is worth quoting in its entirety, particularly for its vividness and versatile imagery highlighting eternal life as a banquet feast and as the natural consequence and continuation of faithfully communing at the Lord's Table during the earthly celebration of the Divine Liturgy.

> So they will move from one table to another, from that which is still veiled to that which is already manifested, from the bread to the Body. While they still live the human life, Christ is bread for them, and He is their Passover for they pass from here to the city which is in heaven. But when they "shall renew their strength, and mount up with wings like eagles," as says the admirable Isaiah (40:31), then they will take their position at the very Body which is unveiled. This also blessed John declares when he says, "we shall see Him as He is" (1 Jn. 3:2).
>
> When the life in flesh has ceased Christ is no longer our bread, nor do we still await our passover. In His Body He bears many marks of His passion, for the hands bear the wounds and the feet bear the traces of the nails, and His side still bears the mark of the spear. The earthly banquet brings us to that Body. Apart from it we cannot receive the Body, any more than it is possible for one to look at the light whose eyes have been gouged out. If those who do not feast at this banquet have life in themselves, how could the Immortal One have become the Head of dead members [and have given them life]?
>
> One only is the power of the table, one the Host in both worlds. The one world is the wedding feast with the Bridegroom Himself, the other is the preparation for that wedding feast. Accordingly, those who depart this life without the Eucharistic gifts will have nothing for that life. But those who have been able to receive the grace and preserve it have entered into the joy of their Lord (Mt. 25:21), and have gone in with the Bridegroom to the wedding feast (Mt. 25:10). Already they have enjoyed the other delight of the banquet though they do not obtain it fully yet; but when Christ has been manifested they will perceive more clearly what it is that they have brought with them.
>
> This then is the account of how the kingdom of heaven is within us.[29]

Cabasilas further regards the feasting in God's Kingdom as the ultimate source of contentment because it implies a unity among the saints who have fed upon the risen Lord while alive and continue to do so in the Kingdom. "Because for this reason did the Lord call the enjoyment of the saints in the future a banquet, in order to show that there is nothing more [i.e. greater] beyond this table."[30]

Symeon of Thessalonike provides a stunning eschatological image in the prothesis rite that simultaneously combines the events at the Second Coming together with the banquet feast of the Kingdom. For Symeon, the eschatological gathering of all men before the judgment seat of God (cf. Matt 25:31–46) may also be envisioned as man's fulfillment of God's invitation to dine with Him at table (cf. Matt 22:1–10; Luke 14:16–24). In fact, the centrality of the Lamb upon the paten during the preparation rite projects Christ as "host" of the banquet feast, encircled by both earthly and heavenly beings subject to His authority. Symeon writes in his *On the Sacred Liturgy*:

Ἴδωμεν δὲ πῶς καὶ διὰ τούτου τοῦ θείου τύπου καὶ τοῦ ἔργου τῆς ἱερᾶς προσ-κομιδῆς τὸν Ἰησοῦν αὐτὸν καὶ τὴν Ἐκκλησίαν αὐτοῦ μίαν πᾶσαν ὁρῶμεν μέσον αὐτὸν τὸ ἀληθινὸν φῶς, τὴν ζωὴν τὴν αἰώνιον κεκτημένην, καὶ φωτιζομένην ὑπ' αὐτοῦ καὶ συνεχομένην. Αὐτὸς μὲν γὰρ διὰ τοῦ ἄρτου μέσον ἐστίν· ἡ Μή-τηρ δὲ διὰ τῆς μερίδος ἐκ δεξιῶν· ἅγιοι δὲ καὶ ἄγγελοι ἐξ' ἀριστερῶν· ὑποκάτω δὲ ἅπαν τῶν αὐτῷ πιστευσάντων τὸ εὐσεβὲς ἄθροισμα. Καὶ τοῦτο ἐστι τὸ μέγα μυστήριον· Θεὸς ἐν ἀνθρώποις καὶ Θεὸς ἐν μέσῳ θεῶν, θεουμένων ἐκ τοῦ κατὰ φύσιν ὄντως Θεοῦ σαρκωθέντος ὑπὲρ αὐτῶν. Καὶ τοῦτο ἡ μέλλουσα βασιλεία καὶ τῆς αἰωνίου ζωῆς τὸ πολίτευμα· Θεὸς μεθ' ἡμῶν ὁρώμενός τε καὶ μεταλαμ-βανόμενος....

But let us also see how through this divine model and the work of the holy proskomide we perceive Jesus and His Church all as one, in the middle Him the true light, from whom the Church has acquired life eternal, illumined and sustained by Him. While He is in the mid-dle through the bread, His mother [is present] through the particle on the right, the saints and the angels on the left, and below everyone who has believed in Him, the pious gathering. And this is the great mystery: God among men and God in the midst of gods, who have been made gods by Him who is God by nature and who was truly incarnated for them. And this is the future kingdom and the common-wealth of eternal life: God with us, both seen and partaken of. . . .[31]

THE LITURGICAL EXPECTATION OF THE SECOND COMING

From the aforementioned eschatological image of the gathering of God's elect before Him for judgment and feasting, the implication deriving from it is that the Church must first seek and pray for the Second Coming to occur and bring the *eschaton* in its dramatic fullness. The most ancient prayer of *Marana tha*, "Our Lord, come!" (1 Cor 16:22; cf. Rev 22:20; cf. *Didache* 10.6) stylistically shares the form of a liturgical epiclesis, which the ancient Church used as a prayer not only for the imminent *Parousia* but also for eucharistic consecration.

The connection, however, between eucharistic consecration and eschatological fulfillment is actually far more pronounced than a mere stylistic association would suggest. In one sense, one can qualify any consecratory prayer as eschatological, inasmuch as epicletic consecration traditionally involves an invocation of God for the purpose of "coming" (cf. 1 Cor 16:22; Rev 22:20; *Didache* 10.6) upon the holy gifts and the recipients of the gifts for the ultimate purpose of sanctifying the latter through the former. The deliberate nature of this advent furthermore implies the eventual encounter of God with man and of the heavenly with the earthly, in which the sublime and uncreated God definitively transforms the entire created order of which humans are naturally a part, thus renewing the whole creation (cf. Rev 21:5). The very idea then of descending ("coming down") from heaven and "coming upon" the people translates into an eschatological act; it implies a completion or realization of a hope and promise now brought to their fruition. The epicletic prayer may be found in almost every ancient eucharistic prayer, regardless of which Person of the Trinity is addressed, as well as in the priestly prayer offered during the prothesis rite.

Even the incarnation of the Logos—Christ's initial "descent" into the world—can be understood as an eschatological moment insofar as history itself enters its final phase before consummation with the preaching of the Gospel to the ends of the earth (Matt 24:14), and man himself is confronted daily with judgment and salvation (2 Cor 6:2), prior to the *Parousia*. Through this first advent, the Kingdom of God is inaugurated in the world, albeit in an inchoative manner. The earthly Church, for all intents and purposes, takes on the characteristics of this inchoate Kingdom, at once perfect but incomplete, the very embodiment of God's divine presence and the precursor of God's final reign over the world, which aspires toward Christ's glorious second coming. The fullness then of God's dominion will be manifested openly and conclusively following the *Parousia*, which Christ Himself affirms will happen by way of promise. "The kingdom of God, though a present reality since the coming of Jesus Christ, is now *hidden*, but it will be made *manifest*."[32]

As previously mentioned, Symeon of Thessalonike presents a dual image of the Second Coming and the festal banquet of the Kingdom when he interprets the allegorical significance of the paten holding the Lamb and adjoining particles. He also envisions the Great Entrance as being that moment in the Divine Liturgy that most closely corresponds to the *Parousia*, as does Maximos the Confessor. Wainwright affirms this stance, saying that

> we cannot do other than salute his vision of the liturgy as a dramatic prefiguration of the parousia and the final kingdom made possible by the presence of the one Christ who came once bringing the divine kingdom in His own person and who will come again at the end to establish God's universal kingdom in power and glory.[33]

ESCHATOLOGICAL BLESSINGS AND JUDGMENT IN THE EUCHARIST

Liturgical scholars agree that practically every eucharistic prayer lists several blessings or benefits associated with the reception of Holy Communion. Such benefits typically fall under the realm of eschatological blessings, since they are provisionary for the Kingdom to come and surpass the boundaries of the temporal material world. They are: (1) the Eucharist becomes the sacramental food for eternal life; (2) Communion cures sin by reestablishing the right relationship between man and God, which makes eternal life possible for man once again; (3) Communion becomes the indirect cause of future glory because it provides grace to conquer sin and persevere in good works, thus making eternal life possible; (4) Communion secures a meeting with the glorified Christ; and (5) Communion transforms the individual communicant into the glorified Body of Christ or into the ecclesial Body of Christ, thus clearly becoming the very source of ecclesiastical unity.

The Church, as the embodiment of the final Kingdom to come, believes that the risen Lord bestows His eschatological blessings not only as provisionary measures in preparation for the end, but also as gifts to be enjoyed now during one's lifetime. In the Liturgy, Christ essentially exercises here and now the functions that he will exercise at the Second Coming. Hence, reward or judgment are previewed in a reserved or contained state before their final eruption and complete distribution at the *Parousia*. Christ's coming then in the Eucharist is a "throwing forward," so to speak, of Christ's final advent into the present.

Cabasilas understands the consecration of the eucharistic gifts as necessary for the transformation of the communicants, the latter of which is considered an eschatological blessing that flows out of the former. He writes: "In the celebration of the holy mysteries the work done is the transformation of the gifts into the divine body and blood, and the aim is the sanctification of the faithful who, through these mysteries, receive the remission of sins and the inheritance of the kingdom of heaven."[34] Along the same lines, John of Damascus likewise agrees that the consecrated holy gifts can provide great spiritual blessings for the communicant, but they can also bring severe judgment if they are partaken of unworthily (ἀναξίως). Interestingly, his reference to the offering at the prothesis elevates the unconsecrated gifts to a special level of potentiality, capable of effecting either eschatological benefits or judgment.

> . . . The bread of the prothesis, and the wine and water, are by the invocation and coming of the Holy Spirit changed in a supernatural way into the body and blood of Christ. . . . [The Body of Christ] is to them that receive it rightly (ἀξίως) and in faith (πίστει), for the remission of sins, for eternal life, and for the protection of soul and body; but to them that receive it unworthily (ἀναξίως) and in unbelief (ἐν ἀπιστίᾳ), it is unto punishment and retribution; just as the Lord's death is, for those who believe, life and incorruption unto the enjoyment of eternal bliss; but to unbelievers and those who killed the Lord, it is unto punishment and eternal retribution.[35]

Because of each man's continuation in sin, every eucharistic celebration becomes a repeated projection of the Final Judgment, which each Liturgy partly fulfills and therefore strengthens the promise of judgment. In 1 Corinthians 11:27–34, Paul generally warns against unworthy participation in the Eucharist, but specifically addresses the abuse in which certain Christians who attended the pre-Eucharist meal, or *agape*, sometimes devoured all the food without moral consideration for others who arrived later. Paul thus formulates this imagery of judgment by aligning moral obligations with the worthy reception of Christ's Body and Blood in the weekly eucharistic synaxis.

How can the severity of the Final Judgment be offset? Paul answers that this may be achieved through the worthy (ἀξίως) reception of the Eucharist by exercising discernment (διακρίνων) of the Lord's Body and Blood, which implies fulfilling first one's moral obligations towards others. The Eucharist received in faith and clear conscience secures justification in Christ, or the divine acquittal of sins (Matt 26:28), a direct eschatological benefit of Holy Communion. Intimately related to eternal life, which is another eschatological gift granted inchoately by Communion, forgiveness of sins brings about a unity between God and the communicant and, consequently, lessens the estrangement that can prove unprofitable for man at the *eschaton*.

ESCHATOLOGICAL TIME IN THE LITURGY: CHRONOS AND KAIROS

Within the context of ecclesiastical worship, the Eastern Church regards two distinct but interrelated conceptions of eschatological time: *chronos*, or historical time, and *kairos*, or salvational time. Both coexist side by side in a manner by which the former is ultimately absorbed via the constant penetration of the latter during the Divine Liturgy.

The origins of this differentiation and the inherent unity between these two concepts of time, the profane and the sacred, lie in popular philosophical views held by the ancient Hellenic world which, generally speaking, had a cyclical view of time and the world. In the *Phaedo*, Plato's account of the Socratic dialogue regarding the themes of death and afterlife sheds light upon this unique concept of *chronos*, in which Socrates argues for the existence of an afterlife and the immortality of the soul by building upon the premise that death (nonexistence) naturally follows human life (existence) and birth naturally comes from a state of previous nonexistence (death), thus indicating this cyclical phenomenon.[36] Georgios Metallinos points out, "Worldly time was in its essence a continuous recycling and eternal return"[37] to the past (*illud tempus*).

For the ancient Greeks, the whole concept of liturgical anamnesis was an escape from the material world and human history, a re-visitation of the world of ideals and archetypes, which were impervious to corruption and decay. Within the context of ritual, it was believed that the corruptive power of *chronos* could be abolished. As an activity, worship was not regarded as a simple, nostalgic recollection of the past, but the actual reproduction of sacred time and of the changeless archetypes. Hence, worship became the only true escape, albeit a transient one, from this cyclic repetition of secular time, since outside of worship the possibility of change or sanctification were clearly absent.[38]

Sharon Gerstel identifies "the profane with terrestrial hours (time measured by a beginning and an end)," while "the sacred is associated with liturgical time (time of transhuman, indeterminate duration)."[39] Gerstel further indicates how the demarcation between profane and sacred is eliminated both liturgically and artistically, via the usage of prayers and, by extension, hymnology that "erase the boundaries of human time"[40], and by iconographic imagery:

> Saints of the Byzantine Church, for example, stand next to one another without regard for the period in which they actually lived. This blending of centuries suspends all notion of real time and draws the

viewer into an alternate frame of reference where all saints flourish simultaneously and on the same sacred plane.[41]

The dualistic dichotomy between profane and sacred that Gerstel suggests is perhaps better understood, from the Eastern perspective, as the transformation of the former by the latter when it comes into contact with the divine or, more accurately, the transformation of the profane *into* the latter at their point of intersection, which is the Liturgy.[42]

In the Christian view, unlike the overtly dualistic Platonic view, salvation did not suggest an escape from the material world and historical *chronos* but rather the transformation of both, which can be understood in the sense of victory. Hence, Christ's proclamation of "overcoming the world" (νενίκηκα τὸν κόσμον) in John 16:33 indicates that *kairos* has neither circumvented nor abolished earthly time but has permeated it and made the reality of salvation more accessible and immediately relevant to man within the context of his earthly existence. In the Divine Liturgy then, one cannot realistically fathom the complete eradication of *chronos*, in which worship occurs in the first place, and which becomes the very channel for the advent and full implementation of *kairos* as God's transformation of "chronic" time. In other words, without the actual existence of historical time, the Liturgy itself is rendered pointless, and *kairos* realistically possesses no medium by which to introduce itself into man's realm of existence. Patricia Rumsey writes:

> If creation is to fulfil its God-given sacramental purpose, then it needs redemption. But for redemption to operate there must be an object to redeem, so redemption needs creation. This sacramental, eschatological and ontological principle also applies to time as part of creation, so the fact of time needing redemption and redemption also needing time, must be born in mind. . . .[43]

From this perspective, namely, historical *chronos* needing salvation, *kairos* may signify "opportunity" or "fit time", in which God's presence and involvement in human history is seen as providential for man's redemption.[44]

This concept of "mutual need" further connotes the fact that the *eschaton* is not the expected termination of historical development, but more so the fulfillment of that which develops within historical time and progresses ultimately toward union with God. Metallinos notes:

> The eschaton is less a chronological category and more a qualitative one, and it is associated with the entrance into the eternal kingdom, the union, i.e., with divine Grace (enlightenment and glorification) as the realization of the purpose of one's existence in Christ.[45]

Given this qualification, the Church must be characterized as a historico-eschatological community, which gradually becomes within history what it is destined to be beyond history.

In summary, the inherent goodness of both time and the material world—as created, God-sanctioned entities—is obvious, since God's *kairos* cannot be said to antagonize *chronos* but rather claims it as its own and transforms it into salvational time. John Romanides sums up this traditional anti-dualistic Christian view when he writes,

Man's salvation does not consist at once of a Platonic escape of the soul from the world and matter, but on the contrary it involves the destruction of evil within the world and time, through the resurrection and renewal of all. Salvation is not from the world, but from evil . . . [and man's] restoration upon the road leading toward perfection and immortality through communion with the Holy Spirit.[46]

On another level, the Christian view of time contends to be a linear progression of events that move onward toward their final consummation at the end of history, without any repetition or recycling of these events. Christ stands at the very epicenter of this timeline, nestled in between creation (the beginning of time) and the *eschaton*, or final track of human history leading up to the Second Coming and ushered in by Christ's incarnation.

As the center of human history, the individuality of Jesus' death as having occurred only once is affirmed by the Apostles Paul and Peter (ἐφάπαξ: Rom 6:10; ἅπαξ: 1 Pet 3:18), signifying the implausibility and impossibility of its reproduction. Nevertheless, since the world has already entered the *eschaton* in Christ, the Eucharist does not actually reproduce the Lord's sacrifice but rather relives and participates in the very same sacrifice offered by Him once and for all. In a sense, one can boldly claim that Christ's acts of salvation, achieved and completed within history, have never truly ended because of the trans-historical nature of the benefits that flow from them to subsequent generations. Hence in the Liturgy, the *kairos* of the Kingdom of God is experienced in part within the "historical *eschaton*," the final segment of the linear timeline leading to the consummation of all. "The kingdom of God then is not life beyond time, but the life in God lived here in this life."[47]

Liturgical time, also called "soteriological (or salvational) time" (σωτηριολογικὸς χρόνος)[48] mystically makes past events in the life of Christ and future blessings immediately accessible and relevant in the present. Not only does the Liturgy transport the believer to the actual Christ event by overstepping the very laws of time, which necessarily require any event to possess a beginning and end, but it also makes him a recipient of endless graces flowing from this timeless event. Christ's absolute dominion over time essentially prompts the Church to center each of its experiences in Him. As Alkiviadis Calivas rightly observes, "Within the Church memory of the past constitutes memory in Christ, and hope in the future constitutes hope in Christ." [49]

Consequently, man enters into the timelessness and ever-presence of God through the portal of the "here and now" experienced in the Liturgy. "Time, therefore, within the context of ecclesiastical worship experience, does not operate so much as past, present and future, but as 'concentrated liturgical time,' as the 'here' and 'now' of salvation." [50] This Eastern concept of "concentrated liturgical time" is best observed in the hymnological tradition of the Church by the widespread usage of the word "today" (σήμερον) during its celebration of Great Feasts and festivals of the saints, in order to indicate the immediacy of salvation which breaks through time and space and appears in the present reality. This "making present" of not only the salvific event but of the very graces flowing from the event is called παροντοποίησις,[51] in which the salvific event introduced within history never quite ended in the past but is simply perpetuated for the Christian into *today*.

Similarly, John Chrysostom affirms the realism of the eucharistic celebration by claiming that each Eucharist *is* the actual Last Supper (and not a memorial or past remembrance), which is not repeated but made present as an unending event for the Church.[52] Likewise, the Eucharist—and liturgical worship in general—does not replicate heavenly worship but is itself the earthly expression of the very same heavenly worship. "Besides, the Eucharist on earth is not a simple parallel reality with the heavenly (reality), but the same heavenly reality, conducted upon earth." [53]

The Church provides the content for this marriage between *chronos* and *kairos* in the form of the liturgical feast, which becomes man's point of entrance into God's eternity. The feasts of the Church draw people back into the biblical event, whose purpose during their first occurrence is to save those who came into contact with them and to continue to save man who participates in this perpetual event from age to age. "For the first Christians [and, by extension, for subsequent generations that followed], the feast was not a simple 'historical remembrance', but (a continuous) entrance into the new reality that Christ brought with His death and resurrection." [54]

Sunday became for the early Church at prayer the special day of the week in which man's entrance into the *kairos* of God was effected, although weekday celebrations of the Eucharist later in history ruled out its exclusivity. Within the patristic mindset, the rationale for elevating Sunday above the other days of the week was clear. Since Christ Himself entered into His glory following His death and resurrection, and since the first day of the week was *when* this entry was accomplished, it followed quite naturally for the Church to claim Sunday as that meeting point between *chronos* and *kairos*, the moment in which man likewise enters into the glory of eternal and true life in God. Hence, Sunday became labeled as the "eighth day" of the week, the day of the "new creation" wrought by Christ's resurrection, a day retaining its own unique character and belonging as much to the historical week as it did to the timelessness of the future age.

So long as the Divine Liturgy is celebrated and commemorates a particular event in the life of Christ or the saints, the Church is capable of transforming *every* day bound by historical time into a festival of the eternal Kingdom. "With the synthesis of the calendar of feasts (ἑορτολόγιον), secular time is transformed into sacred (time), a type of the future age, and every day becomes a feast, the 'memory' of the saints or salvific events, a continuous living within the presence of God in the world and the ability for man to receive sanctification."[55]

THE SERVICE OF KAIROS—
ENTRANCE INTO SOTERIOLOGICAL TIME

The transformation of *chronos* into the *kairos* of salvation, i.e. the very sanctification of time in the eternal Christ, is also achieved when the Church enters the sublimity of divine ritual. This initial entrance into soteriological time is marked by a special preparatory rite for clergy preceding the celebration of the Divine Liturgy, appropriately called *Kairos*, or the "Service of *Kairos*."[56]

The very brief service involves the offering of prayers and penitential hymns, the veneration of the icons upon the iconostasis, and the asking of forgiveness, all of which may be understood as liturgical acts with an intrinsic eschatological value. For example, the Trisagion prayers at the beginning of the service are strongly penitential in content and implore God to show clemency upon man's sinfulness in His righteous judgment. Second, the veneration of icons on the iconostasis brings the clergy face to face, so to speak, with God and the saints, to whom one would naturally turn for comfort and encouragement at the consummation of time. Finally, the offering and receiving of forgiveness, which occurs at the end of the service by means of a respectful bow toward fellow clergy and the congregation, is an act intrinsically related to the *eschaton* and becomes, for man, his final act of reconciliation with others before Christ's Second Coming and the Final Judgment.

The image here is vividly reminiscent of the eschatological reality, in which man finds himself here and now (and will find himself) standing before God's judgment seat, engaged in a prayerful plea for mercy and salvation, bowing in worship before the Lord, and seeking forgiveness from both God and his fellow man. The Service of *Kairos* situates the celebrant outside of the confines of historical worship and elevates him to the eternal worship of the angelic host, making him a concelebrant of heavenly beings without necessarily becoming completely dislodged from his current human state of life.

Despite the affinity and codependence of both concepts of time and the capability of experiencing both within liturgical worship, the fact remains that *chronos*, as created time, will also have an end, only to be absorbed and replaced once and for all by *kairos*, which is God's ever-presence within the universe. Gregory of Nyssa makes this transient nature of earthly time abundantly clear when he writes:

> . . . (and) the temporal nature of time will cease, actions according to birth and corruption being no more; in any case, (time) will stand still, even the week which measures time, and that eighth (day) will succeed it, which is the following age becoming altogether one day, as one of the prophets says, calling it the 'great day', the life that is hoped for.[57]

ESCHATOLOGICAL ELEMENTS IN THE DIVINE LITURGY

The late Alexander Schmemann had indicated that the Divine Liturgy as celebrated in the Eastern Church is traditionally understood as a "downward movement"; in other words, the priest receives grace from on high and transmits it down to the people. This particularly Western perception of the priest as isolated minister rather than co-worshipper is countered with the view of the Liturgy as the whole Church's ascent toward heaven. The end and the fulfillment of the eucharistic synaxis "is found in the entrance of the Church into heaven, her fulfillment upon the table of Christ, in His kingdom."[58] This eschatological, upward movement is perhaps best expressed in the Presanctus prayer of the Byzantine Liturgy of Chrysostom: "You did not cease doing everything *until You led us (up) to heaven* and granted us Your kingdom to come" (. . . οὐκ ἀπέστης πάντα ποιῶν, ἕως ἡμᾶς εἰς τὸν οὐρανὸν ἀνήγαγες καὶ τὴν βασιλείαν σου ἐχαρίσω τὴν μέλλουσαν).[59] Chrysostom then does not so much view the eschatological reality as a metaphysical event dawning upon man, but rather envisions the Church as ascending into this ubiquitous reality that was conclusively established following its inception at Pentecost.

In the Divine Liturgy, the liturgical evidence that prefigures the final advent and the Church's provisional ascent into the eschatological Kingdom abounds. Certain liturgical actions and movements possess a distinctively eschatological character, discussed and identified as such by the Byzantine liturgical commentators. For example, Maximos the Confessor, like Symeon of Thessalonike, sees the greater part of the Liturgy, especially from the reading of the Gospel and Cherubic Hymn onward, as a pre-enactment of the final *Parousia* and the faithful's assumption into heaven.[60]

Eastern liturgical practices then are structured upon an eschatological model that pervades the entire eucharistic liturgy. One may cite several examples. For instance, the typical assembling of the faithful in the Divine Liturgy is reminiscent of the eschatological gathering of the nations before God for judgment (Matt 25:32ff). Before the altar-throne of God, not only is man's equality affirmed but his actions and intentions are fully exposed as well.

In addition, the assembly of faithful at each Eucharist recalls Christ's self-offering for the world, accomplished for the sake of bringing together the scattered children of God (John 11:52), a prophecy also expressed by Caiaphas the High Priest in John 11:51–52: ". . . he prophesied that Jesus should die for the nation, and not for the nation only, but to gather into one the children of God who are scattered abroad." Reunion and unity then are central themes in the Divine Liturgy, which point to their ultimate fulfillment in the *eschaton*. The *Didache* makes a virtually identical eschatological plea for unity: " . . . as this bread was scattered atop the mountains and when gathered together become one, so *let Your Church be gathered together from the ends of the earth into Your kingdom*" (. . . ὥσπερ ἦν τοῦτο τὸ κλάσμα διεσκορπισμένον ἐπάνω τῶν ὀρέων καὶ συναχθὲν ἐγένετο ἕν, οὕτω συναχθήτω σου ἡ ἐκκλησία ἀπὸ τῶν περάτων τῆς γῆς εἰς τὴν σὴν βασιλείαν).[61] The prothesis rite very clearly renders the entire Church present and is seen as the implementation of this eschatological reunion, rejoining the living and dead and bridging together the heavenly and earthly worlds into one.

Another example of a liturgical act that is founded upon an eschatological model is the Small Entrance, which precedes the reading of Scripture. Whereas a more historical interpretation of this original procession into the church proper saw it as the commencement of Christ's earthly ministry of teaching and healing, in an eschatological sense, the Church itself enters into the already established Kingdom in order to stand before God's presence and partake of the promised banquet (Luke 22:30). Unfortunately in modern practice, the redefinition of this entrance into a procession of the clergy with the Book of the Gospels from the altar to the solea obscures this meaning of the Church entering into the sublime eschatological mystery and rather suggests a more "incarnational" movement of the Son of God into the world.

During the Great Entrance as well as the holy anaphora, a historical rendering envisions Christ's entry into Jerusalem, as well as His ascent to the place of crucifixion, Golgotha, and His imminent death. A more eschatological perspective, however, sees both sections of the Liturgy as the community of faith's own translation into the Kingdom, as well as the transformation and perfection of man and nature, brought to fulfillment in the single most important sacrifice of Christ. From the bread and wine offering initiated at the table of oblation (προσφορά) to the offering up of the eucharistic gifts at the holy table (ἀναφορά), the Church enters into the eschatological mystery of God's eternal reign and achieves its eschatological fulfillment in the divine Eucharist.

The commemoration of names for the living and the dead, especially during the prothesis rite, Great Entrance, and the diptychs at the anaphoral intercessions, is yet another key eschatological feature of the Liturgy. The faithful Christian always seeks to be remembered by his Lord and especially at the consummation of the age (cf. Matt 25:34–40), when the final judgment and retribution will come to pass. Indeed, to have oneself exist in God's memory is truly to live in eternity, but to be forgotten by God for reasons of lack of faith or immoral living or impropriety means to enter into a state of oblivion and non-existence. Such a state of "conscious non-existence," so to speak, is understood in Eastern theology as the ultimate torment or hell since it intimates a complete separation from the divine life and its Source. The prayer uttered by clergy and laity alike—"Remember me (us), O Lord, when You come in Your kingdom" or "May the Lord God remember you in His kingdom"—serves as the eschatological plea of a desperate people fearful of losing the ultimate bliss of eternal life which they provisionally enjoy at every Eucharist.

The liturgical act familiarly known as the "kiss of peace" also possesses a key eschatological significance, in that it points to the obligatory reconciliation of all people with one another prior to their entrance into eternal life. Christ highlights the urgent need for mutual reconciliation and acceptance as a prerequisite for the Kingdom when He exhorts: "So if you are offering your gift at the altar, and there remember that your brother has something against you, leave your gift there before the altar and go; first be reconciled to your brother, and then come and offer your gift" (Matt 5:23–24). Along the same lines, Bishop Kallistos of Diokleia remarks: "Without such an exchange of forgiveness, there can be, in the true and deep sense, no full eucharistic celebration,"[62] since every Eucharist allows for a vision of, and a partial participation in, the *eschaton*.

Finally, the reception of Holy Communion, the culmination of the Church's upward pilgrimage into the eschatological reality, enables the Christian pilgrim to receive a foretaste of eternal life by entering into a very real and sacramental union with the risen Christ. This deifying union with God (θέωσις) of course presupposes the necessary passage through two foregoing stages: κάθαρσις (purification), achieved through repentance and reconciliation (as mentioned above), and φώτισις (illumination), achieved through faith in the Gospel proclaimed by the Son of God.

In the next chapter of this book, we shall embark upon the task of analyzing the themes of sacrifice and eschatology as they pertain specifically to the prothesis rite, using as our reference text the 2001 critically revised *Hieratikon*. The rite will be divided into three distinct segments, with each successive chapter corresponding to each division. The next chapter will deal specifically with the first part of the rite: the preparation of the Lamb.

NOTES

1. Jürgen Moltmann, *The Theology of Hope: On the Ground and Implications of a Christian Eschatology.*(New York, 1991), 16.

2. Karl Rahner, *Zur Theologie der Zukunft* (München, 1971), 43.

3. Geoffrey Wainwright, *Eucharist and Eschatology* (London, 1971), 147–51.

4. Ibid., 141–46.

5. Ibid., 151.

6. Martin Karrer, "Eschatology – NT", in *The Encyclopedia of Christianity*, eds. Erwin Fahlbusch et al. (Grand Rapids, 2001), 124–25.

7. Wainwright, 152.

8. Ibid., 154.

9. Ibid.

10. Ibid., 67.

11. As interpreted by Frank Moore Cross, Jr. in his study, *The Ancient Library of Qumran and Modern Biblical Studies* (Sheffield, 1995).

12. Gregory Dix, *The Shape of the Liturgy* (London, 1945), 130–31; and Hugh Wybrew, *The Orthodox Liturgy* (Crestwood, 1990), 44.

13. Origen, *On Prayer* 27, PG 11.505–21.

14. Cyril of Jerusalem, *Mystagogical Catecheses* V.15, PG 33.505A–524B.

15. Cf. Augustine, who despite his usage of the Latin *quotidianum* ("daily"), understood the eucharistic bread as "material" or "substantial" bread upon which the

Christian feeds when he listens to the preaching of the Gospel and lives the Christian life. See Augustine, *On the Lord's Sermon on the Mount* II.7, 27; PL 34.1280f.

16. St. John Chrysostom, *Homilies on the Gospel of Matthew* XIX.8; PG 57.280.

17. Wainwright, 31.

18. Ibid., 31–32.

19. Ibid., 32.

20. Ibid., 34.

21. Ibid., 104.

22. Ibid., 58.

23. Jerome, *Epistles* 120.2; PL 22.985f; Gregory Nazianzus, *Discourse on Holy Easter* 45.23; PG 36.653f; Cyril of Jerusalem, *Mystagogical Catecheses* IV.9; Theodore of Mopsuestia, who calls the Eucharist a "τύπος—of blessings to come": *Catechetical Homilies*, XII.5–7, XV, XVI, in *Les homélies catéchetiques de Théodore de Mopsueste. Reproduction phototypique du Ms. Mingana 571, traduction, introduction*, index. Séries 145, *Studi e Testi*, eds. R. Tonneau and R. Devreesse (Vatican City, 1949); Maximos the Confessor, *Mystagogia* 24; PG 91.704f); and John of Damascus, who sees the earthly altar as the "heavenly table" which connects both eucharistic celebrations: *On the Orthodox Faith* IV.13; PG 94.1136–53.

24. Irenaeus of Lyons, *Against Heresies* V, 33.1f., 36.3; PG 7.1212, 1224.

25. Ibid. IV, 18.5; PG 7.1027–29.

26. Augustine of Hippo, *Quaestiones Evangelorum* I, 43; PL 35.1331f.

27. Georgios D Metallinos, Ἡ θεολογική μαρτυρία τῆς ἐκκλησιαστικῆς λατρείας. [*The Theological Witness of Ecclesiastical Worship*], (Athens, 1995), 235–36.

28. Nicholas Cabasilas, *Explanation of the Divine Liturgy* 43; PG 150.461f.

29. Idem., *The Life in Christ*. trans. Carmino J. deCatanzaro (Crestwood, 1974), 147-48; 4.20; PG 150.625.

30. Idem., *Explanation of the Divine Liturgy* 46.3; PG 150.465. Translation mine.

31. Symeon of Thessalonike, *On the Sacred Liturgy* 94; PG 155.285AB.

32. Wainwright, 15.

33. Ibid., 90–91.

34. Cabasilas, *Explanation of the Divine Liturgy*; PG 150.368.

35. John of Damascus, *On the Orthodox Faith* IV.13; PG 94.1145f.

36. Plato, *Five Dialogues: Euthyphro, Apology, Crito, Meno, Phaedo*. trans. G.M.A. Grube (Indianapolis, 1981), 106–10.

37. Georgios Metallinos, Ἡ θεολογική μαρτυρία [*The Theological Witness*], 112. All translations hereafter from Fr. Metallinos' book are mine.

38. Ibid., Metallinos, 112–13.

39. *Thresholds of the Sacred: Architectural, Art Historical, Liturgical, and Theological Perspectives on Religious Screens, East and West*, ed. Sharon E.J. Gerstel (Washington, 2006), 2.

40. Ibid.

41. Ibid., 2–3.

42. See, e.g., Leonid Ouspensky, "The Problem of the Iconostasis," in *Saint Vladimir's Theological Quarterly*, vol. 8 (1964), 186–218. See also the studies by Roy A.

Rappaport, *Ecology, Meaning, and Religion* (Berkeley, 1979); and Mircea Eliade, *Das Heilige und das Profane* [*The Sacred and the Profane: The Nature of Religion*], trans. Willard R. Trask (San Diego, 1987).

43. Patricia M. Rumsey, "The Different Concepts of Sacred Time Underlying the Liturgy of the Hours," in *Worship,* vol. 78, no.4 (2004), 300–01.

44. See *A Patristic Greek Lexicon.* ed. G.W.H. Lampe (Oxford, 1961), 693.

45. Metallinos, 232.

46. John S. Romanides, Τὸ προπατορικὸν ἁμάρτημα [*Original Sin*], (Athens, 1957), 51.

47. Metallinos, 116.

48. Ibid.

49. Alkiviadis C. Calivas, Χρόνος τελέσεως τῆς Θείας Λειτουργίας. [*The Time of the Celebration of the Divine Liturgy*], (doctoral dissertation), (Thessalonike, 1982), 102. Translation mine.

50. Metallinos, 116.

51. Ibid., 117.

52. John Chrysostom, *Homily on the Gospel of Matthew* 50.3; PG 58.744.

53. Metallinos, 235.

54. Ibid., 122.

55. Ibid.

56. See Chapter One, 2–4 of this book.

57. St. Gregory of Nyssa, *Treatise on the Inscriptions of the Psalms*; PG 44.505A. Translation mine.

58. Alexander Schmemann, *The Eucharist: Sacrament of the Kingdom.* trans. Paul Kachur (Crestwood, 1987), 31.

59. *The Divine Liturgy of Saint John Chrysostom*, trans. Faculty of Hellenic College and Holy Cross Greek Orthodox School of Theology (Brookline, 1985), 20.

60. Maximos the Confessor, *Mystagogia*, 14–21; PG 91.692–97.

61. *Didache* 9.4. Emphases mine.

62. Bishop Kallistos Ware, "'It Is Time for the Lord to Act': The Divine Liturgy as Heaven on Earth", in *Sobornost*, vol. 23, no. 1 (2001), 11.

6

THE MYSTICAL PROTHESIS I: BLOODLESS
IMMOLATION OF THE LAMB

The overwhelming prevalence of both sacrificial and eschatological
themes in Eastern Christian theology and liturgical worship, in general, has been amply proven in the previous two chapters. Centuries of
mystagogical development in the Liturgy by the five great Byzantine commentators essentially followed parallel advancements in theological thought
in the East. The notion of Christ's sacrifice and its corresponding historical
and ethical ramifications (respectively, the bodily sacrifice of the first Christian martyrs and the spiritual sacrifice of Christ's followers to eschew the
worldly ways of evil and obey the Gospel) permeated the mindset of the
early Church and was expressed by the Fathers in their polemical theological discourses and commentaries on the Scriptures. Thus, for example, St.
Nicholas Cabasilas documents this connection between Christ's sacrifice
and those of His believers when he explains:

> But how did he, by inheritance, become Lord of our minds and wills?
> In this way: we subjected them to him . . . who was crucified and who
> rose from the dead; . . . we submitted our wills in giving him our love,
> accepting his rule, and taking his yoke upon our shoulders with joy.[1]

Assimilation with the sacrificed Lamb implied, for the early Christians, a
unity of purpose and a readiness to give of themselves unconditionally like
their prototype. Expressed in baptism, this integration into the new life in
Christ was sealed in various ways: first, by sacramental communion, and
finally, by inclusion on the liturgical paten as "co-sufferers" and "co-victors"
with Christ, to paraphrase the Pauline discourse on baptism in Romans
6:3–11.

In addition, the eschatological expectations shared by the earliest Christian communities, which redefined preexisting Judaic conceptions of the end times, likewise gave the Church a unique orientation and identity as Christ's own eschatological community of followers. And since the Church had always regarded the Divine Liturgy as the natural outgrowth of life itself, as the arena for the expression of one's beliefs and expectations, these themes of sacrifice and eschatology steadily made their way into the liturgical worship of the Church as well. Consequently, from as early as the Late Byzantine period, they constitute the bulk of the thematic content in the Eastern Church's celebration of the Eucharist.

The themes of Christ's sacrifice upon the Cross, together with the eschatological mystery of the "here and not yet" of God's rule in the risen Jesus, cannot be conceived as separate and unrelated entities, and nowhere is this more true than in Eastern liturgy. On the liturgical calendar, the divine economy of God's salvation is portrayed as a progressive series of interrelated events, or phases, each of which is immediately dependent upon the one or ones previous. However, each event, when relived as a liturgical feast of the Church, can also stand alone as a self-sustaining unit, complete with its own thematology that never once fails to connect the feast with the significance of God's overall economia. For example, the birth of Christ did not simply bring a transitory delight to the faithful as an isolated event in His human life, but rather a permanent joy in the knowledge that the Nativity was the first step in God's plan of salvation, which culminated at Golgotha and at the Empty Tomb. Hence, Christ's birth, death, and resurrection are intimately connected, since each event contains in itself the very purpose of the divine plan. This specific connection between the Nativity and the Passion are perhaps best expressed liturgically in a classification of hymns in the Byzantine tradition known as *Stavrotheotokia*.[2] This particular hymnography depicts the Virgin Mary, the source of Christ's human life, at the foot of the Cross, contemplating the mystery of her Son's death and, by extension, the mystery of His imminent resurrection and inauguration of the eschatological Kingdom.

Following the Ascension and Pentecost, the final events of the divine economy within human history, the institution of the Church finalizes the establishment of the eschatological age, which partially reveals the meta-historical reality of God's eternal reign within the limited confines of liturgical synaxis and worship. The Church, as the very embodiment of God's eschatological Kingdom on earth, draws its thematic content and its very raison d'être from the progression of Christological events that led to the birth of the Church, each of which advances the notion of the

Kingdom to come. Hence, for example, the birth of Christ led the way for his impending suffering and death, without which the post-Crucifixion events could never have occurred and without which the Church, the earthly portal to the heavenly Kingdom, could never have been brought into existence.

In the Byzantine prothesis rite, the elaborate arrangement of rubrics and prayers inspires an inherent mystagogical realism that harmoniously ties together both sacrificial and eschatological themes as rudimentary constituents of the divine economy. The initial section of the Byzantine prothesis rite encompasses the preparatory excision of the portion of the prosphora called the Lamb and the pouring of wine and water into the eucharistic chalice. These two practical acts elevate the as-of-yet unconsecrated eucharistic gifts to a level of prime distinction (without necessarily rendering them symbolic) by bestowing upon them a special identity: that of Christ Himself, who appears as the already (in the prothesis) and yet-to-be-sacrificed Lamb of God (in the Divine Liturgy), and who simultaneously is seated upon His celestial throne, encircled by His worshipping Church (Rev 5:1–14).

However, this new identity by which the ritualized gifts of bread and wine came to be reckoned was met historically with as much opposition as it was with espousal. Cabasilas, for example, leveled accusations at perpetrators who prostrated themselves before the gifts carried in procession during the Great Entrance. He argues: "The bread [of the prothesis] therefore remains bread and has received no more than a capacity to be offered to God. That is why it typifies the Lord's body. . . ."[3] On the other hand, St. Symeon of Thessalonike opposed his predecessor's view, claiming that the unconsecrated gifts are worthy of veneration "since they are already images [he uses the Basilian term ἀντίτυπα]of the Body and Blood of Christ, comparable to, though greater than, icons."[4] For Symeon, even the holy vessels are worthy of veneration because they "all partake of sanctification, the holy gifts being offered in sacrifice in them."[5]

Thus, the established Byzantine practice of honoring the gifts from the moment of their preparation in the prothesis until their consumption at the conclusion of the Liturgy closely follows the rationale employed by Symeon, namely, that they are already "antitypes" of Christ's Body and Blood and have been designated to become such following their consecration. Rather than yielding to the temptation of "quantitatively" justifying the presence of God in the gifts both before and after the consecration, the Church, observing its eschatological orientation, instead utilizes the tool of liturgical mystagogy to suspend time and identify the gifts as forever imbued with the sanctifying presence of the risen Lord. This sublime presence is "shown forth" (to use St. Basil's expression) during the anaphoral consecration.⁶

THE RITES OF CLERICAL PREPARATION

Service of *Kairos*⁷

Several Medieval codices, such as the fourteenth-century liturgical order *Panteleimon Codex 6277–770*, dictate that the celebrant clergy must first reconcile with their fellow Christians (ὀφείλει προηγουμένως μὲν κατηλλαγμένος εἶναι μετὰ πάντων)⁸ and not have anything against anyone (καὶ μὴ ἔχειν κατά τινος),⁹ shielding their heart from evil thoughts (καὶ τὴν καρδίαν ὅση δύναμις ἀπὸ πονηρῶν τηρῆσαι λογισμῶν)¹⁰ and keeping abstinence and vigilance until the time of the holy service (ἐγκρατεύεσθαί τε μικρὸν ἀφ' ἑσπέρας καὶ ἐγρηγορέναι μέχρι τοῦ τῆς ἱερουργίας καιροῦ).¹¹ Such exhortations, though not delineated specifically in the critical edition of our prothesis text, are implied. With a clean conscience then, the clergy proceed into the church, make a prostration before the episcopal throne, and stand before the central doors of the icon screen to offer prayers for their own worthiness before undertaking the holy work of the eucharistic liturgy.

The prostration, Symeon remarks, is as much a visible sign of the clergy's plea for forgiveness as it is an indication of their love for God, "for it is necessary to offer prayer before the divine works, and to ask for forgiveness" (δεῖ γὰρ εὐχὴν προηγεῖσθαι τῶν θείων ἔργων, καὶ αἰτεῖσθαι συγχώρησιν).¹² Symeon further says that by prostrating himself before the altar table, the priest "shows his love toward God and (his) union, and that he is sanctified from the altar" (δεικνὺς τὴν πρὸς Θεὸν ἀγάπην αὐτοῦ καὶ τὴν ἔνωσιν, καὶ ὅτι ἀπὸ τοῦ θυσιαστηρίου ἡγίασται).¹³ Contrary to Cabasilas, Symeon understands prostrating oneself before the table of oblation as not a veneration of those sites where the divine economy was enacted, but as the moral initiative of the celebrant clergy to repentance as they enter into the eschatological *kairos* of God's service. This veneration, for Symeon, may also be regarded, albeit arguably, as the appropriate way to "greet" God before embarking on the formal ceremonial (. . . προσκυνήσας τρὶς τῷ Θεῷ, ποιεῖται εὐλογητόν).¹⁴ The clergy then enter into the *kairos* of God, the eschatological reality of the Kingdom invisibly here and yet to come, and proceed to put on the liturgical vestments of their respective offices.

Symeon's insistence on the need for personal reconciliation among clergy (he deliberately brings up the binary unit εὐλογία-συγχώρησις three times in Chapter 83 of *De Sacra Liturgia*) seems to coincide with the architectural and iconographic developments of the Late Byzantine period, in which artistic programs particularly on the inside of sanctuary screens and apses intended to evoke a sense of piety and moral responsibility among the celebrants, "in a period when priests were routinely blamed for their inability to behave in a manner befitting their profession."[15] Sharon Gerstel identifies two specific iconographic motifs that convey this responsibility for clergy to live up to their moral obligations and to receive the Eucharist worthily: (1) a Late Byzantine scene of the Final Judgment that depicts the punishment for priestly infractions; and (2) the medieval depiction of the apostolic communion (from as early as the sixth century), in which Christ appears twice in the same image, standing before a canopied and columned altar and distributing the holy bread to six of the disciples approaching reverently on one side (ἡ ἱερὰ μετάδοσις) and communing the other six with the chalice who approach on the alternate side (ἡ ἱερὰ μετάληψις). (In the church of St. John the Theologian in Veroia, this apostolic procession to communion is momentarily halted by the conciliatory embrace of two of the apostles.) The second icon resourcefully renders a pictorial exegesis of the Liturgy by joining the historical event of the Last Supper to the medieval ceremonial familiar to everyone.[16]

For Symeon, maintaining the proper solemnity and decorum in the Divine Liturgy was highly contingent upon the proper moral demeanor of the bishop, priest, and deacon before God and the watchful eye of the congregation. If, for example, an unrepentant celebrant remained engrossed in sin, not only would the Eucharist not benefit him (though its validity would remain intact), but it would also scandalize the congregants who would want to see in the priest something more than a mere liturgical functionary. Thus Symeon, always the concerned pastor and staunch advocate for proper liturgical order, understands liturgical *taxis* in a truly holistic manner: unless the priest has his own soul in order, his service to God will likewise lack the full potential to transform him and the faithful entrusted to his spiritual care. The rite of *kairos* and the iconography within the altar are coalesced in such a carefully thought-out manner so as to arrive at this "internal order," inducing repentance in the celebrants and setting in them a rightful mindset that will assist them in the proper execution of their liturgical service. And this "arrival" at a proper spiritual disposition via participation in the *kairos* rite can be characterized in terms of a spatial crossing from the profane world of the nave into the sacred realm represented by the sanctuary. Gerstel writes:

> For, in stepping through the wall and across the sacred boundary, the
> priest undertook his own passage from "unworthy servant" to ordained

celebrant, elevating himself above the plane of his profane experience, a passage that was accompanied by specific prayers and changes in wardrobe. The rite of spatial passage, in other words, became a rite of spiritual passage.[17]

This particular stance by Symeon regarding clergy, however, poses a problem when one considers to what degree the iconographic programs on icon screens prepare the laity for their own co-celebration of the Eucharist and their reception of Holy Communion. Research has suggested that the decline in lay communion in the East through the later Byzantine centuries[18] was arguably further exacerbated by iconographic programs in murals on the inside of churches and sanctuary screens, which apparently served to evoke among lay worshippers distanced physically from visual contact with the eucharistic ritual, a sense of devotional piety and cultic attraction to a saint. This notion, in addition to the lack of a formal preparatory *kairos* for the laity, implies an exclusivity to communion, reserved only for the ordained clergy and reinforces a sense of disunity within the liturgical gathering, even in modern practice, as church attendance often possesses different notions for different people. Nevertheless, lay preparation before communion, though perhaps not as formalized as that for clergy in the Byzantine tradition, cannot be viewed as optional. It is incomprehensible how Symeon, despite his silence on the communion of the laity (his liturgical discourses are addressed to the clergy), or any eucharistically-minded Eastern Church Father for that matter, would have accepted icon veneration as a substitution for communion. The corpus of private liturgical prayers for communion, together with the renowned iconographic programs in the sanctuary of the Church of Peribleptos at Mystra,[19] and the various post-sixth century renderings of the apostolic communion mentioned above, which served "as a visual prototype for their [the laity's] own communion and that of the clergy,"[20] clearly indicate the universality of communion for all Christians of orthodox belief who have adequately prepared themselves. In this regard, genuine repentance and entrance into divine *kairos* is expected of all worshippers, clerical and lay alike, although the outward methods and moments of participation may differ.

The Vesting and Washing of the Hands[21]

The liturgical vestments themselves are significant not only of each celebrant's clerical rank, but also adorn in remarkable apparel and glory the chosen earthly ministers who will stand around the eternal throne of the sacrificed Lamb of God. In Revelation 4:4, the twenty-four elders (πρεσβύτεροι), presumably angelic beings representing the twelve Patriarchs of Israel and the twelve Apostles, or, respectively, the Old and New Testament priesthoods, are depicted "clad in white garments, with golden crowns upon their heads," each sitting upon a throne and encircling the more majestic Throne in their midst. The image is reminiscent of the Byzantine *synthronon*, in which the bishop, as the icon of Christ, sits upon a central throne in the sanctuary, flanked by his presbyterate. In time, all the clergy ultimately enclose the altar table, which represents God's mystical throne. The liturgical vestments then are visible, external proof of an invisible, internal reality, that the Church on earth has departed from a profane mode of life and has ushered its faithful into a new mode of existence, whose main activity is the worship and praise of the sacrificed yet eternal Lamb of God.

Cabasilas' general silence on this service of clerical preparation does not eclipse its central importance for the celebrant preparing to conduct the prothesis rite, nor can the service of *kairos* be dismissed as a mere addendum to an otherwise independent series of mini-rites that "must occur" before one enters the eucharistic liturgy. He does, however, offer a fleeting remark on the action of vesting, regarding the clerical vestments as possessing a practical purpose, serving outwardly as distinguishing clothing for the ordained ministers of the Church. By the same token though, they function to raise the conscience of the worshipper to virtuous living, as well as to sanctify those who execute the divine services and those for whom they are conducted.[22]

Symeon of Thessalonike, quite the contrary, dedicates a good portion of his commentary to the mystagogical significance of the holy vestments worn by both bishops and priests, as well as the corresponding prayers recited by the clergy during vesting.[23] He concentrates on the spiritual state of the priests and deacons and regards the actual vesting of all orders of the clergy as an actual vesting in the incarnate Lord's humility. He states:

> ... καὶ ἀρχιερεῖς καὶ ἱερεῖς εἰσί τε καὶ κληρικοί, καὶ τῆς εὐλογίας μετέχουσι, καὶ τὴν ταπείνωσιν ἀποσῴζουσι καὶ τὴν τάξιν· καὶ ὅτι προσέρχονται τῷ Θεῷ μετ' εὐλογίας καὶ συγχωρήσεως· καὶ μετ' ὑποταγῆς τε καὶ εἰρήνης τὸ τῆς διακονίας ἐκτελέσαι ἕκαστος ἔρχεται.
>
> ... and both bishops and priests are clergy, and they participate in the blessing [of the bishop who ordained them], and they are girded with humility and their rank; and they approach God with a blessing and forgiveness; and each one comes forth both submissively and peacefully to execute the service.[24]

In his *Commentary on the Divine Liturgy*, Cabasilas prefaces his explanation of the prothesis rite by establishing its relationship to the rest of the eucharistic celebration. His method employs the use of a parable that is, for all intents and purposes, highly eschatological. The prothesis is a preliminary act of preparation by the Church that follows the sowing of the seed by Christ. The cultivation of the soil will then yield in due time the proper fruit expected of the seed. He writes:

> A sower went forth . . . 'to sow'—not to plough the earth, but to sow: thus showing that the work of preparation must be done by us. Therefore, since in order to obtain the effects of the divine mysteries we must approach them in a state of grace and properly prepared, it was necessary that these preparations should find a place in the order of the sacred rite.[25]

In this example from Christ's parable of the sower (Matt 13:3–23), the act of preparation falls back on the past for its content but simultaneously looks forward to the historical future, when the eucharistic benefits will be reaped in part during the Liturgy, as well as to the eschatological future, when the inheritance of the Kingdom of God will be achieved in its fullness.

A final preparatory rubric for the clergy that precedes the prothesis ritual is the ceremonial washing of the hands, accompanied by Psalm 26:6–12, which connects the need for external and internal purification with the service of God's holy altar. Research indicates that this ceremonial washing is absent from the *Barberini 336* Codex (eighth–ninth century), as well as from the Codex of the *National Library 662* (twelfth–thirteenth century) and *Panteleimon 6277–770* (fourteenth century). Neither Cabasilas nor Symeon make any reference to it, which in all likelihood appears that it was inserted much later, as Brightman's nineteenth-century modern text of the prothesis and Liturgy of St. John Chrysostom affirms.[26] The absence then of any particular witness to this preparatory *lavabo* makes it difficult to surmise its mystagogical significance, except to verify its value for purposes of hygiene, and to connect it surely with Old Testament and inter-Testamental ritual washings prior to one's reception of a blessing or commencement of a holy work—religious acts common among Jews and other religious groups in the Middle East.[27]

Having thus entered into eschatological time and having donned the proper clothing characteristic of God's Kingdom, the priest and deacon proceed to relive the divine *economia* of God's love: they position themselves before the holy table of oblation in order to reenact the first major rubric of the prothesis rite, namely, the immolation of the sacrificial Lamb.

Preparation of the Precious Gifts I— The Immolation of the Lamb[28]

After these, coming to the Prothesis they make three venerations saying:

O God, be gracious to me the sinner and have mercy on me.

Then the deacon says: Bless, master.

And the priest: Blessed is our God always . . .

And taking the prosphora he lifts it with the lance saying:

You have purchased us from the curse of the law by your precious blood; nailed to the cross and pierced by the lance, you have made immortality gush forth for men. O our Savior, glory to you.

The Opening Blessing and the Sacrificial Troparion (Ἐξηγόρασας ἡμᾶς)

The table of oblation is perceived as the historical setting where the Lord not only began and ended His human life but also initiated and fulfilled the divine plan of *economia*, thus earning this momentary display of veneration by the celebrant clergy. Cabasilas alludes in an indirect way to the dual historical significance of the table of oblation as Bethlehem and Golgotha by writing:

> As long as it remains in the prothesis the bread thus separated from the rest is still only bread. But it has acquired a new characteristic – it is dedicated to God; it has become an offering, since it represents our Lord during the first phase of his life on earth, when he became an oblation. Now this happened at the moment of his birth, as has been said, for, as the first-born, he was offered up from birth, in accordance with the Law. But the pains which Christ endured afterwards for our salvation, His Cross and Death, had been symbolized beforehand in the Old Testament. That is why the priest marks the loaf with these symbols before carrying it to the altar and sacrificing it.[29]

The bread offering then is identified with Christ, who offered Himself from the very beginning of His life and brought this self-sacrifice to its fruition at Calvary.

The opening blessing simply assures that the preparatory acts that follow are not simply practical in nature, but highly mystagogical and representative of Christ's own sacrifice. Hence, the acts are contextualized and formalized in the prothesis ceremonial.

Another significant rubric involves the recitation in modern euchologia of the well-known dismissal hymn sung during Holy Friday matins, "You have purchased us" (Ἐξηγόρασας ἡμᾶς), noteworthy because of its sacrificial content. Neither Cabasilas nor Symeon mention it in their commentaries, and the fourteenth-century diataxis of Philotheos Kokkinos (*Codex Panteleimon 770*) only offers a suggestion regarding its use.[30] Nevertheless, its insertion at this juncture of the rite indicates an obvious attempt towards identifying the predominance of the sacrificial notion by way of preface. Clearly taking its content from the Pauline notion of "being bought" from death through the sacrifice of Christ (1 Cor 6:20, 7:23), the hymn points out that the gift of freedom from sin bestowed upon man was purchased at the expense of Christ shedding His own blood. Cabasilas implies that the reenactment of the Passion by marking the Lamb with the emblems of suffering and sacrifice helps man not only to define his emancipation in terms of an uneven exchange or transaction but also, in light of this, to move him to a deeper sense of contrition and closeness to God. He explains:

> The aim of setting all this before us is to influence our souls the more easily thereby (ἵν' ἐκείνῳ μὲν εἰς τὰς ψυχὰς εὐκολώτερον δράσῃ); not merely to offer us a simple picture but to create in us a feeling (ἀλλὰ καὶ πάθος ἡμῖν ἐντεθῇ); for the very good reason that an idea is more deeply impressed upon us if we can see it depicted.[31]

The selection of this hymn as a prelude to the ceremonial immolation of the Lamb emphasizes the permanent abolition by Christ of the Judaic sacerdotal practice of offering up to God periodic sacrifices for one's own sins and the sins of the people (cf. Heb 5:1–3). Christ's self-sacrifice upon the Cross, seen as far more valuable and effectual before God than the animal sacrifices performed by mortals, is relived at each Divine Liturgy and offers a permanent beneficence to the faithful Christian. Whereas the nature of the sacrifice in the Old Testament was considered inadequate and limited in its capacity to achieve full reconciliation with God, insofar as it was offered by fallen man, it had to be repeated. On the contrary, Christ's perfect self-offering, offered just once (cf. Rom 6:10), erased the debt of sin separating man from God since the Fall and required no repetition, except on man's part. In other words, through each celebration of the Divine Liturgy, man receives constant access to the benefits that flow from the one-time (ἐφάπαξ) sacrifice of Christ.

> *Then he seals [crosses] the prosphora three times with the lance saying at each sealing:*
>
> In remembrance of our Lord and God and Savior Jesus Christ.

The deacon: Always, now and forever and to the ages of ages. Amen.

The Sealing and the Significance of Anamnesis

The celebrant first proceeds to "seal" the bread with the lance, invoking upon it the Name of Jesus Christ, in whose remembrance the offering is made. The act of "sealing" the prosphora by marking it with the sign of the cross is equivalent to a preliminary setting aside of the bread and assigning to it a new identity as "depicting the saving passion of Christ" (τὸ σωτήριον πάθος ἐξεικονίζων Χριστοῦ).[32] The expression εἰς ἀνάμνησιν cannot fairly be translated as simply "in memory" (εἰς μνήμην), which typically connotes a sense of past, or historical, remembrance of someone or something absent. The term, rather, biblically signifies a "'re-calling' or 're-presenting' of a past event involving the providence of God toward mankind, so that it becomes *here and now operative by its effects.*"[33] Similarly, the original Greek texts for the dominical Words of Institution (Luke 22:19; 1 Cor 11:24, 25) make use of the same word ἀνάμνησις to express precisely the identical notion of participation in an economical event initiated in the past but with spiritual benefits that remain effectual *ad infinitum*. The term itself certainly broadens the true implication of liturgical mystagogy, in which the parameters of time and space are suspended so that the Church may enter into and participate in the mystery of Christ's once-for-all but eternal self-offering. Hence, Christ's command to His disciples was not one in which he exhorted them to commit to memory a series of past words and actions, but instead to relive the timeless nature of the eucharistic sacrifice, validated by and perpetuated after His own suffering and triumph over death.

Cabasilas indicates that the Church acts out of obedience to its Lord[34] when it performs the sacred acts of the prothesis in His remembrance, without which the eucharistic liturgy cannot soon after be conducted. Hence, the priest "begins [the entire Divine Liturgy] with this commemoration and ends with it."[35] In this sense, the whole span of the eucharistic celebration, from the prothesis to the final dismissal of the worshippers, is a virtual reliving of the divine economy, from its historical inception to its eschatological fulfillment.

Cabasilas is careful to specify that what is commemorated in the prothesis is not the earlier life of Christ, such as His teachings and miracles, but rather the events surrounding His passion. "Rather, we must remember those events which seem to denote nothing but weakness: his Cross, his Passion, his Death—these are the happenings which he asks us to commemorate."[36] As Cabasilas soon after explains, "he did not refer his disciples to his miracles, saying, 'I raised the dead' or 'I healed lepers', but he spoke only of his Passion and Death, saying, 'Which is broken for you'; 'which is shed for you.'"[37] Also, Christ's passion was seen as the determining factor for man's salvation, whereas the miracles wrought during His life were of secondary importance[38] and constituted, according to the Johannine evangelical tradition, the σημεῖα, or signs, which gradually lead one to a deeper understanding of the divine economy fulfilled at Golgotha. In fact, Cabasilas calls the miracles "corroborative" (ἀποδεικτικά), "that men might have faith in Jesus as the true Saviour" and the events surrounding the Passion as "more necessary" (ἀναγκαιότερα) for the general salvation of man rather than the miracles performed on individual recipients.

Interestingly, however, in his interpretation of the Divine Liturgy as a whole, Cabasilas interprets the earlier part of the Liturgy as corresponding to the prophetic utterings announcing the advent of Christ, as well as Christ's earlier life before His final journey to Jerusalem. This is especially evident in Chapter 11 of his *Commentary*, in which Cabasilas regards the Old Testament and Christ's hidden life, prior to His public ministry and saving Passion, as a period concealing the divine will: "Thus the power of the Incarnate God was veiled up to the time of his miracles and the witness from heaven."[39]

> *Consequently, the priest inserts the lance into the right side of the seal, where the IC [portion] is, and cutting he says:*
>
> As a sheep he was led to the slaughter.
>
> *And into the left, where the XC [portion] is:*
>
> And as a blameless lamb before its shearer (is) silent, so he also opens not his mouth.
>
> *Into the top section:*
>
> In his humility his judgment was taken away.
>
> *Into the bottom section:*
>
> Who shall tell of his generation?
>
> *The deacon:* Lift up, master.
>
> *And the priest lifts up the Lamb with the lance saying:*
>
> For his life is lifted up from the earth.

The Four Incisions and Extraction of the Lamb

The next solid indication of the sacrificial nature of the rite involves the ceremonial cutting of the Lamb on all four sides with the lance, the purpose of which is the practical excision of the portion from the rest of the loaf. This first phase of the ritualization of the Lamb is absent in *Codex Barberini 336*, as well as from other *euchologia* and liturgical manuscripts dating from the tenth to the twelfth century, although other sources, such as the well-known ninth century Latin version of St. Germanos of Constantinople's *Ecclesiastical History* by Anastasios the Librarian, explicitly mention the rubric with the corresponding prophetic verses. Thomas Pott is probably correct in explaining this fluctuation between texts as an indication of the resistance exerted by some in the Church to formalize an otherwise practical act of preparing the eucharistic gifts for the Divine Liturgy, a service reserved specifically for the deacon from antiquity. The eventual surrender of the prothesis rite to the presidency of the priest, with the deacon relegated to the lesser role of "ritual assistant," helped to complete its formalization as an independent and highly symbolical (mystagogical) liturgy in itself. He also indicates that several *euchologia* from the periods mentioned were intended for usage by hierarchs who traditionally did not participate in the prothesis rite anyway.[40]

Each individual liturgical action is assigned a mystagogical significance, accompanied by the recitation of a verse from the Messianic chapter 53, verses 7–8 of the Book of Isaiah. Cabasilas states: "As the priest thrusts the lance into the loaf several times in making the incisions, so also he divides the words of the Prophet into a corresponding number of sections, combining the different parts with the several strokes of the lance, to show that the action is an application of the word."[41] He adds that the prophetic writings accompany a rite that consists of "ceremonies which symbolize the Cross and Death of Christ."[42] Symeon also explains that the "second among priests [in seniority]" (τῶν ἱερέων ὁ δεύτερος)[43] undertakes the responsibility of overseeing the prothesis rite, precisely because he takes on the prophetic role of announcing the sacrifice of the Lamb of God that will be fulfilled in the Divine Liturgy, as did Isaiah and, most especially, John the Baptist. Thus, the second-ranking priest

> conducts the introduction to the holy work [liturgy] and so is like the one who has the secondary responsibility behind the first [priest] (καὶ ὡς τὰ δευτεραῖα τοῦ πρώτου ἔχων ἐστιν), that is, to speak of the typical mysteries and things and preachings revealed by the prophets, from Isaiah and the rest, for in the prothesis he speaks about the slaughter and the

death of Christ, and in preparing the gifts [he imitates] the Baptist in
everything, until the Lord came. For the Baptist, by baptizing, taught
about Christ, and he preached about Him, and he served as His servant, and in such a manner the second among the priests serves.[44]

In his explanation, Symeon establishes the prothesis as the προοίμια τῆς
ἱερουργίας and attaches to it a preparatory character within the context of
the Messianic prophecy. The prophetic utterings are themselves part and
parcel of the divine *economia*, announcing the sacrifice that will be accomplished during the Eucharist. Hence, the performance of this rubrical excision and the executor himself together constitute a prophetic unit which
announces the advent of Christ and His imminent sacrifice in the Divine
Liturgy.

The announcement of Christ's sacrifice is enacted visually by the actual
liturgical incision of the Lamb with the lance and its removal from the rest
of the prosphora. Symeon himself indicates that this excised portion of the
loaf, upon which is imprinted the insignia of Jesus Christ the Victor [ICXC
/ NIKA], must also bear the emblems of His suffering if it is truly to be an
image of the Savior (. . . τὸ σωτήριον πάθος ἐξεικονίζων Χριστοῦ; . . . representing the salvific passion of Christ).[45] Even the very separation of the Lamb
from its loaf and its apparent distinction from the other particles upon the
paten affirms Symeon's claim that only the Lamb is consecrated during the
Liturgy (and no other loaf or particle), because it is only the Lamb of God
that was sacrificed for the entire creation. The Archbishop of Thessalonike
states:

> Do you understand that the particles stand for the saints? And [they
> are offered] in their memory and honor, and through them for our sal-
> vation. For they too participate in this terrible mystery as co-sufferers
> of Christ. . . . Except that the particles are not changed into the Body
> of the Master, or into the bodies of the saints; instead they are only
> gifts and offerings and sacrifices through the bread in imitation of the
> Master.[46]

Symeon's concept of realism that begins in the prothesis rite is trans-
mitted through to the anaphora: the Lamb whose sacrifice is announced at
the prothesis is the same Lamb who consecrates Himself in the Divine Liturgy and thus has the capacity to heal and save. The other particles for the
saintly and angelic orders, though witnesses and participants in the divine
economy, are not themselves the source of sanctification and hence ought
not to be used to commune the people. Otherwise, the act of communion
is reduced, theoretically, to a mere hierarchical participation in the energies

of God (no different than receiving a blessing) and not a true ingesting of the only true Savior, Christ the Lamb of God. For Symeon, consecration is the fulfillment of the sacrifice that has been foretold in visual form in the prothesis and the impetus that releases the spiritual benefits that proceed from it.

Symeon's directive is backed by his own exegesis of how the saints function in the whole process of sanctification via the Pseudo-Dionysian hierarchical configuration. The saints operate as "liturgical mediators," receiving first their own sanctification directly from God and then transmitting it to the faithful in worship. This sanctification occurs by virtue of their "participation" in the Lamb's sacrifice, indicated by their proximity to the sacrificial Lamb on the paten. Symeon, in characteristic form, strings along prototype, antitype, and recipient of grace in one successive progression. He extends his exegesis on the role of the particles for the saints:

> . . . and they [the particles for the saints] are offered in His Name, and through the celebration of the mysteries, by both union and communion they are sanctified, and to those whom they are [represent], they transmit sanctification, and through those [particles] for the saints [they likewise sanctify] to us; . . . On the one hand, they are immediately sanctified by God; on the other, by receiving our offerings they sanctify us through them.[47]

This hierarchical procession is further reinforced by the visible arrangement of the particles upon the *diskos*, in which the particles for the saints are situated next to the Lamb while those for the living and dead are directly below the Lamb.

Nevertheless, the very arrangement of the particles around the Lamb, and their intermediary role in conveying sanctification, raise some serious questions. For example, since the reception of the Eucharist implies direct communion with Christ himself, in what sense is the "third-party sanctification" via the saints effectual or even necessary? Could the decline in lay communion in Late Byzantium have led Symeon to suggest the possibility of yet another "secondary blessing" of sorts for those who did not commune? Already in Byzantine liturgical practice, the prayer of the bowing of the head following the Lord's Prayer suggests such a blessing, as does the distribution of the blessed antidoron at the conclusion of the Divine Liturgy. Furthermore, how could one legitimize such a suggestion to a mainly clerical audience (his own priests!), whom the Archbishop would nevertheless have expected to be Eucharist-focused like himself and to teach their flocks accordingly? Finally, along much broader lines, could the Dionysian hierarchical model in Symeon's mystagogy be alleged as counterproductive or even detrimental to frequent communion, appearing as a kind of "substitute" for the latter? Such questions, though outside of the immediate scope of this book, invite further study.

Likewise, Cabasilas undeniably maintains the centrality of the sacrificed Lamb, though he refrains from comment upon the role of the saints like his contemporary. "But it is Christ himself, in his capacity as priest, who set apart the Body of the Lord, offered it up, took it to himself and consecrated it to God, and who sacrificed it. It is the Son of God in person who separated himself from the mass of humankind; it is he who has offered himself to God."[48]

The very act of marking the Lamb with the emblems of sacrifice finds several precedents in antiquity. Cabasilas notes, "This practice of demonstrating, exhorting or prophesying by means of actions is very ancient,"[49] as witnessed by the several accounts quoted by the commentator of men who acted out what they wished to convey or explain. "In the same way," Cabasilas continues, "the priest expresses in words or represents by his gestures all that he knows of the solemn sacrifice, as far as he can with the means at his disposal."[50] The pronouncement of the imminent sacrificial act then, which begins at the prothesis, demands by necessity the participation of the clergy as heralds of this central event of the divine economy, expressed through the media of "types and figures" ($τύποι καὶ γραφαί$).[51] The gifts "both become antitypes of the [Christ's] all-holy Body and Blood" ($ἀντίτυπα γεγονότα τοῦ παναγίου σώματός τε καὶ αἵματος$),[52] by virtue of their ritualized preparation, assuming from the very beginning the potential to inevitably become that for which they have been prepared. Likewise, the Messianic prophecies regarding Christ set the stage for His first appearance in the world, and His very suffering and death bring to completion the divine plan initially begun in His teaching and healing ministry on earth.

The verses from Isaiah 53:7–8 that refer to the sacrifice of the Christ belong to a lengthier passage, which in turn makes up the second chapter of the Messianic couplet (chapters 52 and 53). The biblical verses that correspond to the prothesis rite are italicized:

> And he, because of his affliction, opens not his mouth: *as a sheep he was led to the slaughter, and as a lamb before its shearer is silent, so he also opens not his mouth. In his humiliation his judgment was taken away:* who shall tell of his generation? For his life is lifted up from the earth: because of the iniquities of my people he was led to death. And I will give the wicked for his burial, and the rich for his death; for he practiced no iniquity, nor craft with his mouth (Isa 53.7-9).

Isaiah introduces the Messiah very simply as God's "servant" (Isa 52:13) and proceeds to formulate a description of a physically-afflicted and suffering Messiah:

> As many shall be amazed at thee, so shall thy face be without glory from men, and thy glory shall not be honored by the sons of men . . . We brought a report as of a child before him; he is as a root in a thirsty land: he has no form nor comeliness; and we saw him, but he had no form nor beauty (Isa 52:14; 53:2).

This unique physical characterization of God's Suffering Servant then leads the prophet to offer a description of the distinct mission set before Him, that is, to bear man's griefs and sorrows (Isa 53:4), to be smitten by God and afflicted (Isa 53:4), to be wounded for man's sins and bruised for his iniquities (Isa 53:5), and to take upon Himself the iniquities of all men (Isa 53:6). Mankind's negative response to God's Servant is articulated by the prophet: "But his form was ignoble, and inferior to that of the children of men; he was a man in suffering, and acquainted with the bearing of sickness, for his face is turned from us: he was dishonored, and not esteemed." (Isa 53:3)

In painting this forlorn portrait of the Messiah, Isaiah impressively emphasizes the transcendent moral character of Christ and His exclusive distinction as the sacrificed Lamb. In His perfect innocence, His physical suffering, and His mission to bear the sins and imperfections of the world, Christ is distinguished for all these features and stands far apart from the rest of the human race, all of which are illustrated via the removal of the Lamb from the loaf representing humanity. Cabasilas summarizes: "In the same way that this bread has been separated from other and similar loaves in order that it may be consecrated to God and used in the Holy Sacrifice, so the Lord was set apart from the mass of mankind, whose nature his love had brought him to share."[53]

The symbolism of the leavened loaf as a figure of humanity, from which the Lamb is excised, provides further insight into the meaning of sacrifice as a voluntary but permanent removal from the fallen nature of man, of whom Christ is the primary model for the Church. The subsequent removal from other loaves of the remaining particles for the orders of saints, as well as for the living and deceased, is not coincidental but rather asserts quite clearly that the eschatological Church's membership consists of a humanity that has been (and is expected to become!) transformed through their own voluntary sacrifice after the example of their archetype. In the person of Christ, the dominical words from Leviticus 19:2 resonate in human form for those called to follow Him: "You shall be holy; for I the Lord your God *am* holy." Interestingly, St. Basil of Caesarea, in his not well-known but recently-proven authentic treatise *On Baptism*,[54] implicates how in imitation of Christ, a Christian's moral death to worldly ways all too frequently terminates in his own martyrdom: "To be crucified . . . is to be estranged or set apart (ἀλλοτριοῦν) from those who live according to the 'old man' (Rom 6:6). One who is crucified with Christ is then set apart from all who live according to this world." [55]

This moral dimension of sacrifice, understood as separation from the sinful human condition, interestingly contrasts with a second kind of separation from human biological life, whose final intention is the reunion of all creation with God. Jesus' manhood derives from his human origin as the incarnate Logos of God (the Lamb is part and parcel of the loaf from which it is extracted), but His divinity leads Him to fulfill the very purpose for which He became human; that is, to separate himself from the world (cf. Isa 52:11; Ezek 20:34, 41; 2 Cor 6:17), albeit temporarily, in order to once again draw the world to Himself (cf. John 12:32–33). The applicable Johannine text not only establishes Christ's transitory absence in death as a prerequisite for the final restoration of union between God and man, but also indicates the method of His sacrifice. It would seem then that the preparation of the Lamb in the prothesis niche follows the aforementioned biblical texts well: the rite links Christ's moral distinction among humans, as foretold by the prophecy of Isaiah, with His unique death on the cross, as foretold by Jesus Himself in John's gospel. For the Church then, the notion of sacrifice demands one's rejection of "worldly ways," which often leads to suffering and death, but it also anticipates that the fruits of sacrifice will culminate in the reestablishment of unity between mankind with God.

The Inversion and Crosswise Incision of the Lamb

And he places it upside down on the paten.

The deacon: Sacrifice, master.

The priest slices it, making a deep incision crosswise with the lance and saying:

The Lamb of God, who takes away the sin of the world, is sacrificed for the life and salvation of the world.

And he turns the other part upward, that is, the one having the seal.

In the next phase of the Lamb's immolation, after the eucharistic Lamb is physically removed from its prosphora, it is placed upside down upon the paten, an act possessing both a practical and symbolic purpose. On the one hand, the rubric intentionally helps to prevent condensation from gathering on the bread, which could then possibly oxidize the metallic paten or cause mold to begin forming upon the bread. In addition, the inversion of the Lamb allows the priest to make the appropriate subsequent crosswise incisions on the soft part of the bread without affecting the seal.

On the mystagogical level, however, the vision of the Lamb turned upside down indicates the extreme humility experienced by Isaiah's Suffering Servant Messiah. The inversion of the innocent Lamb prior to its sacrifice stands in radical contrast to the animated and glorified Lamb's upright stance before the celestial throne of God in Revelation: ". . . I saw a Lamb *standing*, as though it had been slain, . . . and he went and took the scroll from the right hand of him who was seated on the throne . . ." (Rev 5:6, 7). Furthermore, the slain yet glorified Lamb receives the praise of His entire Church: "Worthy is the Lamb who was slain, to receive power and wealth and wisdom and might and honor and glory and blessing!" (Rev 5:12). The Lamb's placement on the paten possesses at once both a historical and eschatological significance: the immolation of Christ at a particular point in history immediately transforms His broken Body into the glorified Body characteristic of the new life of the Kingdom. Because of the abolition of space and particularly time within the Eucharist, sacrificial theology and eschatology are not permitted to remain isolated from each other as individual disciplines or even as methods designed to explain the phases of divine economy. The humiliated Isaian Man of Sorrows *is* simultaneously the glorified Lamb of the Johannine Apocalypse. The emblems of the Passion remain real upon the glorified Lamb; they are not expunged but remain as a witness to historical truth. So, the events of history never oppose nor run contrary to the eschatological reality, nor does the *eschaton* completely disengage itself from history. This free-flowing, almost phantasmagorical, assemblage of seemingly paradoxical events indicates clearly that the eucharistic sacrifice *is itself* the Church's establishment and entrance into the eternal *aion*. And the interplay between Isaiah's and John's Lamb, as articulated by the rites over the Lamb and solidified by Symeon's own reworking of the apocalyptic image,[56] helps to further prove the inseparability of sacrificial theology and eschatology.

With the Lamb remaining inverted upon the paten, the priest makes a crosswise incision from the bottom of the bread to the seal (being careful not to cut beyond the seal and thus divide the whole Lamb into two pieces), speaking the words: "The Lamb of God, who takes away the sin of the world, is sacrificed for the life and salvation of the world." Through the aforementioned rubric, the identification of the bread with the sacrificed Lamb is unequivocally expressed. One can see the significance of Antiochene liturgical realism here, devoid of any inkling of metaphorical language or imagery, as visible earlier in this book in the writings of Chrysostom[57] and Theodore of Mopsuestia.[58]

Indeed, Christ's divine ability to remove the stain of sin that taints mankind and to offer life and salvation in the eschatological Kingdom is markedly contingent upon His absolute innocence and selfless gesture to die in place of man. In Revelation 5:9–10, the song of the four beasts and the twenty-four elders lauds the "purchasing power," as it were, of the Lamb's precious Blood, instituting simultaneously both the earthly, historical kingdom of the Church Militant and the heavenly, eternal kingdom of the Church Triumphant: "Worthy art thou to take the scroll and to open its seals, for thou wast slain and by thy blood didst ransom men for God from every tribe and tongue and people and nation, and hast made them a kingdom and priests to our God, and they shall reign on earth." The sacrifice of Christ not only ushers in the Church, the eschatological vehicle of the "here and not yet," but also reveals the eternal Kingdom, toward which all of human history will arrive at its fulfillment.

The entire series of ritual incisions and inversions of the Lamb provides us with paradoxical imagery that highlights both the vulnerability but also the triumphant accolades earned by the Lamb of God in His Kingdom. This imagery is vividly depicted in several iconographic programs particularly common in the West, such as in the sixth-century Church of San Vitale in Ravenna, where a haloed *Agnus Dei* is suspended within a floral medallion by four angels on globes. As the epitome of innocence and purity, the Lamb of God, like any lamb, shares the fate of victim, but in the case of Christ, victim and victor are at once embodied in the same person. In the Late Byzantine era, this interplay between sacrificed and glorified Lamb is rendered through the implementation of a slightly different set of images, namely, the immolated Christ—the Extreme Humility motif (typically, in the prothesis niche) and Christ the celebrant of the heavenly Eucharist (at the highest point of the prothesis apse).[59] Even in this specific assemblage of related iconographic motifs with a more obvious eucharistic theme, sacrifice and eschatology indubitably remain part and parcel of each other.

Preparation of the Precious Gifts II— The Preparation of the Chalice[60]

The deacon: Pierce, master.

And the priest pierces the bread with the lance beneath the name IC saying:

> One of the soldiers pierced his side with a spear, and at once there came out blood and water; and he who has seen it has borne witness and his witness is true.

The deacon pours wine and water into the holy chalice saying:

> Bless, master, the holy union.

And the priest blesses them saying:

> Blessed is the union of your holy things always, now and forever and to the ages of ages. Amen.

The next rubric concludes the series of preparatory acts over the Lamb by marking the eucharistic bread with the final emblem of sacrifice, namely, the piercing of the Lamb's side, and the outpouring of blood and water in the form of wine mixed with water in the chalice. The Johannine text provides the obvious content for the liturgical act. Up until this point, the liturgical instrument known as the lance (or σίδηρον) has been used exclusively in its capacity as a sharp knife, in order to detach the Lamb from the rest of the prosphora. This symbolic piercing with the lance is its only non-practical use, as all future applications of the lance involve extracting the remaining particles that will soon after populate the paten. Pott argues: *"Ensuite la lance sert encore pour enlever des parcelles des autres pains qui, toutefois, ne représentent pas l'agneau immolé et n'ont plus aucun rapport avec l'antique préparation purement fonctionnelle du pain de l'offrande."*[61] Nevertheless, a shift in terminology occurred: the "iron knife" (σίδηρον) was replaced by the "spear" or "lance" (λόγχη), in imitation of the centurion's spear that pierced the side of the already crucified Christ.[62] Here again we see yet another clear example, this time in the area of liturgical vessels, of the supersedure of mystagogical symbolism over practical usage.

Symeon of Thessalonike does not comment exclusively on the sacrificial nature of the liturgical piercing and its biblical antecedent, but rather by expounding upon a diatribe against the Armenian refusal of mixing wine with water,[63] he provides several key insights into the sacrificial notion.[64] He begins his defense of the Orthodox position by making initial reference

to the Scriptures themselves, saying plainly enough that "Blood together
with water was poured out, as the Gospel says, and we drink from this side
[of the Savior]."[65] He continues: "And all that which gushed out of the side
of the Savior is Communion, since it was poured out from the dominical
body."[66] Holy Communion, then, is fundamentally established upon the
immolated flesh of the crucified Savior, as well as the blood and water that
flowed from His sacrificed Body.

In his argument, Symeon emphasizes the indisputable importance of
both the wine and water as elements that are consumed in Holy Communion. He first condemns the heresy of the Ὑδροπαραστάται, or Aquarians
(Lat. *Aquarii*), an extremist Christian ascetical sect belonging to a larger
group known as Encratites, or "Abstainers" who used water instead of fer-
mented wine in the Eucharist. The Aquarians, like the Manichaeans (another extremist but more widespread ascetical sect), harbored a particular
reverence for water as the source of life but an unwavering disdain for wine,
flesh, and marriage as intrinsically evil by nature.

Apparently, for Symeon to be commenting upon the Aquarian practice
in the fifteenth century, is an indication that the heresy was probably still
in existence, although it was probably not as widespread as the Armenian
practice.[67] In his defense against the Aquarians, he writes: "For this reason
is it always necessary for the water to be [placed] in the awesome cup, as [is]
the wine; and not only water, as the impious heresy of the Aquarians states,
which discards the tradition of the [sacramental] mysteries. . . ."[68] Symeon
goes on to associate the severity of this practice of the Ὑδροπαραστάται with
the "godlessness" and "sacrilege" of the Gentiles.[69] The Aquarians, he ac-
cuses, deny the use of wine in the Eucharist but, interestingly, they do not
necessarily absolve themselves from drunkenness! Symeon then follows the
argumentation of Chrysostom, who legitimizes the use of wine in the Eucharist through a reference to the words of Christ spoken during the Last
Supper, as recounted in Luke 22:18:

> "From now on I shall not drink of the fruit of the vine." A vine bears
> wine, not water. For on the one hand he overturns the heresy, on the
> other hand he does not reject the [the use of] water. For he did not
> say wine without water [is to be used] but that the vine bears wine and
> not water.[70]

Symeon next argues against the Armenian practice of using only wine
in the eucharistic chalice. He quotes several sources that support the Orthodox position, such as Christ's words, the Apostolic practice, the witness
of the Fathers (specifically the Byzantine liturgical authors Chrysostom and
Basil), the holy prayers, tradition, and custom.[71] Specifically in the Anapho-

rae of Basil and James, the participle κεράσας ('mixing') is used to indicate the universal use of both wine and water "for," as Symeon observes, "we have received the traditions neither from just a few nor in part, but from all the aforementioned successors to the Apostles and Father Confessors, who also shone forth with miraculous wonders. . . ."[72] Symeon naturally sees the mixture of wine and water as an intricate part of the prothesis rite, precisely because of its direct relation to Christ's sacrifice upon the Cross. For Symeon, the Basilian term ἀντίτυπα applies to the partially ritualized gifts in the prothesis, which together assume the identity of the already sacrificed Lamb of God. It is this onetime sacrifice that the prothesis rite announces and in which the faith community participates and envisions during every eucharistic anaphora.

The prothesis text indicates a blessing that is offered by the priest, and it appears, at least syntactically, that the blessing occurs over the mixing of wine and water into the chalice by the deacon. Both Cabasilas and Symeon, however, remain silent on the significance of the blessing and the meaning of the word "union," although the rubric was well established from antiquity and applied through the late Byzantine era. Leo of Tuscany's twelfth-century Latin translation of Chrysostom's eucharistic liturgy includes the preparation of the chalice. In Leo's euchologion, the pouring of wine and water into the chalice is, logically, accompanied by the Johannine verses referring, respectively, to "blood" and "water." In time, the further formalization of this section of the rite saw this particular rubric abandoned and replaced by a benediction associated with the mixture of wine and water in the chalice.[73]

In the next chapter, the emphasis shifts to a more eschatological orientation with the commemorations, as the entire Church—saints and angelic beings, earthly and heavenly creatures, living and dead—gathers around the glorified Lamb of God to form the image of the redeemed universe in Christ. However, the notion of sacrifice is never fully dismissed in this section of the prothesis, since those who are commemorated appear in God's sight precisely because of their own participation in Christ's example of self-offering. In this sense, the imitation of the Lord's sacrifice secures, as it were, the eschatological reality.

NOTES

1. Nicholas Cabasilas, *A Commentary on the Divine Liturgy*, trans. J.M. Hussey and P.A. McNulty (London, 1960), 93–94; *Commentary on the Divine Liturgy* 40; PG 150.456AB.

2. The *stavrotheotokion*, whose thematic content combines Christ's entrance into earthly life (the Nativity) with His entry into eternal life (the Crucifixion), is typically chanted on Tuesday and Thursday evenings at vespers (or on Wednesday and Friday mornings at matins). According to the weekly liturgical cycle of the Eastern Church, the days commemorate, respectively, the betrayal and death of Christ, and are considered days of obligatory fasting throughout the majority of the year, as dictated also by *Didache* 8.1.

3. Hussey and McNulty, trans., 41; *Commentary on the Divine Liturgy* 11; PG 150.389BC; see also Hugh Wybrew, *The Orthodox Liturgy: The Development of the Eucharistic Liturgy in the Byzantine Rite* (Crestwood, 1989), 161.

4. Wybrew, 169.

5. Ibid.

6. Stylianos Muksuris, *The Anaphorae of the Liturgy of Sts. Addai and Mari and the Byzantine Liturgy of St. Basil the Great: A Comparative Study* (unpublished M.Litt. thesis), (Durham, 1999), 59–60.

7. See pp. 2–4 of this book.

8. P.N. Trembelas, ed. Αἱ τρεῖς λειτουργίαι κατὰ τοὺς ἐν Ἀθήναις κώδικας [*The Three Liturgies According to the Athens Codices*], Texte und Forschungen zur byzantinisch-neugriechischen Philologie (Athens, 1935), 1.

9. Ibid.

10. Ibid.

11. Ibid.

12. Symeon of Thessalonike, *On the Sacred Liturgy* 83; PG 155.261A.

13. Ibid., PG 155.261C.

14. Ibid., 84; PG 155.264AB.

15. Sharon E.J. Gerstel, "An Alternate View of the Late Byzantine Sanctuary Screen," in idem., ed. *Thresholds of the Sacred: Architectural, Art Historical, Liturgical, and Theological Perspectives on Religious Screens, East and West* (Washington, 2006), 155.

16. Idem., *Beholding the Sacred Mysteries: Programs of the Byzantine Sanctuary* (Seattle, 1999), 48–52.

17. Gerstel, "An Alternate View," 155.

18. Robert F. Taft, "The Decline of Communion in Byzantium and the Distancing of the Congregation from the Liturgical Action: Cause, Effect, or Neither?," in Sharon E.J. Gerstel, ed. Thresholds of the Sacred, 27–35.

19. See the Appendix at the conclusion of this book.

20. Gerstel, *Beholding the Sacred Mysteries*, 56.

21. See pp. 5–7 of this book.

22. Hussey and McNulty, trans., 27; Cabasilas, *Commentary* 1, PG 150.372C.

23. Symeon of Thessalonike, *On the Sacred Liturgy* 79–83; PG 155.256B–264A.

24. Ibid., 83; PG 155.261B.

25. Hussey and McNulty, trans., 25; Cabasilas, *Commentary* 1, PG 150.369B.

26. F.E. Brightman, ed., *Liturgies Eastern and Western* (Oxford, 1896), 356.

27. See, e.g., Andrew Fincke, *Background of the Jewish Handwashing Ritual* (master's thesis), (Cambridge, 1987); William Herbert Jones, *Jewish Ritual Washing and Christian Baptism* (master's thesis), (Hamilton, Ontario, 2001); and Jonathan David Lawrence, *Washing in Water: Trajectories of Ritual Bathing in the Hebrew Bible and Second Temple Literature* (Atlanta, 2006).

28. See pp. 7–8 of this book.

29. Hussey and McNulty, trans., 34; Cabasilas, *Commentary* 6, PG 150.380D–381A.

30. Trembelas reports that the hymn is inserted, respectively, either at the beginning of the prothesis rite (Αἱ τρεῖς λειτουργίαι, p. 2) or immediately after the mixing of the chalice and the inversion of the Lamb right side up (p. 233).

31. Hussey and McNulty, trans., 30; Cabasilas, *Commentary* 1, PG 150.376A.

32. Symeon of Thessalonike, *On the Sacred Liturgy* 84; PG 155.264B.

33. Gregory Dix, *The Shape of the Liturgy* (London, 1945), 161, 171.

34. Hussey and McNulty, trans., 35; Cabasilas, *Commentary* 7, PG 150.382D.

35. Ibid.

36. Ibid., 36; PG 150.384A.

37. Ibid., *Commentary* 11, 41; PG 150.384B.

38. Ibid., *Commentary* 7, 36; PG 150.384B.

39. Ibid., *Commentary* 11, 41; PG 150.389D.

40. Thomas Pott, *La réforme liturgique byzantine: étude du phénomène d'évolution non spontanée de la liturgie byzantine* (Rome, 2000), 175–76.

41. Hussey and McNulty, trans., 37; Cabasilas, *Commentary* 7; PG 150.384D.

42. Ibid., 36; PG 150.384C.

43. Symeon of Thessalonike, *On the Sacred Liturgy* 83; PG 155.261B.

44. Ibid., PG 155.261BC.

45. Ibid., 84; PG 155.264B.

46. Ibid., 94; PG 155.281C. See also Wybrew, 167.

47. Symeon of Thessalonike, *On the Sacred Liturgy* 94; PG 155.281CD.

48. Hussey and McNulty, trans., 33; Cabasilas, *Commentary* 5, PG 150.380C.

49. Ibid., 34; Cabasilas, *Commentary* 6, PG 150.381A.

50. Ibid., 35; Cabasilas, *Commentary* 6, PG 150.381BC.

51. Ibid., *Commentary* 6, PG 150.381C.

52. Symeon of Thessalonike, *On the Sacred Liturgy* 96; PG 155.288B.

53. Hussey and McNulty, trans., 37; Cabasilas, *Commentary* 8, PG 150.384D.

54. Basil of Caesarea, *On Baptism*, Book 1; PG 31.1514–1628.

55. Michael Heintz, "Baptismal λόγος and τάξις: Basil of Caesarea, *On Baptism*, Book 1", in *Studia Liturgica*, vol. 35, no. 2 (2005), 153.

56. Symeon of Thessalonike, *On the Sacred Liturgy* 94; PG 155.285AB.

57. John Chrysostom, *Homily on Matthew* 50.3; PG 58.507.

58. Theodore of Mopsuestia, *On the Betrayal of Judas* 1.6; PG 49.382B.

59. This iconographic program is specifically unique to the Church of the Holy Virgin Peribleptos at Mystra. While it is true that the Extreme Humility motif remained the conventional icon to be displayed in the proskomide alcove in practi-

cally all Byzantine churches, the program with Christ as celebrant of the Eucharist appeared less frequently, although the depiction of the apostolic communion at the hand of Christ became more popularized. As I argue in the Appendix, the motivation for combining both themes was to give visual support, as it were, for the orthodox position in the fiery twelfth-century controversy with Soterichos Panteugenes, who denied Christ's role as offerer and receiver of the eucharistic sacrifice.

60. See p. 8 of this book.

61. Pott, 175.

62. Hussey and McNulty, trans., 37; Cabasilas, *Commentary* 8, PG 150.385A.

63. The Armenian practice is nestled in the monophysite stance of the non-Chalcedonian churches, which attributes only a divine nature to the God-Man Jesus Christ. The Armenians traditionally regard the mixing of the chalice as a symbolic representation of the confusion of the two natures of Christ. See Wybrew, p. 88.

64. Symeon of Thessalonike, *On the Sacred Liturgy* 93; PG 155.276A–280C.

65. Ibid., PG 155.276A.

66. Ibid., PG 155.276B.

67. *The Oxford Dictionary of the Christian Church*, eds. F.L. Cross and E.A. Livingstone (Oxford, 2005), 94, 814.

68. Symeon of Thessalonike, *On the Sacred Liturgy* 93; PG 155.276B.

69. Ibid., PG 155.276C.

70. Ibid., PG 155.276D.

71. Ibid., PG 155.277A.

72. Ibid., PG 155.277B.

73. A. Jacob, "*La tradition manuscrite de la liturgie de S. Jean Chrysostome (VIIIe–XIIe siècles)*", in *Eucharisties d'Orient et d'Occident* (Paris 1970), 109–38.

7

THE MYSTICAL PROTHESIS II:
TWO KINGDOMS OF SAINTS UNITED

St. Symeon of Thessalonike's well-known pithy quotation from his masterful treatise *On the Sacred Liturgy*, already referred to earlier in this book,[1] encapsulates concisely the mystagogical realism so characteristic of the prothesis rite, linking the sacrifice of Christ with the inauguration of the Kingdom as one unified scene. The quote is a striking one and for several reasons, not least of which is Symeon's own Dionysian understanding of the hierarchical progression of sanctifying grace, of which more will be said later. Furthermore, it affirms, in the Liturgy, the eschatological unity shared by earthly and celestial realms through the sacrifice of Christ. In spite of its apparent brevity, the citation nevertheless offers several seminal points that support the primary argument of this book, namely, that the prothesis rite contains a strongly sacrificial and eschatological character and that both elements are unavoidably interdependent and complementary.

The initial impression given by the caption reflects Symeon's mystagogical understanding of the *completed* prothesis, i.e. after the excision of particles for the saints and angels, and the living and dead, as an image of the Church Triumphant and Militant, an all-inclusive icon of the entire universe with the glorified Christ at the center, flanked by the members that belong to both the earthly and spiritual realms (cf. Rev 5:1–14). This cosmic image is suggested by Symeon, who states: "On the one hand, the paten symbolizes heaven (τυποῖ τὸν οὐρανόν), and for this reason is it round, and it contains the Master of heaven (καὶ τὸν τοῦ οὐρανοῦ κατέχει Δεσπότην)."[2] This eschatological figure, though certainly not void of any sacrificial intimation, stands in radical contrast to the image of the lone Lamb immolated liturgically in the first phase of the prothesis rite.

Second, Symeon clearly indicates that it is through the mystagogical participation in "this sacred sacrifice" that both angels and saintly men are spiritually united to Christ. In the case of the angels, they are joined to Christ as ethereal, bodiless beings that herald the divine economy, especially the Resurrection. The union of the angelic orders to the triumphant Christ may be understood in one of two ways: (1) in the Dionysian sense, as "reflectors" of the divine glory within their ranks; or (2) as intermediaries between God and humanity, fulfilling a prophetic, or better still, kerygmatic role in proclaiming the news of the Resurrection. Eastern hymns dealing with angelic beings speak of their "communication," as it were, with those who otherwise had lost hope after Christ's death, like the Apostles or women disciples or, at best, were themselves anticipatory of the Resurrection, as in the case with Christ's Mother. In the first instance, for example, the Eighth Morning (*Eothinon*) Doxastikon reads: "Mary's fervent tears are not shed in vain; for behold she was made worthy to be taught by the angels and to behold Your countenance, O Jesus." [3] In the second instance, the Ninth Ode (*Magnificat*) of Pascha says: "The angel cried out to the One Full of Grace: 'O pure Virgin, rejoice, and again I say rejoice: your Son has risen on the third day from the tomb.'" [4] In the case of the saints of the Church, they are joined to their Lord through their own faithful co-suffering with Christ and their symbiotic relationship with Him, as well as their partaking of the Eucharist during their earthly life.

Third, both angels and saints, permanent citizens now of the Church Triumphant, participate forever in the eternal eucharistic celebration that characterizes their heavenly existence and share in the sanctification of the risen and glorified Christ by virtue of their union with Him. Finally, in the eucharistic offering that recalls Christ's own sacrifice upon the Cross, the very same sanctification and union with God experienced *in aeternum* by the angels and saints is bestowed through them ('τούτῳ ἡμᾶς ἑνοῦσιν'), in an inchoative manner, to the clergy and laity that make up the earthly Church. Symeon, an ardent proponent of St. Dionysios the Areopagite's liturgical mystagogy, in which Pseudo-Dionysios comments upon the hierarchical progression of the divine glory from the higher to the lower order of angels,[5] seems to reflect this hierarchical trickling of grace from the heavenly to the earthly realms. Dionysios' lengthy text is worth quoting:

> Following that same harmonious law which operates throughout nature, the wonderful source of all visible and invisible order and harmony supernaturally pours out in splendid revelations to the superior beings the full and initial brilliance of his astounding light, and successive beings in their turn receive their share of the divine beam,

through the mediation of their superiors. The beings who are first to know God and who, more than others, desire the divine virtue have been deemed worthy to become the prime workers of the power and activity which imitate God, as far as possible. In their goodness they raise their inferiors to become, so far as possible their rivals. They ungrudgingly impart to them the glorious ray which has visited them so that their inferiors may pass this on to those yet farther below them. Hence, on each level, predecessor hands on to successor whatever of the divine light he has received and this, in providential proportion, is spread out to every being.

This real spiritual union then between Christ and the Church, in both its earthly and heavenly forms, is achieved through participation by all created beings in the divine glory of the sacrificed and victorious Lamb, be it in a prophetic, ethical, or sacramental manner. The presence of the particles upon the paten, which represent the angelic and saintly orders, achieves the specific purpose of indicating: (1) the unbroken and perpetual communion of the Church on both sides of death (hence, the title of this chapter); and (2) that sanctification for the living is bestowed as a result of the constant intercession before God's celestial throne of those who have been perfected in the faith. This unity, for all intents and purposes, is an eschatological one rooted in the periodic eucharistic celebration of the Church on earth, which in turn imitates the constant eucharistic action of thanksgiving of the Church in heaven. In the Eucharist, man experiences within his given historical context a portion of what the angels and saints experience for eternity—the fullness of life in communion with the living and triune God. This eschatological union is strikingly typified upon the paten with the excision and addition of particles arranged hierarchically upon it, proclaiming:

> the Good News of a new eschatological reality, which had as its center the crucified and resurrected Christ, the incarnation of God the Logos and His dwelling among us human beings, and his continuous presence through the Holy Spirit, in a life of communion, experienced in their "eucharistic" (in the wider sense) life.[6]

The purpose of this chapter is to carefully examine the section of the prothesis rite that is specifically concerned with the excision of particles representing the Mother of God, the angels and saints, and the living and dead, and to identify all critical sacrificial and eschatological elements in these actions. Two particular concerns will be: (1) to prove the interdependence between both themes by establishing the central importance of the ritualized Lamb situated in the midst of His Church, an Apocalyptic image encountered above; and (2) to further comment upon Symeon's intentional reworking of the Pseudo-Dionysian model of sanctification and its hierarchical progression from one realm of the Church to the other.

THE EXCISION OF THE PARTICLE FOR THE MOTHER OF GOD[7] AND THE MEANING OF THE PARTICLES

Then taking another prosphora he says:

In honor and memory of our most-blessed, glorious lady, the Theotokos and ever-virgin Mary, through whose intercessions accept, O Lord, this sacrifice upon your super-celestial altar.

And he cuts from this the particle of the Theotokos and places it to the right of the Lamb saying:

The queen stood at your right hand, clothed and adorned in a garment of pure gold.

The actual placement of particles around the Lamb retains a distinct hierarchical order, and the commemoration of the Mother of God as the first and primary intercessor before Christ is clearly intentional. The honorary position bestowed upon the Virgin Mary by the infant Church following the Resurrection was quite indisputable, as Acts 1:14 verifies. Eastern iconography (as in the depictions of the *Deesis* and the Ascension of Christ) typically depicts Mary in a prominent location in the icon, in relative proximity to Christ, to indicate her importance not only in the Incarnation, but also in her intercessory role. In the case of the *Deesis*, the marked similarities with the populated paten suggest an almost indisputable pattern of influence.[8]

THE PARTICLES FOR THE SAINTS: A SHIFT IN FUNCTION

As evidenced in several *euchologia* from the eleventh century onward,[9] the inclusion of saints in the commemoration portion of the prothesis rite appends the petition, "through whose supplications visit us, O God" (ὧν ταῖς ἱκεσίαις ἐπίσκεψαι ἡμᾶς ὁ Θεός). A similar intercession appears after the remembrance of the Mother of God: "through whose supplications accept, O Lord, this sacrifice at Your super-celestial altar" (ἧς ταῖς πρεσβείαις πρόσδεξαι, Κύριε, τὴν θυσίαν ταύτην εἰς τὸ ὑπερουράνιόν σου θυσιαστήριον). The exact point in time when such insertions occurred in the prothesis rite remains uncertain, but it seems that even after the eleventh century, uniformity of practice had not been achieved everywhere,[10] although the commemorations soon became the standardized norm in the prothesis rite.

A germane point to be made at this juncture is that the hierarchical placement of the saints around the Lamb as participants in the "economical system or 'the history of salvation'"[11] did not necessarily oppose their role as fervent intercessors. Thomas Pott argues rightfully that a radical shift in emphasis had indeed taken place by the twelfth century on the Holy Mountain Athos, whereby the saints commemorated at the prothesis were seen less as intercessors and more as participants in the divine economy. "Now the saints no longer possess the role of interceding for the expiation of the sins of the faithful, that one wishes to commemorate them, but they are seen as contributing to a commemoration in their 'honor and memory.'"[12]

This is evidenced by rubrical modifications in the rite, and he provides helpful manuscripts that in fact witness to this novelty. Three distinct manuscripts are credited with witnessing to this important alteration in wording: (1) an order of service, or *diataxis*, dating from the twelfth or thirteenth century, known as *Codex 662 Ethnike Bibliotheke* (*National Library of Greece*); (2) a *diataxis* of the Divine Liturgy of St. John Chrysostom from the *Codex Panteleimon 5924*, dating from around the beginning of the fourteenth century; and (3) the well-known *Diataxis* of Patriarch Philotheos Kokkinos, from the first half of the fourteenth century.

One will take note of an additional rubrical modification related to the rewording, namely, the displacement of the preparation of the chalice from before the excision of particles to after. The known practice in the Late Byzantine period prior to the change was to prepare the chalice with wine and water *after* all the prosphora were utilized; that is, following the excision of the Lamb and the particles for the Mother of God, the angelic orders and hierarchy of saints, and even the living and dead and their sequential placement upon the *diskos*. Hence, the cup is ritualized immediately after the Lamb has been removed from the first prosphora and placed upon the paten, while the particles and commemorations constitute the final act before the ceremonial covering of the holy gifts. This logical modification accomplished two important tasks: (1) it confirmed the thematic unity between the preparation of the bread and the cup and, supported by the Johannine verse (John 19:34), linked the piercing of the Lamb with the pouring of wine and water into the chalice; and (2) it detracts the saints from their intercessory role before the Lamb by virtue of their proximity and immediate positioning around the Lamb and regroups them in such a manner as to promote the notion of their inclusion in a celestial hierarchy of beings. Pott writes:

They [the particles] are no longer explicitly transporters of the intercessions of the saints beside the immolated Lamb but being "in honor and memory" of such and such a saint, they are regrouped around the Lamb in order to evoke the idea of a celestial hierarchy, in the manner of an iconographic program of the churches from post-Iconoclasm.[13]

This hierarchical categorization of saints in post-Iconoclastic churches is likewise attested to by L. Ouspensky in his discussion of the customary five tiers of Old and New Testament personages and events normally found on sanctuary screens from this period.[14] Thus, the prothesis rite came to be regarded as an extension and mirror of the artistically elaborate church building itself, which in turn, according to Symeon of Thessalonike[15] and Maximos the Confessor,[16] represented a microcosm of not only heaven and its hierarchy of inhabitants but also an image of the cosmos. This cosmos, comprised of all material creation and naturally mankind, both living and dead, is redeemed in the one-time sacrifice of Christ and perpetually united with the celestial hierarchy of beings via the periodic eucharistic celebration.[17]

Pott interestingly abstains from reconciling the saints' roles as intercessors and economical participants, and one must wonder if the new latter "role" assumed by the saints warrants any manner of intercession on their part, at least according to the available liturgical commentaries, which themselves conflict in practice. One could surmise that the construction and restoration of monasteries on Mount Athos had stopped, thus possibly bringing to an end the notion that the saints could be regarded as intercessors on behalf of imperial patrons and affluent civilian donors, who were nonetheless commemorated at the prothesis. The Ottoman occupation of Greece and the Balkans after the first half of the fifteenth century would in all likelihood have restricted or seriously limited such expenditures toward structural and artistic ameliorations on religious buildings.

Contemporary practice, following several Late Byzantine *euchologia* that contain the prothesis rite, including the *Panteleimon Codex 770*,[18] reconciles the saints as both intercessors and participants in a hierarchical structure by affirming that the sacrifice is indeed made "in honor and memory" of the saints but then adding, following the litany of names, "through whose supplications visit us, O God." Despite the aforementioned rubrical redactions made to reflect this new manner of visualizing the saints as mainly participants in the history of salvation, it appears that the discrepancy in texts and practice was extensive and thus the intercessory nature of the saints was never—and could never—be fully eclipsed.

As for the commemoration of the living and the dead and the excision of particles for them, this may simply be understood as the final act completing "the economical system or the history of salvation represented upon the paten, without there being any more explicit relationship with the immolated lamb of God and the forgiveness of sins."[19] Consequently, the dynamic of intercessory prayer by the saints for the living and dead commemorated immediately after them was relegated to a place of secondary importance, but it was certainly not extinguished altogether. In this regard, Pott fails to point out that subsequent evidence in other manuscripts, such as *Panteleimon 770*, clearly indicates that the intercessory quality of the saints *was* retained in the prothesis rite, and the same texts simultaneously did *not* reject the hierarchical notion. Variation in practice thus abounded, and Pott correctly admits the coexistence of the historical and eschatological components in the prothesis rite throughout its developmental history, *"comme une interprétation à plusieurs niveaux d'un unique acte ritual."*[20] In light of this observation, he states that the notion of a celestial hierarchy, a shift toward a more otherworldly vision of the prothesis rite,

> eclipsed the more ancient system according to which the commemoration of the faithful was in direct relation with the gifts that they had offered in view of the anaphora. Now the commemoration of the faithful is equally linked to their offering but in the interior of a system of ritual that depends more upon the theological idea of a celestial hierarchy than on the preparation of the gifts for the anaphora.[21]

"Eclipsed" here may best be replaced by "modified." As Pott himself admits, the significance of offering and, by extension, intercessory prayer by the saints for the offerer, never disappeared, either in theory or in practice, but was assumed into a wholly different mode and context. In other words, intercession is offered by the saints who are not solely constituents of the historical realm, but equally members of a celestial hierarchy capable of transmitting prayer and grace to and from God.

Any polarization of the historicizing and eschatological tendencies of liturgical mystagogy, marking the intercession of the saints with their "new" standing as members of the celestial hierarchy as incompatible, can best be remedied by adhering to the Dionysian understanding of hierarchy, rethought and reworked by Symeon of Thessalonike in his *Interpretation of the Divine Temple and Liturgy.* He offers a general theory of the symbol by utilizing the concept of a liturgical veil, which appears in his discussion of the sanctuary enclosure. He explains that the laity participate in the holy mysteries not directly but indirectly (πλὴν ἐμμέσως, καὶ οὐκ ἀμέσως)[22] and receive grace from God but *via* the celebrant clergy, who "unveil," as it were, the veiled (κεκαλυμμένος),[23] central Mystery of

Christ gradually (κατὰ μικρὸν ἀνοιγόμενος)[24] through the celebration of the liturgical mysteries of the Church. Symeon expounds upon the reason for such an indirect participation by maintaining that the earthly liturgy can only be celebrated "through symbols and veils."[25] Because of man's fleshly nature, he cannot witness the heavenly liturgy in its sublime, "unveiled" immediacy. Consequently, its earthly performance is mediated through liturgical symbols, called "veils," whose intention is not to conceal the divine prototype but rather to make Him and the notions of sacrifice, sanctification, and eschatology more readily comprehended and accessed in the only manner possible to man and consistent with the theology of the Incarnation, "in the 'dual-natured Jesus', who as God 'remained' purely spiritual while 'becoming' fully material as man."[26] Following Pseudo-Dionysius rationalization of the celestial hierarchy, he infers (without stating it openly) that the latter likewise participate in the divine glory but through yet a higher sophisticated network of ethereal beings in closer proximity to God, who unveil the divine glory to man. Symeon does not insinuate here that the ability to perceive God is essentially "controlled" by hierarchy, but the veil that is drawn is seen as the contemplative faculty of each individual being. Hence, all beings can rightly participate in the glory and redemptive movements of God in a manner appropriate to them and their abilities. Constas writes: "No one is by nature excluded from communion with God, but the transcendent deity is imparted only under various symbolic forms, or 'veils,' that are 'analogous' to one's capacity to receive it."[27]

The intercessory capacity of the saints then can be likened to their "unveiling" of the divine truth and glory in Jesus Christ, which in turn prompts the "lower hierarchies of worshipers" to participate in the divine source of salvation through their own contemplative effort. This "upper hierarchy" of saints and angels, in iconographic proximity to the sanctuary, the location of the eucharistic sacrifice but also the throne of God, co-celebrate the divine mystery of human redemption with the Church on earth by conveying to those below what they already know and experience in eternity. Hence, Symeon's reliance on the Areopagitical corpus of writings[28] that denote hierarchical unveiling as "level-appropriate revelation" is not insignificant, despite its superficial treatment in contemporary scholarship, for it not only establishes the doctrine of the Incarnation as the foundational basis for liturgical mystagogy, but it also employs the incarnational model to explain how the unveiling of divine truth is accomplished in accordance with the noetic and spiritual capability of each person to receive and accept it.

Reconciling the Binary Role of the Particles via the Areopagitical Hierarchy

The Dionysian hierarchical structure, which may be likened to the hierarchical positioning of the saints around the immolated Lamb upon the paten, is clearly characterized by a *downward* progression of the divine glory, in which each stratum of angelic beings mediates the thearchic light to the level immediately below it, and not an *upward* movement of glorification or supplication mediated within the Church to God. Nicholas Constas summarizes this participation in the divine glory as follows: "No one is by nature excluded from communion with God, but the transcendent deity is imparted only under various symbolic forms, or 'veils,' that are 'analogous' to one's capacity to receive it."[29] Even Symeon, as the Areopagite's most avid redactor, regards that the proximity of the saints and the living and dead around the Lamb have their purpose of receiving grace downward from the Triune God, rather than making their offering upward to Him.

> Εἰσὶ τοίνυν αἱ μὲν ὑπὲρ τῶν ἁγίων προσαγόμεναι εἰς δόξαν αὐτῶν καὶ τιμὴν καὶ ἀνάβασιν τῆς ἀξίας καὶ τοῦ θείου φωτισμοῦ παραδοχὴν μείζονα· αἱ δὲ ὑπὲρ τῶν πιστῶν, κεκοιμημένων μέν, εἰς λύτρωσιν ἁμαρτιῶν, καὶ θείας χάριτος ἕνωσιν, ζώντων δέ, εἰ μετανοίᾳ μόνον τὴν ζωὴν ἐξοικονομοῖεν, εἰς δεινῶν ἀπαλλαγήν, εἰς ἁμαρτημάτων ἄφεσιν, εἰς ζωῆς αἰωνίου ἐλπίδα.[30]

Pott's reductionism becomes evident when he concludes, "Now the commemoration of the faithful [and the saints] is equally linked to their offering but at the interior of a ritual system which depends more on the theological idea of a celestial hierarchy than on the preparation of the gifts for the anaphora."[31]

On the other end of this spectrum, St. Nicholas Cabasilas explains that the reasons for the excision of particles for the Theotokos and, by extension, for the saints are twofold: to offer thanksgiving to God for their example of true faith and Christian living, and *to make supplication to God through them*.[32] In order to achieve this dual purpose, he proposes that the loaves, from which the particles are removed, are to be regarded as gifts, given in gratitude but also in request for a particular spiritual benefit. He argues: "No gift is made without cause, whether it is a question of worshipping God or of pleasing men, but always some benefit is held in mind, whether it be one already received or merely one which is hoped for."[33] Cabasilas here almost reveals a cyclical pattern of movement and a causal relationship between thanksgiving (εὐχαριστήρια) and supplication (ἱκεσία), with the one inevitably resulting from and generating the other. The connection is a significant one, insofar as both interrelated actions constitute the very foundational components of liturgical life in the Church. Hence, one can say that when a Christian is not supplicating God in prayer, then he is praising Him, and vice versa!

A point of divergence between Cabasilas and Symeon may be found here, where the former seems to emphasize the *upward* movement of praise and supplication from the ones commemorated, mediated through the saints and eventually approaching God. Symeon, on the contrary, stresses the *downward* progression of the divine glory that is mediated through the angelic ranks to the lower strata of creation. In either case, despite the directional flow, not only do intermediaries play a critical role in the communication between God and the entire created order, but each order of the Church, by virtue of its relation to God and function, experiences in a sense a *perichoresis*, or mutual indwelling, with the uncreated deity, as Symeon alludes to when he calls the "whole [church building] the dwelling place of God" (κατοικητήριον ὅλος Θεοῦ καθίσταται).[34]

Cabasilas, however, does draw closer to Symeon's emphasis on the downward progression of grace when he identifies the spiritual benefits bestowed upon the faithful during the Eucharist, for which the particles are offered: "the forgiveness of our sins and the inheritance of the kingdom." He points out that, in one sense, these benefits have already been received in this life, but they are still requested by the Church at the eucharistic synaxis in preparation for the end time. The Pauline eschatological premise of the "already and not yet," which St. Paul used specifically in conjunction with baptism and the spiritual benefits that stem from it, is applied by Cabasilas with regard to the Eucharist in this way: forgiveness of sins, shared by all Christians baptized in Christ, was obtained by Christ as a result of His sacrifice, and "this power [of forgiveness] is contained in Holy Baptism and in the other sacraments, whereby we are made children of God and heirs of the kingdom of heaven."[35] Hence, the power of forgiveness has *already* become a viable reality in the Church, but it is made readily accessible through the Church's sacramental life, in which the Christian participates to inherit the eternal Kingdom that has *not yet* come in its fullness. Hence, adoption into the Body of Christ, achieved via baptism, initiates the neophyte into the mystery of salvation, into which the individual Christian partly immerses himself during the eucharistic liturgy and struggles to attain during his earthly existence. The Church, in offering particles for the living and dead, mediates to the saints on their behalf, who in turn supplicate God for their salvation. On the other hand, the saints commemorated in the prothesis live in the continuous presence of God, as the completed *diskos* clearly indicates, and have already attained the permanent reality of salvation in

God's Kingdom, for which the Church gives thanks. Cabasilas summarizes the prothesis in this manner:

> This is why she [the Church] commemorates the Lord's death and the
> departed saints for whom she has obtained the fullness of perfection;
> she is mindful also of those who are not yet perfect. For the former she
> gives thanks, and for the rest she intercedes.
>
> Thus the first and second parts of the *prothesis* are spent in thanks-
> giving, while the remainder is concerned with supplication; in mem-
> ory of the Lord, for the glory of his Blessed Mother, and in honour of
> the saints.[36]

Cabasilas indicates that the concluding phrases (i.e. "in memory of";
"for the glory of"; "in honor of") can possess a double meaning: one that
can be applied as a thanksgiving for present benefits already received or one
that can take the form of a petition for anticipated blessings yet to come.

Immediately afterward, Cabasilas includes a prayer (not his own) that
not only praises Christ for His voluntary sacrifice, but also expresses the
prominence of the saints as fervent intercessors for their fellow men and
women. The prayer, in its phraseology, cleverly creates a sense of intimacy
between the Mother of God, the saints, and the faithful, an image very
reminiscent of the eschatological reality seen in Revelation 5:8 and 8:3–4.

> We give thanks to thee, [the Church] says (φησίν), that by thy death
> thou hast opened for us the gates of life, that from us thou didst choose
> a mother (ὅτι Μητέρα παρ' ἡμῶν ἔλαβες), that we have as ambassadors
> (πρεσβευτάς) our fellow-men (ὁμοφύλους), and that thou has allowed to
> members of our human family (τοῖς ὁμογενέσιν ἡμῶν) such freedom of
> access to thee.[37]

The verb "φησίν" ("says") indicates that the prayer is not Cabasilas' creation. Hussey and McNulty identify the speaker as the Church. In all likelihood, the prayer appears as an improvised collection by Cabasilas to affirm
the community's thanksgiving for the divine economia of Christ and the
participation in it of Mary and the saints.

Interestingly, the prayer seems to summarize succinctly the Church's
thanksgiving for Christ's sacrifice and for the saints' participation in the
divine economy, through whom and with whom man has access to the gifts
of salvation. Almost a century later, Symeon would make a strikingly similar pronouncement, indicating the timeless and personal nature of God's
economia that stems from the Cross.[38]

Symeon of Thessalonike's commentary on the excision of the triangular particle for the Mother of God is rather limited, although his treat-

ment of her proximity and orientation to her Son is reminiscent of his affinity to the complex hierarchical system of Dionysios the Areopagite. He simply states that a particle in her honor and memory is taken from a second loaf and "placed to the right of the holy bread upon the paten" (ἐκ δεξιῶν τοῦ ἐν τῷ δίσκῳ ἱεροῦ ἄρτου τίθησιν),[39] a place of prime honor given to the Holy Virgin who gave birth to Christ the King (τῆς τοῦτον τεκούσης παρθενικῶς ... τοῦ Υἱοῦ καὶ Βασιλέως Χριστοῦ). Regarding the prominence given to Mary on the Lamb's right, Symeon explains:

> On the one hand, this bread [Lamb] is the antitype of the body of Christ; on the other hand, that particle [for the Theotokos] stands for her who gave birth to him as a virgin. Therefore, by preserving even the very *typos* of the truth, the Queen is represented as in the Psalms [cf. Ps 45.9,13], on the right hand of the Son and King Christ, receiving the first honors as Mother. For the right is also the first [place of honor].[40]

He further adds that Mary is for the Church

> the servant of the great dispensation, the workshop of the divine union toward us, both the root and the birth-giver and reason for the appearance of the Creator. *She receives the glory before all, and is the first to be given the illumination from the One incarnated from her* above explanation in a virginal and holy manner, and from the One who is united to us out of extreme goodness. For this reason she is represented to the right of Him, and likewise we place the particle for her to the right of the holy bread, this indicating as such that *she is higher than anyone else and closest to God.*[41]

Cabasilas, on the contrary, omits commenting specifically on the significance of the particle for Mary being to the right of the Lamb. He offers only a fleeting reference: "To the glory of the all-holy Mother of God, in honour of such and such a saint, and for the remission of the sins of the living and dead."[42] Symeon, the ordained liturgist, appears to have a practical concern here, coupling rubric with theory, whereas Cabasilas, the lay theologian, is particularly interested in establishing the theological premise that the very act of offering is both a thanksgiving and supplication.

The image of Mary's proximity to her Son upon the paten is reflective of her historical and eschatological involvement in, respectively, the earthly life of Christ and the divine *economia* of salvation: in the cave during the Incarnation, at the base of the Cross during the Crucifixion, and at the right hand of Christ's Judgment Seat, as depicted in the icons of the *Deesis* and the Final Judgment. The Virgin then is not only the first witness to and beneficiary of the sacrifice of her Son, but she is also the first among the saints who enjoys the eschatological bliss of God's eternal reign.

The Excision of the Particles for the Saints[43]

Then taking a third prosphora (or the same one, if there is no other) he takes out from it nine particles in honor of the saints and he places them to the left of the Lamb in three columns of three particles each from the top to the bottom, that is, the second one beneath the first, the third beneath the second, the fourth next to the first, the fifth next to the second, etc., saying:

For the first particle:

In honor and memory of the exceedingly great commanders Michael and Gabriel and all the heavenly bodiless powers.

For the second particle:

Of the honorable and glorious prophet, forerunner and baptist John, the holy glorious prophets Moses and Aaron, Elijah and Elisha, David and Jesse, the holy Three Children and Daniel the prophet, and all the holy prophets.

For the third particle:

Of the holy, glorious and all-praiseworthy apostles Peter and Paul, the Twelve and the Seventy, and all the holy apostles.

For the fourth particle:

Of our holy fathers among the saints, great hierarchs and ecumenical teachers Basil the Great, Gregory the Theologian, and John Chrysostom, Athanasios and Cyril, Nicholas of Myra, and all the holy hierarchs.

For the fifth particle:

Of the holy first martyr and archdeacon Stephen, the holy great martyrs George the Triumphant, Demetrios the Myrrh-flowing, Theodore the Recruit and Theodore the Commander, the priest-martyrs Haralambos and Eleftherios, and all the holy [male and female] martyrs.

For the sixth particle:

Of our righteous and God-bearing fathers Anthony, Euthymios, Sabbas, Onouphrios, Athanasios of Athos, and all the [male and female ascetics] righteous.

For the seventh particle:

Of the holy and miraculous unmercenaries Kosmas and Damian, Kyros and John, Panteleimon and Hermolaos, and all the holy unmercenaries.

For the eighth particle:

Of the holy and righteous ancestors of God Joachim and Anna, of Saint (of the day), whose memory we commemorate.

For the ninth particle:

Of our holy father among the saints John Chrysostom, archbishop of Constantinople (or Basil the great and revealer of heaven, archbishop of Caesarea) and all the saints, through whose supplications visit us, O God.

While the categories of saints are a fairly standard feature in Medieval Byzantine liturgical manuscripts, the number and names of commemorated saints vary in different *euchologia* and commentaries. For example, Cabasilas mentions only the Virgin Mary by name, both in the prothesis rite and in the commemorations—intercessions during the Divine Liturgy—while choosing to cluster the remainder of the saints together: "Then he commemorates the whole assembly of the saints (τὸν τῶν ἁγίων ἄπαντα σύλλογον)."[44] However, a little further on during the anaphoral intercessions, Cabasilas does mention the *categories* of the saints, which precede the specific naming of some of the saints themselves.[45] On the other hand, Symeon of Thessalonike, not surprisingly, is much more explicit in his treatment of the saints, categorizing them hierarchically and discussing their significance in reference to Christ's sacrifice and the divine economy.[46] Thus, for example, the order of holy angels "ministered the mystery of the dispensation" (τῷ μυστηρίῳ τῆς οἰκονομίας καθυπούργησαν),[47] while the saints "participate . . . in this fearful mystery as co-sufferers with Christ" (μετέχουσι . . . τῷ μυστηρίῳ τῷ φρικτῷ τούτῳ ὡς συνηγωνισμένοι Χριστῷ).[48]

The variations existing between liturgical texts, in terms of which saints were included in the commemorations, were neither entirely uncommon nor inappropriate, given the fact that some regions possessed a certain affinity to particular saints. Also, the addition of other individuals to the Church's roster of saints, or *hagiologion*, naturally accounts for the absence of some names in earlier manuscripts. The listing is slightly modified and replicated in other non-eucharistic rites (such as the Vesperal Blessing of the Loaves service and Matins), and it is abbreviated to include the Mother of God, St. John the Forerunner, the Apostles, and the saint(s) of the day in the anaphoral intercessions, which follow the consecratory epiklesis of the Liturgy.[49]

Nine triangular particles, each one representing a particular category of saints that in turn corresponds to one of the nine angelic orders, are removed from the third loaf and arranged hierarchically in three sets of three rows to the immediate left of the Lamb. A close comparison between the *National Library Codex 662*,[50] the *Panteleimon Codex*,[51] Symeon's commentary,[52] and various other *euchologia* will reveal expected variations and, in some cases, categorizations that are not always clear-cut, but the following taxonomy is generally representative of most manuscripts: (1) the holy bodiless powers of heaven, i.e., the holy angels; (2) St. John the Forerunner and Baptist [at the head of the Old Testament prophets]; (3) the holy apostles; (4) the holy fathers and hierarchs of the Church; (5) the holy martyrs; (6) the holy ascetics; (7) the holy unmercenary and healing saints; (8) the holy godparents Joachim and Anna [together with the saint(s) commemorated on the day]; and (9) Saint John Chrysostom or St. Basil the Great, whose Divine Liturgy is celebrated on the day.

These particles are excised from the loaf in order to affirm their prominence and their participation in the sacrifice of Christ and the benefits that streamed forth from it. St. Paul's classic line from Hebrews, similar to Revelation 5:1–14, is strongly evocative of this collective witness and sharing in the Lord's sacrifice by the saints:

> Therefore, since we are surrounded by so great a cloud of witnesses, let us also lay aside every weight, and sin which clings so closely, and let us run with perseverance the race that is set before us, looking to Jesus the pioneer and perfecter of our faith, who for the joy that was set before him endured the cross, despising the shame, and is seated at the right hand of the throne of God. (Hebrews 12:1–2).

Symeon's vision of the Church as a united whole, as a union of saints, angels, and men who encircle the celestial throne is revealed in the excision of representative particles placed around the Lamb. For Symeon, ultimate unity with God implies participation in the divine economy or, in the case of the higher beings like the angels, its ministration to the lower strata of the created order. He writes characteristically: "It is necessary to offer [particles] for them [the heavenly powers], for they have ministered the mystery of the dispensation; and because they have been united to us, and we are one Church."[53]

Symeon's reasoning for including the angels at the prothesis is to not identify them as intercessors in the same capacity as the saints, but to honor them for their participation in the divine dispensation, which does not conflict with his celestial imagery motif. Generally speaking, the angelic orders are included in the Medieval Byzantine texts, but not as intercessors. The *Hieratikon* of the Church of Greece (2001) seems to uphold this stance, prefacing the mentioning of the angels with the prepositional phrase "εἰς τιμὴν καὶ μνήμην" (in honor and memory) to identify them as constitutive celestial members of the Church. However, it later appends "ὧν ταῖς ἱκεσίαις ἐπίσκεψαι ἡμᾶς ὁ Θεός" through whose supplications visit us, O God) to the final saints commemorated, in order to specify that the *succession of saints in the remaining eight orders* possess an intercessory role.[54]

Fellowship with the heavenly host is attained by virtue of the common denominator shared by all earthly and celestial beings; that is, participation in the divine economy. Immediately afterward, Symeon quickly indicates that the angels likewise "desire to behold the mysteries of the Church,"[55] referring specifically to the liturgical mystagogy of the Eucharist. In making this subsequent addition, Symeon implies clearly that there is no essential difference between the liturgical celebration of the divine economy and the participation of the angels in the historical sacrifice of Christ: it is one and the same event. The implosion of the eschatological age into history following the event of Pentecost and, expressly, the creation of the Christian Church, has perpetuated the Christ-event into the ages, giving it at once an eternal character and making it readily accessible to virtually every generation of Christians.

Through the mystagogical experience of the Church's eucharistic liturgy, not only have the horizontal constraints of historical time been eliminated, but so have the vertical boundaries separating earthly and heavenly worshippers. The Church's oneness then consists in the transparency of time and space, by which history and eternity, heaven and earth, although retaining their idiosyncratic uniqueness, are fused into the same present reality in such a manner that any differences between them are indistinct and unrecognizable. Thus, for example, the realism with which Maximos the Confessor[56] and Symeon of Thessalonike[57] regard the church building as an image of the redeemed cosmos is very significant and lends further credence to the patristic belief in the abolition of time and space within the context of worship. Ouspensky observes that this mystagogical envisioning of the church temple reveals an eschatological

> cosmos renewed and transfigured, the figure of a universal unity restored, in contrast to the universal disorder and enmity existing in creation now. It represents the world built into the Church, with Christ at its head. . . . To put it in another way, the church is revealed as an

image of the condition in which the universe is destined to be, that state which is now experienced by the Church as the norm, presupposing fulfillment but lying still beyond the edge of history.[58]

Being representative of Antiochene realism, Chrysostom, in his *Second Homily on the Incarnation*, perhaps says it best when he writes:

> I see a strange and wonderful mystery; the shepherds' voices ring in my ears, the shepherds whose pipes play no isolated melody, but chant a heavenly hymn. The Angels chant, the archangels praise, the cherubim hymn, the Seraphim glorify, *all celebrate seeing God on earth and man in the heavens.*[59]

The excised particles for the saints, aside from signifying their participation in the sacrifice of Christ, possess a second function; namely, to receive the thanksgiving of the Church and to direct the supplications of the faithful to God (καὶ τὴν εὐχαριστίαν ἐμφαίνει καὶ τὴν ἱκεσίαν).[60] Both Cabasilas and Symeon remark extensively on these two liturgical acts. Cabasilas avows that the saints "are the cause for which the Church gives thanks to God. It is for them that she offers to him a spiritual sacrifice of thanksgiving"[61] because, as he explains, they are the very embodiment of that "which she seeks and obtains that for which she has prayed—the kingdom of heaven."[62] The eschatological banquet of the Eucharist then comprises a thanksgiving celebration honoring the heroes of the Christian Faith who have made their homecoming and now appear before their sacrificed and risen Lord, the very prototype of their own suffering and victory. The banquet is a testimony not only to the whole progression of the divine economy, but also a laudatory witness to the participants in it.

Similarly, Symeon characteristically labels the particles as offered both "in memory and honor"[63] (εἰς τιμὴν καὶ μνήμην) of the saints who, according to Cabasilas, nevertheless retain their intercessory function as part of this sophisticated hierarchical structure. The Church, Symeon claims, in recalling her past, bestows tribute upon the saints by virtue of either their direct involvement in the work of salvation or through their Christ-like imitation of living the Gospel. Hence, the heavenly host are called "ministers of the mystery" (καθυπουργησάντων τῷ μυστηρίῳ); the Old Testament prophets and the righteous were the first to "proclaim in advance those things concerning the mystery . . . of whom the most excellent and seal is the Baptist" (τῶν προκηρυξάντων τὰ τοῦ μυστηρίου... ὦν ἐξαίρετος καὶ σφραγὶς ὁ Βαπτιστής); the apostles are described as "servants of Christ, as the first priests and teachers of the faith" (ὑπηρετῶν τοῦ Χριστοῦ, ὡς πρώτων ἱερέων καὶ διδασκάλων τῆς πιστέως) who have also "seen God" (θεοπτῶν); the holy fathers are envisioned as the apostolic successors who have "engaged in the study and learning of piety" (τῆς εὐσεβείας ἐσπουδακότων); and the martyrs and righteous ascetics are described as the "fruit of preaching" (καὶ τοῦ καρποῦ τοῦ κηρύγματος, τῶν μαρτύρων καὶ ὁσίων).[64] This propinquity then to the divine economy permits the saints to share a "physical" closeness, as it were, to the sacrificed Lamb, and thus, in the Pseudo-Dionysian sense, to transmit sanctification to the living and dead, represented by the particles placed toward the bottom edge of the paten.

The mediatory function of the saints to convey sanctification from the sacrificed Lamb to the faithful is taken up predominantly by the Archbishop of Thessalonike, who writes:

> Except the particles are changed neither into the Master's Body nor into the bodies of the saints; but they are only gifts and offerings and sacrifices through bread in imitation of the Master, and in their name they are offered to Him, and through the celebration, union, and communion with the mysteries, they are sanctified, and to those for whom they are [represent] they convey sanctification, and through [the particles] for the saints to us.[65]

This hierarchical progression of holiness, that is, from the consecrated Lamb to the particles representing the saints and then to the living and dead represented by those particles below them, is likened by Symeon to the holy relics and churches, which are consecrated at once by God and then become vehicles of grace.[66] This intermediate step in the process of sanctification makes the important theological point of the goodness of created beings and their capability to transmit the eschatological benefits, which are relished never on an individualistic basis but always within the context of a communal celebration, hence the eschatological banquet.

Interestingly, however, Symeon stops well short of explaining how sanctification proceeding from the particles that have been "hallowed" via contact to the consecrated Lamb differs from the sanctification imparted via the reception of communion. It could very well be that Symeon is simply interested in advancing his own Dionysian model of celestial hierarchy. Nevertheless, it remains vague why the sanctified particles upon the paten are understood as possessing the potential to convey eschatological benefits, when Holy Communion, in the general patristic understanding, achieves the same goal. If, in fact, clergy are cautioned to commune themselves and the faithful exclusively from the Lamb and not the particles, then one must wonder if the efficacy of the particles can be seen as benefiting only those commemorated at the prothesis and not necessarily the communicants themselves. Such a stance would no doubt preserve the Dionysian hierarchical model to which Symeon ascribes most vigilantly, and it would also explain Symeon's staunch reluctance to allow the faithful to commune the Holy Mysteries exclusively from the consecrated Lamb and not the particles representing the celestial host.[67] As Robert Taft notes, the decline especially in lay communion in the East after the first millennium may very likely have brought about an increase in commemorations and prayers for the faithful,[68] in which case Symeon's position bears credence.

Cabasilas, in commenting upon the intercessory section of the anaphora, draws a comparison between Chrysostom's understanding of the double aspect of the spiritual sacrifice (i.e. thanksgiving and supplication) and Basil of Caesarea's view, a difference, Cabasilas claims, may simply be one of expression.[69] For the former, a sharp distinction is made between those for whom thanksgiving is offered (the saints) and those for whom supplication is made (the living and dead). The Chrysostomian anaphora makes the distinction between supplication and thanksgiving more palpable by listing first the benefits of Holy Communion and then, in a separate sentence, stating the second reason why the offering is made: "Moreover we offer to you this reasonable worship for the Forefathers who repose in the faith . . . [followed by the litany of generic categories of the saints]."[70] On the contrary, the Archbishop of Caesarea abstains from such a dichotomy and rather groups the two together. He seemingly attaches to the prayer of worthiness for communion the phrase, ". . . but that we may find mercy and grace with all the saints who through the ages have pleased You,"[71] which is indicative of the Church's gratitude for the work wrought by the saints for the glory of God.

This difference between the two Byzantine liturgical commentators is quite conspicuous, and it raises several provocative questions related to this chapter. First, what degree of separation exists between those members of the Church already in heaven and those still on earth and what specific qualities peculiar to each realm, if any, warrant such a separation? Can the Dionysian hierarchical structure of "superior" – "inferior" (i.e. from Creator to creature and, in turn, from "higher" to "lower" strata of created beings) be reasonably applied also to the relationship between the living and the saints, when both groups are essentially mortals who simply exist, as it were, on different "planes?" Can it be implied that Christians belonging to the Church Triumphant and Church Militant are really separated only by the factor of time (i.e. the former have already entered eternity while the latter have not but eventually will), and that sainthood naturally makes them recipients of praise and thanksgiving while at the same time capable of interceding before God for their confreres? Furthermore, does the

Basilian intention of combining thanksgiving and supplication, two inherently ascending movements, seem compatible with the Dionysian hierarchy that only stresses the downward progression of grace? Finally, can thanksgiving and intercession ever exist separately in the first place or are they in fact mutually dependent activities? The interdependence seems rather obvious when Cabasilas lauds the honorable feats of the saints as the very reason for their mediatory grace: "It is as if one said: 'Give us the grace which thou hast already given to the saints; sanctify us as thou hast already sanctified so many of our race.'"[72] Even though the favorable state of sainthood is an ideal that the Church extols, it is also the goal of the Church to seek this standard for her members.

THE EXCISION OF THE PARTICLES FOR THE LIVING AND THE DEAD[73]

Then he takes out particles for the living and places them below the Lamb toward the right saying:

Remember, O loving Master, every diocese of the Orthodox, our archbishop (name), the honorable presbyterate, the diaconate in Christ and every priestly and monastic order [in the monasteries: our father (name) the priest-monk] and all our brother-hood in Christ.

And he commemorates the hierarch who ordained him, if he is alive, and by name all the living and he adds:

And all our brothers, whom you have called to your service through your compassion, O loving Master.

Consequently, he takes out particles for those who have fallen asleep and places them beneath the Lamb toward the left saying:

For the memory and forgiveness of the sins of the blessed and ever-memorable builders of this holy Church (or holy monastery).

And he commemorates the hierarch who ordained him, if he has fallen asleep, and all those who have fallen asleep, and he adds:

And all who in hope of the resurrection of eternal life have fallen asleep in communion with you, our Orthodox fathers and brothers, O loving Lord.

And the deacon commemorates the living and dead which he wants.

And finally the priest lifts up a particle for himself and places it with the particles of the living saying:

Remember also, O Lord, my unworthiness and forgive me every transgression both voluntary and involuntary.

The commemoration of saints for the sake of thanksgiving and supplication is immediately followed by the specific and likewise hierarchical remembrance of the living first and then the dead, via the excised particles for each individual named. A general categorization of those commemorated, however, precedes the litany of individual names. Among the living, the subsequent individuals are commemorated in the following order: (1) the three degrees of the clergy (bishop, priest, and deacon), with the name of the local archbishop mentioned first among this list; (2) in monasteries, the abbot, who is likewise distinguished by name; (3) by implication, the concelebrating clergy and all clergy called to the service of Christ; (4) the ordaining hierarch of the officiant of the prothesis rite, if living; and (5) the rest of the living mentioned individually by name. Medieval manuscripts, not surprisingly, also included the Emperor or Empress as representative of all civil authority,[74] a specification unnecessary in the modern critical text. Among the dead, the following order is observed: (1) the deceased builders of the church or monastery; (2) the deceased hierarch who ordained the clergyman presiding over the prothesis; and (3) the individual names of the deceased, followed by a generic, all-inclusive request for those "fathers and brothers" who have died in the faith of Christ. Finally, the commemorations end with the priest and deacon each excising a particle for themselves and naturally placing it on the side of the living. Symeon follows this line of commemorations in the latter very closely but also adds a specific reason for each individual remembrance.[75] For example, the first to be remembered is the celebrant bishop, "because he is the source of priesthood." Then, the celebrant lower clergy are remembered, since they have been appointed by the Church for the service of the holy mysteries. Symeon here also makes an inference to the Pauline injunction that the laborers should be among the first to receive the fruits of their labors. Next are mentioned the God-fearing kings, who defended the orthodox faith, and then the pious people of the nation. Then, if the Liturgy is performed in the monastery, the abbot, together with the brotherhood, is remembered. Next, the builders and benefactors of the church or monastery, be they alive or dead, are commemorated, followed by the people who brought the gifts to the Liturgy and those for whom they were offered. The dead, as in the *Codex* and all other Byzantine *euchologia*, are listed last, with the deceased clergy again preceding the lay faithful who have fallen asleep in the faith.[76]

Both Byzantine Fathers attempt to identify the spiritual benefits sought by the Church for both the living and the dead. The benefits themselves can best be characterized as eschatological, and they reach the ranks of the living and the dead hierarchically through the saints, whose prayers for those "below" them, as it were, have as their content the spiritual benefits of the faithful leading to their salvation. Symeon includes in his commentary the brief supplicatory prayer attached to the commemoration of the saintly orders: "through whose supplications visit us [he says], O God, and grant to us *all requests unto salvation, and life eternal.*"[77] Cabasilas lists in more detail the benefits awaited by both the living and the dead:

> In particular, that the departed may have rest for their souls, and may, with the saints who have completed their course, inherit the kingdom; and that the living may partake of the holy table, and be made holy, and that none may partake to his own judgement and condemnation; likewise, that they may receive remission of their sins, peace, fruitfulness, and the provision of what is necessary to them; and finally that they may in God's sight appear worthy of the kingdom.[78]

Cabasilas further advocates that *sanctification* via the Eucharist is the ultimate goal for both groups, but it can only be attained by first embarking on a cathartic process highlighted by genuine repentance and the forgiveness of sins. "In what does this sanctification consist? In the remission of sins; that is the chief effect of these sacred offerings."[79] For both Fathers, it is clear that constant and uninterrupted participation in the life in God remains the key to the Christian's existence, which may be extended to include sanctification, salvation, and eternal life.

The insistence on the cathartic effects of eucharistic reception as a prerequisite for sanctification or deification (*theosis*) concurs with St. Maximos the Confessor's three-step process of purification (κάθαρσις), illumination (φώτισις), and deification (θέωσις), although the latter specifically considers man's reception of Holy Communion as his participation in "mystical theology,"[80] or the divine life, rather than as the source of expiation. Nevertheless, the Eastern formula at Communion, "for the forgiveness of sins and life everlasting," explicitly takes into account the stages of purification and deification, implying simultaneously that man's enlightenment ensues as a result of his personal repentance and innate desire to obey the Gospel and perform its statutes.

The three phases delineated by Maximos, quite fascinatingly, also seem to correspond to the various sections of the prothesis rite examined thus far. For example, the step toward κάθαρσις is very plainly reflected in the bloodless immolation of the Lamb and the analogous rites with the chalice, whose obvious purpose is the exoneration of mankind's sins and offenses. The commemoration of the angelic and saintly orders relates to the enlightenment stage, insofar as the angels and saints are themselves the direct recipients and transmitters of divine illumination and grace, and the *par excellence* role models of the Church, to be emulated by the living and dead who aspire to be united with God. Finally, the phase of θέωσις corresponds to the addition of the particles for the living and dead to the paten, joining them into one union with God, and the epicletic prayer of the prothesis, which identifies and establishes Christ as "the heavenly bread" that unites into the one body of the Church the entire world and mystically conjoins into a dynamic union the celestial altar of God with the lesser altars of sanctuaries throughout the world. In actuality, this liturgical act brings to completion Symeon's eschatological vision of the redeemed Church and world, permeated by God's presence.[81]

THE ECCLESIOLOGICAL DIMENSION OF THE PROTHESIS

With the concluding commemoration of the living and dead and the placement of their particles below the Lamb on the paten, all the excisions from the prosphorae are complete and the *diskos* is immediately transformed, in Symeon of Thessalonike's words, into an icon of the Church. Symeon's astute reference to the circular paten as symbolic of heaven[82] also advances his own mystagogical rendering of the church temple as representative of the heavenly, or "super-worldly," realm. He writes: "The church, therefore, even though it is composed of matter, nevertheless possesses a super-worldly grace, for it is perfected by the silent prayers [spoken] by the high priest and is anointed through divine myrrh, and it is established entirely as the dwelling place of God."[83] Symeon thereby introduces in characteristic form a litany of seemingly opposing binaries that reconcile the expressly divine, or intelligible, and the expressly human, or sensible. For example, Symeon indicates the "double nature" of the church temple (διπλοῦς ὁ ναός), stating that there coexists in each building an innermost sanctuary whose entrance is forbidden to the lay people (τῶν ἀδύτων) and the nave outside the altar (τῶν ἐκτός).[84] He then proceeds to identify the divine and human natures of the incarnate Christ (Θεὸν ὁμοῦ καὶ ἄνθρωπον), affirming the invisibility (ἀόρατον) of the former and the visibility of the latter (ὁρατόν).[85]

Even man, Symeon claims, possesses an invisible component, the soul, but also a sensible constituent, the body.[86] Here, Symeon takes his analogical analysis beyond the binary level by identifying a tripartite nature to the church temple, after the Trinity. Thus, for example, the three sections of the church building (the *pronaos*, or narthex, the nave, and the altar correspond to the three orders of the faithful (the penitents, the laity, and the clergy, respectively), as well as to the three celestial planes (again, in order, the earth, the heavens, and the celestial sphere beyond the heavens). Admittedly, the list may go on almost indefinitely, but what is of pertinent value here is that Symeon implements an incarnational mystagogy in his comparative juxtapositions that does not reject the inherent goodness of the sensible item. Quite the contrary, he stresses the magnitude of its value within the context of the created order, which is continually in need of transformation and redemption by the incarnate Christ. In this regard, and perhaps unintentionally, Symeon not only formulates an anti-Gnostic polemic in his symbolic appraisal of the church temple, but he also establishes a basis for the belief that divine sanctification permeates the entire cosmos, represented strikingly by the prothesis rite and, by extension, the church building itself. This unique elucidation then of the prothesis and the Church as images of a historical and meta-historical "redeemed community," worthy of and filled with the divine presence, is likewise significant because it affirms the eschatological reality the Church lives daily and anticipates in its fullness at the end times.

What further proof is there in the patristic writings, aside from the Byzantine commentator's aforementioned reference, that the prothesis rite indeed possesses any sort of ecclesiological dimension? A first indication is Symeon's characteristic envisioning of the entire Church, historical and meta-historical, which has congregated around the sacrificial Lamb of God. Symeon writes: "But let us understand how also through this divine symbol and through the work of the holy proskomide we see Jesus Himself and all His one Church (τὸν Ἰησοῦν αὐτόν, καὶ τὴν Ἐκκλησίαν αὐτοῦ μίαν πᾶσαν ὁρῶμεν). . . ."[87] The nature of the Church is to be understood in terms of the community of faith "called out" (ἐκκλησία) of the world (in imitation of Christ's own extraction from the world) for the purpose of redemption, excised or raised out of the leaven of the physical world in order to form the polity of heaven. The paten then, a symbol of the heavenly realm and the Church, receives the particles for the living and dead from the "earthly" prosphora, in order to bring to completion the constitution of the Kingdom of God. In addition, since the Church also signifies the place where renewal and rebirth are effected via holy baptism, the paten may also be likened to a baptismal font of sorts, a birthing womb of the converted Christian, replete with neophytes redeemed through the blood of the risen Lord and fully alive in Him.

A second proof of the ecclesiological dimension of the prothesis involves the constant offering of supplication and praise to the Holy Trinity, two liturgical acts that form the very crux of the Church's daily life of worship. "The offering of sacrifice," explains Cabasilas, the very reason for the Church's liturgical celebration, "is not only an act of supplication; it is one of thanksgiving as well."[88] St. Cyril of Jerusalem's characteristic acknowledgment of prayer as efficacious when offered "in the presence of the holy and most dread sacrifice"[89] provides the impetus for why the Church offers intercessory petition at the time of consecration in the first place, emphasizing the inherent realism that characterizes the consecrated gifts. In like manner, doxological prayer is also offered before them, since the very presence of God is manifest in the eucharistic elements. Cabasilas extends this realism to include even the pre-consecratory phase of the gifts, which obviously comprises their origin at the prothesis. He writes that both supplication and doxology are part of the offering at the anaphora, "in the same way that, at the beginning of the liturgy, in dedicating the offerings to God, the priest gave thanks and made supplication at the same time; he now, having consecrated and sacrificed these gifts, unites thanksgiving with petition. He states the reasons for his thanksgiving, and names those for whom he prays."[90] Interestingly, the Church's reciprocation of a sacrifice of praise and supplication before the immolated Lamb in worship imitates the almost concurrent offering of petition and doxological confession offered at Golgotha by both the thief and centurion, respectively, strikingly transforming the place of sacrifice into a sort of makeshift local church, the first '"ecclesial community" comprised of supplication and doxology. The thief's plea toward the crucified Lord, "Jesus, remember me when you come in your kingdom" (Luke 23:42) is followed by the centurion's confession, "Truly this was the Son of God!" (Matt 27:54) Both utterances offered before the altar of the Cross become the model *par excellence* for the dual form of prayer subsequently offered in liturgical worship. And each prayer centers around the magnanimity of Christ's sacrifice, which ushers in the eschatological Kingdom.

A third and final proof of the ecclesiological dimension of the prothesis rite is Symeon of Thessalonike's staunch insistence upon the practice of selective and exclusive commemoration of only baptized Orthodox Christians, who remain in good canonical standing with the Church. He states:

And it [the Kingdom of God as exposed upon the paten] is not a land for the unbelievers, nor for those who think (believe) differently. For what communion is there between light and darkness? For even the angels, he says, remove the evil from the midst of the righteous. For this reason is it not proper at all for any priest to offer [particles] for a heterodox or to lift up [pieces] in his memory; but not even for those who have openly sinned or remain unrepentant, because [their] admission [to the paten] is to their condemnation, as it is for those who commune the dread mysteries without having repented, as the divine Paul says.[91]

Symeon's conservatism in the above assessment is plainly obvious, but his conservative attitude seems to lie in the strong realism that characterizes his liturgical mystagogy. His identification of the paten, as an icon of the redeemed Church, with the insinuated "land of believers" apparently drives home this point. In addition, the rejection of unrepentant sinners from commemoration on the paten is an indication of their "bad canonical standing" with the Church, which by extension translates into their exclusion from the blessedness of the eschatological Kingdom.

Symeon's realism in understanding the completed paten as true icon of the redeemed Church is complemented by one particular rubric removed from the modern critical text but included in medieval manuscripts like *Panteleimon*. The Codex orders for the deacon, upon completing his own commemorations, to ensure that all particles excised previously by the priest and himself be gathered toward the center of the paten, "*so that they sit safely and not one falls off.*"[92] This rubric likewise reveals a realism that suggests that the paten, like the Church, is one and the same with the divine Kingdom, and thus the celebrant must take special care in who is and is not admitted to the paten, since this act, at least in Symeon's eyes, has serious implications as to a soul's inclusion in the eschatological Kingdom! Symeon sees salvation as offered through the Body of Christ on earth, which expresses here and now, in an inchoative manner, the reality of a soul's state in the *eschaton*.[93]

The next chapter completes this book's specific examination of sacrificial and eschatological elements in the prothesis, by focusing upon the veiling, censing, and blessing of the ritualized gifts; in other words, the conclusion of the preparatory rite prior to the commencement of the eucharistic liturgy. If, as previously said, the first two chapters dealt, respectively, with establishing the grounds upon which the Church was established, as well as populating the image of the Church upon the paten via the excisions of particles for its members on both sides of death, the subsequent chapter will deal with the actual setting aside, or "sanctification," of the holy gifts via the series of aforementioned liturgical acts. It is now to this concluding segment of the prothesis rite that this book turns.

NOTES

1. See pp. xx–xxi of this book.

2. Symeon of Thessalonike, *On the Sacred Liturgy* 85; PG 155.264C.

3. Παρακλητική, ἤτοι Ὀκτόηχος ἡ Μεγάλη· περιέχουσα ἅπασαν τὴν ἀνήκουσαν αὐτῇ ἀκολουθίαν μετὰ τῶν ἐν τῷ τέλει συνηθῶν προσθηκῶν [*The Parakletike, or the Great Oktoechos: Containing Every Service Belonging to It with the Usual Additions at the End*], (Athens, 1992), 467. Translation mine.

4. Πεντηκοστάριον χαρμόσυνον, τὴν ἀπὸ τοῦ Πάσχα μέχρι τῆς τῶν Ἁγίων Πάντων Κυριακῆς ἀνήκουσαν αὐτῷ ἀκολουθίαν·περιέχον ἐπὶ τέλους δὲ καὶ τὰ ἑωθινὰ Εὐαγγέλια τὰ ἐν τῷ Ὄρθρῳ ἑκάστης τῶν ἐν τῷ μεταξὺ τούτῳ ἑορτῶν ἀναγινωσκομένα, διορθωθέν, καὶ δι' ἑνὸς προλόγου πλουτισθὲν ὑπὸ Βαρθολομαίου Κουτλουμουσιανοῦ τοῦ Ἰμβρίου [*The Joyful Pentekostarion, (with) the Service(s) Belonging to It from Easter to the Sunday of All Saints: Containing in the End the Morning Gospels of Matins Read on Each (Sunday) Between These Feasts, Corrected and Enriched by Bartholomew Koutloumousianos of Imvros*], (Athens, 1992), 5. Translation mine.

5. Dionysios the Areopagite, *Celestial Hierarchies* 13; PG 3.301C; see also Pseudo-Dionysius, *The Complete Works*. trans. Colm Luibheid. *The Classics of Western Spirituality* (New York, 1987), 178; and Διονυσίου Ἀρεοπαγίτου. Περὶ Ἐκκλησιαστικῆς καὶ Οὐρανίας Ἱεραρχίας [*On Ecclesiastical and Celestial Hierarchies*], trans. Ignatios Sakalis (Thessalonike, 1985), 278–81.

6. Petros Vassiliadis, "Eucharistic and Therapeutic Spirituality", in *The Greek Orthodox Theological Review*, vol. 42, no. 1-2 (1997), 4. In this provocative paper, the author staunchly advocates for a return to a more ancient eucharistic, or liturgical spirituality, whose goal is the realization of the Church as the eschatological *community* preparing for the end time. Upon this principle, he dismisses as of secondary importance the therapeutic, or cathartic, spirituality popularized by the development of monasticism and Alexandrian and later Pseudo-Dionysian theology, which focuses primarily on the *individual* attainment of theosis and a return to the prelapsarian state of pristine existence.

7. See pp. 8–9 of this book.

8. Stylianos Muksuris, "The Prothesis Rite and the Icon of the *Deesis*: The Eschatological Vision of Liturgy with Contemporary Implications," American Academy of Religion Annual Meeting (San Diego, November 19, 2007).

9. Thomas Pott indicates that the earliest evidence of commemorations in the prothesis rite comes from the eleventh century *Codex Sinaiticus georg. 89*, an *euchologion* discovered in Jerusalem. See Thomas Pott, *La réforme liturgique byzantine: étude du phénomène d'évolution non spontanée de la liturgie byzantine* (Rome, 2000), 186; also idem., 180, n. 71, and 183, n. 89.

10. Just half a century before the *Sinaiticus* manuscript, one encounters the well-known correspondence between a priest of Crete and his Metropolitan Elias, residing in Constantinople at the time, regarding the "correct" execution of the prothesis rite. The priest's dilemma centered on proper liturgical procedure from conflicting authoritative sources. On the one hand he wished to remain faithful to Patriarch Nicholas III (Grammatikos) of Constantinople (d. 1111) and the liturgical canons that became standardized throughout the churches in the Empire, and on the other to the ancient practice reflected in St. Basil the Great's *Mystagogical History of the Catholic Church* and St. Germanos of Constantinople's *Ecclesiastical History*, which nevertheless conflicted with the canons of Nicholas. In essence, the Metropolitan of Crete affirms the standing tradition in the capital city, namely, the use of four prosphora in the prothesis, signifying that each loaf was offered in honor of a particular figure or group of figures (e.g. the Lamb, the Mother of God, the angelic hierarchies, and the orders of saints). See Pott, pp. 180–82.

Yet another contemporary of the aforementioned sources, but one which omits any commemoration of saints, is the critical edition of Leo of Tuscany's translation of the Liturgy of St. John Chrysostom. See the enlightening articles by A. Jacob, "*La traduction de la Liturgie de S. Jean Chrysostome par Léon Toscan. Édition critique*", in *Orientalia Christiana Periodica*, vol. 32 (1966), 111–62; and idem., ed. "*Une version géorgienne inédite de la liturgie de saint Jean Chrysostome*", in *Le Muséon*, vol. 77 (1964), 65–119.

11. Pott, 186, trans. mine; Robert F. Taft, *The Byzantine Rite: A Short History* (Collegeville, 1992), 87.

12. Pott, 185. Translation mine.

13. Ibid. Translation mine.

14. Leonide Ouspensky, "The Problem of the Iconostasis", in *Saint Vladimir's Theological Quarterly*, vol. 8 (1964), 201–04.

15. Symeon of Thessalonike, *On the Sacred Liturgy* 94; PG 155.281B.

16. Maximos the Confessor, *Mystagogia* 2; PG 91.668D.

17. Nicholas P. Constas, "Symeon of Thessalonike and the Theology of the Icon Screen", in Sharon E.J. Gerstel, ed., *Thresholds of the Sacred: Architectural, Art Historical, Liturgical, and Theological Perspectives on Religious Screens, East and West* (Washington, 2006), 166–67.

18. P.N. Trembelas, Αἱ τρεῖς λειτουργίαι κατὰ τοὺς ἐν Ἀθήναις κώδικας [*The Three Liturgies According to the Athens Codices*], *Texte und Forschungen zur byzantinisch-neugriechischen Philologie* (Athens, 1935), 3.

19. Pott, 186. Translation mine.

20. Ibid., 187.

21. Ibid. Translation mine.

22. Symeon of Thessalonike, *Interpretation of the Divine Temple and Liturgy* 105; PG 155.312B.

23. Idem., *On the Sacred Liturgy* 98; PG 155.296C.

24. Ibid.

25. Idem., *Interpretation of the Divine Temple and Liturgy* 131; PG155.340AB, and *On the Sacred Liturgy* 98–99; PG 155.296CD.

26. Constas, 168.

27. Ibid., 170.

28. Among these works are: *On the Celestial Hierarchy* 1.2; *On the Divine Names* 1.4; *On the Ecclesiastical Hierarchy* 4.2; *Letter* 9.1; and *Letter* 8.1. See also Constas, 176, n. 49.

29. Constas, 170.

30. Symeon of Thessalonike, *Interpretation of the Divine Temple and Liturgy* 102; PG 155.748C.

31. Pott, 187. Translation mine.

32. Nicholas Cabasilas, *Commentary on the Divine Liturgy* 10; PG 150.388A; N. Cabasilas, *A Commentary on the Divine Liturgy*, trans. J.M. Hussey and P.A. McNulty (London, 1960), 39.

33. Ibid., PG 150.388B.

34. Symeon of Thessalonike, *Interpretation of the Divine Temple and Liturgy* 3; PG 155.704A.

35. Hussey and McNulty, trans., 39–40; Cabasilas, *Commentary* 10; PG 150.388C.

36. Ibid., PG 150.388D.

37. Ibid., 40; Cabasilas, *Commentary* 10; PG 150.388D.

38. Symeon of Thessalonike, *On the Sacred Liturgy* 94; PG 155.281B.

39. Ibid., 93; PG 155.280C.

40. Ibid.

41. Ibid., 94; PG 155.284A. Emphasis mine, to indicate Symeon's hierarchical insistence.

42. Hussey and McNulty, trans., 39; Cabasilas, *Commentary* 10; PG 150.388A.

43. See pp. 9–10 of this book.

44. Hussey and McNulty, trans., 84; Cabasilas, *Commentary* 33; PG 150.441D.

45. Ibid.

46. Symeon of Thessalonike, *On the Sacred Liturgy* 94; PG 155.280D–281B.

47. Ibid., PG 155.280D, cf. 284A.

48. Ibid., PG 155.281C.

49. Stylianos Muksuris, *The Anaphorae of the Liturgy of Sts. Addai and Mari and the Byzantine Liturgy of St. Basil the Great: A Comparative Study* (unpublished M.Litt. thesis), (Durham, 1999), 60–61.

50. Trembelas, 3.

51. Ibid.

52. Symeon of Thessalonike, *On the Sacred Liturgy* 94; PG 155.280D–281A.

53. Ibid., PG 155.280D.

54. Ἱερατικόν [*Priest's Service Book*], ed. Constantinos Papayiannis (Athens, 2001), 102, 103.

55. Symeon of Thessalonike, *On the Sacred Liturgy* 94; PG 155.280D.

56. Maximos the Confessor, *Mystagogia* 2; PG 91.668B.

57. Symeon of Thessalonike, *Interpretation of the Divine Temple and Liturgy* 4; PG 155.704AB.

58. Ouspensky, 200.

59. St. John Chrysostom, *Second Homily on the Incarnation, Our Father among the Saints John the golden-Mouthed (Chrysostom): On the Nativity of Our Savior Jesus Christ, Second Homily*, trans. Constantine Terss (Atlanta, 1995), 1; PG 56.385–394. Emphasis mine.

60. Hussey and McNulty, trans., 83; Cabasilas, *Commentary* 33; PG 150.441C.

61. Ibid., PG 150.441D.

62. Ibid., PG 150.441C.

63. Symeon of Thessalonike, *On the Sacred Liturgy* 94; PG 155.281A.

64. Ibid., PG 155.281AB.

65. Ibid., PG 155.281CD.

66. Ibid., PG 155.281D.

67. Ibid., 99; PG 155.300AB. Symeon here mentions that *only* the consecrated Lamb, after its breaking, is immersed into the Blood in preparation for the communion of the faithful.

68. Robert F. Taft, "The Decline of Communion in Byzantium and the Distancing of the Congregation from the Liturgical Action: Cause, Effect, or Neither?," in Sharon E.J. Gerstel, ed., *Thresholds of the Sacred: Architectural, Art Historical, Liturgical, and Theological Perspectives on Religious Screens, East and West* (Washington, 2006), 27–50.

69. Hussey and McNulty, trans., 84–85; Cabasilas, *Commentary* 33; PG 150.444AC.

70. Translation mine. See also F.E. Brightman, ed., *Liturgies Eastern and Western* (Oxford, 1896), 387.

71. Muksuris, *The Anaphorae*, 172.

72. Hussey and McNulty, trans., 85; Cabasilas, *Commentary* 33; PG 150.444C.

73. See pp. 10–11 of this book.

74. Trembelas, 3.

75. Symeon of Thessalonike, *On the Sacred Liturgy* 94; PG 155.284B.

76. Ibid., PG 155.284BC.

77. Ibid., PG 155.281BC.

78. Hussey and McNulty, trans., 83; Cabasilas, *Commentary* 33; PG 150.441B.

79. Ibid., 85; Ibid., PG 150.444C.

80. See the excellent summary of St. Maximos the Confessor's *Mystagogia* and how Maximos analyzes the mystical visions of Pseudo-Dionysios in his *Celestial Hierarchies*, in Chapter Four ("The Church and the Divine Eucharist, according to St. Maximos the Confessor") of Metropolitan of Nafpaktos Hierotheos Vlahos' book *The Mind of the Orthodox Church*, trans. Esther Williams (Levadia, 1998).

81. Symeon of Thessalonike, *On the Sacred Liturgy* 94; PG 155.285AB.

82. Ibid., 85; PG 155.264C.

83. Idem., *Interpretation of the Divine Temple and Liturgy* 3; PG 155.701D–704A.

84. Ibid., 4; PG 155.704A.

85. Ibid.

86. Ibid.

87. Idem., *On the Sacred Liturgy* 94; PG 155.285AB. See also M. Papadopoulos, Λειτουργική: Τὰ τελούμενα ἐντὸς τοῦ ναοῦ [*Liturgics: The Rites Conducted within the Church*], (Athens, 1992), 184–85.

88. Hussey and McNulty, trans., 83; Cabasilas, *Commentary* 33; PG 150.441C.

89. Gregory Dix, *The Shape of the Liturgy* (London, 1945), 199.

90. Hussey and McNulty, trans., 83–84; Cabasilas, *Commentary* 33; PG 150.441C.

91. Symeon of Thessalonike, *On the Sacred Liturgy* 94; PG 155.285B.

92. Trembelas, 4.

93. See Hans-Joachim Schulz, *Die Byzantinische Liturgie: Glaubenszeugnis und Symbolgestalt* [Ἡ Βυζαντινή Λειτουργία· μαρτυρία πίστεως καί συμβολική ἔκφραση] trans. Demetrios V. Tzerpos (Athens, 1998), 181.

8

THE MYSTICAL PROTHESIS III: THE FINAL
PREPARATION IN THE VEILING AND PRAYER

The notion of sanctification (or pre-sanctification) as the formal setting aside and designation of the prepared gifts as the antitypes of
Christ's Body and Blood pervades this final section of the prothesis rite,
which involves the ritual offering of incense, the veiling, and the "consecratory" prayer over the gifts. It is rather interesting that Georges Descoeudres[1]
and Thomas Pott[2] are just shy of calling the prothesis a "mini-anaphora,"
in the sense that the preparatory rite has taken on the significance of "a
prophetic anticipation of the salvation event in Jesus Christ celebrated in
the anaphora."[3] Pott reasonably argues that by at least the last quarter of
the twelfth century (a reference to the important Latin translation of the
Chrysostomian eucharistic liturgy by Leo Tuscan between 1173–1178)[4] the
manner of preparation of the Lamb and the chalice, together with the sacrificial implications attached to the preparation and coupled with the offering of incense over the gifts, had formalized the rite almost to the degree
of a "mini-Eucharist," replete, itself, with its own reserve of sacrificial and
eschatological mystagogy. The prayer of the prothesis, which appears for
the first time in the eighth-century *Barberini Codex 336* and whose successful introduction into the series of preparatory acts was in fact the first
step toward the prothesis' formalization into a rite, complements these later
rubrics in giving the prothesis a distinctly anaphoral idiosyncrasy.

These observations raise several questions. First, how similar are the sacrificial and eschatological notions in the prothesis to those in the Eucharist
and in what sense do the common anaphoral elements assist in the similarity of these notions? Second, in what sense are the offering of incense and
the corresponding veiling of the gifts sacrificial and eschatological? Third,

what sacrificial and eschatological undertones, if any, can be extracted from the ancient prayer of the prothesis and can any of them seriously be considered intentional? Finally, in which way does the "consecratory" language in the prothesis prayer[5] preserve the sacrificial and eschatological fiber in the prothesis rite? Before we proceed to answer these specific questions, which essentially seek to address "the dialectic between the ritual and its horizon of symbolic understanding"[6] (i.e. the relationship between the rite as it stands at a particular stage in its historical development and its theological significance, which Pott insists always go hand in hand), it is more pertinent to assess, in a more general sense, his central thesis of the non-spontaneous development of the Byzantine Liturgy.

THE NON-SPONTANEOUS DEVELOPMENT OF THE PROTHESIS RITE

If the evolution of theological thought and ideas were expressed by changes reflected in the prothesis rite, could this conscious process likewise be held accountable for transferring such themes from the eucharistic liturgy to the prothesis? Like the Divine Liturgy, did the rite of the prothesis evolve deliberately or in an "organic" manner, that is, in a sporadic, irregular way? For the purposes of this book, Pott's stance is crucial for the simple reason that the sacrificial and eschatological elements that permeate both Liturgy and prothesis are far too numerous and closely interrelated to warrant a stamp of "casual development." The Byzantine liturgical tradition, in all its ritual modes, expresses its sacrificial and eschatological theology consistently and in faithful continuation of the beliefs of the primitive Church, albeit in a far more refined and "material" fashion.

In Support of T. Pott: The Dynamics of the Prothesis' Non-Spontaneous Development

In his *La réforme liturgique byzantine: étude du phénomène d' évolution non-spontanée de la liturgie byzantine*, Thomas Pott offers keen arguments in favor of the conscious (though not always systematic)[7] development of the Byzantine Liturgy, all interwoven within the four specific examples of ritual modification or expansion. These examples are: (1) the Studite reforms of the ninth century; (2) the formation of the Byzantine Triduum; (3) the development of the prothesis rite; and (4) the liturgical reforms of the seventeenth century within the Slavic churches.[8] In his chapter regarding the prothesis, Pott cautions that his purpose is not to reproduce a complete history of the prothesis rite in all its practical aspects, a task already accomplished by Descoeudres,[9] but rather to build upon his predecessor's work and identify historical factors that can explain the course of the rite's evolution.

Insinuated of course in this preliminary remark is that the prothesis rite expanded its theological understanding of itself, so to speak, by accepting modifications, or additions, to its execution that did not necessarily annul its earlier intended symbolism. As Andrew Louth observes, "Even with Nikon's reforms it was a matter of the modification of an existing liturgy, rather than the devising of a fresh one: there was more continuity than change."[10] The evolution of the Liturgy then in the East has typically involved a modification of an existing rite or key elements within it, without the need to eliminate them completely. Consequently, the introduction of new elements in a rite would create not a new theology per se, but rather a shift in emphasis or a readjustment of theological thought for the purpose of preserving the unity between the said elements. This seemingly unbalanced yet nevertheless viable coexistence of older sacrificial elements with the newer view of the prothesis as an image of the celestial hierarchy is denotative of the Church's theological reflection throughout the centuries, which did not replace "unwanted" or "incorrect" elements but rather shifted emphasis in a non-threatening and non-damaging way. Hence, the Bread of Life and Lamb, typified by the wording of the prothesis rite and later by the introduction of the liturgical spear used to "immolate" the Lamb, is, at the very end of the prothesis' evolution, the same glorified Lamb of the Apocalypse who receives, in hierarchical fashion, the doxological praises and supplications of the orders of saints and angelic beings, in whose honor and memory the Liturgy is offered.

Pott identifies three stages that highlight the evolution of the prothesis rite (*les trois horizons de compréhension symbolique*):[11] (1) the introduction of the prothesis prayer by the beginning of the seventh century and the designation of the procession of the gifts at the Great Entrance by Maximos the Confessor as "the entrance of the holy mysteries" (Ἡ δὲ τῶν ἁγίων μυστηρίων εἴσοδος);[12] (2) the introduction of the lance, evidenced by Germanos of Constantinople in his Ecclesiastical History by the year 730; and (3) the post-Iconoclasm formalization of the rite, including the further preparation of the Lamb and chalice and the rite of incense; the multiplication of particles; and the celestial hierarchy imagery via the rearrangement of particles in categories. Each stage essentially functions not so much as a gradual formalization of the rite but more so as a theological reflection by the Church, expanding upon ritual modifications by building upon the elements of the previous phase and broadening the dimensions by which the rite may be comprehended. The idea of theological reflection is actually a critical aspect of Pott's argumentation and will be revisited a little later in this section.

Pott correctly establishes that Theodore of Mopsuestia's characterization of the Great Entrance as the procession of Christ to the place of execution serves as the impetus for subsequent developments in the prothesis rite. Hence, from the very beginning of the rite's mystagogical formation, the notion of sacrifice occupies a central place in the theology of the rite, as it certainly did in the theological consciousness of the Church. The sacrificial notion is then reworked and expanded, so that the Body of Christ is identified not only as the heavenly manna that feeds the world, thus introducing the prayer of the prothesis, but also as the Isaian Lamb of God to be immolated before His accusers, thus introducing the use of the liturgical spear. This imagery, set in the Church's consciousness for several centuries, converts the prothesis into a sort of liturgical Golgotha, which then evokes the history of salvation. Consequently, the Church begins to see the divine economy in cosmic terms, encompassing the entire created universe, thus leading to a hierarchical arrangement of particles around the Lamb much reminiscent of the apocalyptic vision of John the Theologian.[13]

In this description of the rite's evolution, the Church's theological awareness, expressed and revised through the centuries, is evident in each step of development without necessarily preempting or delegitimizing the already existent elements that characterize the Church's thought for a particular period. In fact, and specifically with the prothesis rite, one may suppose that the Church's theological meditation after the Iconoclast era essentially assumes a secondary dimension, a more vivid eschatological vision articulated in terms of the new rubrical redactions to the rite. This is not to say by any means that the Church's belief in the eschatological reality is introduced for the first time now, during the Middle to Late-Byzantine era. On the contrary, the eschatological dimension of Christian life was well established by the primitive Church, which saw the sacrifice of the Lamb of God as the historical event that opened Paradise, where the same Lamb appears upon the divine throne of glory (Rev 5:1ff). Hence, the Lamb of sacrifice is simultaneously the Lamb of the Apocalypse, and this most critical juxtaposition has been embedded in the Church's theological meditation for almost two millennia. It just so happens that this secondary dimension is channeled through the ritual form of the prothesis, with the various rubrical additions (especially the increase in excised particles and their hierarchical arrangement on the paten) transforming the prothesis niche from a historical grotto or place of execution into a more cosmic or apocalyptic icon of heaven. The very reciprocity of influence between the theological commentary and the liturgical act is yet another important indication of the non-spontaneous nature of the prothesis rite's evolution. Pott writes:

> In conclusion one can say that theology, by explaining and interpreting the liturgical gesture, has taken it under its wings of systematic theory in order to instruct it and condition it. In return, the ritual has deployed before theology a richness of meaning which characterizes all symbolic language and represents for theology a healthy nourishment.[14]

Pott rightly maintains that the role of theology vis-à-vis the rite is to explain in greater detail that which the gesture already symbolizes or, better yet, to verbalize the symbol's inner meaning. The inherent implication of the liturgical act is understood then as the base symbolism upon which the liturgical commentary expounds. Thus, for example, the lance's representation as the spear at Golgotha, used in conjunction with the extraction and piercing of the Lamb, creates a defining sacrificial theology that goes well beyond the mere symbolic representation of a single item; the liturgical spear not only corroborates the imagery perceived at the Great Entrance as Christ's procession to the place of execution, first put forth by Theodore of Mopsuestia, but it also transforms the entire first section of the prothesis rite into a reenactment, or exegesis of sorts, of Christ's sacrifice.

For Pott, this theological exegesis of the prothesis rite may likewise be understood as the personal and thus unique reflection of each Christian at prayer, each of which is nestled among the greater and more representative collection of liturgical commentaries handed down in the Church throughout the ages. And it is through such paradigms of personal theological contemplation, all rooted in a more or less universally accepted symbolism of the rite, that the Church has ensured a conscious evolution for the prothesis. Pott observes that man

> contemplates theologically on the meaning of the mystery he celebrates by confronting the rite with all that is theologically sensible to him; the rite receives and mirrors these reflections and, like an icon that bears the marks of veneration from generation to generation, it becomes a living archive—although perhaps not a very ordered one—of a diachronic liturgical theology.[15]

As Pott argues, the two reforms of privatization and clericalization ("*la hiératisation*") of the prothesis rite, meaning the execution of the rite within the enclosed sanctuary, hidden from public view, and its celebration by one priest assisted by a deacon, were major factors explaining the accelerated rate at which the rite developed its more sophisticated theology at the turn of the first millennium. Such a radically new method of performing the prothesis meant that the celebrant was allotted more time to consciously reflect upon the sacrificial and eschatological themes inherent in the rite, as a once practical act of preparation was formalized into a liturgy whereby personal devotions and private theological musings were given an adequate context, both in terms of proper space and time. "Consequently," writes Pott, "having become a clerical rite of sorts, the prothesis presented itself as a handy mirror to reflect the theological tendencies and devotions of the clergy and above all the monks."[16]

In the end, such theological meditation on themes distinctly biblical and immersed in patristic tradition, with the aid of ritual form, may be perceived as exclusive or even elitist, reflecting only the beliefs of a select few, and frequently accepted as the official "opinion" (δόξα) of the Church. What was once a less elaborate and non-symbolic act of liturgical preparation before the commencement of the Eucharist, under the supervision of the deacon, is now expanded, as it were, into a more "theological" service but one under the exclusive direction of the priest. Does this not contradict the very nature of theology as the intended domain of all God's people, including the laity? To disprove this argument is quite difficult, given the prothesis rite's privatized character. On the other hand, one must wonder how reverting to a once again public and very practical execution of the prothesis could ever be capable of preserving the sacrificial and eschatological ideas that have permeated the Church's teaching from the beginning, but never fully delineated liturgically until the prothesis was formalized into an independent rite. It is unfortunate that Pott avoids this discussion by choosing to focus rather on the reformer or commentator's witness as the factor that secures the non-spontaneous evolution of the prothesis rite. He concludes:

> But the second approach does not consider the liturgy as an end in itself: it attempts to fathom the theological and ecclesial dimension of the reform in order to discover the liturgical theology of the reformer and his time, so as to obtain a more complete picture of the history of the prothesis and above all the circumstances which have rendered to it the form we know today.[17]

Whichever the case, the formation and re-formation of theological views serve a distinctly exegetical purpose: to enhance the basic Christological doctrines of sacrifice and eschatology by creating a mystagogical structure for the Church's periodic celebration of the prothesis, an act that can hardly be termed spontaneous or coincidental.

THE OFFERING OF INCENSE AT THE VEILING OF THE GIFTS[18]

Then the deacon takes the censer and placing incense (in it) says to the priest:

Bless, master, the incense.[19]

And the priest blessing says the prayer of the incense:

We offer incense to you, O Christ our God, as a scent of spiritual fragrance; receiving it upon your super-celestial altar, send down to us in return the grace of your all-holy Spirit.

The offering of incense at the prothesis introduces the third and final section of the rite, which also consists of the veiling of the gifts, the prayer, and the dismissal. Casimir Kucharek concurs that the offering of incense at the prothesis, which naturally coincides with the veiling of the gifts, is found in most manuscripts between the twelfth and fifteenth centuries.[19] Descoeudres agrees that incense accompanied the ritual covering of the gifts by the second half of the twelfth century, citing Tuscan's translation, and further identifies the prayer at the offering of incense, which he maintains appears at other points in the Divine Liturgy, at least by the beginning of the tenth century.[20] On the contrary, Pott holds that the offering of incense at the prothesis probably began around the ninth century and accompanied the prayer of the prothesis, thus basing his argument on Anastasius the Librarian's (AD 869–870) Latin translation of Germanos of Constantinople's *Ecclesiastical History*.[21] *Barberini 336*, however, does not mention any offering of incense accompanying the prayer.[22]

Nicholas Cabasilas and Symeon of Thessalonike remain relatively silent as to the sacrificial and eschatological significance of the incense offering at the prothesis and in all likelihood assume that their audiences are presumably mindful of its symbolic meaning. Cabasilas, for example, discusses the significance of the veiling of the gifts,[23] as does Symeon,[24] and both simply make passing references to the rubric of censing each individual veil separately and the gifts collectively at the conclusion of the rite.

It would be unwarranted, however, to completely dismiss Symeon's treatment of incense in general, since the mystagogue takes up the general use of incense in lengthy fashion, regarding the rite as "yet another mark of continuity between the tabernacle and the church, for it symbolizes the effusions of divine glory emanating from the divine presence."[25] Symeon explains that the purpose for the offering of incense by the priest is twofold: to show the Church's "thanksgiving for the work of the Spirit, and [to typify] the descent of [His] operational power [upon the people]" (εἰς εὐχαριστίαν τοῦ ἔργου καὶ τῆς ἐνεργείας ἐπιδημίαν τοῦ Πνεύματος),[26] hardly deviating from the content of the incense prayer. He says something similar a little later in his text, calling the offering of incense "the grace and gift and fragrance of the Spirit, poured upon the world from heaven through Jesus Christ, which again later ascends up to heaven through Him" (τὴν ἀπ' οὐρανοῦ χάριν καὶ δωρεὰν ἐκχυθεῖσαν τῷ κόσμῳ διὰ Ἰησοῦ Χριστοῦ καὶ εὐωδίαν τοῦ Πνεύματος, καὶ πάλιν εἰς τὸν οὐρανὸν δι' αὐτοῦ ἀναχθεῖσαν).[27] Symeon indicates that the censing of the church building by the acolytes was deliberately done to signify the glory of God,[28] in imitation of the OT tabernacle into which Moses and Aaron could not enter until it dissipated. Elsewhere, Symeon regards the incense as a type of the Holy Spirit,[29] filling the tabernacle and the temple of Solomon. In this instance, Symeon's fidelity to the prayer of incense becomes obvious. In yet another place, Symeon admonishes his deacons "not to cense a heretic, should one chance to be present out of curiosity, for incense is the impartation of divine grace."[30] The association in Symeon of incense with the Spirit is quite clear then, but one may further glean the eschatological significance of the aforementioned references: at the *eschaton*, the cosmos, of which the church temple and paten are but a representation, will be completely permeated by and surrendered completely to God.

In the absence then of any substantial commentary from our primary sources regarding the mystagogical significance of incense at the prothesis, it is not particularly difficult to glean the significance of incense from the prayer of incense itself. The heavenward ascent of incense is understood as the collective sacrificial offering (προσφέρομέν σοι) of the earthly Church to God, "a sweet-smelling fragrance" whose base elements (flowers, oils, etc.) were first collected and later used to manufacture incense, at the expense of human toil and time. The sacrificial notion is likewise advanced by the very expectation of the Church to receive in turn something from God, namely, the "grace of Your most-holy Spirit," to sanctify and complete the rite.

Michael Solovey's insightful observation regarding the sacrificial nuances of the Temple loaves and their association with the altar of incense suggests a striking resemblance to the prosphora of the prothesis and the accompanying rite of incense. Visible emblems of the Covenant, the showbread is offered weekly in the Temple as an ongoing sacrifice of remembrance for God's manifold blessings in the past and His continuous providence toward the House of Israel. Likewise, the prosphora loaves are offered "in remembrance of our Lord and God and Savior Jesus Christ," a sacrifice of remembrance by the Church for the *economia* of salvation in the person of the Incarnate Logos, who is the New Adam and the New Covenant. The censing of the loaves in both cases signifies that they have already become dedicated to God (ὡς ἀφιερωμένα τῷ Θεῷ, καὶ ὡς αὐτῷ προσαχθέντα),[31] set aside for the purpose of affirming the centrality of the Covenant relationship between God and His people via the act of worship, which Walter Brueggemann calls a "practice of covenant."[32] Consequently, in this affirmation, the divine presence draws near to the faithful and bestows upon them blessings in exchange for their sacrifice.

The eschatological significance of incense is evident in the heavenly worship as depicted in Revelation 8:3–4:

> And another angel came and stood at the altar with a golden censer; and he was given much incense to mingle with the prayers of all the saints [i.e. Christians] upon the golden altar before the throne; and the smoke of the incense rose with the prayers of the saints from the hand of the angel before God.

In this text, incense may be understood in one of two ways: (1) either as a "transporter" of earthly prayers from worshippers below to God's celestial throne above; or (2) as a "co-sacrifice" (cf. Lev 16:12–14), together with the prayers and other acts of worship by the Church.

The prayer of the prothesis, read immediately after the censing of the veils and the gifts, supplicates God: "[Do] You the same bless this prothesis, and accept it upon Your super-celestial altar." In this instance, the Church, together with its offering of incense, co-offers a prayer, seeking entrance into the liturgy of the *eschaton*, in order to make its earthly eucharistic celebration and its designation of the bread and wine as antitypes of the Body and Blood of Christ (καὶ ὡς ἀντίτυπα γεγονότα τοῦ παναγίου σώματός τε καὶ αἵματος),[33] acceptable before God's throne, that the worship within human *chronos*—and the grace proceeding from this worship—may emulate the angelic liturgy celebrated in divine *kairos*.

THE ASTERISKOS AND THE VEILING OF THE GIFTS[34]

The deacon censing the asteriskos says:

Make firm, master.

And the priest places the asteriskos upon the paten saying:

By the word of the Lord the heavens were made firm and by the breath of his mouth all their power.

The deacon censing the first veil says:

Beautify, master.

And the priest covers with it the holy paten saying:

The Lord has reigned, he has clothed himself with beauty; the Lord has clothed and girded himself with power.

The deacon censing the second veil says:

Cover, master.

And the priest covers with it the holy chalice saying:

Your virtue, O Christ, covered the heavens, and the earth (is) full of your praise.

The deacon censing the aer says:

Shelter, master.

And the priest covers both holy vessels saying:

Shelter us under the shelter of your wings; drive away from us every enemy and adversary; pacify our lives; Lord, have mercy on us and your world and save our souls as (one who is good) and loves man.

Introduced in the eleventh century, this four-pronged metallic support was used to prevent one of the smaller cross-shaped veils draped over it from touching the Lamb and brushing against the other excised particles on the paten. From the perspective of mystagogical symbolism, however, a discrepancy seems to arise when the patristic commentaries identify the *asteriskos* as the star that appeared over Christ's birth cave and attach to it the Matthean verse 2:9, but other contemporary *euchologia* append to the rubric the Psalmic verse 32:6. The incongruity is further exacerbated by the question of the actual significance of the *asteriskos*: does it represent the star over Bethlehem or the firmament of heaven (Gen 1:6), beneath which is found Symeon's cosmic image of the entire redeemed universe with Christ at its center?

Michael Papadopoulos maintains that a preliminary verse, compounded from several smaller verses, preceded the Matthean witness, namely: "By the word of the Lord the heavens were established (Ps 32:6); let the earth be established and not be moved (1 Chr 16:30), with a [by his] strong hand and [his] an outstretched arm (Ps 135:12)." He claims that apart from this introductory verse, which is found in other manuscripts) the existing Matthean text accompanying the *asteriskos* makes no sense.[35] Surely, the Matthean verse referring to the star logically corresponds to the later Byzantine view of the prothesis as the nativity cave (in addition to the more commonly accepted symbolism of the *diskos* as representing heaven), and this is well corroborated by Cabasilas[36] and Symeon,[37] both of whom faithfully follow

Nicholas of Andida's tendency toward the historicization of the prothesis and Divine Liturgy.[38]

Cabasilas, however, places Psalm 32:6 *after* Matthew 2:9, but while he makes it clear that the latter corresponds to the placement of the asterisk over the bread, he seems to identify the former not with the asterisk *per se*, but with the first veil. Nevertheless, the inclusion of the Psalmic verse moments later in the rite is deliberate, and Cabasilas gives a theological reason for this, arguing for a balance between Christ's two natures that he perceives upon the paten.

> Then he goes on to recite the agelong prophecies about him as God, so that the lowliness of the flesh and outward appearance shall not lead men to form a wrong conception of him, unworthy of his Divinity. 'At the word of the Lord the heavens were established' . . . While he is saying these words, the priest covers the gifts, that is the bread and the chalice, with fine veils.[39]

In this regard, Cabasilas proceeds to "reconcile," as it were, the possible dual significance of the *asteriskos*, preserving especially its originally intended cosmic symbolism as the firmament of heaven.

Cabasilas, more so the literal historian than his allegorist counterpart Symeon, agrees with Nicholas of Andida that the prothesis is a succinct summary of Christ's birth and early years, but he also makes the interesting observation that Jesus "himself was an offering from his birth onwards" (ὅτι κἀκεῖνο ἐξ ἀρχῆς δῶρον ἦν),[40] with "ἀρχὴ" here referring back to "πρώτην ἡλικίαν." This characterization of Christ's self-offering from the very beginning of his earthly life indicates that His sacrifice cannot be seen as belonging exclusively to the Passion events at Golgotha. The notion of sacrifice then is expanded to include *all* the events of the divine *economia* surrounding Christ's existence in the flesh, of which the Nativity is simply the commencement point. Cabasilas explicitly says that it is the Passion, Resurrection, and Ascension—the events in which the Body of Christ is the "central figure in all these mysteries" (εἰς Κυριακὸν μεταβάλλει σῶμα, τὸ ταῦτα πάντα δεξάμενον, τὸ σταυρωθέν, τὸ ἀναστάν, τὸ εἰς τὸν οὐρανὸν ἀνεληλυθός)—that are relived in the Liturgy and that are directly responsible for man's salvation, not the miracles and teachings which specifically serve to induce more fervent faith in Christ.[41] In this regard then, the prothesis becomes, as the *prooimion* of the Divine Liturgy, not only the visible sign of the Nativity, but more importantly the noticeable herald that announces the beginning of Christ's life of self-offering, experienced mystically within the confines of the eucharistic celebration.

According to Kucharek, the veiling of the gifts at the prothesis was introduced between the twelfth and fourteenth centuries,[42] with various symbolic interpretations attached to their use, either representing the cosmic firmament over the earth, the swaddling clothes of the infant Jesus, or the burial shroud of Christ.[43] The general notion, however, of the veils as signifying a formal dedication of the gifts runs prominent in Cabasilas, since the gifts represent the Savior, who was himself a gift offering to God the Father from infancy.[44]

For Cabasilas, the veils, like the *asteriskos*, serve as a proclamation of God's economia in the incarnate Christ, because they are draped over the antitypes that denote His "physical" liturgical presence. Cabasilas, however, progresses a step further by saying that "the power of the Incarnate God was veiled up to the time of his miracles and the witness from heaven."[45] In the natural progression of the Divine Liturgy, if the historical interpretation of the prothesis is adhered to, namely that it represents the Nativity, then the beginning of the Liturgy relives Christ's epiphany as an adult in the world, marked by His baptism in the Jordan and the beginning of His teaching and healing ministry.

Cabasilas' significant statement is indicative of the fact that the authority with which God the Father has invested the Son from the beginning, like the mystery of the divine *economia*, has been hidden from the knowledge of man or, as Cabasilas seems to insinuate in his next statement ("But *those who know* say of him: 'The Lord hath reigned . . .'"),[46] from the eyes and hearts of those who have not yet been initiated into the Christian mysteries regarding Christ as Savior and Redeemer.

By the same token, the liturgical use of veils possesses as much a revelatory, or apocalyptic, notion as it does one in which the veils seek to conceal the divine mysteries. The paradoxical interplay between the concealing and revealing aspect of the veils is taken up by Symeon of Thessalonike below, who not only reworks the mystical theology of Dionysios the Areopagite, but does so in the light of his own affinity to the hesychast movement and in conjunction with the polemical theology of Gregory Palamas. In general terms, one may assume this dual function of a veil anyway, and the very opening and closing of the veils during the Liturgy apparently demonstrates this phenomenon. Nicholas Constas takes up this issue in part in an important study that focuses on developing Symeon of Thessalonike's architectural and iconographic theology vis-à-vis the iconostasis.[47]

Symeon offers his own explanation of the mystical significance of the veils at two points in the Liturgy: (1) during the Small Entrance, in which he makes reference, oddly, to a more ancient custom whereby the celebrant bishop enters the church from the outside (more a true entrance than a procession), exchanging the psalmic dialogue from Psalm 23:7 with the one designated to open the doors to the Church; and (2) immediately following the Great Entrance, which involves a closing of the altar curtain. In the first instance, he mentions that "Christ is the One who gives us entrance into the holy things through the veil of His flesh" (διὰ τοῦ καταπετάσματος τῆς σαρκὸς αὐτοῦ),[48] clearly an inference to the Pauline text of Hebrews 10:19–20. In the second instance, he states: "Then the doors are closed, for this is the order in the future, and the lofty things are not comprehensible to the lowly and those below, neither are the mysteries known to all, for even then Jesus is completely veiled to many (ἐπεὶ καὶ τότε κεκαλυμμένος ἔσται πολλοῖς), and He is revealed little by little" (καὶ κατὰ μικρὸν ἀνοιγόμενος).[49] This gradual revelation, Symeon indicates, occurs through subsequent liturgical acts, such as the drawing of the sanctuary curtain, the communal recitation of the Creed, and the mutual exchange of the kiss of peace, all of which reveal to the Church the sacrificial Lamb of the Apocalypse:

> Then Jesus, the most excellent victim, will be in the midst of all His saints, the peace of all and unity, both priest and sacrificial offering, joining all and joined to all but analogically; for not all can participate in Him immediately; but some will be near [the divine Godhead] unhindered and without veils, within reach like the priests and those who have been perfected.[50]

Constas rightly identifies Symeon's insistence on the non-dualistic coexistence between the sensible and the intelligible, a notion that actually converts the function of a veil from a mere vehicle of concealment into more of a medium for revelation. Symeon bases his position almost verbatim on his mentor Dionysius the Areopagite,[51] as well as his own theological stance as a hesychast within the Palamite mystical tradition. For Symeon, as for Emperor and later monk John VI Kantakouzenos,[52] Patriarch Philotheos Kokkinos,[53] the monk Theophanes of Nicaea,[54] and Gregory Palamas,[55] the symbol of Christ's flesh in the Pauline text from Hebrews is the veil that simultaneously hides the Godhead but also reveals it fully, an incarnational model extended to qualify the liturgical symbol in general. In the *Triads*, Palamas' description of Moses' entrance into the sacred cloud creates a distinction "between the sensory perception of liturgical symbols and the deeper insight available to those who, like Moses, have 'entered the mystical cloud' and behold the 'things themselves', devoid of 'every covering.'"[56] The end of this passage concludes with a Dionysian paradox, which finds these same unveiled mysteries still "veiled in the brilliant darkness of the cloud." The paradox is reconciled by Palamas and Symeon himself by affirming a vision of the divine that is unmediated by veils and symbols, a pure and unhindered (ἀκραιφνῶς) *theoptia* that transcends sense perception and all forms of being, but which is possible only after one's passage from the sensible world of symbols into the purely spiritual realm of the heavenly Kingdom. Finally, following the Areopagitical envisioning of the entire creation as a theophany,[57] Symeon's fellow hesychasts regard living creatures in nature as "'symbols' of intelligible reality—'veils' of the uncreated divine energies,"[58] which mediate the reality and presence of God. Hence, all creation becomes a theophany, an incarnation of sorts, that points to God whose sensuous apprehension cannot otherwise be attained. In this regard, Constas correctly assesses that such Dionysian principles, reworked by Palamas and other hesychasts, "unequivocally affirm that human beings know God by sense perception no less than by intellection,"[59] the definitive argument used against the attacks against Eastern hesychast practice by the Calabrian monk Barlaam.

The veils covering the gifts in the prothesis are thus symbols that hide the mystery of Christ until their gradual removal during the Divine Liturgy, signifying the revelation of divine mysteries but in a manner appropriate to the sensible world. Constas concludes, "God is present only in the created symbols, accessible only in the veils that conceal him, because the nature of the symbolic is to conceal and reveal simultaneously, or, 'to speak more divinely,' to reveal by concealing."[60]

The use of the liturgical veils in the rite of the prothesis then denotes both a dedication and a revelation within the concealing of the divine economy in Christ, a "veiled unveiling."[61] In another sense, what is hidden at first and later revealed during the Eucharist (when the veils are partially lifted from the gifts during the Great Entrance and completely at the beginning of the anaphora) is also Symeon of Thessalonike's magnificent eschatological envisioning of the redeemed Church, the culmination of God's work of salvation.[62] Hence, unveiled in the Divine Liturgy are several things that have already been set into motion, so to speak, and announced in the prothesis rite: the notion of Christ as a gift offering from His infancy; the sacrifice of Christ in the flesh, marked with the emblems of His passion and death; and the eschatological Kingdom yet to come.

The Psalm verses that accompany the censing of the smaller veils and the veiling of the paten and chalice are treated by Symeon, who insistently ties them with the Incarnation.[63] Cabasilas likewise maintains that the verses serve as specific references to Christ's humanity (i.e. Incarnation) as well as His divinity, careful not to compromise one nature for the other: "Then he [the priest] goes on to recite the agelong prophecies about him as God, so that the lowliness of the flesh and outward appearance shall not lead men to form a wrong conception of him, unworthy of his Divinity." [64] Either way, the intent of the verses is purely Christological in scope, to preserve in the incarnate Christ His dual natures. Each veiling with its corresponding verse will be treated separately below.

The First Verse for the Veil over the Paten

The mystagogical symbolism of the first two veils representing the swaddling clothes of the infant Jesus and His burial shroud seems to contradict the specific verse that makes palpable reference to God being arrayed in celestial majesty. [65] The inconsistency would appear to be one between the two Christological natures. How does one reconcile the simple, material clothing of the infant Jesus, born meekly in the cave in Bethlehem, with the awe-inspiring and immaterial apparel of glory with which the eternal God enwraps Himself in the presence of the Holy Host (cf. Ps 103:2)? Is not the verse perhaps unsuitable in such a context?

On the contrary, it is here that the rich Byzantine mystagogical tradition appears useful and actually makes an authoritative dogmatic statement by combining the rubric of the veiling and Psalm 92:1. The fullness of the glory of God in Christ is concealed in the incarnate Logos until the fulfillment of His *economia* at the Resurrection, but it exists precisely in the simplicity and humility of His human nature. In addition, it is this human nature that Christ seeks to transform and redeem by assuming it. Dual interpretation not only of events in Christ's life (Nativity – Passion) but also of contrasting conditions in the Person of Christ (humility – sublimity; weakness – power) is a common occurrence among the Byzantine mystagogues, who naturally do not believe that one view is necessarily exclusive of the other. The final outcome of Christ's earthly life, much like the end result of the Eucharist—which is the Church's reliving of the former—makes this co-existence of seemingly contradictory elements possible. The mystagogical symbolism then of the prothesis veils as the infant Jesus' swaddling clothes, in this regard, does not reject the sublime majesty of God; if anything, it endorses a theology of salvation that views man as a potential participant in the divine glory. For the Greek Fathers, God's majesty and reign over the created world are traditionally ascribed to the divine Logos (as affirmed by the Nicaeo-Constantinopolitan Creed of the fourth century: "through whom all things were made"), but it is specifically through the Incarnation of the Word that man has recourse once again to his original place of glory within the splendor of divine creation.

There is also an ecclesiastical dimension associated with the censing and rubrical implementation of the first veil. Symeon's vision of the paten as representing the redeemed Church is applicable here. God's sublimity and sustaining power overshadows not only the universe, but also the Church, the created and uncreated worlds subject to God's authority. Sanctifying grace that streams forth from the mystical presence of the Godhead, the driving force that gives existence and meaning to the created order, envelops both sensible and spiritual creatures, who affirm the lordship of Christ at the center of human history and human existence. And since Christ's absolute authority remains paramount within the created order, it follows naturally that neither His Church nor the universe, as the psalm dictates, can be shaken or overcome by opposing enemies (cf. Matt 16:18), either in history or after its consummation.

The Second Verse for the Veil over the Chalice

In contrast to the first veil as representing God's sublime power over the universe and the Church, which is fulfilled in the Son's *economia*, the second veil, by reason of the verse attached to it, seems to refer to the ethical properties of Christ. Symeon comments: "He is the one who covers heaven with virtues [τὸν οὐρανὸν καλύπτει ταῖς ἀρεταῖς] as God [and Lord] Jesus Christ."[66] To this category naturally belong Christ's teachings on proper moral attitude and behavior toward one's fellow man, the always necessary ethical side of the Gospel message that measures the human response to the gift of salvation.

In the completed prothesis then, one observes a neatly arranged correspondence between the two sides of the evangelical message and the veiled paten and chalice. In the patristic mindset, the paten is a "visual Gospel," the proclamation of God's *economia* in Jesus Christ, the incarnate and crucified Logos encircled by His Church. One may say that the chalice, on the other hand, is also a "visual Gospel" that declares the relevance of Christ's teachings and the "pleasantness" of living the virtuous life. In this regard, the link between both paten and chalice becomes obvious: through adherence to the statutes of the Christian life, one becomes an active partaker in the eschatological victory of the risen Christ and enjoys the full and irrevocable membership of the eternal Kingdom.

Symeon also regards both veiled paten and chalice, like the Christian Gospel, as a theophany that reveals the Trinity to the world. The revelation is a result of the Incarnation of the Son of God, whose Body and Blood are mystically represented in the paten and chalice, ceremoniously set aside for the Eucharist.[67] "For when he was incarnated, the entire earth knew him with the Father and the Spirit" (Σαρκωθέντος γὰρ αὐτοῦ πᾶσα ἡ γῆ αὐτὸν σὺν τῷ Πατρὶ ἐπέγνω καὶ Πνεύματι).[68]

The Verse for the Aer

Robert Taft explains that the *aer* was alternately called: ἡ ἁγία νεφέλη (*the holy cloud*), ἡ ἀναφορά (*the anaphora*), and τὸ ἱερὸν ἔπιπλον (*the holy veil*), and it was originally the large, unembroidered veil used to cover both paten and chalice. After the fourteenth century, the *aer* began to be called *epitaphios*, which initially had an image of Christ's dead body and gradually came to include other figures present at the site of the Crucifixion. This same scene was also transposed to the *antimension*, the "portable altar" cloth that replaced the corporal (*eiliton*), which was unfolded upon the altar and used to receive the gifts at the Great Entrance.[69] As Taft insightfully observes, "The cloths used at the eucharist were interpreted as elements in the historical passion of Christ."[70]

The final veiling of the ritualized gifts with the larger rectangular *aer* is treated at length by Symeon. Taft's observation of the *aer*'s Passion symbolism is corroborated by Symeon's own strong conviction when the latter calls it *epitaphios* (Εἴτα τελευταῖον τὸν ἀέρα θεὶς ὁ ἱερεὺς θυμιάσας, ὅς ... καὶ ἐπιτάφιος λέγεται).[71] While Cabasilas is relatively silent on its significance, Symeon sees in it a dual symbolism, namely: (1) an image of the vast universe that contains the star which shone over the cave in Bethlehem at the Nativity (. . . ὃς δὴ καὶ τὸ στερέωμα ἐν ᾧ ὁ ἀστήρ . . .—. . . which [signifies] both the firmament where the star is . . ."[72]); and (2) the burial shroud of Christ (. . . καὶ τὴν σινδόνα σημαίνει, διὰ τοῦτο γὰρ καὶ ἐσμυρνισμένον νεκρὸν πολλάκις περιφέρει τὸν Ἰησοῦν καὶ ἐπιτάφιος λέγεται, . . .—. . . and it signifies the shroud, for this reason many times it bears on it Jesus' myrrh-anointed dead body, and is called epitaphios . . ."[73]). As the outermost veil that is immediately discernible, how does the verse associated with it, which now takes the form of a supplication rather than a prophetic or psalmic utterance of confession, assimilate to the nativity and burial cortege symbolism?

Symeon identifies the efficacy of God's protective power over the Church only *after* the completion of the divine *economia* in Christ, announced first in the prothesis rite and fully accomplished in the eucharistic liturgy. The prophetic utterings regarding the Lamb of God and the sacrificial acts performed to it, the multiplication of particles adjoining the Lamb and representing the orders of saints and angels, and the excision of crumbs for the living and deceased are all necessary steps that identify the gradual process by which the Church was born, and it is precisely the Church after Pentecost, the depository of divine grace and the continuation of Christ's salvific work, which now offers supplication to its Founder and Lord on behalf of the world. In this sense, one can reasonably argue that the first section of the prothesis rite, dealing specifically with the preparation of the paten and chalice, lays the Christological and ecclesiological groundwork, as it were, for the Christian Faith, whose practical application, in terms of prayer and outreach, becomes unquestionably evident at the end of the rite, with the verse for the *aer* and the prayer of the prothesis.

Hence, we now have liturgical proof of how *orthopraxia* is born out of *orthodoxia*, and how the *lex credendi* of the Church gives rise to the *lex orandi*. However, it must be made clear that unlike other similar juxtapositions in which an original theory may be regarded as "functionally superior" to its practical application—meaning that the latter derives its validity distinctly from the truth of the former—Christian faith and praxis are mutually interdependent and, quite avowedly, one and the same because each subsists in and derives its intrinsic value from the other. In other words, the message of the Gospel cannot be perceived to be an elaborate system of doctrinal truths or ethical codes upon which altruistic acts are based; the Gospel proclaims the person of Christ who is Himself the living origin and embodied expression of love and compassion. So, belief and knowledge of Christ translates into a selfless love of others (1 John 4:7–8); likewise, selfless love is nothing else than a confession of belief in the Son of God (John 13:35).

In summary, the veiling with the *aer* of the paten and chalice signifies a completion, a fulfillment of the prophecy regarding the immolation of the Lamb of God. Following Christ's sacrifice the Church is brought into existence at Pentecost, and the *eschaton*, an age of ceaseless prayer and supplication in anticipation of the imminent Second Coming of Jesus (cf. Rev 22:20), has already dawned. In the prayer of the veiling, the Church seeks God's physical and spiritual protection for all its members, who already enjoy a sense of proximity and unity to the Lamb of God, in expectation of the end of time, which will finalize God's dispensation of mercy and redemption over the cosmos.

A word must be said regarding the incremental unveiling of the gifts during the anaphora (the smaller veils after the Great Entrance and the aer during the Creed and immediately before the anaphora). Cabasilas remains silent on the subject, but Symeon undertakes the interpretation of the veils by drawing an engaging analogy between them and the sanctuary enclosure, whose own curtain or veil (τὸ καταπέτασμα) is similarly opened and closed during the progression of the Liturgy. Symeon begins by identifying the sanctuary enclosure with the firmament of heaven, which explains his perspective on the relationship between the tabernacle of Moses and the church building, both microcosms of creation in themselves. The tripartite structure of the church building (i.e. narthex, nave, and altar), he explains, was prefigured in both the tabernacle of Moses and the Temple of Solomon, with such divisions corresponding to the spiritual cosmos. An example given is God's immaterial throne, elevated on high within the spiritual realm but typified by the altar table within the sanctuary.[74] He then proceeds to envision the tabernacle-sanctuary enclosure as a typos of Christ's own body, and it is here that the tabernacle veil becomes especially significant, inasmuch as it is identified by the mystagogue as the flesh concealing the incarnate Logos (cf. Heb 10:19–20), who is also the "door" of the sheep in the corresponding Johannine pericope (John 10:7).[75] In fact, Symeon extends the symbolism of the veil to the altar cover, "which is the glory and grace of God, by which he himself is concealed (καλυπτόμενος), 'clothing himself with light as with a garment' (Ps. 103:2)."[76] As Constas observes, "Here the deity is said to be hidden, not by invisibility or darkness, but paradoxically by light itself. . . . Contrary to expectation, it is light (or vision itself) that simultaneously reveals and conceals the presence of God. . . ."[77]

Following this line of thinking, the "enfleshment" of the divine Logos, typified in the prothesis rite which serves as the prooimion of the Liturgy where the whole of the divine economy is accomplished, is well represented by the veils that not only conceal the incarnate Lamb and the mystery of salvation, but over the course of the eucharistic liturgy reveal the mystery of Christ to the Church. On another plane altogether, the essential nature of the divine Logos is hidden from human intellection via the medium of the "veil" of His flesh, in which case the flesh becomes a necessary buffer to "shield," as it were, the human mind from incomprehensible, intelligible realities.[78] By the same token, the veil functions as a symbol that alone can reveal the unintelligible in the only manner comprehensible to the limited human mind. "Thus one cannot," Constas notes, "in a gnostic ascent from sense perception to 'pure' intellection, strip away the symbols, or remove the veils because when these are removed, there is 'nothing' there, nothing, that is, which can be given to human comprehension."[79] "God," Constas continues, "is present only in the created symbols, accessible only in the veils that conceal him, because the nature of the symbolic is to conceal and reveal simultaneously."[80] He adds: "What is required is a movement into the signs, an understanding of the veils of creation as ontological symbols. One does not encounter God by discarding created symbols, but by experiencing them as symbols, as visible mirrors of the invisible."[81] And yet, what is revealed—the Logos of God—remains concealed, a divine mystery, just like the eschatological fulfillment of history that can only be prefigured in part by the prothesis rite and by the Eucharist.

Hence, in regard to both the veils over the gifts and the altar vellum, or curtain, the central theme is one of divine knowledge and revelation, which paradoxically but necessarily translates into a deeper concealment of the divine mysteries. Taking up yet again the baton of the Dionysian hierarchical structure, Symeon reminds his readers that the mysteries are privy to only those who are capable of transcending to higher theoriai,[82] to angelic beings and to members of the earthly Church, who hold the privilege of participating in the eucharistic liturgy.

This stance is further backed by the fact that the paten and chalice are unveiled at the Great Entrance, at a point when the Catechumens have already been dismissed from the eucharistic celebration and only the Christian faithful are allowed to remain and receive the revelation of the divine mysteries.

THE PRAYER OF THE PROTHESIS[83]

The deacon: Bless, master.

And the priest taking the censer censes the Prothesis three times saying:

Blessed is our God, who has so deigned; glory to you.

And the deacon adds each time:

Always, now and forever and to the ages of ages. Amen.

Then the deacon says:

Upon the offering of the precious gifts let us pray to the Lord. Lord, have mercy.

And the priest the prayer.

PRAYER OF THE PROTHESIS

O God, our God, who sent forth as food for the entire world, the heavenly bread, our Lord and God Jesus Christ as savior and deliverer and benefactor, blessing and sanctifying us; do you the same bless this prothesis, and accept it upon your super-celestial altar. As a good and loving one, remember those who have brought forth offerings and those for whom they were brought forth, and protect us without condemnation in the holy work of your divine mysteries.

For sanctified and glorified is your all-honorable and magnificent name, of the Father and the Son and the Holy Spirit, now and forever and to the ages of ages. Amen.

The prayer of the prothesis constitutes the very core of the preparatory rite in that, from antiquity, it was the only ritual element that accompanied the chiefly practical acts of preparing bread and wine for the Eucharist. The most ancient *euchologia* mention that the priest was responsible for reading the prayer in the *skeuophylakion*, at least from the witness of Maximos the Confessor (early seventh century) until the appearance of *Barberini Codex 336* (second half of the eighth century).[84] Originally read by the priest in the *skeuophylakion*, the prayer's reference to Christ as the "heavenly bread" is intrinsically linked to a new conception of the Great Entrance as "[l'] entrée des saints et vénérables mystères", an entrance that G. Descoeudres contrasts with Maximos' entrance of the bishop (Small Entrance) to commence the eucharistic liturgy.[85] Thus in a sense, the heavenly bread is elevated to the status of almost possessing a *hypostasis*, for as Pott writes: "Henceforth, the heavenly bread symbolically represented Jesus Christ, the heavenly bread sent by the Father."[86] Pott likewise postulates that the rite of incense typically would have accompanied the prayer, thus further supplying the prothesis with a "sacrificial" dimension and more official status.[87] In the prayer, one receives a sense of the rite's initial mystagogical meaning. Schulz states: "As the most ancient, as we have seen, euchological element of the proskomide, the priestly prayer makes up the most authentic expression of its initial meaning."[88]

At first glance, the designation of Christ as "heavenly bread" and as "food for the whole world" is suggestive of the very obvious: the human need for physical and spiritual nourishment and, by extension, the divine resolution to fulfill this need. Aside from the evident eucharistic overtones in the prayer, Christ's self-pronouncement as the Bread of Life (John 6:35–39, 49–51), in view of the palpable sacrificial atmosphere that pervades the entire rite, indicates a sacrificial offering not only to feed His followers with His Body and Blood, but also with His words of virtue (cf. Matt 4:4) and His acts of righteousness (cf. John 4:34), which possess life in themselves for those who are united mystically to Christ and thus participate in the divine life. Christ's self-offering to God the Father on behalf of the world and His offering to mankind as the heavenly bread serves as a reciprocation for the Church's obedient (cf. Luke 22:19) and periodic offering of

the Eucharist (cf. 1 Cor 11:26). What is reciprocated goes beyond a tempo-
rary satiation of material and spiritual hunger; the "supersubstantial bread"
(ὁ ἐπιούσιος ἄρτος) continues to feed the faithful with divine life well beyond
history and into the timelessness of the eschatological age.[89]

Hence, the sacrificial and eschatological notions in the prayer are very
clear by virtue of the "Bread of Life" imagery: Christ offers Himself as food
for His Church, and it is precisely this divine food and drink, or mystical union with Christ, that guides and sustains each individual Christian
within this temporal age and transports him to the eschatological reality of
the eternal Kingdom. Symeon extends the "Bread of Life" eschatological
imagery via a reference to the Byzantine rite of the Elevation of the Panagia,
a purely monastic service conducted at monastery refectories during meal-
time and preferably in the eucharistic liturgy at the Diptychs. He speaks
of the elevated bread offered in honor of Mary at the conclusion of the
monastic meal, to whom the monks make prayerful intercession. For it is
she, he explains, who brought forth the heavenly bread (τὸν οὐράνιον ἄρτον),
the living manna, who feeds the souls of the faithful.[90] This portrayal of
the Theotokos as the mother of the living Bread reroutes the prothesis rite
back to an incarnational typology, identified most ardently by Nicholas of
Andida who, as we have already seen, preferred to see the Divine Liturgy as
representative of the entire earthly life of Christ.[91]

Interestingly, neither Cabasilas nor Symeon (nor even the earlier Byzantine commentators, for that matter!) comment significantly on the mystagogical significance of the prayer, an odd omission for this most ancient
element of the prothesis rite, which can only be explained by the commentators' assumption that the clergy were already well informed as to the
prayer's "Bread of Life" symbolism. Symeon brushes over the prayer's meaning by simply listing, item by item, what requests the prayer makes to God
and nothing more. He writes:

> . . . he [the celebrant] recites the prayer of the proskomide, and he
> calls upon God the Father, who sent His Son, the heavenly bread,
> to us, to bless [the gifts] placed forth, and to accept these upon His
> super-celestial altar, to remember both those who have brought them
> and those for whom these have been brought, and to protect without
> judgment the celebrants in the liturgy.[92]

Immediately prior to this, however, he mentions that the gifts have
now been dedicated to God (by virtue of their having been censed) and
have become the antitypes of Christ's Body and Blood.[93] For Symeon, this
ordering—i.e. the prayer following the dedication—suggests, as seen ear-

lier in this chapter, that with the completion of the divine economy at the beginning of the prothesis, the immolated but now glorified Lamb of the Apocalypse has now assumed full lordship over the whole of the redeemed cosmos and thus receives the prayers and praises of His Church into the *eschaton* (cf. Rev 8:3ff).

THE PRAYER OF THE PROTHESIS AND THE PRAYER OF THE PROSKOMIDE AT THE GREAT ENTRANCE

Much confusion typically arises with the indiscriminate, interchangeable usage in English of the expressions "prayer of the prothesis" and "prayer of the proskomide." Both prayers are often thought to possess characteristics of an offertory, a position that immediately raises the query why the Byzantine eucharistic liturgy would even need two such prayers in the first place, let alone one. For according to Taft, the East never truly possessed a formal offertory procession as did the West, thus nullifying any possibility that the prayer of the proskomide, which precedes the ceremonial transfer of gifts to the altar, is the collect associated with it.[94] This, however, does not rule out an offertory in the strict sense in the Liturgy (the anaphora), nor even a pre-offertory (the prothesis).

One possible reason behind the interchangeability of the expressions "prayer of the prothesis" and "prayer of the proskomide" may lie in the evidence Taft provides in Germanos of Constantinople's Ecclesiastical History (as well as in other sources), who writes that a second preparation of gifts apparently occurred in the skeuophylakion immediately prior to the Great Entrance, called the proskomide (Ἡ προσκομιδὴ ἡ γενομένη ἐν τῷ θυσιαστηρίῳ, ἤτοι ἐν τῷ σκευοφυλακίῳ, ἐμφαίνει τοῦ κρανίου τὸν τόπον...). This additional preparation did not refer to the actual prothesis rite, which Germanos was careful to distinguish by placing it at the beginning of the Divine Liturgy. Hence, Germanos was in all likelihood referring to an act of immediate preparation of the gifts before their transfer to the altar—possibly censing and uncovering them.[95] Taft, however, also proposes that this final, immediate preparation of the gifts before the Great Entrance may have involved only the chalice, since some sources claim that

> the traditional Constantinopolitan prothesis prayer is a prayer over the bread only, and why canon 12 of the 10–11th century canonical writings attributed to Nicephoras I, Patriarch of Constantinople (806–815) states that the chalice is not blessed at the prothesis

prayer: Ὅτι οὐ χρὴ σφραγῖδα ποιεῖν ἐν τῇ εὐχῇ τοῦ σκευοφυλακίου, ἐπὶ τὸ ἅγιον ποτήριον.[96]

A second possible reason for this interchangeability may be due to the fact that certain elements of the prothesis rite at the Great Entrance are still found during hierarchical liturgies, which seemingly retain the ancient practice of a preparation of the gifts just prior to the anaphora. (The permanent fusion of the Liturgy of the Word, or Synaxis, to the Liturgy of the Eucharist after the fourth century no doubt contributed to the difficulty in seeing the prothesis as the immediate antecedent to the Eucharist, which typically began with the transfer of gifts to the altar, i.e. the Great Entrance.) Although a considerable amount of variety exists between service books as to the presiding bishop's direct involvement in the prothesis rite (either before the Divine Liturgy or just prior to the Great Entrance), the fact remains that the prothesis prayer is read by the celebrant bishop, who typically concludes the preparatory rites anyway, regardless of their positioning in the Divine Liturgy.[97]

P. Trembelas qualifies this distinction between prothesis and proskomide by explaining that the latter refers to the selection of only those elements to be used for the "sanctification and showing forth of the body and blood of Christ" (πρὸς καθαγιασμὸν καὶ ἀνάδειξιν σώματος καὶ αἵματος Χριστοῦ), as compared to the more general connotation of prothesis, referring to all the offerings of bread (εἰς ὁλόκληρον τὴν πρόθεσιν τῶν ἄρτων) made by the faithful (εὐλογίαι), which were, understandably, not all used in the Eucharist.[98] In this regard, preserved is the burial cortege imagery at the Great Entrance that the proskomide etymologically possesses, as well as the processional "movement" of the gifts into the altar.

Interestingly, the individual wording of the prayers hardly provides any indication of the distinction between the terms, since both prayers share the common themes of offering and worthy acceptance of the gifts by God. This thematic similarity would account for their interchangeability in usage, but their positioning in different places within the Divine Liturgy is clearly indicative of their uniqueness in function.

Barberini 336's placement of the prayers at different locations in the Byzantine Liturgy (the prothesis prayer at the beginning of the rite and the proskomide prayer at the completion of the Great Entrance, following the transfer of the gifts to the altar)[99] clearly indicates that both prayers were originally designated to fulfill different functions. In addition, the wording in the prayer of the proskomide is indicative of the celebrant's plea for the worshipping community's worthiness before offering the gifts of bread and

wine during the anaphora. Below is the entire text of the prayer of the proskomide from Byz-CHR, a more succinct version than the one in Byz-BAS:

O Lord God Almighty, the only Holy One who receives a sacrifice of
praise from those who call upon You with all their heart, accept also
the prayer of us sinners and lead [it, i.e. the prayer] toward Your holy
altar, and enable us to bring forth to You gifts and spiritual sacrifices
for our own sins and for the offences of the people, and make us completely worthy to find grace before You, so that our sacrifice may be
acceptable and that the good Spirit of Your grace may dwell upon us
and upon these gifts set forth and upon all Your people.[100]

A portion of the longer proskomide prayer of Byz-BAS is included
below, whose scope is likewise a plea for worthiness prior to the actual
anaphora.

Accept us as we draw near to Your holy altar, according to the multitude of Your mercy, that we may be worthy to offer You this spiritual
sacrifice without the shedding of blood, for our sins and for the transgressions of Your people. Grant that, having accepted this sacrifice
upon Your holy, heavenly, and spiritual altar as an offering of spiritual
fragrance, You may in return send down upon us the grace of Your
Holy Spirit.[101]

In both instances, the two prayers of the proskomide look forward to
the as-of-yet unaccomplished sacrifice, whereas the prayer of the prothesis
seeks a blessing, a "pre-consecration" of the gifts and God's acceptance
of the ritualized gifts upon His celestial altar in preparation for the eucharistic sacrifice. This "pre-consecration" during the prothesis rite, in
Cabasilas' view, is a sort of necessary transformation (he calls it a "dedication") of the ordinary bread and wine into an antitypical representation of
Christ before His death and resurrection. Cabasilas writes: "That is why
the oblations, which represent the body of Christ, are not immediately
taken to the altar and sacrificed. The sacrifice comes at the end. They are
dedicated first. . . ."[102]

For the purpose of this book, the distinction between the two prayers
is a significant one. Given the entire nature of the prothesis rite as a somewhat condensed "mini-anaphora" (or "mini-epiklesis," as will be seen in the
next chapter), the prothesis prayer rightfully retains its status as a sort of
pre-offertory, whereas the prayer of the proskomide, as Robert Taft thoroughly proves, does not progress beyond being simply a prayer of *accessus
ad altare*.[103]

The attention of this book now turns to a formal consideration of how the prothesis rite shares elements with the eucharistic anaphora. The examination is a crucial one, to say the least, since it raises the issue of the very probable influence exerted by the Byzantine Liturgy upon the prothesis to adopt various sacrificial and eschatological elements, thus proving the universality of these all-important and always relevant themes.

NOTES

1. Georges Descoeudres, *Die Pastophorien im syro-byzantinischen Osten. Eine Untersuchung zu architektur- und liturgiegeschichtlichen Problemen. Schriften zur Geistesgeschichte des östlichen Europa*, 16 (Wiesbaden, 1983), 87.

2. Thomas Pott, *La réforme liturgique byzantine: étude du phénomène d'évolution non-spontanée de la liturgie byzantine* (Rome, 2000), 178.

3. Ibid. Hereafter, all translations from Pott are mine.

4. Pott, 177, and especially A. Jacob, *"La traduction de la Liturgie de S. Jean Chrysostome par Léon Toscan.* Édition critique," in *Orientalia Christiana Periodica* 32 (1966), 111–62.

5. F.E. Brightman, ed., *Liturgies Eastern and Western* (Oxford, 1896), 309.

6. Pott, 189ff.

7. The Roman Church's systematic modifications to the Liturgy via the convening of an ecumenical council, such as Vatican II in the beginning of the 1960s, is often compared to the lack of such "organized" activity in the East, which then yields erroneously the judgment that the East lacked any true sense of *reformatio* in its own liturgical tradition, and that any changes were, at best, spontaneous. See Andrew Louth, "Review: *La réforme liturgique byzantine: étude du phénomène d'évolution non-spontanée de la liturgie byzantine.* By Thomas Pott", in *Journal of Theological Studies*, vol. 53 (2002), 358–61.

8. Pott, 99ff.

9. Descoeudres, 85–126.

10. Louth, 360.

11. Pott, 171.

12. Maximos the Confessor, *Mystagogia* 16; PG 90.693C..Cf. *Maximus Confessor: Selected Writings.* trans. George C. Berthold (New York, 1985), 201.

13. Pott, 189.

14. Ibid., 190.

15. Ibid.

16. Ibid., 192.

17. Ibid., 195–96. Emphasis mine.

18. See p. 11 of this book.

19. Casimir Kucharek, *The Byzantine-Slav Liturgy of St. John Chrysostom: Its Origin and Evolution* (Combermere, 1971), 312.

20. Descoeudres, 89.

21. Pott, 179.

22. Brightman, 309–10.

23. Nicholas Cabasilas, *Commentary on the Divine Liturgy* 11; PG 150.389BD; Nicholas Cabasilas, *A Commentary on the Divine Liturgy*, trans. J.M. Hussey and P.A. McNulty (London, 1960), 41–42.

24. Symeon of Thessalonike, *On the Sacred Liturgy* 96; PG 155.285D–287C.

25. Nicholas P. Constas, "Symeon of Thessalonike and the Theology of the Icon Screen", in Sharon E.J. Gerstel, ed., *Thresholds of the Sacred: Architectural, Art Historical, Liturgical, and Theological Perspectives on Religious Screens, East and West* (Washington, 2006), 171.

26. Symeon of Thessalonike, *On the Sacred Liturgy* 95; PG 155.285BC.

27. Ibid., 96; PG 155.289A.

28. Idem., *Interpretation of the Christian Temple and Its Rituals*; PG 155.624C.

29. Ibid., PG 155.329BC.

30. Ibid. PG 155.644A.

31. Idem., *On the Sacred Liturgy* 96; PG 155.288B.

32. Walter Brueggemann, *Worship in Ancient Israel. An Essential Guide Series* (Nashville, 2005), 8.

33. Symeon of Thessalonike, *On the Sacred Liturgy* 96; PG 155.288B.

34. See pp. 11–12 of this book.

35. Michael Papadopoulos, Λειτουργική: Τὰ τελούμενα ἐντὸς τοῦ ναοῦ [*Liturgics: The Rites Conducted within the Church*], (Athens, 1992), 191.

36. Hussey and McNulty, trans., 41; Cabasilas, *Commentary* 11; PG 150.389C.

37. Symeon of Thessalonike, *On the Sacred Liturgy* 96; PG 155.285D.

38. Nicholas of Andida, *Protheoria* 10; PG 140.429C–432A.

39. Hussey and McNulty, trans., 41; Cabasilas, *Commentary* 11; PG 150.389CD.

40. Ibid., Cabasilas, *Commentary* 11; PG 150.389C.

41. Ibid., 27, 36; Cabasilas, *Commentary* 1, 7; PG 150.372A, 384BC.

42. Kucharek, 319–20.

43. Hans-Joachim Schulz. *Die Byzantinische Liturgie: Glaubenszeugnis und Symbolgestalt*. (Ἡ Βυζαντινὴ Λειτουργία· μαρτυρία πίστεως καί σθμβολική ἔκφραση), trans. Demetrios V. Tzerpos (Athens, 1998), 180.

44. Hussey and McNulty, trans., 31, 34; Cabasilas, *Commentary* 2, 6; PG 150.376D, 380D.

45. Ibid., 41; Cabasilas, *Commentary* 11; PG 150.389D. Emphasis mine.

46. Ibid., Emphasis mine.

47. Constas, 163–83.

48. Symeon of Thessalonike, *On the Sacred Liturgy* 98; PG 155.293A.

49. Ibid., PG 155.296BC.

50. Ibid., PG 155.296C.

51. Dionysios the Areopagite, *On the Celestial Hierarchy* 1.2; PG 3.372D.

52. John VI Kantakouzenos, *Refutio Prochori Cydonii* 1.5.

53. Philotheos Kokkinos, *Antirrheticus contra Gregoram*, oratione 2.

54. Theophanes of Nicaea, *De lumine Thaborio*, oratione 3.

55. Gregory Palamas, *Triads* 2.3.55.

56. Constas, 178.

57. Cf. Dionysios the Areopagite, *On the Divine Names* 4.13.

58. Constas, 178.

59. Ibid., 179.

60. Ibid.

61. Ibid.

62. Symeon of Thessalonike, *On the Sacred Liturgy* 94; PG 155.285AB, and most especially, ibid., 98; PG 155.296C.

63. Ibid., 96; PG 155.285D.

64. Hussey and McNulty, trans., 41; Cabasilas, *Commentary* 11; PG 150.389D.

65. Symeon of Thessalonike, *On the Sacred Liturgy* 85; PG 155.264C.

66. Ibid., 96; PG 155.288A.

67. Ibid.

68. Ibid.

69. Robert Taft, *The Great Entrance: A History of the Transfer of Gifts and Other Pre-anaphoral Rites of the Liturgy of St. John Chrysostom* (Rome, 1978), 216–17.

70. Ibid., 217.

71. Symeon of Thessalonike, *On the Sacred Liturgy* 96; PG 155.288A.

72. Ibid.

73. Ibid.

74. Idem., *Interpretation of the Christian Temple and Its Rituals*; PG 155.337D; cf. also Hebrews 1:8, 4:16, 8:1, 12:2.

75. Ibid., PG 155.645A, 697AB; cf. also idem., *On the Sacred Liturgy* 98; PG 155.293A.

76. Idem., *Interpretation of the Christian Temple and Its Rituals*; PG 155.348CD. Translation Constas, 172.

77. Constas, 172.

78. Symeon of Thessalonike, *On the Sacred Liturgy* 83; PG 155.261B.

79. Constas, 179.

80. Ibid.

81. Ibid.

82. Ibid.

83. See pp. 12–13 of this book.

84. S. Parenti and E. Velkovska, eds., *L'euchologio Barberini gr. 336* (Rome, 1995), 1–263 *et passim*; and R. Taft, *The Great Entrance*, 274.

85. Descoeudres, 93.

86. Pott, 173.

87. Ibid., 179–80; see also Taft, *The Great Entrance*, 274.

88. Schulz, 258. Translation mine.

89. See specifically Geoffrey Wainwright's enlightening patristic interpretation of the "eschatological day" in the Lord's Prayer: G. Wainwright, *Eucharist and Eschatology* (London, 1971), 31ff.

90. Symeon of Thessalonike, *Treatise on Prayer* 65; PG 155.664f. For the rite itself, see: Ὡρωλόγιον τὸ Μέγα, περιέχον ἅπασαν τὴν ἀνήκουσαν αὐτῷ ἀκολουθίαν κατὰ τὴν τάξιν τῆς Ἀνατολικῆς Ἐκκλησίας καὶ τῶν ὑποκειμένων αὐτῇ εὐαγῶν μοναστηρίων μετὰ τινῶν ἀπαραιτήτων προσθηκῶν. [*The Great Book of Hours, Containing Every Service Belonging to It and the Venerable Monasteries Under It, with Some Necessary Additions*], (Athens, 1986), 130–35, and especially the footnote on p. 132.

91. Schulz, 153.

92. Symeon of Thessalonike, *On the Sacred Liturgy* 96; PG 155.288BC.

93. Ibid., PG 155.288B.

94. Taft, 259.

95. Taft, 260; René Bornert, *Les commentaires byzantins de la Divine Liturgie du VIIe au XVe siècle* (Paris, 1965), 149; and Germanos of Constantinople, *Ecclesiastical History*, PG 98.396B.

96. Taft, 274–75; see also PG 100.856.

97. Taft, 265–70.

98. P.N. Trembelas, ed., Αἱ τρεῖς λειτουργίαι κατὰ τοὺς ἐν Ἀθήναις κώδικας [*The Three Liturgies According to the Athens Codices*], *Texte und Forschungen zur byzantinisch-neugriechischen Philologie* (Athens, 1935), 19.

99. Brightman, 309–10 and 319–20.

100. Ibid., 319. Translation and emphases mine.

101. *The Divine Liturgy of Our Father among the Saints Basil the Great*, trans. Faculty of Hellenic College and Holy Cross Greek Orthodox School of Theology (Brookline, 1988), 20. Emphases mine.

102. Hussey and McNulty, trans., 31; Cabasilas, *Commentary* 2; PG 150.376D.

103. Taft, 257–275.

9

THE PROTHESIS RITE AS IMAGE
OF THE ANAPHORA

"The entire performance of the proskomide consists of a mini-sketch (σμικρογραφία) of the Divine Liturgy and is embodied theologically and liturgically within its confines."[1] This critical statement, made by one of the world's foremost experts on the Byzantine Divine Liturgy, forms the basis for the argumentation to be presented in this final chapter. In essence, Ioannes Fountoules contends that the prothesis rite, both in terms of structure and theological content, represents a condensed version of the more elaborate and significant eucharistic liturgy. The mystery of God's divine *economia*, aimed at the salvation of mankind and the restoration of the fallen universe through the grace of renewal wrought in the Person of the sacrificed and resurrected Christ (cf. Rev 21:5), is amply expressed throughout the Divine Liturgy by the intricate combination of words, acts, and symbolism that constitute the rite. This mystery of salvation, however, which is unavoidably comprised of sacrificial and eschatological themes, is first articulated in the prothesis rite, the abridged version of the eucharistic celebration and its most immediate antecedent.

This position is similarly shared by Hans-Joachim Schulz and other liturgiologists, who have carefully examined the mystagogical ramifications of the prothesis rite and have found the dual themes of *economia* and eschatology to permeate the rite of the prothesis as they do the liturgical anaphora. Schulz writes:

> Thus, the prayer of the prothesis corresponds to the basic thought of the relative teleturgical acts with the Offertorium and of the prayers

of the Roman canon. Like the Offertorium, so too does the prothesis serve as a depiction of the anaphora, which especially emphasizes that side which is expressed with the term προσφέρομεν.[2]

For Schulz, the prothesis resembles the anaphora because both rites are characterized by the act of mutual *offering*, a rubric that very easily ties into the theme of Christ's sacrificial self-offering as well as the concept of the eschatological Kingdom, which Christ "offers" to His followers (cf. Matt 25:34), who in turn "offer" their lives to the dictates of the Gospel. He writes that the prayer of the prothesis,

> as the most ancient euchological component of the proskomide . . . constitutes the most authentic expression of its original meaning. For it resounds with the ancient practice of the offering of the gifts by the faithful, through which is expressed the idea of this offering as a sacrifice of humanity's very existence.[3]

Paul Evdokimov observes: "This service consists of a small, realistic, and very succinct drama, which depicts the sacrifice of the Lamb, thus creating a miniaturization (σμικρογραφία) of the sacrifice which will take place during the Divine Liturgy."[4]

Along these same lines, Casimir Kucharek identifies the *prophetic* orientation of the prothesis rite vis-à-vis the Eucharist, which brings to completion the mystagogical truths highlighted in abbreviated form in the prothesis. He comments: "In the *proskomidia*, then, the priest acts as a prophet of the unbloody death of Christ to be re-enacted in the Eucharistic Sacrifice."[5] The relationship between the prothesis rite and the Divine Liturgy is best understood as a prophetic prefiguration of the sacrifice and eschatological promise that will be experienced in all their intensity during the mystery of the Eucharist. Kucharek continues:

> Even in the *proskomidia*, before it becomes the Eucharistic Christ, the main host is called the *lamb* because of what is to come. The proskomidia rite prepares, prophesies, and prefigures what will take place in the Eucharistic Sacrifice just as the Old Testament was a time of preparation, prophecy, and prefiguration as regards the historical events of the redemption.[6]

More specifically, the incisions around the Lamb to excise it from the rest of the prosphora "is prophecy in liturgical action relative to the Eucharistic Sacrifice: the bread, which is still not the Eucharist, is called the Lamb of God sacrificed for mankind."[7]

One may argue that most Byzantine liturgical services and sacraments typically do resemble one another anyway with common structural elements, a phenomenon defined by their nature as communal events that once found expression in the public celebration of the Eucharist, later detaching themselves from it but retaining several of its elements. For example, the *enarxis* (opening) and *apolysis* (dismissal), both doxological in nature, form the tail ends of any formal rite in the Byzantine liturgical tradition. In between this opening and closing doxology, the content of the rite typically revolves around two poles: (1) an *anamnesis*, or remembrance of the divine economy, made possible in the Person of the incarnate Son of God; and (2) an *epiklesis*, or entreaty for the full realization of the eschatological Kingdom of God, which is partially experienced during life and is channeled to each individual Christian believer through various other spiritual and material blessings (i.e. the remission of sins, the granting of mercy, bodily health, etc.). The more pertinent question, however, is: To what degree, if any, does the formalization, or codification, of a rite contribute to its deeper immersion in mystagogical concepts? On the contrary, does not the formalization of a rite serve as a deterrent, stifling any further growth in terms of the theological understanding of the Liturgy?

No one can deny that the prothesis gradually evolved into a full-blown rite from a simple act of preparation; it is equally unfounded to claim as arbitrary the development of mystagogical concepts, which as Thomas Pott argued in the previous chapter, were given a fertile context up until the eventual privatization and clericalization of the prothesis. Pott struggles with the question of whether or not the codification of the rite led to the termination of any accompanying theological thought, although he appears to think that it, in fact, did stifle the latter's growth, stating that "it appears as though theology was no longer able to find the inspiration for 'a subsequent evolution' (*une évolution ultérieure*),"[8] although he refrains from specifying what such a secondary evolution would entail. He wonders if, by the fourteenth century, the Liturgy and its theological exegesis could have actually evolved independently, apart from each other, "in a state of perfection or saturation that excluded the need for the development of subsequent material."[9] Despite the fluidity of mystagogical meaning in any Byzantine rite (we see minor variations in the witnesses of all the major liturgical commentators), reflected by oftentimes slight differences in rubrical practice, it would seem that codification neither prevents alternate ideas from seeping into liturgical practice nor does it standardize—or rather absolutize—theological meaning. As a classic example, Germanos of Constantinople characteristically offers evidence of the binary significance of several prominent

ecclesiastical items (e.g. the apse as the cave where Christ was born and
the cave where He was buried; the altar table as tomb and divine throne),
indicative of such variety.[10] Of course, one may argue that Germanos'
period was still a formative one for the Liturgy, but Nicholas Cabasilas
and Symeon of Thessalonike, writing almost a century apart and during
a period considered the apex of liturgical development, in which liturgical practice throughout the Byzantine East was more or less solidified
in the traditions of the Great Church of Christ, still differed in their
exegetical perspective, with the former preferring a more historical orientation and the latter an eschatological one. In either case, neither mystagogue disqualifies the view of the other, and this is so for the simple
reason that in Eastern liturgical mystagogy, theological interpretation is
not exclusive but, by nature, complementary. Hence, the whole process
of codification, in terms of liturgical exegesis is, in one sense, a misno-
mer. Whereas practice may become "set in stone," as it were, and be dis-
seminated throughout a region for the sake of universal compliance and
conformity, interpretation is far more subjective in its dynamics. And it
is perhaps in this regard that Pott is quite accurate in characterizing the
prothesis as receiving "a personal or subjective stamp (*"une empreinte
personelle ou subjective"*) by its almost private character."[11] It should come
as no surprise then that the prothesis rite, a one-time practical act of
preparation and transfer, likewise evolved into a formal service and was
modeled after the various sections of the eucharistic anaphora, becoming an icon depicting in synoptic form the economic and eschatological
mysteries of God, without necessarily experiencing a "freeze" or cessation
of theological development.

The intent of this final chapter is geared toward supporting and sub-
stantiating this very claim, namely, that the prothesis rite is indeed a
miniaturization of the Divine Liturgy both in structure and, most especially, in theological content. The two unanswered questions raised at the
beginning of the previous chapter will be dealt with here: (1) How similar
are the sacrificial and eschatological notions in the prothesis to those in
the Eucharist and in what sense do the shared anaphoral elements assist in the similarity of these notions?, and (2) In which way does the
"consecratory" language in the prothesis prayer preserve the sacrificial
and eschatological fiber in the prothesis rite? We shall likewise revisit
Thomas Pott's line of argumentation regarding the non-spontaneous development of the prothesis rite and apply it to the question of whether
the rite's shaping into a "mini-anaphora" was intentional or coincidental.

THE INTENTIONAL SHAPING OF THE PROTHESIS INTO A 'MINI-ANAPHORA'

As we have already seen, Thomas Pott, in his important study on Byzantine liturgical reform, argues that the gradual evolution of Byzantine liturgical rites throughout history "depends neither on historical events nor on the liturgy itself, but only on man and his manner of living."[12] Pott assesses this hypothesis by putting to the test four "paradigms," or important historical events in the East, which prompted the Church during each epoch to initiate certain liturgical reforms as a *witness and expression of man's experience in eucharistic worship*: (1) the reforms of Theodore the Studite (759–826) during the unstable period of Iconoclasm; (2) the reforms surrounding the Byzantine Paschal Triduum, from as early as the fourth-century accounts of the nun Egeria up until the sixteenth century; (3) the evolution of the prothesis preparation into a full-blown rite, mainly between the eleventh and fourteenth centuries; and (4) the seventeenth-century liturgical reforms outside the Byzantine Empire and after the fall of Constantinople, in mainly Slavic lands that adopted the Byzantine liturgical traditions.[13] Pott points out that although history may, in fact, exert some degree of influence upon the Liturgy, the effect is normally an indirect one, "creating favorable circumstances for the birth of a new élan of liturgical evolution"[14] that is inevitably focused upon the human experience. Hence, this anthropocentric slant to liturgical reform sets man as the indispensable catalyst responsible for upgrading liturgical worship to a deeper theological level, which is more evocative of the collective faith of the Church during his time.

As a viable example, the standardized iconographic program on sanctuary screens, depicting Christ as an infant with His Mother and Christ as judge, borders the holy doors on each side, the space of the present where the periodic celebration of the Liturgy draws the two poles of the divine economy, past and future, into a cohesive and indissoluble union.[15] These two prominent Christological dogmas, Christ's sacrifice and Second Coming, have not only been definitive for the Church throughout history, but they were also deeply engrained in the early Christians' consciousness, thus rendering all future enhancements in theological expression, liturgical and otherwise, as deliberately centered around these two themes.

While it is surely man's external expression of faith that undergoes the aforesaid evolutional reforms—which, as history has inevitably shown, has yielded rather sophisticated and oftentimes "uncompromising" systems of liturgical worship—it is the primary *kerygma* of the Gospel, the basic tenets and revealed truths of the Christian Faith (i.e. the divine economy and the eschatological dawning of the Kingdom of God), which ultimately provide the content for these reforms and become normative for the Church throughout the ages. It was foreseeable that the collective liturgical expression of the first Christians would incorporate the sacrifice of Christ and the eschatological Kingdom, since it stood at the very core of their belief system and essentially defined their manner of living. In imitation of their Lord, many early Christians identified the transient nature of their earthly lives, which they were convinced would in all likelihood culminate in sacrificial martyrdom. However, their continuous otherworldly outlook and assurance in the eschatological Kingdom beyond human history made their impending death to the world not only bearable but meaningful as well.[16] The periodic celebration of the Eucharist served as a constant reminder to the Christian of the divine economy in Christ, from beginning to end, which all adherents of the Gospel were called to participate in through a faithful disposition and conduct of their lives. Even the famous Pauline injunction on the Eucharist drives home this point quite clearly (cf. 1 Cor 11:26).

Thus, the content of any particular liturgical rite, originally fixed within the confines of the Eucharist (or at least attached to it), intentionally identifies the sacramental act as an expression of the Church's belief in the consecratory efficacy of the one-time sacrifice of Christ, as well as orients the act so that it is understood in terms of a partial fulfillment of the eschatological Kingdom. Every liturgical rite, replete with prayers and symbolic acts, is a "movement of consecration,"[17] drawing its power from the mystical but real presence of the sacrificed Lord, whose present dominion is but a foretaste of His eternal reign that will be realized fully at the end of human history.

From a purely thematic perspective, we may conclude that the early Church's insistence on the centrality of the Cross and the eschatological Kingdom gave to all subsequent liturgical rites a definitive thematic content around which to structure public worship. Both prothesis and eucharistic anaphora undoubtedly share this content, and it is this common ground that provides the impetus to initially suggest that a level of influence was indeed exerted by the eucharistic anaphora on the prothesis rite. Both rites share then the Church's fundamental Christological *credo*: "Christ crucified" [Χριστὸν ἐσταυρωμένον (1 Cor 1:23)]; and "Come, Lord Jesus" [Ἔρχου, Κύριε Ἰησοῦ (Rev 22:20)]. In accordance with Pott, the likelihood of any possible spontaneity or haphazardness in the formulation of the prothesis rite is virtually nonexistent, given the fact that the conscience of the Church has always sought to convey, though not always in a systematic manner, the evangelical message of the divine *economia* and the *eschaton*, both ἐν λόγοις (written Gospel) καὶ ἔργοις (divine worship).

These two basic tenets of Christian doctrine take the form of confession (*anamnesis*) and supplication (*ikesia-epiklesis*), which simultaneously constitute the two most rudimentary segments of any Eastern liturgical prayer. Such a fact then gives credence to the claim that all formal liturgical prayers within the context of collective worship, regardless of specific content, are unequivocally sacrificial and eschatological in their overall thematic orientation, as are all liturgical rites.

COMMON THEMES: PROTHESIS AND ANAPHORA

The Prothesis Prayer as 'Mini-Anaphora

The first and most crucial element of the preparatory rite that deserves our attention is the ancient prayer of the prothesis. As previously discussed, it was in fact the first major shift made toward a formalization of the rite. In Schulz' estimation, the prayer constituted the most genuine articulation of the prothesis' original meaning, which was essentially to see the eucharistic bread as Christ's immolated Body, the sacrificial food designated to feed man provisionally until the consummation of the Kingdom of God and then to become the food of the Kingdom, that Christ would eat and drink anew with His followers into the *eschaton* (cf. Matt 26:29). Byz-BAS' prothesis prayer from *Barberini 336*[18] matches up rather neatly to four of the constitutive ten[19] sections of most eucharistic anaphorae, rendering it a miniaturized version of an anaphora itself.

PRAYER OF THE PROTHESIS	LITURGICAL/ ANAPHORAL ELEMENTS
Barberini 336: Byz-BAS	in the Byzantine Divine Liturgy
(Εὐχὴ ἣν ποιεῖ ὁ ἱερεὺς ἐν τῷ σκευοφυλακίῳ ἀποτιθεμένου τοῦ ἄρτου ἐν τῷ δίσκῳ)	
— Ὁ Θεός, ὁ Θεὸς ἡμῶν, ὁ τὸν οὐράνιον ἄρτον τὴν τροφὴν τοῦ παντὸς κόσμου τὸν Κύριον ἡμῶν καὶ Θεὸν Ἰησοῦν Χριστὸν ἐξαποστείλας Σωτῆρα καὶ Λυτρωτὴν καὶ Εὐεργέτην εὐλογοῦντα καὶ ἁγιάζοντα ἡμᾶς·	*Postsanctus (summary of the economia in the Person of Christ as the "heavenly bread")
— αὐτὸς εὐλόγησον τὴν πρόθεσιν ταύτην καὶ πρόσδεξαι αὐτὴν εἰς τὸ ὑπερουράνιόν σου θυσιαστήριον·	*Epiklesis (prayer of consecration and acceptance upon God's heavenly altar)
— μνημόνευσον ὡς ἀγαθὸς καὶ φιλάνθρωπος τῶν προσενεγκόντων καὶ δι' οὓς προσήγαγον καὶ ἡμᾶς ἀκατακρίτους διαφύλαξον ἐν τῇ ἱερουργίᾳ τῶν θείων σου μυστηρίων·	*Intercessions (supplication for the living and dead, for whom the sacrifice is offered)
— ὅτι ἡγίασται καὶ δεδόξασται τὸ πάντιμον καὶ μεγαλοπρεπὲς ὄνομά σου τοῦ Πατρὸς <καὶ τοῦ Υἱοῦ καὶ τοῦ Ἁγίου Πνεύματος, νῦν καὶ ἀεὶ καὶ εἰς τοὺς αἰῶνας τῶν αἰώνων.>	* Doxology

The opening of the prothesis prayer corresponds to the postsanctus, which in eucharistic anaphorae typically follows the Isaian Sanctus (6:3) and expresses a thanksgiving for who God is (the "theological" Trinity) and for the divine economy wrought in the incarnation of the Second Person of the Holy Trinity (the "economical" Trinity).[20] The prayer is addressed to God the Father (as are most Eastern anaphorae), gratefully acknowledging the incarnation of the Son as "Savior," "Redeemer," and "Benefactor." In order to fulfill the divine economy, the Savior's point of contact with humans is to be consumed by them eucharistically; that is, as "the heavenly bread." However, prior to this consumption—and certainly before any consecratory transformation of the gifts can take place—the Person of Christ and the salvific works accomplished by Him must first be confessed by the communicants for, as a general rule, what remains unknown can hardly ever be approached or entreated. This recognition becomes the task of the postsanctus in the anaphora and is present in virtually all liturgical prayers of the Byzantine rite, regardless of length or complexity. In a sense, it serves as a kind of prophetic preamble to the "heart" of the prayer, which is normally supplicatory in character, and it authenticates the request made immediately afterward by identifying the central figure and agent of divine grace (i.e. the incarnate Christ), as well as the capacity in which the agent acts (i.e. as "the bread from heaven").

The second part of the prothesis prayer clearly corresponds to the epiklesis of the anaphora, entreating God to "bless" (εὐλόγησον) and "accept" (πρόσδεξαι) the ritualized gifts. Interestingly, two more verbs that constitute the intercessions, or third section, of the prothesis prayer ("remember" (μνημόνευσον) and "protect" (διαφύλαξον) seem to extend the epicletic nature of the prayer, but in all Byzantine anaphorae, the intercessory section has precisely this purpose anyway: to petition God for "worldly" or "material" blessings directed toward individuals or groups of people ("those who have offered (these gifts) and for whom they were offered" (τῶν προσενεγκόντων καὶ δι' οὓς προσήγαγον),[21] whereas the epiklesis proper focuses upon the transformation of the gifts (τὴν πρόθεσιν ταύτην) and the "spiritual" benefits that will be reaped by the communicants of faith.[22] With the epicletic section of the prothesis prayer, the ritualized bread becomes an antitype[23] of Christ as the "bread from heaven," who already bears the marks of His impending suffering and death and stands flanked by His Church as the Lord of history and meta-history.

The fourth and final section of the prothesis prayer concludes with the typical Byzantine doxology of the Holy Trinity, which corresponds to the doxological conclusion of the anaphora rite, with a slight variation in wording.[24] Not much more can be added here, except to point out the obvious attempt at formalizing the prothesis via a structural conformation to the parent rite, especially in both rites' focus upon the magnificence of the Name of God.

Consequently, based upon the above examination of the prayer of the prothesis and its section-by-section correlation to anaphoral components of the Basilian eucharistic celebration, one may reasonably conclude that this most ancient and core element of the proskomide rite has retained the economical and eschatological themes, which have concurrently designated it a "mini-anaphora."

FROM ENARXIS TO EPIKLESIS: HISTORY AND SACRIFICE

The introductory troparion and doxological enarxis of the prothesis rite, like the conclusion, appear as later elements appended to the service to make it more analogous in structure to the sequence of Matins[25] immediately preceding the Divine Liturgy (at least according to Greek parochial practice but not necessarily the norm in monasteries). The actual trinitarian enarxis of the Byzantine Liturgy appears first in the writings of Pseudo-Sophronios of Jerusalem[26] (560–638), then in Theodore the Studite[27] (758–826), and finally in Cabasilas[28] (fourteenth century). P. Trembelas, basing his argumentation on the Western nun Egeria's *Itinerarium Egeriae,* or *Travels* (381–384), and Anton Baumstark's classic work *Comparative Liturgy,*[29] makes the case that, by the fourth century, a primitive form of the Matins service was already in full use by the Church of Jerusalem and constituted the beginning of the Divine Liturgy (ὅτε ὄρθρος καὶ λειτουργία ἀπετέλουν μίαν ἀναπόσπαστον ἀκολουθίαν— "when matins and liturgy constituted one inseparable service").[30]

The content of both troparia makes the necessary connection between the two main events in the Christological economia—the Crucifixion and Resurrection—with theologically and biblically expressive language. The suffering and death of Christ are seen as a "purchasing" (ἐξηγόρασας) of mankind from the curse of the Law, a first-century theme taken up ardently by the Apostle Paul (1 Cor 6:20; 7:23) and to which the patristic tradition thereafter bears ample witness. Likewise, Christ's sacrifice becomes the gateway to immortality (τὴν ἀθανασίαν) and victory (τὸ νῖκος) over sin and great mercy (τὸ μέγα ἔλεος), the fruits of the eschatological Kingdom now savored by the faithful as a result of the vacant Tomb.

Theologically, the doxological enarxis and conclusion, in the form of a blessing of either the divine Name or Kingdom, signifies an acknowledgement of God's sovereignty and goodness toward all mankind,[31] both before (cf. Matt 25:34) *and* after the divine economy has taken place. The imminence of Christ's sacrifice, together with the future establishment of the post-Resurrection eschatological Kingdom, together constituted the "master plan of salvation" that was devised by the wisdom of God. Consequently, the praise of God precedes the enactment of the sacrifice in the prothesis, as a testimony to the σοφία τοῦ Θεοῦ, and follows it, as a thanksgiving for its completion and the dawning of the new *aion* of God's reign.

The anamnesis in both the prothesis and eucharistic anaphora simply constitutes a remembrance of the Person of Christ and the distinct salvific activities accomplished in Him. The more succinct anamnetic section in the prothesis seems to make unique reference to the Crucifixion, as evidenced by the threefold signing with the lance over the seal of the first prosphora, from which the Lamb is extracted. The eucharistic anamnesis extends the remembrance to include the post-Crucifixion events, and it makes specific mention of Christ's "enthronement at [God the Father's] right hand"[32] (τῆς ἐκ δεξιῶν καθέδρας) and "His glorious and awesome second coming"[33] (τῆς δευτέρας καὶ ἐνδόξου πάλιν παρουσίας) of Christ, both of which are clearly eschatological themes.

As already affirmed by Symeon of Thessalonike and Nicholas Cabasilas, the antiphons in the Divine Liturgy function as prophetic utterings of Christ's impending coming in the flesh and His sacrificial death. The modified Isaian verses (53:7-9), which complete removal from the prosphora, likewise proclaim the imminent immolation of the Lamb of God before His enemies. In both circumstances, what is noteworthy is that the sacrifice is not yet effected; it is simply announced, but the actual prophetic declaration also retains a high degree of significance because it indicates that from the beginning of each rite, the divine economy of man's salvation in Christ has already been placed into motion. In other words, the certainty of man's deliverance is sealed by virtue of the certainty of God's word, spoken through the prophets. Cabasilas recognizes the importance of the divine announcement as he recognizes the value in first dedicating the correspond to the four practical incisions on each side of the Lamb in preparation for its precious gifts to God before offering them to Him.[34] God's spoken word through the prophet Isaiah is, in one sense, a dedication that designates the Lamb to become in the Eucharist what it is preordained to become—the life-giving sacrifice that ushers in the eschatological Kingdom.

The piercing of the extracted Lamb and the pouring of wine and water into the chalice are accompanied by the Johannine verse 19:34. This further act of physical destruction inflicted upon Jesus' body corresponds to the moments immediately following Jesus' physical end, and both actions may be regarded as additional symbolic representations of the voluntary immolation of the sacrificed Lamb, which is itself supported by the numerous prophecies from Scripture (cf. Exod 12:46; Num 9:12; Ps 34:20; Zech 12:10; Rev 1:7). In like manner, the offering of the sacrifice in the anaphora marks Christ's death and simultaneous glorification during the elevation of the precious gifts with the words: "Offering to You these gifts from Your own gifts in all and for all . . ."[35] The anaphoral rubric calls for the cross-armed raising of the paten and chalice, which gives obvious weight to the crucifixion as Christ's free-will offering to God the Father.

The epiklesis section in both prothesis and anaphora is a natural continuation of the offering of the sacrifice and, rubrically speaking, is dominated by the blessing gesture of the celebrant priest over both the paten and chalice. In both cases, the gifts are mystically "transformed" from plain bread and wine to antitypes of Christ's Body and Blood, and from antitypes representing Christ to

> the true Victim, the most holy Body of the Lord, which really suffered the outrages, insults and blows; which was crucified and slain, . . . In like manner, the wine has become the blood which flowed from that Body. It is that Body and Blood formed by the Holy Spirit, born of the Virgin Mary, which was buried, which rose again on the third day, which ascended into heaven and sits on the right hand of the Father.[36]

Up until now, the Church has predominantly relived the events of Christ's earthly life, His incarnation, passion, and finally His crucifixion. The hymns, prophetic utterings, and liturgical gestures all look to this end; namely, to advance the thematic content of the history of salvation, centered on the sacrifice of Jesus. Once the historical sacrifice has been accomplished, there is an immediate transition into meta-history, into the "eighth day" of God's eternal reign. It is at this point that the eschatological Church, having received its Lord resurrected and glorified, looks henceforth toward the slain yet enthroned Lamb of the Apocalypse in adoration (cf. Rev 5:6–14). The prothesis rite, like the Divine Liturgy, now shifts toward a vision of this eschatological Kingdom, which is broadcast through the sections known as the commemorations and the intercessions.

FROM COMMEMORATIONS TO CONCLUSION: META-HISTORY AND THE ESCHATON

Upon the completion of the prothesis rite, with the addition of particles upon the paten representing the saints as well as the living and dead, Symeon of Thessalonike envisions the eschatological Kingdom of God's glory and victory in Jesus Christ, "God in the midst of gods."[37] As already indicated, this characteristic phrase coined by Symeon is highly apocalyptical, but it is also representative of the Church still in formation prior to the fulfillment of the divine economy. In other words, the ritualized paten in the prothesis rite is not simply an icon of the Kingdom yet to come; it simultaneously signifies the synaxis of earthly and heavenly beings from every place and time in history, eagerly anticipating the binary event of Christ's sacrifice and His resurrection, achieved in the anaphoral epiklesis.

During the prothesis, the multiplication of particles upon the paten and the accompanying commemoration of saints are matched by a similar remembrance in the anaphora. The standard hierarchical listing of saints in the anaphora, beginning first with the Mother of God and then continuing with John the Forerunner and the Apostles, naturally corresponds to the order in which the particles are excised and placed next to the Lamb in the prothesis. This taxonomy, very reminiscent of the Pseudo-Dionysian angelic hierarchy,[38] designates not only the order in which Christ became known to man in history (i.e. first to His mother, and then to the Baptist, and finally to His disciples et al.) but also the inverse; that is, the order in which man has recourse to the risen Christ of the *eschaton*. Hence, the Eucharist, in its capacity as a celebration "in honor and memory" (εἰς τιμὴν καὶ μνήμην) of the saints of history who have received and accepted the revelation of the divine *economia* in Christ, is also offered as a supplication to them, to intercede on man's behalf that he too may share in their meta-historical bliss as co-inhabitants of the eschatological Kingdom.

A concise (and practically identical) intercessory petition to God immediately follows the commemoration of saints in both the prothesis and the anaphora rites, which then opens up to a longer and more complex series of supplications making requests for individual persons and needs. The insertion of the intercessions, i.e. *following the consecratory epiklesis*, holds much significance. Interestingly, the saints, congregated around the as-of-yet unsacrificed Lamb in anticipation of His fulfillment of the divine economy, are not readily identified as intercessors. In one sense, one can surmise that the pre-formative period of the Church was not yet fully conducive to miracles performed via intercessions since the grace of the Holy Spirit had not yet given birth to the Church and, consequently, the era of New Testament Christian saints had not yet been inaugurated. With the instantaneous transition into meta-history that the divine economy achieved, the Church advances from being simply a closely-knit brotherhood of men and women witnessing to the sacrifice of their Lord, to a true, divinely-sanctioned, and transformative force empowered by God to continue the sanctifying and salvific work of Christ in the world. Hence, the act of consecration in both prothesis and anaphora renders a mystagogical vision of a newly-formed Church, a heavenly Jerusalem whose members have not only received the divine revelation of Christ's *economia*; they have actively entered into it as full participants who perpetuate the divine economy from age to age.

The content of the intercessions in both rites centers on the repose of the dead and the spiritual welfare of the living, clergy and laity alike. The spiritual benefits for both groups, as Cabasilas painstakingly notes, are of paramount importance since the ultimate end of all membership in the

Church is inheritance of the eschatological Kingdom. However, it is an
inheritance achieved on the basis of the accomplishment of the sacrifice,
which Cabasilas again equates with God's acceptance of the Church's offerings.[39] Hence, after the sacrifice is accomplished and God has accepted the
anaphora of the faithful, the Church pleads for the spiritual benefits leading
to the eschatological inheritance of the Kingdom, which Cabasilas terms
"effects." He writes:

> What are these effects? They are common to the living and the de-
> parted: that for the gifts which he has been pleased to accept, God
> will send grace in return. In particular, that the departed may have
> rest for their souls, and may, *with the saints who have completed their
> course, inherit the kingdom* (καὶ βασιλείας κληρονομίαν μετὰ τῶν τετελειω-
> μένων ἁγίων); and that the living may partake of the holy table, and
> be made holy, and that none may partake to his own judgement and
> condemnation; likewise, that they may receive remission of their sins,
> peace, fruitfulness, and the provision of what is necessary to them; and
> finally, *that they may in God's sight appear worthy of the kingdom* (τὸ
> τελευταῖον, βασιλείας ἀξίους φανῆναι παρὰ τῷ Θεῷ).[40]

From a patristic perspective, the commemorations and intercessions
may be viewed as a single unit, not only structurally but thematically as
well. In fact, both sections are oriented toward the eschatological Kingdom.
Cabasilas makes this point abundantly clear when he remarks:

> The offering of sacrifice is not only an act of supplication [interces-
> sion]; it is one of thanksgiving [commemoration] as well, in the same
> way that, at the beginning of the liturgy, in dedicating the offerings to
> God, the priest gave thanks and made supplication at the same time;
> he now, having consecrated and sacrificed these gifts, *unites thanksgiv-
> ing with petition* (καὶ εὐχαριστεῖ . . . καὶ ἱκεσίαν προσάγει). He states the
> reasons for his thanksgiving, and names those for whom he prays.[41]

He immediately continues:

> The reasons for thanksgiving . . . are the Saints; *for in them the Church
> finds that which she seeks and obtains that for which she has prayed—the
> kingdom of heaven* (ἐν τούτοις γὰρ ἡ Ἐκκλησία τὸ ζητούμενον εὗρε, καὶ τῆς
> εὐχῆς ἔτυχε τῆς βασιλείας τῶν οὐρανῶν). Those for whom she prays are they
> who have not yet reached perfection and are still in need of prayer.[42]

Hence, the purpose of the commemoration-intercession unit is clearly
to couple thanksgiving with supplication, using the saints not only as the
recipients of the Church's veneration and the embodied representations of
the fulfilled eschatological Kingdom, but also as empowered intercessors

for the living, who are still in the process of completing their course toward perfection and the Kingdom of God.

"CONSECRATORY" LANGUAGE IN THE PRAYER OF THE PROTHESIS: A FURTHER INDICATION

A final indication of the sacrificial and eschatological importance within the rite of the prothesis revolves around the "consecratory" language used in the prothesis prayer. Although the conventional definition of liturgical consecration among Eastern and Western Christians typically comprises some sort of qualitative transformation of the eucharistic bread and wine,[43] raising the ritualized elements to a higher and more sublime ontological state, the Basilian notion of consecration as chiefly a form of divine revelation to the worshiping Church seems more conducive to our purposes here. Basil of Caesarea uses the term ἀνάδειξις ("declaration"; "showing forth") as the very purpose of the epiklesis in his important work *On the Holy Spirit* (27.66). The Basilian anaphoral triplet 'to bless—to sanctify—to declare' (εὐλογῆσαι-ἁγιάσαι-ἀναδεῖξαι) includes three infinitives used in the Byz-BAS prayer of consecration and associates the act of the consecration of the gifts with their revelation as the Body and Blood of Christ, possessing in full the divine presence. In fact, according to the Cappadocian Father, ἀνάδειξις is the final sequence in the process of consecration, not the result of a singular consecratory act. The eucharistic pronouncement by Christ in the Institution Narrative, "This is My Body . . . this is My Blood" (εὐλογία), leads to the actual transformation of the elements by the Spirit (ἁγιασμός - καθαγιασμός), which in turn declares them, or shows them forth, to the worshiping Church as containing the fullness of Christ (ἀνάδειξις). Without this final revelation, the first two steps in the "consecration movement" would seemingly have no meaning, since a main purpose of the Eucharist, according to Cabasilas, is communion of the gifts[44] and, theoretically, the Church cannot confess or commune with what is not revealed to her from above.[45] It is noteworthy also to mention that for the Eastern liturgical tradition, consecration is best understood as the very act of worship itself, with the Church's collective thanksgiving and supplication coupled together, and not one of many isolated acts in the eucharistic rite. The above explanation of the significance of the Basilian liturgical triplet is not an attempt to undermine this truth by scientifically dichotomizing the consecratory act into constitutive parts but rather to demonstrate the significance of the consecratory movement, first as an upward offering (from Christ to God) and then as a downward offering (from God to the Church).

In the prothesis rite, while no specific transformation of the antitypical elements into Christ's Body and Blood occurs, the prayer clearly indicates a showing forth of the eucharistic bread upon the paten as the "heavenly bread, the food of the whole world, our Lord and God Jesus Christ." How is this possible when, in fact, the Basilian triad calls for ἀνάδειξις to be the final step in the movement of offering but has not yet been preceded by the conventional hallowing of the gifts, as it were? With this disruption in the Cappadocian's liturgical sequence, is not what is shown forth still only plain bread and wine?

On the contrary, Basil's characteristic naming of the ritualized gifts as "antitypes" just prior to his epiklesis implies that they already signify Christ by virtue of the anamnetic dramatization of His life to which they have contributed, begun in the prothesis and continued during the eucharistic liturgy. Via anamnesis, the ritualized bread of the prothesis, having received the marks of Christ's passion and positioned in the middle of the paten—an indication of Christ's centrality in the Church, in history, and in the universe—is shown forth to already be the very bread and source of life. In a sense then, although the term ἀνάδειξις is absent from the prayer of the prothesis, Christ is immediately identified with and declared to be the heavenly bread in the prayer. This serves as a form of "pre-consecration," or initial revelation of Christ's person and mission. In other words, Christ is the heavenly bread, the *Lamb of God* who voluntarily sacrifices Himself later in the Liturgy (a "second proclamation," *revealing* Christ as the crucified and risen Lord) and, soon after, is eucharistically consumed for the life of mankind (a "third proclamation," revealing Christ as Healer and Savior of those who receive Him in Holy Communion). As a combined unit, the prothesis and eucharistic rites do not only relate the story of the divine economy in the person of Christ; they also engage the Church and its worshiping membership to participate in this economy, marked by this aforementioned series of "revelations" (ἀναδείξεις) that occur during the important moments of liturgical offering.

According to the prayer, Christ the heavenly bread already bears the capacity to "bless and sanctify" man. This capability, to be sure, exists in Him as much before His death and resurrection as it does after, but the benefits to the faithful are released only after the fulfillment of the divine *economia*, that is, after the heavenly bread progresses through the aforementioned three cycles of revelatory consecration.

Finally, one will note that the remainder of the prothesis prayer, addressed specifically to God the Father, makes entreaty for the full sanctification of the prothesis rite, its acceptance by God upon His heavenly altar, and the remembrance by God of all those who offer the gifts to Him and for whom they are offered. However, this full sanctification does not imply any transformation in the substantive composition of the ritualized bread upon the paten (Christ the heavenly bread does not become "greater" or "more blessed"), as there was never any essential change in the hypostasis of God the Son either before or after the Incarnation. The Church simply entreats God to accept the prothesis rite as the work of salvation wrought through the hands of the incarnate Christ, the heavenly bread, who prior to His crucifixion likewise prays the Father to accept and glorify Him for the work of divine economy He accomplished (cf. John 17:4–5) during His earthly existence.

NOTES

1. Ioannes M. Fountoules, Ἀπαντήσεις εἰς λειτουργικὰς ἀπορίας [*Answers to Liturgical Questions*], vol. 3 (Athens, 1994), 43. Translation mine.

2. Hans-Joachim Schulz, *Die Byzantinische Liturgie: Glaubenszeugnis und Symbolgestalt* [Ἡ Βυζαντινή Λειτουργία· μαρτυρία πίστεως καί συμβολική ἔκφραση], trans. Demetrios V. Tzerpos (Athens, 1998), 259. Translation from the Greek mine.

3. Ibid., 258. Translation mine.

4. Paul Evdokimov, *La prière de l'Église d'Orient: La liturgie byzantine de saint Jean Chrysostome* (Mulhouse, 1966), 152.

5. Casimir Kucharek, *The Byzantine-Slav Liturgy of St. John Chrysostom: Its Origin and Evolution* (Combermere, 1971), 269.

6. Ibid., 270.

7. Ibid., 271.

8. Thomas Pott, *La réforme liturgique byzantine: étude du phénomène d'évolution non spontanée de la liturgie byzantine* (Rome, 2000), 190. All subsequent translations from Pott are mine.

9. Ibid.

10. Germanus of Constantinople, *On the Divine Liturgy*, trans. Paul Meyendorff (Crestwood, 1984), 59.

11. Pott, 190.

12. Ibid., 227.

13. Ibid., 99–223.

14. Ibid.

15. This striking image is taken up by Thomas Elavanal, *The Memorial Celebration: A Theological Study of the Anaphora of the Apostles Mar Addai and Mari* (Kerala, 1988), 182, who reworks Edward Schillebeeckx's view of Christianity and, by extension, Christian worship, as a religion of *Maranatha*. See also E. Schillebeeckx, *Christ: The Sacrament of the Encounter with God* (London, 1963), 41.

16. "The Martyrdoms of Saints Perpetua and Felicitas", in *Readings in the Humanities: First Year Program. Saint Anselm College, Seventeenth Edition* (Acton, 2004), 294–308.

17. Stylianos Muksuris, *The Anaphorae of the Liturgy of Sts. Addai and Mari and the Byzantine Liturgy of St. Basil the Great: A Comparative Study* (Durham, 1999), 261; see also C.C. Richardson, "The So-Called Epiclesis in Hippolitus", in *Harvard Theological Review*, vol. 40 (1947), 108.

18. F.E. Brightman, *Liturgies Eastern and Western* (Oxford, 1896), 309–10.

19. Liturgiologists typically identify ten sections to any Christian eucharistic anaphora, while others fewer than ten, since some of the sections are grouped together: (1) the opening dialogue; (2) the preface; (3) the *presanctus*; (4) the *sanctus*; (5) the *postsanctus*; (6) the words of institution; (7) the anamnesis; (8) the epiklesis; (9) the intercessions; and (10) the doxology. See also my *The Anaphorae*, 90 *et passim*.

20. Ibid., 114, 126 (note 10), and 132–33; see also Elavanal, 107.

21. Muksuris, 200–02.

22. Ibid., 172.

23. Ibid., 255–56.

24. Ibid., 244.

25. Ὡρολόγιον τὸ Μέγα, περιέχον ἅπασαν τὴν ἀνήκουσαν αὐτῷ ἀκολουθίαν κατὰ τὴν τάξιν τῆς Ἀνατολικῆς Ἐκκλησίας καὶ τῶν ὑποκειμένων αὐτῇ εὐαγῶν μοναστηρίων μετὰ τινῶν ἀπαραιτήτων προσθηκῶν. [*The Great Book of Hours, Containing Every Service Belonging to It and the Venerable Monasteries UnderIt, with Some Necessary Additions*], (Athens, 1986), 83–84, 87.

26. Sophronios of Jerusalem, *Liturgical Commentary* 11; PG 87.3992BC.

27. Theodore the Studite, *Interpretation of the Presanctified Liturgy*; PG 99.1690.

28. Nicholas Cabasilas, *Commentary on the Divine Liturgy* 11; PG 150.392A; Nicholas Cabasilas, *A Commentary on the Divine Liturgy*, trans. J.M. Hussey and P.A. McNulty (London, 1960), 43.

29. Anton Baumstark, *Comparative Liturgy*, trans. F.L. Cross (Oxford, 1958).

30. P. Trembelas, Αἱ τρεῖς λειτουργίαι κατὰ τοὺς ἐν Ἀθήναις κώδικας [*The Three Liturgies According to the Athens Codices*], *Texte und Forschungen zur byzantinisch-neugriechischen Philologie* (Athens, 1935), 21–25.

31. Hussey and McNulty, trans., 43; Cabasilas, *Commentary* 12; PG 150.392B.

32. Muksuris, 138.

33. Ibid.

34. Hussey and McNulty, trans., 31; Cabasilas, *Commentary* 2; PG 150.376C–377A.

35. Muksuris, 138.

36. Hussey and McNulty, trans., 70; Cabasilas, *Commentary* 27; PG 150.425CD.

37. Symeon of Thessalonike, *On the Sacred Liturgy* 94; PG 155.285AB.

38. Dionysios the Areopagite, *Celestial Hierarchies* 13; PG 3.301C.

39. Hussey and McNulty, trans., 83; Cabasilas, *Commentary* 33; PG 150.441B.

40. Ibid. Emphases mine.

41. Ibid., 83–84; PG 150.441C. Emphases mine.

42. Ibid., Emphases mine.

43. For a general summary of the Eastern and Western Christian perspectives on consecration, see Robert Sokolowski, *Christian Faith and Human Understanding: Studies on the Eucharist, Trinity, and the Human Person* (Washington, 2006); and David Berger, *Thomas Aquinas and the Liturgy* (Naples, 2005).

44. Hussey and McNulty, trans., 25; Cabasilas, *Commentary* 1; PG 150.369A.

45. Cf. Muksuris, 153–54, especially note 36.

CONCLUSION

LITURGICAL MYSTAGOGY AS THE EXPERIENCE OF DIVINE REALITY

Byzantine liturgiologist Robert F. Taft has noted that "one of the distinguishing characteristics of the Byzantine Rite is precisely its intimate symbiosis of liturgical symbolism (ritual celebration), liturgical setting (architecture/iconography), and liturgical interpretation (mystagogy)."[1] The celebration of the Eucharist, in other words, which is the Church's preeminent act of worship, can be defined and understood in terms of what is done, the context in which the liturgical act is performed, and the innate, intrinsic meaning of the liturgical act, which can accomplish no less than transcend its immediately outward form, although it remains inherently dependent upon it.

These components of the Byzantine Divine Liturgy are not intended to serve as optional and thus dispensable ameliorations to an otherwise mundane service, capable of transforming the act of worship into a more vivid and enjoyable experience for the believer. Quite the contrary, Taft's assertion is thoroughly indicative of the fact that the effectiveness of each component is mutually dependent upon the existence *and* magnitude of the other two. Hence, for example, the proper execution of the prothesis rite *requires* the liturgical vessels and "holy space" of the table of oblation within the altar, along with the appropriate iconography. Similarly, the proper execution of the prothesis rite, combined with the appropriate context conducive for its celebration, assists in revealing the fullest extent of its mystagogical significance that, as this book has sought to prove, revolves around the sacrificial and eschatological themes central to Christology.

This third component, liturgical explanation or mystagogy, has concerned us most in this book, precisely because it is mystagogy that stands at the threshold of theological understanding and reveals vital Christological truths, without whose acceptance genuine healing, salvation, and restoration are virtually impossible for the believer. Hence, liturgical mystagogy not only provides insight into the divine *economia* fulfilled within history in the sacrifice of Jesus Christ, but it naturally draws each individual and the Church as a whole to actively participate in the eschatological victory of God's dominion that this divine sacrifice has wrought.

Of course, one may ponder how mystagogy actually differs from a mere designation of meaningful symbols to various liturgical objects or actions (the first component), since the latter's intent is also to arrive at a deeper knowledge of theological truths via the liturgical celebration. In what sense is mystagogy truly distinct from liturgical symbolization? After all, were not the mystagogical commentaries of Nicholas Cabasilas and Symeon of Thessalonike—as well as their predecessors in the East, Theodore of Mopsuestia, Pseudo-Dionysios, Maximos the Confessor, Germanos of Constantinople, Nicholas of Andida, and even Sophronios of Jerusalem—merely objective and oftentimes exhaustive exegeses of the Divine Liturgy, which over the course of several centuries gained the sophistication and grandeur that characterize it today? Could it be that these liturgical commentaries actually surpassed the level of mere textbook explanations and became characterized by a distinctiveness all their own?

The answer becomes apparent within the consistency of the patristic witness, namely, that true mystagogy is above all else *experiential*; it is lived and breathed during the moments of prayer and the hours dedicated to worship. Liturgical mystagogy is not limited to a cerebral exercise in symbology, neither can the mystagogue (a calling ideally shared by all worshipping Christians) be considered a symbologist. On the contrary, the uniqueness of the Byzantine Divine Liturgy is such that it summons the Church each time to attain a very real vision of the divine life—to the extent, of course, that man is capable of beholding and allowed to behold this vision—and further welcomes the earthly community to participate in it. By incorporating the eternal reality of God into one's own finite reality, albeit on a provisional basis, the worshipper not only understands the truths leading to salvation, but he also participates in them and thus becomes himself a co-participant in salvation history.

René Bornert's admission, namely that "the liturgy is above all a life, perhaps more so in Byzantium than elsewhere,"[2] gives credence to the idea that mystagogy (theology) becomes the primary activity of the Christian at prayer, who is rightly to be called a mystagogue (theologian), in keeping with the conventional Evagrian axiom: "If you are a theologian, you will pray truly; and if you will pray truly, you are a theologian"

(*Εἰ θεολόγος εἶ, προσεύξῃ ἀληθῶς, καὶ εἰ ἀληθῶς προσεύξῃ, θεολόγος εἶ*).[3] Evagrios illustrates that the work of theology is tantamount to a Christian's own struggle for truth and union with God, which he bears with faith and a prayerful disposition. Theology then—and, by extension, mystagogy—becomes for the Christian the application of the divine economy to his own life and reality. It would seem then that by constantly seeking and thus broadening one's knowledge of Christological truths, the Christian is simultaneously drawn into the divinely-ordained plan of salvation, realizing that together with the rest of humanity, he shares the privilege of being a prospective inheritor of the Kingdom of God. To this end, he is confronted with important faith-based decisions that he must inevitably make, which will ultimately bear consequences on his own salvation and, oftentimes, on the salvation of others. Hence, mystagogy involves far more than simply understanding theological truths; it entails making those theological truths pertinent to one's life experience. Hence, the Christian no longer remains a third-party observer of the sacrificial and eschatological aspects of *economia*; he becomes a firsthand partaker in them.

The central themes in God's *economia*, Christ's sacrifice and the reign of His eschatological Kingdom, are events which, by virtue of their divine initiator, are both historical and trans-historical entities; that is, they belong to the realm of *chronos* but are also free of the constraints of time, thus belonging to God's *kairos*. Liturgical mystagogy, within the rites of the prothesis and the Eucharist, gives historical man provisional access to God's timelessness, allowing him to participate in the mystery of the Cross and, inchoately, in its fruit, which is the eschatological Kingdom.

In the prologue to the Greek translation of Paul Evdokimov's book *The Prayer of the Eastern Church*, Metropolitan Anastasios of Androusi makes the point that in the eucharistic liturgy:

> Here is revealed and realized the salvific event in Christ. The Kingdom of God is doxologically announced as a reality that "has come" and "is coming." With the operation of the Holy Spirit, who transforms the dimension of time, we become eyewitnesses of the events which compose the economia of salvation – from the Nativity until Pentecost and the Second Coming.[4]

By suspending the concept of time in any singular celebration of the Divine Liturgy, either present or future, liturgical mystagogy renders real and effectual the movement from Christ's sacrifice to the dawning of the eschatological Kingdom. In other words, Christ is not sacrificed anew, neither is a new kingdom established. It is the *original* sacrifice and the *original* arrival of the eschatological age that the believer encounters and is challenged to accept for his own benefit.

The theological themes then of sacrifice and eschatology not only constitute the very content and core of divine economy in the person of the crucified and resurrected Christ, but they also summarize the central confession of faith of each Christian, whose salvation may be gauged in terms of his response to the Christ event. Liturgical mystagogy, replete with countless references to Christ's sacrifice and the eschaton, constantly reminds the Church at prayer of three important things: (1) its history (i.e. its origins whereby it exists and is authorized to act in the spirit of its eternal Lord); (2) its future fulfillment as the redeemed community awaiting the consummation of history; and (3) its responsibilities in the present, namely, to affirm and bear witness to the already sacrificed and glorified Lamb of the Apocalypse, rooted in faith in its past and remaining focused on its final aim, its very raison d'être, which is none other than the sanctification and restoration of the entire created order back to God.

LITURGICAL PRAYER: Σμικρογραφία AND ICON OF LITURGICAL MYSTAGOGY

The point has already been made that the prothesis rite represents, both in terms of structure as well as theological content, a mini-version of the entire Byzantine Anaphora. Even the eucharistic prayer itself, the central anaphoral component, is full of sacrificial and eschatological references, a notion which leads to the proposition that *all* liturgical prayer forms may quite possibly be justified as images of liturgical mystagogy, whose principal focus is God's work of redemption (*economia*).

From antiquity, early Christians tenaciously regarded the eucharistic prayer of the anaphora as the archetypal liturgical prayer of the Church, after which other smaller liturgical prayer units (e.g. litanies with a prayer collect and a trinitarian *ekphonesis*, or proclamation) were modeled. The usual Christological content (Christ's sacrificial death and the post-Resurrection Kingdom) was duplicated in these shorter prayer forms and found expression via various approaches (e.g. thanksgiving for Christ's sacrifice, supplication for the inheritance of the Kingdom of God, confession before "the awesome Judgment Seat of Christ", etc.).

Interestingly, a random analysis of Eastern liturgical prayers, regardless of size or complexity, indicates that at least one of the two aforementioned themes is always present in each prayer. This observation does not in any way minimize the importance of the other theme that may appear to be visibly absent, for the simple reason that both subjects are interdependent and mutually derivative of one another. Christ's suffering and death was the necessary means by which the eschatological age dawned upon the world, and the post-Exilic prophetic expectations of the final establishment of God's reign in the world served as the necessary precedent for the divine sacrifice. Commenting on the cohesive nature of the relationship between sacrifice and eschatology as components of divine *economia*, Cabasilas intimates that in the Divine Liturgy, the acts preceding the sacrifice of the Savior (e.g. His birth and His manifestation to the world via His teaching and healing ministry) and those following the sacrifice (i.e. the Ascension, the descent of the Holy Spirit, and the birth of the Church) were all indispensably tied to "Christ's work of redemption" (ἡ τοῦ Χριστοῦ οἰκονομία): "But first, let us remind ourselves that the sacrifice is a figure of the whole mystery of Christ's redemptive work [τὸ μυστήριον τῆς οἰκονομίας τοῦ Χριστοῦ]; likewise, all the ceremonies and prayers which precede and follow the sacrifice symbolize this work."[5]

Two smaller prayers from the Byzantine Liturgy of Saint John Chysostom, which contain at least one of the aforesaid economical themes, are: (1) the Prayer of the Third Antiphon; and (2) the Second Prayer of the Faithful. As will be seen below by their structure and content, both prayers are true σμικρογραφίαι, or miniature sketches, of the larger eucharistic prayer, as well as true exemplars representative of our two major mystagogical themes.

From a purely structural perspective, it may be particularly helpful for one to bear in mind that like the eucharistic prayer, each smaller prayer consists of four constitutive parts, each of which typically (though not always) corresponds to at least one of the two themes of divine economy: (1) the opening address; (2) the confession; (3) the petition; and (4) the doxology. As a general rule, in these smaller prayers as in the eucharistic prayer itself, when the Church offers confession, the content is distinctly Christological and focuses on some aspect of Christ's life or sacrifice; when it offers petition or doxology, the content changes to a more eschatological tone, as the Church prays for the coming of the Kingdom and glorifies the Trinity.

Model 1: The Prayer of the Third Antiphon[6]

Ὁ τὰς κοινὰς ταύτας καὶ συμφώνους ἡμῖν χαρισάμενος προσευχάς, ὁ καὶ δυσὶ καὶ τρισὶ συμφωνοῦσιν ἐπὶ τῷ ὀνόματί σου τὰς αἰτήσεις παρέχειν ἐπαγγειλάμενος· Αὐτὸς καὶ νῦν τῶν δούλων σου τὰ αἰτήματα πρὸς τὸ συμφέρον πλήρωσον, χορηγῶν ἡμῖν ἐν τῷ παρόντι αἰῶνι τὴν ἐπίγνωσιν τῆς σῆς ἀληθείας, καὶ ἐν τῷ μέλλοντι ζωὴν αἰώνιον χαριζόμενος.

Ὅτι ἀγαθὸς καὶ φιλάνθρωπος Θεὸς ὑπάρχεις καὶ Σοὶ τὴν δόξαν ἀναπέμπομεν, τῷ Πατρὶ καὶ τῷ Υἱῷ καὶ τῷ Ἁγίῳ Πνεύματι, νῦν καὶ ἀεὶ καὶ εἰς τοὺς αἰῶνας τῶν αἰώνων.

O You [*address*] who has granted to us these common and united prayers, [*confession #1*] who has promised to grant the requests of two or three who are joined together in Your name. [*confession #2*] Do you the same now fulfill the petitions of Your servants for [*their*] benefit, providing us in the present age with the knowledge of Your truth and granting us in the future [age] eternal life. [*petition*]

For You are a good and loving God, and to You we send up glory, to the Father and the Son and the Holy Spirit, now and forever and to the ages of ages. [*doxology*]

In this first prayer, all four constitutive parts are clearly present, although any explicit sacrificial references are absent. At first glance, this may be because in keeping with the mystagogical explanations of more "historically-minded" Byzantine commentators such as Nicholas of Andida and Nicholas Cabasilas, the antiphonal singing in the first part of the Liturgy represents only a preparatory stage in Christ's life, the prophetic announcement of "the coming of Christ and his work," nevertheless leading up to His sacrifice on the Cross.[7] This nonappearance of the sacrificial theme in the text does not necessarily suggest its nonexistence, given Cabasilas' mystagogical treatment of the first three antiphons that serve as the prayer's immediate context. It is noteworthy that Cabasilas treats the first three antiphons as doxological commentaries praising the person and imminent redemptive work of Christ who, "although present on earth [he] was not known to the multitude; when 'he was in the world and the world knew him not' (John 1:10)." For Cabasilas, these praises imply thanksgiving for, naturally, the *whole* work of economy, culminating in Christ's sacrifice and the establishment of the eschatological Kingdom.[8] Hence, one may see how the doxological nature of any prayer, chant, or section in the Liturgy by necessity can only loop back to the sacrifice of the slain Lamb of God and the eschatological Kingdom that He inaugurated. The second confession alludes to Christ's promise of His presence to His followers in the evangelical passage Matthew 18:20, but the text is deliberately modified to assert instead Christ's granting of requests made by the faithful in His name. This important manipulation of the scriptural pericope then sets the stage for the eschatological content that follows: the request for the knowledge in this life that secures eternal life in the world to come.

The "knowledge" within the prayer goes beyond a simple recognition and acceptance of rules for proper Christian living. It entails familiarity with the very person of Christ in every one of His capacities: Christ as Teacher and Healer (the prophetic office), Christ as "Offerer" and "Offered" upon the Tree of sacrifice (the priestly office), and Christ as resurrected Lord and Conqueror over evil and death (the kingly office). Knowledge of the divine economy with Christ at the very epicenter of God's plan of redemption for the world becomes a prerequisite for sharing eternal life with Him in the eschaton, for the simple reason that a personal choice of either acceptance or rejection must then be made based upon the Christological information at hand. In sum, the intent of the prayer is to beseech God to make the eschatological reality attainable for the worshipper too, who inevitably must attain the "knowledge" of Christ as protagonist in the divine work of redemption.

As stated earlier, the doxological closing to the prayer (and indeed to any liturgical prayer in the Byzantine tradition) reminds the Church of the present that God, who is not bound by the limitations of *chronos*, worthily receives ("now") and will receive ("and to the ages of ages") the glorification due to Him, from not only believers subject to history but also from the angelic orders in the spiritual realm who live *in aeternum* together with God ("and forever").

Model 2: The Second Prayer of the Faithful[9]

Πάλιν καὶ πολλάκις Σοὶ προσπίπτομεν καὶ Σοῦ δεόμεθα, ἀγαθὲ καὶ φιλάνθρωπε, ὅπως ἐπιβλέψας ἐπὶ τὴν δέησιν ἡμῶν, καθαρίσῃς ἡμῶν τὰς
ψυχὰς καὶ τὰ σώματα ἀπὸ παντὸς μολυσμοῦ σαρκὸς καὶ πνεύματος, καὶ
δῴης ἡμῖν ἀνένοχον καὶ ἀκατάκριτον τὴν παράστασιν τοῦ ἁγίου Σου θυσιαστηρίου. Χάρισαι δέ ὁ Θεὸς καὶ τοῖς συνευχομένοις ἡμῖν προκοπὴν
βίου καὶ πίστεως καὶ συνέσεως πνευματικῆς· δὸς αὐτοῖς πάντοτε μετὰ φό-
βου καὶ ἀγάπης λατρεύειν Σοι, ἀνενόχως καὶ ἀκατακρίτως μετέχειν τῶν
ἁγίων Σου Μυστηρίων καὶ τῆς ἐπουρανίου Σου βασιλείας ἀξιωθῆναι.

Ὅπως, ὑπὸ τοῦ κράτους Σου πάντοτε φυλαττόμενοι, Σοὶ δόξαν ἀναπέμπομεν, τῷ Πατρὶ καὶ τῷ Υἱῷ καὶ τῷ Ἁγίῳ Πνεύματι, νῦν καὶ ἀεὶ καὶ εἰς
τοὺς αἰῶνας τῶν αἰώνων.

Again and many times we fall before You and pray to You [*confession*], O good and loving One [*address*], that having looked upon our prayer, You cleanse our souls and bodies from every defilement of flesh and spirit [*petition #1*]; and that You give to us to stand without blame and condemnation at Your holy altar [*petition #2*]. And grant also, O God, to those who pray with us progress in life and faith and spiritual understanding. [petition #3] Grant them always to worship You in fear and love, to participate in Your holy Mysteries blamelessly

and uncondemned and to be made worthy of Your heavenly kingdom.
[*petition #4*]
   That always guarded by Your power, we may send up glory to You,
the Father and the Son and the Holy Spirit, now and forever and to
the ages of ages. [*doxology*]

   In this particular prayer, the worthy realization of God's gift of the
"heavenly kingdom" is clearly the definitive goal and aspiration of the
Christian. Arrival at and incorporation into the eschatological reality of
God, however, requires a series of further preparatory stages that must be
responsibly traversed by the Christian. These steps are outlined hierarchically by way of supplication.

   For example, purification from the "defilement of flesh and spirit" (forgiveness of sins by God and genuine repentance on the part of the worshipper) enables each Christian, clergy and laity alike, to stand worthily before
God's throne of judgment, which is mystagogically represented by the holy
altar table (Maximos the Confessor and Symeon of Thessalonike). Acceptance by God then leads to the proper worship of the Holy Trinity "in fear
and love" by the faithful who, like the angels and saints, congregate around
or stand before the throne of God.   Finally, full union in God is achieved
through one's participation in the eschatological feast of the Kingdom. This
sublime unity is experienced *in aeternum* by all heavenly dwellers permeated by the full radiance of God's glory, which emanates from the sacrificed
and exalted Lamb (Rev 5:9–10). It is also accomplished on a provisional and
inchoative basis by the members of the earthly Church via the bloodless
sacrifice of the Lamb in the Eucharist and their reception of the consecrated
elements as Holy Communion.

   Hence, within the context of the eucharistic liturgy, the acceptance of
the person of Christ and His redemptive work, culminating in His sacrifice
upon the Cross and the triumphant events that follow, becomes the key
that unlocks the eschatological life of God's Kingdom. Accordingly, via the
conduit of liturgical mystagogy, sacrifice and eschatology become the *sine
qua non* of each other's existence.

FROM PROTHESIS TO REAL LIFE: THE CHALLENGE
OF LITURGICAL MYSTAGOGY

The general intent of this book has been to comprehensively examine the
umbrella theme of divine economy and its derivative concepts of sacrifice
and eschatology within their unique context in the prothesis rite. The vehicle of liturgical mystagogy, nestled within the Byzantine eucharistic tradi-

tion, has proven that the actual celebration of the prothesis and its parent rite, the Divine Liturgy, together proclaim the Church's most fundamental Christological mystery that lies at the heart of the Gospel, namely, that all of existence derives its essential *raison d'être* in the death, resurrection, and glorious return of Christ. This Christological pronouncement occupies not only the very crux of the redemptive theology of the Christian Church, but it likewise permeates virtually every service and prayer that comprises the gamut of the Eastern Church's liturgical literature. Hence, the Divine Liturgy—and, for that matter, any liturgical rite in the East—serves as a living witness to the Christ event and as the Church's daily "broadcast" and reminder to the world of God's eschatological victory in the Son's sacrifice.

As this book has shown, the objective of Byzantine liturgical mystagogy is twofold: (1) to situate the celebration of the Liturgy within the history of salvation; that is, to mystically draw the worshipping community and the individual worshipper of the present into the timeless nature of salvation in God; and (2) to personalize the redemptive act for each participant in worship.[10] Hence, without a mystagogical orientation, the Eucharist may be perceived as a simple statement of God's redemption in Christ, which is not necessarily engaging and completely objective. However, through the verbalized mystagogy of the Byzantine liturgical commentators, most especially Sts. Nicholas Cabasilas and Symeon of Thessalonike, the prothesis rite and the Divine Liturgy are transformed into an interactive crucible of sorts, where man acquires the potential to become, through faith, an active "partaker of divine nature" (cf. 2 Pet 1:4) and an actual co-creator and player of salvation history rather than a mere sideline observer.

The work of liturgical mystagogy as theology in action is, for all intents and purposes, experiential. In their liturgical commentaries, Cabasilas and Symeon seek earnestly to share their faith-based visions of God's *economia* in Christ and the inauguration of the eschatological Kingdom with their readers. Their principal intention is not merely to assign symbolic significance to words or acts or liturgical vessels, which to the predominantly clerical audience of their day, were already familiar concepts. While the *penultimate* aim may very well be this exercise in symbology, the final objective is clearly the arrival at a spiritual vision of the divine economy, with both Christ and the Christian "mystagogue-theologian" as the protagonists. In the words of Bishop Kallistos Ware: "Invoking the term used by Byzantine commentators on the Liturgy, we may say that there is no true 'mystagogy' that is not firmly based on lived experience."[11]

This aforementioned final objective, to arrive at a vision of God's love for mankind and creation and to behold oneself in the midst of God's plan of redemption, comprises the greatest challenge that faces the Christian when confronted with the demands of liturgical mystagogy. Is this vision, however, one to be attained only during the eucharistic celebration? How can mystagogy have a positive effect on a Christian *outside* the confines of liturgical worship? How can an implemented mystagogical approach to everyday life prove beneficial for the Christian worshipper?

Although these questions are perhaps not of immediate interest to this book, they do raise relevant issues nonetheless that beg for answers if, in fact, the meaning of mystagogy is extended to cover the flow of human life and the complexities associated with it, of which liturgical experience is but an image of the way life was intended to be. Indeed, the eminent value of liturgical mystagogy may appear quite underrated and subdued when confined only to formal worship; by its very nature, liturgical mystagogy must transcend the eucharistic liturgy and become incorporated into the Christian's everyday life in the Spirit, that is, into his own "liturgy after the Liturgy." Better yet, mystagogy must abolish the divisional barriers between "liturgical life" and "everyday life" and render the latter as an extension of the former. Thus, this new mystagogical approach to life is extracted from the mystagogical image of the Divine Liturgy, with the sacrifice of Christ and the eschatological Kingdom as the Christian's absolute points of reference. A proper mystagogical orientation to life possesses the enormous potential to assist the Christian in not only making morally-based decisions that will prove beneficial in his relationships with others, but also placing into perspective critical existential questions that may lead to answers regarding life's overall meaning and purpose. Consequently, when an individual comprehends his existence contextually as a part of God's greater design to emancipate man from evil and restore the created order back to its pristine state, his behavior and outlook will undergo a maturation in which the oftentimes frivolous pursuits of life will appear all the more insignificant, and he will by necessity remain focused on the "one thing needful" (cf. Luke 10:42).

In theory, this view of the significance of mystagogy when applied to everyday life may seem appealing, but the intent of the Byzantine liturgical commentators was clearly to impress upon their readers the vital connection between worship and faith (*lex orandi* [*est*] *lex credendi*), where the "rule of faith" here represents belief in the two basic Christological tenets of divine *economia*: the sacrifice of Christ and the inauguration of the Kingdom. Hans-Joachim Schulz has written: "Indeed, the liturgical writings of the lay theologian and mystic Nicholas Cabasilas and the metropolitan of Thessalonike Symeon, which appeared in this time [14th–15th century], acquired such validity, that until today they remain unsurpassed in the area of Orthodoxy,"[12] and this partly because they are the most recent and complete extant commentaries on the modern execution of the prothesis rite and the Divine Liturgy. However, these timeless writings are unrivaled for another more important reason: their ability to envision and explain the liturgical rites of the Church in terms of "lived theology," as the eternal continuation of God's plan of redemption to save mankind and as God's ongoing invitation to man, from age to age, to enjoy the fruits of divine *economia*.

Cabasilas explains the method by which mystagogy draws the worshipper participating in the Eucharist and the celebrant priest conducting the prothesis rite toward the divine economy.

> This is why the symbolism of which I have spoken was conceived. It does not confine itself to the indication of all this by words alone, but *it places it before our eyes in its entirety throughout the liturgy* [ἀλλὰ καὶ ἐπ' ὄψιν ἄγων ἅπαντα]. The aim of setting all this before us is *to influence our souls the more easily thereby; not merely to offer us a simple picture but to create in us a feeling* [ἵνα ἐκείνῳ μὲν εἰς τὰς ψυχὰς εὐκολώτερον δράσῃ, καὶ οὐ θεωρία ψιλὴ μόνον, ἀλλὰ καὶ πάθος ἡμῖν ἐντεθῇ], for the very good reason that an idea is more deeply impressed upon us if we can see it depicted.[13]

The usage of particularly visual symbols, a necessary part of the mystagogical process, creates the psychological and spiritual disposition within the Christian to enter a frame of mind conducive to better comprehending and participating in the divine economy. When faith is induced within the worshipper, the very dynamic of mystagogical activity commences, in which the liturgical rite is perceived with a dynamic, interactive realism.

Arrival at this realism is the ultimate goal of liturgical mystagogy, to observe God drawing the human race and each individual person, clergy and lay alike, into the divine work of redemption and restoration, to envision oneself before the sacrificial Lamb of God and in the eschatological Kingdom where true love and right judgment reign, to see in life as upon the paten of the prothesis rite, together with the renowned Archbishop of Thessalonike, the wondrous vision of "God among men and God in the midst of gods, observed by Him who is God by nature and who was truly incarnated for them. And this is the future kingdom and the commonwealth of eternal life: God with us, both seen and partaken of."[14]

NOTES

1. Robert F. Taft, *The Byzantine Rite: A Short History* (Collegeville, 1992), 18.

2. René. Bornert, *Les commentaires byzantins de la Divine Liturgie du VIIe au XVe siècle* (Paris, 1965), 7. Translation mine.

3. Evagrios of Pontos, *On Prayer* 61.

4. Paul Evdokimov, *La prière de l'Église d'Orient: La liturgie byzantine de saint Jean Chrysostome* (Mulhouse, 1966), 7. Translation mine.

5. Nicholas Cabasilas, *Liturgical Commentary* 16; PG 150.404A; N. Cabasilas, *A Commentary on the Divine Liturgy*, trans. J.M. Hussey and P.A. McNulty (London, 1960), 52.

6. *The Divine Liturgy of Saint John Chrysostom*, trans. Faculty of Hellenic College and Holy Cross Greek Orthodox School of Theology (Brookline, 1985), 6–7. English translation mine.

7. Hussey and McNulty, trans., 53; Cabasilas, *Commentary* 16; PG 150.404D.

8. Ibid., 54–58; Cabasilas, *Commentary* 17-19; PG 150.405B–411B.

9. *The Divine Liturgy of Saint John Chrysostom*, 12. Translation mine.

10. Bornert, 269–70.

11. Bishop Kallistos Ware, "'It Is Time for the Lord to Act': The Divine Liturgy as Heaven on Earth", in *Sobornost*, vol. 23, no. 1 (2001), 8.

12. Hans-Joachim Schulz, *Die Byzantinische Liturgie: Glaubenszeugnis und Symbolgestalt* ['Η Βυζαντινή Λειτουργία· μαρτυρία πίστεως καί συμβολική ἔκφραση], trans. Demetrios V. Tzerpos (Athens, 1998), 155. Translation mine.

13. Hussey and McNulty, trans., 30; Cabasilas, *Commentary* 1; PG 150.376A.

14. Symeon of Thessalonike, *Dialogue* 94; PG 155.285AB.

Appendix

The Relation of the Prothesis Rite to the Eucharistic Liturgy: An Architectural and Iconographic Approach

The availability of sources exclusively dedicated to the historical development of the prothesis rite in the Byzantine liturgical tradition is scarce. To my knowledge, the closest "critical" commentary on the development of the prothesis rite appears in Georges Descoeudres, *Die Pastophorien im syro-byzantinischen Osten*,[1] whose conclusions, as Thomas Pott observes, "contrast perceptibly with those of his predecessors on the matter like Dmitrievskij, Petrovskij, de Meester, Bârlea, Mandalà and others,"[2] all of which reflect scholarship outdated by contemporary standards. Evidence that the prothesis has undergone, over time, substantial modification both in terms of setting and meaning can be gleaned easily from a simple comparison of liturgical manuscripts or commentaries reflecting a different point in Church history. Nevertheless, even such original works, however necessary for liturgical scholarship of any kind, typically suffer from a lack of critical engagement. Most Byzantine liturgical texts and commentaries, geared toward the priestly class of celebrants anyway, are apt to be more descriptive and in certain cases even corrective, but rarely critical editions highlighting the complexities and nuances of how rites evolve or even employing an interdisciplinary or alternative approach to the matter

Sharon E.J. Gerstel offers a refreshing interdisciplinary perspective on the development of the prothesis rite itself and its accompanying theology by situating the rite into its historically final location in the Byzantine temple (in the semicircular side apse within the sanctuary) and then commenting on the *architectural* novelties characteristic of the Late Byzantine epoch that affected the rite.[3] Gerstel, it must be made clear, refrains from making direct mystagogical affirmations, but her well-informed observations of the church interior, as a Byzantine art historian, give the liturgiologist substantial material with which to draw his own conclusions.

INTERCESSORY AND DEVOTIONAL MOTIFS
IN ICONOGRAPHY AND PROTHESIS RITE

Gerstel's examination of sixty masonry altar screens from the Late Byzantine period (thirteenth–fifteenth centuries) indicates a building plan making use of local fieldstones coated in plaster and adorned with sacred imagery.[4] The immediate predecessor of the ornate altar screen, the chancel barrier was popularized as a practical innovation for keeping proper order and decorum within liturgical services. Its main purpose, in keeping with the dictates of Canon 69 of the Sixth Ecumenical Council (Constantinople III or Trullo, 681), was to keep the laity (except the Emperor) from entering the altar area, reserved only for the ordained clergy.[5] This prohibition is furthermore echoed by Germanos of Constantinople[6] and Pseudo-Sophronios.[7] By the Medieval period, the barrier was raised and the slabs became separated by columns, in an attempt to prevent the laity from viewing the liturgical ceremony inside the sanctuary.[8] Gradually, *proskynetaria* icons were placed on adjacent tiers, probably as a means of pacifying the faithful whose "exclusion" from visual participation in the eucharistic ceremony led to a devotional shift in piety among the laity, i.e. from the Eucharist to icons.[9] Despite conflicting literary and visual sources, the general consensus among scholars typically places the final evolution of the chancel barrier into the current iconostasis from the eleventh century to the post-Byzantine period. Hence, during this final phase, the insertion of icons into the sanctuary screen occurred with varying frequency throughout the different regions of the Byzantine Empire.[10]

Characteristic of this period, on each iconostasis, is an intercessional program consisting of Christ, either as Teacher (full body) or Judge (enthroned), and the Virgin with Child.[11] Sometimes, these two icons, on either side of the holy doors, are supplemented by an icon of a titular saint (i.e. for whom the church is named) and, in some cases, by saints of significance to donors. On the southern half (right) of the altar screen, the popular *Deesis* icon may also have been included.[12] Leonide Ouspensky notes that from the eleventh to the fourteenth century, the *Deesis* icon was placed on the architrave above the holy doors, a more prominent location than the southern end of the iconostasis, thus drawing the attention of the worshipers to the themes of intercession and the cultic veneration of saints, both characteristic of the shift in piety during this period. He later adds that "the

Deisis was the kernel out of which the whole thematic treatment of the iconostasis was to grow"[13] and, by extension, the rationale behind the particular excision and arrangement of particles during the prothesis. In general terms, the mounting or painting of icons directly on the masonry closures of the screen came to reflect a change in devotional piety. Gerstel observes:

> The screen's closure through the insertion of icons into the intercolumnar spaces came at a time of broad changes in lay spirituality, changes that may have encouraged a type of private piety that was best served by large-scale, yet highly personal, images in closest proximity to the sacred.[14]

This change affected not only the laity who often felt "excluded" from visually witnessing the liturgical celebration within the sanctuary, but also the clergy in the sanctuary, where various iconographic programs on the inside of the altar screen and apses likewise provided visual support for such devotional tendencies. Thus, for example, the service of priestly preparation (καιρός) was believed to have been developed during the Late Byzantine era and thus coincided with the inclusion of images on the inside of the sanctuary screen for the celebrant clergy, which depicted scenes of spiritual transformation or elevation. This link is a crucial one and seems to have been a corrective attempt to dissuade clergy from abuses and behavior unbecoming of their calling and position within society. Hence, crossing from the nave (where the service of *kairos* begins) into the sanctuary (where it ends) was equated with a sort of spiritual traversing from the profane to the sacred.[15]

"The large icons [that eventually filled the intercolumnar cavities of the iconostasis]," writes Gerstel, "were intended primarily for the laity, who could address devotional prayers to these intercessory figures both during the Liturgy and at moments of private supplication,"[16] actions not all too different in contemporary liturgical practice. However, it is not entirely clear, based on the available evidence, to what degree this shift away from a traditional Eucharist-centered worship toward a more "personal" or "privatized" cultic veneration of saints was intentional.

Could the further decline in Communion among the faithful during this era have led the Church to "accommodate" the laity by providing a replacement for Communion? Robert Taft, in good company with other liturgical historians, argues that the apparent decline in the reception of Communion among the laity began after the formal institutionalization of the Church following the Peace of Constantine in AD 312. He pinpoints four "datable phenomena" leading to this liturgical deterioration: from the fourth century, (1) the penitential crisis regarding the sudden reincorporation of apostates into the Church via a new series of canonical penances that naturally involved abstention from Holy Communion, as well as an expanded catechumenate that saw candidates for the Christian Faith refraining from Communion for a preparatory period of at least three years; (2) the vision of the Eucharist as something fearful and sacred, at completely opposite poles of anyone or anything profane; and (3) the cordoned-off or hidden sanctuary; and from the fifth to the sixth century, (4) the multiplication and silent recitation of the liturgical prayers vs. the audible recitation of the solitary eucharistic prayer common from the first three centuries of Christian worship. Taft concludes that, paradoxically, while the frequency of the celebration of the eucharistic liturgy increased in the East after the fourth century, the frequency of Communion among the laity dropped in the first millennium, followed by a similar trend among monastics during the second millennium.[17] Leonide Ouspensky blatantly rejects any notion of such a replacement, arguing against Dom H. Leclerq's Western criticism of the iconostasis as a hindrance to the full eucharistic participation of the laity who, according to the latter, "are left to take part in the Eucharistic sacrifice in their imagination (sic!), and can merely wait patiently until it is completed."[18] Since the Eucharist, he contends, is ultimately meant to be consumed and not gazed upon or adored as in the Roman Church, one's physical position in the church building or proximity to the altar is irrelevant. Nevertheless, with the established post-sixth century Byzantine practice of the clergy's silent recitation of the prayers, coupled with the spatial separation between clergy and laity via the construction of larger church structures and higher iconostases, the fact remains that the factors for active lay participation in the eucharistic liturgy had all but increased.

It would certainly seem unfathomable that the East would sacrifice the centrality of the Eucharist in its liturgical celebration, only to lessen its importance by creating a parallel rite or cult of adoration for the saints, very reminiscent of the West's own attempt to counter the decline in Communion among the faithful via the establishment of the Veneration of the Blessed Sacrament. I do not believe, however, that the eventual trend toward a more privatized devotional spirituality was at all intentional on behalf of the always eucharist-minded Church, but consequential—the result of centuries of conditioned abstinence by the laity from Communion, for the reasons outlined by Taft above. Neither do I accept the insinuation that the iconographic programs of the Late Byzantine period contributed to this shift in worship. The connection between the eucharistic sacrifice in all its critical phases (offering, consecration, and distribution) and Christ's own sacrifice was adequately and vividly displayed at the Church of the

Holy Virgin at Peribleptos, which contains a unique iconographic program within the sanctuary, visibly to clergy and lay worshipers alike. The emphasis then on Communion is made in the context of Christ's self-sacrifice on the Cross, which as Cabasilas affirms is the *sine qua non* of and very basis for attending and co-celebrating the eucharistic liturgy. The mystagogical representations of Christ's work of redemption in the Divine Liturgy help to create a faith-inducing feeling (καὶ πάθος ἡμῖν ἐντεθῇ) among worshippers, a proper mindset which in turn will lead them to consume the consecrated gifts and not merely be united with Him intellectually or emotionally, but also "ontologically" via a real sacramental union.[19] Nevertheless, the fact remains that this swing in devotional piety led to a series of distinct iconographic programs focusing on intercessory prayer, which in turn was replicated in the prothesis rite, namely, in the manner in which the particles for the orders of saints and angels were henceforth viewed.

THE CHURCH OF THE VIRGIN PERIBLEPTOS AT MYSTRA

Gerstel correctly affirms that the iconographic programs on sanctuary screens, both on the outside and inside of the iconostasis, targeted the devotional inclinations of lay worshipers as much as the proper ethical demeanor of celebrant clergy. However, in the case of the latter, viewing iconography solely for its corrective value suffers from an oversimplification of its manifold purposes. It is equally pertinent to acknowledge the fact that religious art within the sanctuary, both on the inside of the icon screen and in the apses within the altar, was intended for clergy celebrants in order to *remind* them, during their performance of the prothesis rite, and the eucharistic liturgy, of the connection between Christ the High Priest and offerer of the sacrifice and Christ the sacrificed Lamb who is offered for the sins of the world. The Church of the Virgin Peribleptos at Mystra provides a very unique program of iconography in the central apse, as well as the prothesis apse, which elucidates this correlation.

There can be no doubt that for the Byzantines, Peribleptos functioned as a vociferous artistic response to the scathing twelfth-century controversy in the East involving Soterichos Panteugenes who denied Christ's binary role as offerer and receiver of the eucharistic sacrifice.[20] In this unique iconographic plan within the apse of the prothesis, in the northeastern section of the sanctuary, three tiers of familiar images (except for the top tier, which is by all indications inimitable in its content) are arranged in such a manner as to invoke a strong sense of connectedness between the periodic celebration of the eucharistic liturgy in history and its constant celebration into eternity by Christ the High Priest. Suzy Dufrenne writes: "This ensemble, impregnated with the spirit and the letter of the rites of the Liturgy, utilizes iconographic forms created well in advance, in different contexts, according to techniques or for different functions."[21] In her helpful diagram,[22] the third level, closest to the ground and flanking the niche in the apse where the prothesis rite is conducted, depicts two bishops standing and looking inward toward the eucharistic oblation. The second level directly above the niche portrays the busts of bishops likewise turned inward and framing the familiar Christ of Sorrows, or icon of the Extreme Humility (the crucified and lifeless Jesus, half-dressed with arms crossed over the chest, His body descending halfway in an upright tomb that resembles a sarcophagus, with the Cross in the background). According to Dufrenne, the icon of the Extreme Humility was sometimes situated in a portion of the central apse in some churches, while in others in the diakonikon. However, its primary location was typically in the prothesis apse and the niche carved into the wall that served as the oblation table.[23] The icon itself serves as an indication of how the Byzantines regarded the Passion of the Christ in the fourteenth century. The thematic content of Holy Saturday, with its solemn anticipation of the Resurrection, most closely corresponds to the significance of the prothesis rite as the quiet preparatory period preceding the jubilation of the Eucharist. The icon's usage on Holy Saturday to convey this hope for victory and new life is further enhanced when, on some versions of the same icon, the inscription "The King of Glory" (a theological modification of the historical Johannine caption in John 19:19–20), is placed at the head of the Cross, to affirm that Christ's death is but the harbinger of His victory over death. Consequently, one can detect the necessary interdependence between the Crucifixion and the Resurrection, the sacrifice of Christ and the dawning of the eschatological Kingdom in the risen Lord.

Finally, on the top level and in radical contradiction to the thematic content of the tier below it, there is a magnificent image of a living and glorified Christ, standing before an altar as chief celebrant of the eucharistic mystery and surrounded by hosts of angels adorned in diaconal attire and assisting Him, reminiscent of the deacons during the procession of the Great Entrance. Directly above Christ but theoretically still belonging to this top tier, situated in a celestial vista of sorts, are the Father and the Holy Spirit, both of whom are represented in unity with Christ, the chief celebrant and High Priest of the sacrifice. The iconographic renderings of the Father and the Spirit, depicted as the Ancient of Days (*Antiquus Dierum*; Παλαιὸς τῶν Ἡμερῶν; *Atik Yomin*, Aramaic; cf. Dan 7:9, 13, 22) and a dove, respectively, were innovations in the Byzantine tradition and inconsistent with the Church's strong insistence upon its centuries-old incarnational theology, which assigned the privilege of iconographic depiction to the Son alone. Nevertheless, one will find several churches in places like Romania and Bulgaria that depict the Trinity in this aforementioned unconventional style.[24]

"The eucharistic décor of Mystra," Dufrenne observes, "in effect must be placed in parallel with the mystagogical commentaries of Nicholas Cabasilas."[25] Such a stance is not difficult to disprove when one identifies within Cabasilas' liturgical commentaries the intentional correlation between Calvary, the earthly liturgy, and the heavenly liturgy, all linked together and vividly evident in the Byzantine eucharistic celebration. The Eucharist does not initiate a new sacrifice each time, believes Cabasilas, but rather brings the Church before the one-time sacrifice of Christ at Golgotha, truly immolated by the transformation of the bread and wine.[26] In the prothesis niche at Peribleptos, the crucified Christ is also the "King of Glory," sacrificed and resurrected and, as depicted in the top tier, capable of rendering real the eucharistic sacrifice[27] as High Priest throughout eternity. As Cabasilas indicates, "For after once offering himself, and being made a sacrifice he did not end his priesthood, but is continually offering the sacrifice for us, by virtue of which he is our advocate before God forever."[28] Thus each image, in its unique arrangement with the others, acquires literary corroboration and elaboration in the liturgical commentary.

In the Late Byzantine period, the theological and artistic interplay between Christ the victim and victor over death is expressly played out in the simultaneous rendering of Christ as the undignified Man of Sorrows (Isa 53:2–12) and Christ as the glorified celebrant of the heavenly liturgy. Naturally, this remarkable contrast can only be grasped by an all-inclusive envisaging that assigns a mutual interdependence between the murals in question. At the core of this visualization lies the belief in Christ's omnipresence; He is as much present at the Cross as He is in the bowels of Hades and in the bosom of God the Father in heaven. In each milieu, Christ retains the fullness of His divinity and is perceived as such by both the living and dead, and by the created and uncreated realms, as St. Paul plainly asserts in Philippians 2:10 and to which Isaiah alludes in Isaiah 45:23. The familiar Eastern hymn, typically assigned to the deacon to be read at the conclusion of the prothesis rite,[29] likewise captures this notion of omnipresence:

Ἐν τάφῳ σωματικῶς, ἐν ᾅδῃ δὲ μετὰ ψυχῆς ὡς Θεός,
ἐν παραδείσῳ δὲ μετὰ λῃστοῦ, καὶ ἐν θρόνῳ ὑπῆρχες, Χριστέ,
μετὰ Πατρὸς καὶ Πνεύματος, πάντα πληρῶν ὁ ἀπερίγραπτος.

Bodily you were in the grave, with (your) soul You were in Hades
as God,
you were in paradise with the thief, and you were upon the throne,
O Christ,
with the Father and the Spirit, filling all things, O indescribable one.

Hence, the combination of religious art and hymnology marks out a
distinctive theology of the prothesis rite[30] that encapsulates the dual themes
of sacrifice and eschatology: the historical Christ, subject to suffering and
death, is simultaneously the champion over sin and death and as High Priest
offers eternally the celebration of the Eucharist in His celestial Kingdom.
As Dufrenne makes clear, "The Christ of Sorrows of Mystra, between the
depictions of the bishops, under the image of the Divine Liturgy, answers
this double evocation of the Cross and victory."[31]

In closing, our research has proven that the mystagogical interplay between the central themes of sacrifice and eschatology in the eucharistic liturgy in general (and the prothesis rite specifically) is evidenced not only
through a review of relevant texts and comments highlighting historical
and theological elements, but equally through Eastern ecclesiastical art and
architecture which, as we have witnessed, exude their own theological nuances.

NOTES

1. Georges Descoeudres, *Die Pastophorien im syro-byzantinischen Osten. Eine Untersuchung zu architektur- und liturgiegeschichtlichen Problemen. Schriften zur Geistesgeschichte des östlichen Europa* (Wiesbaden, 1983).

2. Thomas Pott, *La réforme liturgique byzantine: étude du phénomène d'évolution
non spontanée de la liturgie byzantine* (Rome, 2000), 170. Translation mine.

3. Sharon E.J. Gerstel, *Beholding the Sacred Mysteries: Programs of the Byzantine Sanctuary* (Seattle, 1999); and her essay, "An Alternate View of the Late Byzantine Sanctuary Screen," in idem., ed. *Thresholds of the Sacred: Architectural, Art
Historical, Liturgical, and Theological Perspectives on Religious Screens, East and West*
(Washington, 2006), 135–61. I also found the following study to be an indispensible
supplement for Gerstel's work: Suzy Dufrenne, "Images du décor de la prothèse," in
Revue des Études Byzantines vol. 26 (1968), 297–310, which details the most unique
iconographic program of the prothesis apse of the Church of the Virgin Peribleptos
at Mystra. See also Leonide Ouspensky, "The Problem of the Iconostasis", in *Saint
Vladimir's Theological Quarterly* vol. 8 (1964), 186–218.

4. Gerstel, "An Alternate View," 136.

5. Idem., *Beholding the Sacred Mysteries*, 6.

6. Germanus of Constantinople, *On the Divine Liturgy*, trans. Paul Meyendorff (Crestwood, 1984), 63.

7. Pseudo-Sophronios, *Liturgical Commentary* 4; PG 87.3984D–3985A.

8. Gerstel, *Beholding the Sacred Mysteries*, 7.

9. Ibid., 7, 10.

10. Ibid., 8.

11. Gerstel, "An Alternate View," 139.

12. Ouspensky, 195.

13. Ibid.

14. Gerstel, "An Alternate View," 157.

15. Ibid., 155.

16. Ibid., 139.

17. Robert F. Taft, "The Decline of Communion in Byzantium and the Distancing of the Congregation from the Liturgical Action: Cause, Effect, or Neither?," in Sharon E.J. Gerstel, ed., *Thresholds of the Sacred*, 27–35.

18. Ouspensky, 189.

19. Nicholas Cabasilas, *A Commentary on the Divine Liturgy*, trans. J.M. Hussey and P.A. McNulty (London, 1960), 26–30; and *Explanation of the Divine Liturgy* 1; PG 150.369D–376C.

20. See pp. 66–69 of this book.

21. Dufrenne, 305. Translation mine.

22. Ibid., 304.

23. Ibid., 298–99.

24. Ibid., 304.

25. Ibid., 306. Translation mine.

26. Hussey and McNulty, trans., 81; Cabasilas, *Commentary* 32; PG 150.440C.

27. Ibid., 27; *Commentary* 1; PG 150.372A.

28. Ibid., 71; *Commentary* 28; PG 150.428B.

29. F.E. Brightman, ed., *Liturgies Eastern and Western* (Oxford, 1896), 361.

30. Dufrenne, 300.

31. Ibid., 301. Translation mine.

BIBLIOGRAPHY

PRIMARY SOURCES

Biblical Texts

Ἡ Ἁγία Γραφή: Ἡ Παλαιὰ Διαθήκη καὶ ἡ Καινὴ Διαθήκη· ἐγκρίσει τῆς Μεγάλης τοῦ Χριστοῦ Ἐκκλησίας καὶ τῆς Δ. Ἱερᾶς Συνόδου τῆς Ἐκκλησίας τῆς Ἑλλάδος [*The Holy Scripture: The Old Testament and the New Testament; by Approval of the Great Church of Christ and the Permanent Holy Synod of the Church of Greece*]. Athens: Brotherhood of Theologians "Zoe", 1991.

Ἡ Καινὴ Διαθήκη· τὸ πρωτότυπο κείμενο μὲ μετάφραση στὴ δημοτική [*The New Testament: the Original Text with Translation in Modern Greek*]. Edited by Savvas Agourides. Athens: Greek Biblical Society, 2003.

Ἡ Παλαιὰ Διαθήκη κατὰ τοὺς Ἑβδομήκοντα· ἐγκρίσει τῆς Δ. Ἱερᾶς Συνόδου τῆς Ἐκκλησίας τῆς Ἑλλάδος [*The Old Testament According to the Seventy; by Approval of the Permanent Holy Synod of the Church of Greece*]. Athens: Brotherhood of Theologians "Zoe", 1950.

The New Oxford Annotated Bible with the Apocrypha (Revised Standard Version). Edited by Herbert G. May and Bruce M. Metzger. New York: Oxford University Press, 1977.

The Septuagint Bible. Edited by C.A. Muses. Indian Hills: The Falcon's Wing Press, 1954.

The Septuagint Version of the Old Testament and Apocrypha: With an English Translation and with Various Readings and Critical Notes. Edited by Charles Lee Brenton. Grand Rapids: Zondervan Publishing House, 1978.

Concordances

A Concordance to the Septuagint and the Other Greek Versions of the Old Testament (Including the Apocryphal Books). Edited by Edwin Hatch. Grand Rapids: Baker Books, 1998.

Analytical Concordance of the Greek New Testament. Edited by Philip S. Clapp, Barbara Friberg, and Timothy Friberg. Grand Rapids: Baker Book House, 1991.

The Exhaustive Concordance to the Greek New Testament. Edited by John R. Kohlenberger III, Edward W. Goodrick, and James A. Swanson. Grand Rapids: Zondervan Publishing House, 1995.

The New Strong's Exhaustive Concordance of the Bible. Edited by James Strong. Nashville: T. Nelson Publishers, 1984.

Patristic Texts

Augustine of Hippo. *Enarrationes in Psalmos 1–150*. In *Corpus Scriptorum Ecclesiasticorum Latinorum*, Volumes 1–3. Edited by Franco Gori *et al.* Vienna: Verlag der Osterreichischen Akademie der Wissenschaften, 2001–2004.

———. *The City of God*. In *The Fathers of the Church Series*, Volumes 8, 14, 24. Translated by Demetrius B. Zema, Gerald G. Walsh, *et al.* New York: Fathers of the Church, 1950–1954.

———. *The Confessions*. Edited and translated by Philip Burton. New York: A.A. Knopf, 2001.

———. *On Christian Doctrine*. Translated by D.W. Robertson, Jr. New York: Liberal Arts Press, 1958.

Cabasilas, Nicholas. *A Commentary on the Divine Liturgy*. Translated by J.M. Hussey and P.A. McNulty. London: SPCK, 1960.

———. *Explication de la divine liturgie*. In *Sources Chrétiennes*, Volume 4. Translated by Sévérien Salaville. Paris : Éditions du Cerf, 1967.

———. *La Vie en Christ*. In *Sources Chrétiennes*, Volume 355. Translated by Marie Hélène Congourdeau. Paris: Éditions du Cerf, 1989.

———. *The Life in Christ*. Translated by Carmino J. deCatanzaro. Crestwood: St. Vladimir's Seminary Press, 1974.

Clement of Alexandria. *Paedagogus*. Edited by M. Marcovich. Boston: Brill, 2002.

———. *Stromateis: Books 1-3*. Translated by John Ferguson. Washington, DC: Catholic University of America Press, 1991.

Cyril of Jerusalem. *Lectures on the Christian Sacraments*. Edited by F.L. Cross. Crestwood: St. Vladimir's Seminary Press, 1986.

Dionysius the Areopagite. *La gerarchia ecclesiastica*. Translated by Salvatore Lilla. Rome: New City, 2002.

———. *La hiérarchie céleste*. In *Sources Chrétiennes*, Volume 58. Translated by Maurice de Gandillac. Paris : Éditions du Cerf, 1970.

———. Περὶ Ἐκκλησιαστικῆς καὶ Οὐράνιας Ἱεραρχίας [*On Ecclesiastical and Celestial Hierarchies*]. Translated by Ignatios Sakalis. Thessalonike: P. Pournaras, 1985.

———. *The Complete Works*. Translated by Colm Luibheid. In *The Classics of Western Spirituality*. New York: Paulist Press, 1987.

———. *The Ecclesiastical Hierarchy*. Translated by Thomas L. Campbell. Washington: University Press of America, 1981.

Germanus of Constantinople. *On the Divine Liturgy*. Translated by Paul Meyendorff. Crestwood: St. Vladimir's Seminary Press, 1984.

Hippolytus of Rome. *La Tradition apostolique d'après les anciennes versions*. In *Sources Chrétiennes*, Volume 11. Translated by Bernards Botte. Paris : Éditions du Cerf, 1968.

Holmes, Michael W., ed. and trans. *The Apostolic Fathers: Greek Texts and English Translations*. Grand Rapids: Baker Academic, 2007.

Irenaeus of Lyons. *Against the Heresies*. Translated by Dominic J. Unger and John J. Dillon. New York: Paulist Press, 1992.

John Chrysostom. *On the Nativity of Our Savior Jesus Christ, Second Homily*. Translated by Constantine Terss. Atlanta, s.n., 1995.

John of Damascus. *On the Divine Images: Three Apologies Against Those Who Attack the Divine Images*. Translated by David Anderson. Crestwood: St. Vladimir's Seminary Press, 1980.

———. *Three Treatises on the Divine Images*. Translated by Andrew Louth. Crestwood: St. Vladimir's Seminary Press, 2003.

Justin Martyr. *Dialogue avec le Tryphon, édition critique*. Edited by Philippe Bobichon. Fribourg: Academic Press Fribourg, 2003.

Lactantius. *Divine Institutes*. Translated by Anthony Bowen and Peter Garnsey. Liverpool: Liverpool University Press, 2003.

Maximus Confessor: Selected Writings. In *The Classics of Western Spirituality*. Translated by George C Berthold. New York: Paulist Press, 1985.

Migne, J.P., ed. *Patrologiae cursus completus. Series Graeca*. (= PG) Volumes. 1–161. Paris, 1857–1868.

———. *Patrologiae cursus completus. Series Latina*. (= PL) Volumes. 1–221. Paris, 1844–1855.

Nicholas of Methone. Ἀνάπτυξις τῆς Θεολογικῆς στοιχειώσεως Πρόκλου πλατωνικοῦ φιλοσόφου [*Refutation of Proclus' Elements of Theology*]. Athens: Academy of Athens, 1984.

———. *Refutation of the Writings of Soterichos [Panevgenos]*. In *Bibliotheca Ecclesiastica 1*. Edited by A Demetrakopulos. Leipzig: Nachdruck, 1866, 321–59.

Symeon of Thessalonike. *Politico-Historical Works of Symeon, Archbishop of Thessalonica (1416/17 to 1429)*. Edited by David Balfour. Vienna: Verlag der Österr, 1979.

―――. Τὰ Ἄπαντα ἐκ τῆς ἀρχαίας εἰς τὴν ὁμιλουμένην μετενεχθέντα πρὸς ψυχοφελῆ χρῆσιν τῶν εὐλαβῶν Ὀρθοδόξων ἱερέων καὶ λαϊκῶν, μετὰ πολλῶν διορθώσεων κατὰ τὸ ἀρχαῖον κείμενον [*All His Works Rendered from Ancient into Modern Greek for the Beneficial Use of Pious Orthodox Clergy and Laity, with Many Corrections according to the Ancient Text*]. Thessalonike: Regopoulos, 1950.

―――. *Treatise on Prayer*. Translated by Harry L. N. Simmons. Brookline: Hellenic College Press, 1984.

―――. *Über die Göttliche Mystagogie*. Translated by Wolfram Gamber. Regensburg: Kommissionsverlag Friedrich Pustet, 1984.

Theodore of Mopsuestia. *Catechetical Homilies*. In *Les homélies catéchetiques de Théodore de Mopsueste. Reproduction phototypique du Ms. Mingana 571, traduction, introduction, index. Studi e Testi*, 145. Edited by R. Tonneau and R. Devreesse. Vatican City : Biblioteca apostolica vaticana, 1949.

―――. *Catechetical Homilies*. In *The Awe-Inspiring Rites of Initiation*. Edited by Edward J Yarnold. Slough: St. Paul Publications, 1972.

Lexica and Dictionaries

A Greek-English Lexicon. Compiled by Henry G. Liddell and Robert Scott and edited by Henry S. Jones, Roderick McKenzie, *et al.* New York: Oxford University Press, 1996.

A Greek-English Lexicon of the New Testament and Other Early Christian Literature. Edited by William Arndt. Chicago: University of Chicago Press, 2000.

A Greek-English Lexicon of the Septuagint: Chiefly of the Pentateuch and Twelve Prophets. Edited by T. Muraoka. Dudley, MA: Peeters, 2002.

A Patristic Greek Lexicon. Edited by G.W.H. Lampe. Oxford: Clarendon Press, 1961.

Λεξικὸν Ἀρχαίας Ἑλληνικῆς Γλώσσης [*Lexicon of the Ancient Greek Language*]. Edited by Ioannes Stamatakos. Athens: Phoenix Publishing Company, 1972.

Oxford Latin Desk Dictionary. Edited by James Morwood. New York: Oxford University Press, 2005.

Critical Liturgical Texts

Brightman, F.E., ed. *Liturgies Eastern and Western*. Oxford: Clarendon Press, 1896.

Parenti, Stefano, and Elena Velkovska, eds. *L' Euchologio Barberini gr. 336*. Rome: CLV – Edizioni Liturgiche, 1995.

Trembelas, P.N., ed. Αἱ τρεῖς λειτουργίαι κατὰ τοὺς ἐν Ἀθήναις κώδικας [*The Three Liturgies According to the Athens Codices*]. In *Texte und Forschungen zur byzantinisch-neugriechischen Philologie*. Athens: Zoe Publishers, 1935.

Modern Liturgical Texts

Ἱερατικόν [*Priest's Service Book*]. Edited by Constantinos Papayiannis. Athens: Apostolike Diakonia, 2001.

Ἱερατικόν Α΄, περιέχον ἄπασαν τὴν τοῦ ἱερέως διάταξιν εἰς τὸν Ἑσπερινόν, τὸν Ὄρθρον, καὶ εἰς τὴν Θ. Λειτουργίαν τοῦ ἐν ἁγίοις πατρὸς ἡμῶν Ἰωάννου τοῦ Χρυσοστόμου, ὡς καὶ εἰς ἑτέρας ἱερᾶς ἀκολουθίας καὶ τελετάς [*Priest's Service Book (Volume 1), Containing the Entire Order of Service for the Priest, for Vespers, Matins and the Divine Liturgy of Our Father among the Saints John Chrysostom, as Well as for Other Holy Services and Rites*]. Daphne, Holy Mountain: Holy Monastery of "Simonopetra", 1992.

Ἱεροδιακονικόν, περιέχον ἄπασαν τὴν διάταξιν τῆς ἱεροδιακονίας εἰς τὸν Ἑσπερινόν, τὸν Ὄρθρον, καὶ εἰς τὰς τρεῖς Λειτουργίας, ὡς καὶ εἰς ἑτέρας ἱερὰς ἀκολουθίας καὶ τελετάς [*Deacon's Service Book, Containing the Entire Order of Service for the Deacon, for Vespers, Matins and the Three Liturgies, as Well as for Other Holy Services and Rites*]. Karyai, Holy Mountain: "Panselenos" Publications, 1989.

Μηναῖον, περιέχον ἄπασαν τὴν ἀνήκουσαν αὐτῷ ἀκολουθίαν, διορθωθὲν τὸ πρὶν ὑπὸ Βαρθολομαίου Κουτλουμουσιανοῦ τοῦ Ἰμβρίου καὶ παρ' αὐτοῦ αὐξηθὲν τῇ τοῦ τυπικοῦ προσθήκῃ κατὰ τὴν διάταξιν τῆς Ἁγίας τοῦ Χριστοῦ Μεγάλης Ἐκκλησίας ἧς τῇ ἐγγράφῳ ἀδείᾳ ἀναθεωρηθὲν καὶ ἀκριβῶς ἐπιδιορθωθὲν [*The Menaion, Containing Every Service Belonging to It, Previously Corrected by Bartholomew Koutloumousianos of Imvros and Augmented by Him through the Addition of the Typikon according to the Order of the Great Church of Christ, which through Written Permission Has Been Revised and Accurately Corrected*]. Volumes 1–12. Athens: Apostolikē Diakonia, 1990–1994.

Παρακλητική, ἤτοι Ὀκτόηχος ἡ Μεγάλη· περιέχουσα ἄπασαν τὴν ἀνήκουσαν αὐτῇ ἀκολουθίαν μετὰ τῶν ἐν τῷ τέλει συνηθῶν προσθηκῶν [*The Parakletike, or the Great Oktoechos: Containing Every Service Belonging to It with the Usual Additions at the End*]. Athens: Apostolike Diakonia, 1992.

Πεντηκοστάριον χαρμόσυνον, τὴν ἀπὸ τοῦ Πάσχα μέχρι τῆς τῶν Ἁγίων Πάντων Κυριακῆς ἀνήκουσαν αὐτῷ ἀκολουθίαν·περιέχον ἐπὶ τέλους δὲ καὶ τὰ ἑωθινὰ Εὐαγγέλια τὰ ἐν τῷ Ὄρθρῳ ἑκάστης τῶν ἐν τῷ μεταξὺ τούτῳ ἑορτῶν ἀναγινωσκομένα, διορθωθέν, καὶ δι' ἑνὸς προλόγου πλουτισθὲν ὑπὸ Βαρθολομαίου Κουτλουμουσιανοῦ τοῦ Ἰμβρίου [*The Joyful Pentekostarion, (with) the Service(s) Belonging to It from Easter to the Sunday of All Saints: Containing in the End the Morning Gospels of Matins Read on Each (Sunday) Between These Feasts, Corrected and Enriched by Bartholomew Koutloumousianos of Imvros*]. Athens: Apostolike Diakonia, 1992.

The Divine Liturgy of Our Father among the Saints Basil the Great. Translated by the Faculty of Hellenic College and Holy Cross Greek Orthodox School of Theology. Brookline: Holy Cross Orthodox Press, 1988.

The Divine Liturgy of Saint John Chrysostom. Translated by the Faculty of Hellenic College and Holy Cross Greek Orthodox School of Theology. Brookline: Holy Cross Orthodox Press, 1985.

Τριῴδιον κατανυκτικόν, περιέχον ἅπασαν τὴν ἀνήκουσαν αὐτῷ ἀκολουθίαν τῆς Ἁγίας καὶ Μεγάλης Τεσσαρακοστῆς· ἀπὸ τῆς Κυριακῆς τοῦ Τελώνου καὶ τοῦ Φαρισαίου μέχρι τοῦ Ἁγίου καὶ Μεγάλου Σαββάτου, μετὰ τῶν Τριαδικῶν ὕμνων καὶ φωταγωγικῶν, στιχηρῶν τε καὶ καθισμάτων διαφόρων ἐν τῷ τέλει [*The Solemn Triodion, Containing Every Service of Holy and Great Lent Belonging to It, from the Sunday of the Publican and the Pharisee until Great and Holy Saturday; with the Hymns to the Trinity and the Hymns of Light, Both Various Stichera and Sessional Hymns at the End*]. Athens: Apostolike Diakonia, 1994.

Τυπικὸν τῆς τοῦ Χριστοῦ Μεγάλης Ἐκκλησίας, ὅμοιον καθ' ὅλα πρὸς τὴν ἐν Κωνσταντινουπόλει ἐγκεκριμένην ἔκδοσιν, ἥτις δὶς ἐξεδόθη ὑπὸ Κωνσταντίνου πρωτοψάλτου· μὲ πολλὰς προσθήκας καὶ ἐπιδιορθώσεις ὑπὸ τοῦ πρωτοψάλτου Γεωργίου Βιολάκη, ἐργασθέντος μετὰ δύο ἀλλεπαλλήλων ἐπιτροπῶν, ἐπὶ τούτῳ Πατριαρχικῇ διαταγῇ ὁρισθεισῶν [*Typikon of the Great Church of Christ, Similar in Everything to the Approved Edition in Constantinople, which Was Published Twice by Constantine Protopsaltis, with Many Additions and Corrections by the Protopsaltis George Violakis, who Labored with Two Successive Committees Appointed for this by Patriarchal Order*]. Athens: Basil D. Saliveros, 1940.

Ὡρολόγιον τὸ Μέγα, περιέχον ἅπασαν τὴν ἀνήκουσαν αὐτῷ ἀκολουθίαν κατὰ τὴν τάξιν τῆς Ἀνατολικῆς Ἐκκλησίας καὶ τῶν ὑποκειμένων αὐτῇ εὐαγῶν μοναστηρίων μετὰ τινῶν ἀπαραιτήτων προσθηκῶν. [*The Great Book of Hours, Containing Every Service Belonging to It and the Venerable Monasteries Under It, with Some Necessary Additions*]. Athens: Apostolike Diakonia, 1986.

Other Liturgical References

Dictionary of the Liturgy. Edited by Jovian P. Lang, OFM. New York: Catholic Book Publishing Company, 1989.

The Liturgical Dictionary of Eastern Christianity. Edited by Peter D. Day. Collegeville: Liturgical Press, 1993.

The New Dictionary of Sacramental Worship. Edited by Peter E. Fink. Collegeville: Liturgical Press 1990.

The New SCM Dictionary of Liturgy and Worship. Edited by Paul Bradshaw. London: SCM Press, 2002.

The Oxford Dictionary of the Christian Church. Edited by F.L. Cross and E.A. Livingstone. Oxford: Oxford University Press, 2005.

SECONDARY SOURCES

Articles

Baldovin, John F., "The *Fermentum* at Rome in the Fifth Century: A Reconsideration." *Worship* 79, no. 1 (2005): 38–53.

Balfour, David, "Symeon of Thessalonike as a Historical Personality." *The Greek Orthodox Theological Review* 28 (1983): 55–72.

Bobrinskoy, Boris, "Nicholas Cabasilas: Theology and Spirituality." *Sobornost* 5, no. 7 (1968): 483–505.

Brightman, F.E., "The *Historia Mystagogica* and Other Greek Commentaries on the Byzantine Liturgy I-II." *The Journal of Theological Studies* 9 (1908): 248–57 and 387–97.

Constas, Nicholas P., "Symeon of Thessalonike and the Theology of the Icon Screen." Sharon E.J. Gerstel, ed. *Thresholds of the Sacred: Architechtural, Art Historical, Liturgical, and Theological Perspectives on Religious Screens, East and West*. Washington: Dumbarton Oaks, 2006, 163–83.

Craig, R.N.S., "Nicholas Cabasilas: *An Exposition of the Divine Liturgy*", in Texte und Untersuchungen zur Geschichte der alterchristlichen Literatur Vol. II. Eds. Kurt Aland and F.L. Cross. Berlin: Akademie Verlag, 1957, 21–28.

Dalmais, I.H., "Place de la Mystagogie de saint Maxime le Confesseur dans la théologie liturgique byzantine." *Studia Patristica* 80 (1962): 277–83.

Daly, Robert J., "Sacrifice Unveiled or Sacrifice Revisited: Trinitarian and Liturgical Perspectives." *Theological Studies* 64, no. 1 (2003): 24–42.

———. "Robert Bellarmine and Post-Tridentine Eucharistic Theology." *Theological Studies* 61 (2000): 239–60.

Davies, J.G., "Review: *Comparative Liturgy*. By A. Baumstark." *Journal of Theological Studies* 10 (1959): 427–29.

Dufrenne, Suzy, "Images du décor de la prothèse." *Revue des Études Byzantines* 26 (1968): 297–310.

Eisler, Robert, "Das Letzte Abendmahl." *Zeitschrift für die neutestamentliche Wissenschaft* 24 (1925): 161–92.

Engberding, H., "Die εὐχὴ τῆς προσκομιδῆς der byzantinischen Basileiosliturgie und ihre Geschichte." *Muséon* 79 (1966): 287–313.

Fahlbusch, Erwin, Horst Dietrich Preuss, et al. "Eschatology." *The Encyclopedia of Christianity*. Edited by Erwin Fahlbusch *et al.* Grand Rapids: William B. Eerdmans Publishing Company, 2001.

Felmy, Karl Christian, "Der Christusknabe auf dem Diskos. Die Proskomidie der orthodoxen Liturgie als Darstellung von 'Schlactung des Lammes' und Geburt des Herrn." *Jahrbuch für Liturgie und Hymnologie* 23 (1979): 95–101.

Galadza, Peter, "Restoring the Icon: Reflections on the Reform of Byzantine Worship." *Worship* 65 (1991): 238–55.

Gerstel, Sharon E.J., "An Alternate View of the Late Byzantine Sanctuary Screen." Sharon E.J. Gerstel, ed. *Thresholds of the Sacred: Architechtural, Art Histori-cal, Liturgical, and Theological Perspectives on Religious Screens, East and West.* Washington: Dumbarton Oaks, 2006.

Gharib, Georges, "Nicolas Cabasilas et l'explication symbolique de la liturgie." *Le Proche-Orient chrétien* 10 (1960): 114–33.

Giraudo, Cesare, "Anafore d'Oriente per le Chiese d'Occidente." *The Christian East, Its Institutions and Its Thought: A Critical Reflection. Papers of the Interna-tional Scholarly Congress for the 75th Anniversary of the Pontifical Oriental Insti-tute, Rome, 30 May – 5 June 1993.* Edited by Robert F. Taft. Rome: Pontificio Istituto Orientale, 1996, 339–51.

Gouillard, J., "Le Synodikon de l'Orthodoxie." *Travaux et Mémoires* 2 (1967): 73–75.

Heintz, Michael, "Baptismal λόγος and τάξις: Basil of Caesarea, *On Baptism*, Book 1." *Studia Liturgica* 35, no. 2 (2005): 148–57.

Henninger, Joseph, "Sacrifice." *Encyclopedia of Religion.* Vol. 12. New York: Mac-millan, 1987.

Hussey, J.M., "Symeon the New Theologian and Nicolas Cabasilas: Similarities and Contrasts in Orthodox Spirituality." *Eastern Churches Review* 4 (1972): 131–40.

Jacob, A., "La tradition manuscrite de la liturgie de S. Jean Chrysostome (VIIIe – XIIe siècles)." *Eucharisties d'Orient et d'Occident.* Paris: Éditions du Cerf, 1970.

———. "La traduction de la Liturgie de S. Jean Chrysostome par Léon Toscan. Édition critique." *Orientalia Christiana Periodica* 32 (1966): 111–62.

———. ed. "Une version géorgienne inédite de la liturgie de saint Jean Chrysos-tome." *Le* Muséon 77 (1964): 65–119.

Keefe, Donald J. "The Reality of the Real Presence." *Adoremus Bulletin: Society for the Renewal of the Sacred Liturgy* (online edition) 8, no. 1 (March 2002).

Kilmartin, Edward J., "The Catholic Tradition of Eucharistic Theology: Towards the Third Millenium." *Theological Studies* 55 (1994): 405–457.

Laurent, Vitalien, "Le rituel de la proscomidie et le métropolite de Crète Élie." *Révue des études byzantines* 16 (1958): 116–42.

Lingas, Alexander, "Festal Cathedral Vespers in Late Byzantium." *Orientalia Christiana Periodica* 63 (1997): 421–55.

Loenertz, Raymond J., "Chronologie de Nicolas Cabasilas: 1345-1354." *Orienta-lia Christiana Periodica* 21 (1955): 205–31.

Louth, Andrew, "Review: *La réforme liturgique byzantine. Étude du phénomène de l'évolution non-spontanée de la liturgie byzantine.* By Thomas Pott." *Journal of Theological Studies* 53 (2002): 358–61.

McKenna, John H., "Eucharist and Sacrifice: An Overview." *Worship* 76, no. 5 (2002): 386–402.

Muksuris, Stylianos, "The Prothesis Rite and the Icon of the *Deesis*: The Eschatological Vision of Liturgy with Contemporary Implications." *American Academy of Religion Anuual Meeting.* San Diego: November 19, 2007.

Nassif, Bradley, "Kissers and Smashers." *Christian History* 54 (1997): 20–23.

Nybroten, Arvid, "Possible Vestiges of the *Afikoman* in the Elevation of the *Panagia.*" *The Greek Orthodox Theological Review* 43 (1998): 105–27.

Ouspensky, Leonide, "The Problem of the Iconostasis." *Saint Vladimir's Theological Quarterly* 8 (1964): 186–218.

Patapios, Hieromonk, "The Alexandrian and the Antiochene Methods of Exegesis: Towards a Reconsideration." *The Greek Orthodox Theological Review* 44 (1999): 187–98.

Richardson, C.C., "The So-Called Epiclesis in Hippolitus." *Harvard Theological Review* 40 (1947): 101–08.

Rumsey, Patricia M., "The Different Concepts of Sacred Time Underlying the Liturgy of the Hours." *Worship* 78, no. 4 (2004): 290–309.

Ševčenko, Ihor, "Nicholas Cabasilas' 'Anti-Zealot' Discourse: A Reinterpretation." *Dumbarton Oaks Papers* 11 (1957): 79–171.

———. "Nicolaus Cabasilas Correspondence." *Byzantinische Zeitschrift* 47 (1954): 54–56.

Stevenson, Kenneth, "Review: The Byzantine Liturgy. Symbolic Structure and Faith Expression. By Hans-Joachim Schulz." *Journal of Theological Studies* 38 (1987): 287–88.

Taft, Robert F., "Mass without the Consecration?" America: *The National Catholic Weekly* 188, no.16 (May 12, 2003): 7–11.

———. "The Decline of Communion in Byzantium and the Distancing of the Congregation from the Liturgical Action: Cause, Effect, or Neither?" Sharon E.J. Gerstel, ed. *Thresholds of the Sacred: Architechtural, Art Historical, Liturgical, and Theological Perspectives on Religious Screens, East and West.* Washington: Dumbarton Oaks, 2006.

———. "The Liturgy of the Great Church: An Initial Synthesis of Structure and Interpretation on the Eve of Iconoclasm." *Dumbarton Oaks Papers* 34–35 (1980–1981): 45–75. Reprinted in Robert F. Taft, *Liturgy in Byzantium and Beyond.* Brookfield: Ashgate Publishing Company, 1995.

Tchéremoukhine, Paul, "Le Concile de 1157 à Constantinople et Nicholas, évêque de Méthone." *Messager de l'Exarchat du Patriarche Russe en Europe Occidentale* 67 (1969): 137–73.

"The Martyrdom of Saints Perpetua and Felicitas." *Readings in the Humanities: First Year Program. St. Anselm College.* Acton: Copley Custom Publishing, 2004.

Timiadis, Emilianos, "The Renewal of Orthodox Worship." *Studia Liturgica* 6 (1969): 95–115.

Vassiliadis, Petros, "Eucharistic and Therapeutic Spirituality." *The Greek Orthodox Theological Review* 42, no. 1-2 (1997): 1–23.

Ware, Bishop Kallistos, "'It Is Time for the Lord to Act': The Divine Liturgy as Heaven on Earth." *Sobornost* 23, no. 1 (2001): 7–22.

———. "Prayer in Evagrius of Pontus and the Macarian Homilies." *An Introduction to Christian Spirituality*. Edited by Ralph Waller and Benedicta Ward. London: SPCK, 1999.

———. "The Meaning of the Divine Liturgy for the Byzantine Worshipper." *Church and People in Byzantine Society for the Promotion of Byzantine Studies (Manchester, 1986)*. Edited by Rosemary Morris. Birmingham: University of Birminham, 1990.

———. "The Tension between the 'Already' and 'Not Yet'." *Returning Pilgrims. Insights from British and Irish Participants in the Fifth World Faith and Order Conference Santiago de Compostela 3-14 August 1993*. Edited by Colin Davey. London: Council of Churches for Britain and Ireland, 1994.

Yiannias, John J., "The Elevation of the Panaghia." *Dumbarton Oaks Papers* 26 (1972): 225–36.

Zizioulas, John, "Εὐχαριστία καὶ Βασιλεία τοῦ Θεοῦ" ["The Eucharist and the Kingdom of God"] (in three parts), Suvnaxh 49 (January – March 1994): 7–18; 51 (July – September 1994): 83–101; 52 (October – December 1994): 81–97.

Books

Altripp, Michael. *Die Prothesis und ihre Bildausstattung in Byzanz unter besonderer Berücksichtigung der Denkmäler Griechenlands*. Frankfurt: P. Lang, 1998.

Angelopoulos, Athanasios A. Νικόλαος Καβάσιλας Χαμαετός· Ἡ ζωή του καὶ τὸ ἔργον του [*Nicholas Cabasilas Chamaetos: His Life and His Work*]. Thessalonike: Patriarchal Institute of Patristic Studies, 1969.

Balfour, David. Ἁγίου Συμεὼν Θεσσαλονίκης, Ἔργα Θεολογικά [Saint Symeon of Thessalonike: Theological Works]. *Analecta Vlatadon* 34. Thessalonike: Patriarchal Institute of Patristic Studies, 1981.

———. *Politico-Historical Works of Symeon Archbishop of Thessalonica*. Weiner Byzantinistische Studien 13. Vienna: Verlag der Österreichischen Akademie der Wissenschaften, 1979.

Baumstark, Anton. *Comparative Liturgy*. Translated by F.L. Cross. Oxford: Oxford University Press, 1958.

Beasley-Murray, George R. *Jesus and the Future: An Examination of the Criticism of the Eschatological Discourse, Mark 13, with Special Reference to the Little Apocalypse Theory*. New York: St. Martin's Press, 1956.

Behr, John, Andrew Louth, and Dimitri Conomos, eds. *Abba: The Tradition of Orthodoxy in the West. Festschrift for Bishop Kallistos (Ware) of Diokleia*. Crestwood: Saint Vladimir's Seminary Press, 2003.

Berger, David. *Thomas Aquinas and the Liturgy*. Naples: Sapienta Press of Ave Maria University, 2005.

Bornert, René. *Les commentaires byzantins de la Divine Liturgie du VIIe au XVe siècle*. Paris: Institut Français d'Études Byzantines, 1965.

Boyer, Louis. *Liturgical Piety*. Notre Dame: University of Notre Dame Press, 1955.

Brueggemann, Walter. *Worship in Ancient Israel. An Essential Guide Series*. Nashville: Abingdon Press, 2005.

Bultmann, Rudolf. *History and Eschatology*. Edinburgh: University Press, 1957.

Cabrol, Fernand. *Liturgical Prayer: Its History and Spirit*. London: Burns, Oates, and Washbourne Ltd., 1922.

Calivas, Alkiviadis C. Χρόνος τελέσεως τῆς Θείας Λειτουργίας [*The Time of the Celebration of the Divine Liturgy*] (doctoral dissertation). Thessalonike: Patriarchal Institute for Patristic Studies, 1982.

Chauvet, L.M. *Symbol and Sacrament: A Sacramental Reinterpretation of Christian Existence*. Translated by P. Madigan and M. Beaument. Collegeville: The Liturgical Press, 1995.

Chrysostomos, Archimandrite. *Orthodox Liturgical Dress*. Brookline: Holy Cross Orthodox Press, 1981.

Connolly, Dom R.H., ed. and trans. *The Liturgical Homilies of Narsai*. Cambridge: University Press, 1909.

Conticello, Carmelo Giuseppe and Vassa Conticello, eds. *La théologie byzantine et sa tradition. Corpus Christianorum*. Turnhout : Brepols, 2002.

Cross, Frank M. *The Ancient Library of Qumran and Modern Biblical Studies*. Sheffield: Sheffield Academic Press, 1995.

Cullmann, Oscar. *Christus und die Zeit*. Zollikon-Zürich: Evangelischer verlag, a.g., 1946.

Dalmais, I.H. *Liturgies d'Orient: rites et symboles*. Paris: Les Éditions du Cerf, 1980.

Daly, Robert J. *Christian Sacrifice: The Judaeo-Christian Background before Origen. Studies in Christian Antiquity*, 18. Washington: Catholic University of America, 1978.

———. *The Origins of the Christian Doctrine of Sacrifice*. Philadelphia: Fortress, 1978.

Daube, David. *He That Cometh*. London: London Diocesan Council for Christian-Jewish Understanding, 1966.

Day, Peter D. *Eastern Christian Liturgies: The Armenian, Coptic, Ethiopian and Syrian Rites*. Shannon: Irish University Press, 1972.

Deiss, Lucien, ed. *Early Sources of the Liturgy*. Translated by Benet Weatherhead. New York: Alba House, 1967.

Demetrakopulos, A., ed. *Bibliotheca Ecclesiastica 1*. Leipzig: Nachdruck, 1866.

————. ed. Νικολάου Μεθώνης: λόγοι δύο [*Nicholas Methones: Two Discourses*]. Leipzig: Nachdruck, 1865.

Descoeudres, Georges. *Die Pastophorien im syro-byzantinischen Osten. Eine Untersuchung zu architektur und liturgiegeschichtlichen Problemen. Schriften zur Geistesgeschichte des östlichen Europa*, 16. Wiesbaden: Harrassowitz, 1983.

De Vaux, Roland. *Les institutions de l'ancien testament*. Paris: Éditions du Cerf, 1997.

Dix, Gregory. *The Shape of the Liturgy*. London: A & C Black Publishers Ltd., 1945.

Dodd, Charles H. *The Parables of the Kingdom*. New York: Scribner, 1961.

Dragas, George D. *On the Priesthood and the Holy Eucharist according to St. Symeon of Thessalonica, Patriarch Kallinikos of Constantinople, and St. Mark Eugenikos of Ephesus*. Rollinsford: Orthodox Research Institute, 2004.

Ducellier, Alain. *L'Église byzantine: entre pouvoir et esprit (313–1204)*. Paris: Desclée, 1990.

Elavanal, Thomas. *The Memorial Celebration: A Theological Study of the Anaphora of the Apostles Mar Addai and Mari*. Kerala: M.C.B.S. Publications, 1988.

Eliade, Mircea. *The Sacred and the Profane: The Nature of Religion*. Translated by Willard R. Trask. San Diego: Harcourt Brace Jovanovich, 1987.

Evdokimov, Paul. *La prière de l'Église d'Orient: La liturgie byzantine de saint Jean Chrysostome*. Mulhouse: Éditions Salvator, 1966.

Fenwick, John R.K. *The Anaphoras of St. Basil and St. James: An Investigation into Their Common Origin*. Rome: Edizioni Orientalia Christiana, 1992.

Fincke, Andrew. *Background of the Jewish Handwashing Ritual* (master's thesis). Cambridge: Harvard University, 1987.

Fleming, W.K. *Mysticism in Christianity*. New York: Fleming H. Revell Company, 1913.

Fountoules, Ioannes M. Ἀπαντήσεις εἰς λειτουργικὰς ἀπορίας [*Answers to Liturgical Questions*]. Volumes 1–4. Athens: Apostolike Diakonia, 1994.

————. Λειτουργική Α΄ [*Liturgics I*]. Thessalonike: s.n., 1993.

————. Τὸ λειτουργικὸν ἔργον τοῦ Συμεὼν τῆς Θεσσαλονίκης: συμβολὴ εἰς τὴν ἱστορίαν καὶ θεωρίαν τῆς θείας λατρείας [*The Liturgical Work of Symeon of Thessalonike: Symbolism in the History and Theory of Divine Worship*]. Thessalonike: s.n., 1968.

Fouskas, Konstantinos M. Ὁ Νικόλαος Μεθώνης καὶ ἡ Διδασκαλία Αὐτοῦ περὶ Θείας Εὐχαριστίας [*Nicholas of Methone and His Teaching Regarding the Divine Eucharist*]. Athens: s.n., 1992.

Fuller, Reginald H. *The Mission and Achievement of Jesus: An Examination of the Presuppositions of New Testament Theology*. London: SCM Press, 1954.

Gerstel, Sharon E.J. *Beholding the Sacred Mysteries: Programs of the Byzantine Sanctuary*. Seattle: University of Washington Press, 1999.

————. ed. *Thresholds of the Sacred: Architectural. Art Historical, Liturgical, and Theological Perspectives on Religious Screens, East and West.* Washington: Dumbarton Oaks, 2006.

Girard, René. *The Scapegoat.* Translated by Yvonne Freccero. Baltimore: Johns Hopkins University Press, 1986.

————. *Violence and the Sacred.* Baltimore: Johns Hopkins University Press, 1977.

Gogol, Nikolai V. Ἡ Θεία Λειτουργία [*The Divine Liturgy*]. Translated by Vasileios Moustakes. Athens: I. Rossolatos Press, 1962.

Harrington, L. Michael, ed. and trans. *A Thirteenth-Century Textbook of Mystical Theology at the University of Paris. The Mystical Theology of Dionysius the Areopagite in Eriugena's Latin Translation with the Scholia Translated by Anastasius the Librarian and Excerpts from Eriugena's Periphyseon. Dallas Medieval Texts and Translations* 4. Leuven: Peeters, 2004.

Heath, Dale E. *The Orthodox Septuagint.* Lake City: Dale E. Heath, 1997.

Jacob, A. *Histoire du formulaire grec de la liturgie de Saint Jean Chrysostome* (unpublished doctoral dissertation). Louvain: University of Louvain, 1968.

Jeremias, Joachim. *Die Gleichnisse Jesu.* Göttingen: Vandenhoeck and Ruprecht, 1952.

————. *Rediscovering the Parables.* New York: Scribner, 1966.

Jones, Cheslyn, Geoffrey Wainwright, Edward Yarnold, and Paul Bradshaw, eds. *The Study of Liturgy.* New York: Oxford University Press, 1992.

Jones, William Herbert. *Jewish Ritual Washing and Christian Baptism* (master's thesis). Hamilton, Ontario: McMaster University, 2001.

Kavanagh, Aidan. *On Liturgical Theology.* Collegeville: The Liturgical Press, 1992.

Kazhdan, Alexander P., ed. *Oxford Dictionary of Byzantium.* Vols. I–III. New York: Oxford University Press, 1991.

Kilmartin, Edward J. *Christian Liturgy: Theology and Practice. Systematic Theology of Liturgy,* Volume 1. Kansas City: Sheed and Ward, 1988.

————. *The Eucharist in the West: History and Theology.* Edited by Robert J. Daly. Collegeville: The Liturgical Press, 1998.

Knupp, Josef. *Das Mystagogieverständnis des Johannes Chrysostomus. Benediktbeurer Studien* 4. Munich: Don-Bosco-Verl., 1995.

Kucharek, Casimir. *The Byzantine-Slav Liturgy of St. John Chrysostom: Its Origin and Evolution.* Combermere: Alleluia Press, 1971.

Kunzler, Michael. *Gnadenquellen: Symeon von Thessaloniki . . . als Beispiel für die Einflussnahme des Palamismus auf die orthodoxe Sakramententheologie und Liturgik.* Trier: Paulinus – Verlag, 1989.

Ladd, G.E. *Jesus and the Kingdom: The Eschatology of Biblical Realism.* New York: Harper and Row, 1964.

Lawrence, Jonathan David. *Washing in Water: Trajectories of Ritual Bathing in the Hebrew Bible and Second Temple Literature.* Atlanta: Society of Biblical Literature, 2006.

LaVerdiere, Eugene. *The Eucharist in the New Testament and the Early Church.* Collegeville: The Liturgical Press, 1996.

Loenertz, Raymond-Joseph, ed. *Démétrius Cydonius: correspondance.* Vatican City: Biblioteca apostolica vaticana, 1956.

————. *Les recuils de lettres de Démétrius Cydonès. Studi e testi* 131. Vatican City: Biblioteca apostolica vaticana, 1947.

Lot-Borodine, Myrrha. *Un maître de la spiritualité byzantine au XIVe siècle: Nicolas Cabasilas.* Paris: Éditions de l'Orante, 1958.

Louth, Andrew. *Denys, the Areopagite.* Wilton, CT: Morehouse, 1989.

Lyman, J. Rebecca. *Christology and Cosmology: Models of Divine Activity in Origen, Eusebius, and Athanasius.* Oxford: Clarendon Press, 1993.

Mandalà, Marco. *La protesi della liturgia nel rito Bizantino-Greco.* Grottaferrata: Scuola Tipografica Italo-Orientale "S. Nilo", 1935.

Mateos, J. *La célébration de la parole dans la liturgie byzantine.* Rome: Pontifical Institute of Oriental Studies, 1971.

Mazza, Enrico. Mystagogy: *A Theology of Liturgy in the Patristic Age.* Translated by Matthew J. O'Connell. New York: Pueblo Publishing Company, 1989.

————. *The Celebration of the Eucharist: The Origin of the Rite and the Development of Its Interpretation.* Translated by Matthew J. O'Connell. Collegeville: The Liturgical Press, 1999.

————. *The Origins of the Eucharistic Prayer.* Translated by Ronald E. Lane. Collegeville: The Liturgical Press, 1995.

Metallinos, Georgios D. Ἡ θεολογικὴ μαρτυρία τῆς ἐκκλησιαστικῆς λατρείας [*The Theological Witness of Ecclesiastical Worship*]. Athens: Armos Publications, 1995.

Meyendorff, John. *Byzantine Theology: Historical Trends and Doctrinal Themes.* New York: Fordham University Press, 1979.

Mitchell, Leonel L. *Worship: Initiation and the Churches.* Washington: The Pastoral Press, 1991.

Moltmann, Jürgen. *The Theology of Hope: On the Ground and Implications of a Christian Eschatology.* New York: Harper Collins Publishers, 1991.

Monk of St. Tikhon's Monastery, A., ed. *These Truths We Hold.* South Canaan: St. Tikhon's Seminary Press, 1986.

Moore, Arthur L. *The Parousia in the New Testament.* Leiden: E.J. Brill, 1966.

Muksuris, Stylianos. *The Anaphorae of the Liturgy of Sts. Addai and Mari and the Byzantine Liturgy of St. Basil the Great: A Comparative Study* (unpublished M.Litt. thesis). Durham: University of Durham, 1999.

Nautin, Pierre. *Origène: sa vie et son oeuvre.* Paris: Beauchesne, 1977.

Nellas, Panayiotis. *Deification in Christ: Orthodox Perspectives on the Nature of the Human Person. Contemporary Greek Theologians*, Volume 5. Crestwood: St. Vladimir's Seminary Press, 1987.

———. *Le vivant divinisé: l'anthropologie des Pères de l'Église*. Translated by Jean-Louis Palierne. Paris: Éditions du Cerf, 1989.

———. Προλεγόμενα εἰς τὴν μελέτην Νικολάου τοῦ Καβάσιλα [*Introduction to the Study of Nicholas Cabasilas*]. Athens: s.n., 1968.

Ostrogorsky, George. *History of the Byzantine State*. New Brunswick, N.J.: Rutgers University Press, 1999.

Papadopoulos, Michael. Λειτουργική: Τὰ τελούμενα ἐντὸς τοῦ ναοῦ [*Liturgics: The Rites Conducted within the Church*]. Athens: Heptalofos A.B.E.E., 1992.

Patrones, George P. Σχέσεις παρόντος καὶ μέλλοντος εἰς τὴν περὶ βασιλείας τοῦ Θεοῦ διδασκαλίαν τῆς Ὀρθοδόξου Θεολογίας [*The Relationship between the Present and the Future in the Teaching about the Kingdom of God in Orthodox Theology*]. Athens: s.n., 1975.

Plato. *Five Dialogues: Euthyphro, Apology, Crito, Meno, Phaedo*. Translated by G.M.A. Grube. Indianapolis: Hackett Publishing Company, 1981.

Porter, W.S. *The Gallican Rite. Studies in Eucharistic Faith and Practice*. London: A.R. Mowbray and Co., Ltd., 1958.

Pott, Thomas. *La réforme liturgique byzantine: étude du phénomène d'évolution non spontanée de la liturgie byzantine*. Rome: CLV – Edizioni liturgiche, 2000.

Rahmani, J.E., ed. *Testamentum Domini nostri Jesu Christi*. Mainz: s.n., 1899.

Rahner, Karl. *Zur Theologie der Zukunft*. München: Deutscher Taschenbuch-Verl., 1971.

Rappaport, Roy A. *Ecology, Meaning, and Religion*. Berkeley: North Atlantic Books, 1979.

Rigo, Antonio, ed. *Gregorio Palamas e oltre: studi e documenti sulle controversie teologiche del XIV secolo bizantino. Orientalia Venetiana*, 16. Florence: Leo S. Olschki, 2004.

Romanides, John S. Τὸ προπατορικὸν ἁμάρτημα [*The Ancestral Sin*] (doctoral dissertation). Athens: Apostolike Diakonia, 1957.

———. *The Ancestral Sin*. Translated by George S. Gabriel. Ridgewood, NJ: Zephyr Publishing, 2002.

Roques, R. *L'univers dionysien. Structure hiérarchique du monde selon le pseudo-Denys*. Paris: Aubier, 1954.

Schillebeeckx, Edward. *Christ: The Sacrament of the Encounter with God*. London: Sheed and Ward, 1963.

Schmemann, Alexander. *Introduction to Liturgical Theology*. Crestwood, NY: St. Vladimir's Seminary Press, 1986.

———. *Liturgy and Life: Christian Development through Liturgical Experience*. New York: OCA Department of Religious Education, 1993.

————. *The Eucharist: Sacrament of the Kingdom*. Translated by Paul Kachur. Crestwood, NY: St. Vladimir's Seminary Press, 1987.

Schnackenburg, Rudolf. *God's Rule and Kingdom*. New York: Herder and Herder, 1963.

Schulz, Hans-Joachim. *Die Byzantinische Liturgie: Glaubenszeugnis und Symbolgestalt*. [Ἡ Βυζαντινή Λειτουργία· μαρτυρία πίστεως καί συμβολική ἔκφραση]. Translated by Demetrios V. Tzerpos. Athens: Akritas Publications, 1998.

————. *The Byzantine Liturgy. Symbolic Structure and Faith Expression*. Translated by Matthew J. O'Connell. New York : Pueblo, 1986.

Schweitzer, Albert. *Das Messianitäts – und Leidensgeheimnis: eine Skizze des Lebens Jesu*. Tübingen: J.C.B. Mohr, 1956.

————. *Die Mystik des Apostels Paulus* [*The Mysticism of Paul the Apostle*]. New York: Macmillan, 1955.

————. *Geschichte der Leben – Jesu – Forschung* [*The Quest of the Historical Jesus*]. Edited by John Bowden. Translated by W. Montgomery, J.R. Coates, et al. Minneapolis: Fortress Press, 2001.

————. *Reich Gottes und Urchristentum* [*The Kingdom of God and Primitive Christianity*]. Edited by Ulrich Neuenschwande. Translated by L.A. Garrard. New York: Seabury Press, 1968.

Sellers, R.V. *Two Ancient Christologies: A Study of the Christological Thought of the Schools of Alexandria and Antioch in the Early History of Christian Doctrine*. London: SPCK, 1954.

Sokolowski, Robert. *Christian Faith and Human Understanding: Studies on the Eucharist, Trinity, and the Human Person*. Washington: Catholic University of America Press, 2006.

Solovey, Meletius Michael. *The Byzantine Divine Liturgy*. Washington: Catholic University of America Press, 1970.

Taft, Robert F. *Beyond East and West: Problems in Liturgical Understanding*. Washington: The Pastoral Press, 1984.

————. *The Byzantine Rite: A Short History*. Collegeville: The Liturgical Press, 1992.

————. *The Diptychs: A History of the Liturgy of St. John Chrysostom*. Volume IV. Rome: Pontifical Institute of Oriental Studies, 1991.

————. *The Great Entrance: A History of the Transfer of Gifts and Other Pre-anaphoral Rites of the Liturgy of St. John Chrysostom*. Rome: Pontifical Institute of Oriental Studies, 1978.

————. *The Precommunion Rites*. Rome: The Pontifical Institute of Oriental Studies, 2000.

Thomas, John and Angela Constantinides Hero, eds., *Byzantine Monastic Foundation Documents: A Complete Translation of the Surviving Founders' Typika and*

Testaments. Dumbarton Oaks Studies, Volume 35. Washington, DC: Dumbarton Oaks, 2000.

Tsirpanlis, Constantine. *The Liturgical and Mystical Theology of Nicholas Cabasilas* (masters thesis). New York: Tsirpanlis, 1979.

Vasileios, Archimandrite. *Hymn of Entry: Liturgy and Life in the Orthodox Church.* Translated by Elizabeth Briere. Crestwood: St. Vladimir's Seminary Press, 1984.

Vatican Council II. *Constitution on the Sacred Liturgy of the Second Vatican Council and the Motu Proprio of Pope Paul VI.* Glen Rock: Paulist Press, 1964.

Verheul, A. *Introduction to the Liturgy: Towards a Theology of Worship.* London: Burns & Oates Ltd., 1968.

Vlahos, Hierotheos. *The Mind of the Orthodox Church.* Translated by Esther Williams. Levadia: Birth of the Theotokos Monastery, 1998.

Völker, Walther. *Die Sakramentsmystik des Nikolaus Kabasilas.* Wiesbaden: Steiner, 1977.

Wainwright, Geoffrey. *Eucharist and Eschatology.* London: Epworth Press, 1971.

Walker, P.W.L. *Holy City, Holy Places? Christian Attitudes to Jerusalem and the Holy Land in the Fourth Century.* Oxford: Clarendon Press, 1990.

Ware, Timothy. *The Orthodox Church.* New York: Penguin Books, 1963.

Wiles, Maurice and Mark Santer, eds. *Documents in Early Christian Thought.* Cambridge: Cambridge University Press, 1975.

Winkler, Gabriele. *Studies in Early Christian Liturgy and Its Context.* Brookfield: Ashgate Publishing Company, 1997.

Zizioulas, John. *Eucharist, Bishop, Church: The Unity of the Church in the Divine Eucharist and the Bishop during the First Three Centuries.* Translated by Elizabeth Theokritoff. Brookline: Holy Cross Orthodox Press, 2001.

———. Θέματα Ἐκκλησιολογίας [*Themes in Ecclesiology*]. Thessalonike: s.n., 1992.

ABOUT THE AUTHOR

THE REVEREND PROTOPRESBYTER DR. STELYIOS S. MUKSURIS, PH.D., is Professor of Liturgy at the Byzantine Catholic Seminary in Pittsburgh, PA. A native of Boston and a graduate of Hellenic College and Holy Cross Greek Orthodox School of Theology in Brookline, MA, he received his postgraduate degrees and his doctorate in liturgical theology from the University of Durham in the United Kingdom. A member of the international *Societas Liturgica* and the *Society of Oriental Liturgy*, he has lectured at numerous academic conferences and is the author of several journal articles and book chapters in his area of expertise.